The Luxury Guide to Walt Disney World® Resort

"Luxury means different things to different travelers: an elegant guest suite, a hotel atrium full of exotic blooms, a romantic dinner with fireworks as a backdrop. However you define it, Cara Goldsbury's book tells you where to find it."

—Faye Wolfe, *Disney Magazine*

"Expertly written by a former travel agency owner . . . an impressively informative vacation planning guide for any individual or family seeking to maximize their experience of the 'Disney magic' to the fullest."

—James A. Cox, *Midwest Book Review*

Help Us Keep This Guide Up to Date

Every effort has been made by the author and editors to make this guide as accurate and useful as possible. However, many things can change after a guide is published—establishments close, phone numbers change, facilities come under new management, etc.

We would love to hear from you concerning your experiences with this guide and how you feel it could be improved and kept up to date. While we may not be able to respond to all comments and suggestions, we'll take them to heart and we'll also make certain to share them with the author. Please send your comments and suggestions to the following address:

The Globe Pequot Press
Reader Response/Editorial Department
P.O. Box 480
Guilford, CT 06437

Or you may e-mail us at:

editorial@GlobePequot.com

Thanks for your input, and happy travels!

INSIDERS' GUIDE®

The Luxury Guide to Walt Disney World® Resort

How to Get the Most Out of the Best Disney Has to Offer

Cara Goldsbury

INSIDERS' GUIDE®

GUILFORD, CONNECTICUT
AN IMPRINT OF THE GLOBE PEQUOT PRESS

The prices, rates, and hours listed in this guidebook were confirmed at press time. We recommend, however, that you call establishments to obtain current information before traveling.

INSIDERS' GUIDE®

ISSN 1555-6050
ISBN 0-7627-3957-6

Manufactured in the United States of America
First Globe Pequot Edition/First Printing

Grande Lakes rose garden

Top: *Christmas at Epcot.* PHOTO BY BRUCE CARLSON
Bottom: *Hyatt Regency Grand Cypress pool*

The Golf Club

Walt Disney World Dolphin lobby

Top: *Disney's Grand Floridian Resort.* PHOTO BY BRUCE CARLSON
Bottom: *Massage Room at the Ritz-Carlton Spa*

Top: *Presidential Suite at the Ritz-Carlton*
Bottom: *Disney's Beach Club Resort*

Disney's Polynesian Resort

Top: *Portofino Bay Hotel*
Bottom: *Disney's Wilderness Lodge lobby.* PHOTO BY BRUCE CARLSON

Top: *JW Marriott Grande Lakes*
Bottom: *JW Marriott Grande Lakes lobby*

Hyatt Regency Grand Cypress grounds

Top: *Disney's Animal Kingdom Lodge*
Bottom: *Disney's Contemporary Resort lobby*

Top: *Ritz-Carlton Grande Lakes pool*
Bottom: *Disney's Wilderness Lodge*

CONTENTS

ACKNOWLEDGMENTS

Many thanks to the creative and caring people of The Globe Pequot Press. To my editor Erin Joyce who is a joy to work with and Laura Strom whose enthusiasm for my book was delightful.

My appreciation to Walt Disney World for their guidance and assistance, in particular Geoffrey Pointon in Media Relations and Chris Ware, Concierge Guest Services Manager at Disney's Grand Floridian Rersort.

Thanks go to Susan Flower at Discovery Cove, Greg Smith at SeaWorld, Jennifer Hodges and Chrissy Gillette at Universal Orlando, Michelle Valle at Grande Lakes Orlando, Keith Salwoski and Suzanne Stephan at Gaylord Palms Resort, and Kris Michalson at the Hyatt Regency Grand Cypress.

To all my readers whose enthusiasm for Disney inspires me, and to the many Disney webmasters, authors, and travel agents who have been such a support.

And to Robert, my husband and biggest champion, whose patience is endless.

INTRODUCTION

Walt Disney World.

These three words instantly fill the mind with images of Mickey Mouse, Peter Pan, Cinderella, and Snow White. For children they send the imagination soaring to places only dreamed of in their wildest fantasies. For adults they offer a trip back to the idyllic innocence of childhood when nothing was unattainable and the world was filled with unlimited possibilities. What other place could be all this to so many people?

Walt Disney World is a destination that renews hopes and dreams, an adventure of the heart, true magic. Disney's four theme parks are so totally distinct that it's almost like taking a different vacation each day of your visit. Enhancing the experience are Disney's themed resorts, transporting you to a unique time and place: early twentieth-century New England, nineteenth-century Florida, even a lodge in deepest Africa. With only a small percentage of its 30,000 acres fully developed, you'll find lush grounds dotted with lakes, wetlands, and stunningly landscaped resorts and parks. With so many delightful diversions, it's difficult to know where to begin. Allow this guidebook to step in and show you the way.

Is it possible for sophisticated travelers to really enjoy themselves in the land of Mickey Mouse? Absolutely! This unique travel guide overflowing with tips and techniques for a splendid vacation is designed for those who wish to tour Walt Disney World but also want to reside in luxurious resorts and dine at many of the best restaurants. I'm prepared to direct you in planning a visit in which each day comes with the best Disney has to offer. Together we will arrange a relatively stress-free vacation by utilizing each component of this travel guide to best suit your needs. Together we will decide the most convenient time of year for your vacation, which resort best fits your personality, how to obtain the finest room at the lowest possible price, where to dine, and much, much more. Helpful tips throughout can make the difference between a mediocre trip and a fantastic one. Now let's get going!

HOW TO USE THIS GUIDE

To help you choose which accommodations and restaurants best suit your needs, we've developed the following codes:

Accommodations

The following symbols represent the average cost (without any discounts) of standard through concierge-level rooms for one night in regular season, excluding tax; and studio through three-bedroom villas at home-away-from-home resorts:

$. $200 or less
$$ . . . . $201 to 350
$$$ . . . . $351 to 500
$$$$ . . . . $501 to 700
$$$$$. . . . . $701 to 1,900

Restaurants

The following symbols represent the average cost of an adult dinner entree or buffet, excluding tax and tip:

$. . . . . $10 or less
$$. $11 to $15
$$$. . . . . $16 to $25
$$$$ . . . . $26 and over

 This symbol indicates the most luxurious accommodations, restaurants, and entertainment.

PLANNING YOUR TRIP

The most successful vacations are those that are carefully planned and researched months ahead of time. In fact, the planning is, for some, half the fun. Disney is so extensive and offers so many choices to fit the personalities of so many types of vacationers that it demands at least some forethought. You'll discover a wealth of options, some suitable for just about everyone, others ridiculously frivolous for some but perfect for others. Neglecting to do your homework oftentimes results in disappointment and frustration. The outcome can mean the difference between a smooth trip or an exasperating one.

Begin by reading this book cover to cover and visiting its companion Web site at www.luxurydisneyguide.com. Send for a free Disney vacation planning video or CD-ROM (800–205–3002 or www.disneyworld.com to order), call the Orlando/Orange County Convention and Visitors Bureau (800–551–0181 or 407–363–5871), or visit www.orlandoinfo.com for maps of the area as well as a visitor's guide on the many area attractions. For those interested in visiting Universal Orlando (and you should be), call (800) 837–2273 or visit www.universalorlando.com. Check out the sites listed in the following section, and remember, the help of a good travel agent may be the key to your best vacation ever.

Disney Internet Sites

Log on to these excellent Disney-related sites for hundreds of tips along with pictures, menus, and much, much more.

The Luxury Guide to Walt Disney World (www.luxurydisney guide.com). Companion site to this guidebook with continual book updates, menus, recipes, photos, and loads of information on Disney, Universal Orlando, and SeaWorld.

Walt Disney World Online (www.disneyworld.com). Walt Disney World's official Web site, with a wealth of information useful in planning your trip. Especially helpful are diagrams of guest rooms, park hours, and up-to-date ticket pricing.

AllEarsNet (www.allearsnet.com). A top pick! Fabulous for up-to-date detailed information including complete Disney restaurant menus. Sign up for the great free weekly newsletter.

Carlson's Disney Resort and Parks Picture Site (www.wdwfun.com). Featuring more than 1,800 photos of the Walt Disney World Resort.

The DIBB (www.thedibb.co.uk). A UK–based Disney and Orlando interactive site with information, tips, and planning advice along with an active forum and photo gallery.

The DIS (www.wdwinfo.com). Great information site with the best Disney discussion group around.

Discovery Cove (www.discoverycove.com). Discovery Cove's official Web site.

Disney Echo (www.emuck.com). A fun and friendly online connection to like-minded Disney fans from all over the world.

Disney World and Orlando Unofficial Guide (www.wdisneyw.co.uk). Includes Walt Disney World theme park info and tips, resort descriptions and reviews, money-saving advice, photos, maps, and more.

Disney World Trivia (www.disneyworldtrivia.com). From the author of the *Walt Disney World Trivia Book,* Lou Mongello's site contains trivia, secrets, and fun facts about Walt Disney World, as well as photo galleries, discussion forums, weekly trivia games, author Q&A, and guest columnists.

INTERCOT (www.intercot.com). A comprehensive guide to Walt Disney World featuring information covering the major theme parks, travel information, pictures, audio clips, video clips, tips, trivia, and interactive discussion about the world's most popular vacation destination.

Magical Mountain (www.magicalmountain.net). Disney information, news, reviews, guest columns, and photos.

MagicTrips (www.magictrips.com). Practical information, reader restaurant reviews, and a discussion site.

Mickey News (www.mickeynews.com). The latest Disney news as well as park photos, dining, and movie reviews. Check out the column sections for great tips and information.

The Mouse for Less (www.themouseforless.com). An online community that makes Disney vacation planning easy and affordable. Members have access to exclusive discounts, money-saving techniques, rate-reducing codes, and a completely free Disney specialized travel agency to assist with all of their vacation arrangements.

MousePlanet (www.mouseplanet.com). Practical advice, news, and reader reviews.

MouseSavers (www.mousesavers.com). A running list of current discounts available at Walt Disney World and Universal resorts.

MouseTyme Vacations (www.mousetyme.com). Planning information for Florida theme parks and the Disney Cruise Line. Includes news, forums, articles, photos, even Disney recipes.

My Disney World (www.mydisneyworld.com). Discounts, tickets, resorts, news, forums, and information for the Disney World tourist.

Our Laughing Place (www.ourlaughingplace.com). Photos and virtual tours of resorts and restaurants as well as a wide array of planning and review articles, and forums.

SeaWorld (www.seaworld.com). Official Web site of SeaWorld.

Tikiman's Polynesian Resort Pages (www.tikiman2001.homestead .com). Loads of pictures and information on Disney's Polynesian Resort.

Universal Orlando (www.universalorlando.com). Official Web site includes park hours, ticket options, theme park attractions, and hotel information.

Walt Disney World Live Entertainment (http://pages.prodigy.net/steve soares). Current Walt Disney World entertainment schedules, descriptions, photos, and links.

WDW Magic (www.wdwmagic.com). Information on upcoming Disney attractions and plenty of park photos.

Important Walt Disney World Phone Numbers

Behind-the-Scenes tours (407) WDW–TOUR or (407) 939–8687

Boating and tennis (407) WDW–PLAY or (407) 939–7529

Child care center reservations (407) WDW–DINE or (407) 939–3463

Fishing information and reservations (407) WDW–BASS or (407) 939–2277

General information (407) 824–4321

Golf tee times (407) 938–4653

Park tickets (407) WDW–MAGIC or (407) 939–6244

Advance reservations for restaurants (407) WDW–DINE or (407) 939–3463

Switchboard (407) 824–2222

Transportation information (407) 939–7433

Updated park hours (407) 824–4321

When to Go

Always a tough decision. Should you plan a summer trip when the children are out of school, knowing full well the parks will be sweltering and jam-packed? What about a slower time of year when parks are half-empty but with shortened operating hours in which to tour them? How about over a long holiday weekend, or would it be preferable to simply take the children out of school? These are all questions you must weigh, questions that will help you reach a decision best for you and your family.

Each season has its pros and its cons. The busy season brings congested parks, long lines, and higher resort rates but also greatly extended park hours. The slower seasons bring half-filled parks, little waiting in line, and lower resort rates along with later opening times, earlier closing times, and attractions that are closed for rehab. For me, slow season can't be beat. If you are able to do so, avoid the busiest times of the year. If not, the summer months or holidays are certainly better than nothing and, with a bit of planning and a lot of energy, can be more than enjoyable.

The following guidelines may not be exact since each year comes with different Florida resident offers, special celebrations, conventions, and so forth that affect crowd size. Use them as a general guide to avoiding the parks at their worst.

Park Attendance

Busiest: President's Day week; the last three weeks of March to the week after Easter (staggered spring break around the country); the second week

TRAVEL TIPS FOR THE BUSIEST TIMES

If at all possible, avoid like the plague the summer months and most importantly any major holiday at Walt Disney World. The busiest holiday periods are President's Day, the two weeks surrounding Easter, July 4, Thanksgiving weekend, and Christmas through New Year's—the busiest time of year. Memorial Day is a toss-up, with the only exception to the rule being Labor Day, Columbus Day, and Veterans Day, when parks are crowded but not unbearable.

If you must travel in busy seasons, remember to use priority seating and FASTPASS (described in chapter 4 on the parks) whenever possible, and pick a resort close to the parks for easy access and midday breaks. When parks reach full capacity, and they do during the busiest of times, only Disney resort guests are allowed admission, making it even more important to stay on-property if visiting in high season. Those staying off-property should arrive at the parks well before opening time, when a large percentage of Disney resort guests are still sleeping, to assure themselves access. Although such information is never released in advance, Disney sometimes opens earlier than official opening time during holiday periods in anticipation of record crowds.

of June to the third week of August; Thanksgiving weekend; the week of Christmas to just after New Year's.

Busy: The last two weeks of February (avoid President's Day week) to the first part of March before the onset of spring break; the month of October (a big convention month, the PGA Golf Classic, and Halloween celebrations at the Magic Kingdom and Universal Orlando); the week after Easter until the second week of June.

Least busy: The second week of January to the first week of February (avoiding the Martin Luther King holiday weekend in January); the third week of August to the beginning of October; the month of November excluding Thanksgiving weekend; just after Thanksgiving and again the week preceding Christmas week, a special time when the parks and resorts are festively decorated for the holidays.

The Weather at Walt Disney World

Because Orlando is a year-round vacation destination, you probably won't encounter bitter cold weather. Winter has many days of sunshine along

Month	Average High Temp (°F)	Average Low Temp (°F)	Average Rainfall (inches)
January	72	50	2.3
February	72	50	4
March	78	56	3.2
April	84	61	1.3
May	88	67	3.1
June	91	72	7.5
July	92	74	7.2
August	91	74	7.1
September	89	73	6.3
October	84	67	2.9
November	77	57	1.7
December	73	52	2

with the occasional cold snap, while summer brings uncomfortably muggy and warm days with almost daily afternoon showers. Peak hurricane season begins in August and runs through October, so be prepared for a washout (just about every store in the parks sells inexpensive Mickey-motif rain ponchos for that afternoon shower). The best months of the year—with delightfully mild and low-humidity weather, relatively small amounts of rainfall, and little if no danger of hurricanes—are November, April, and early May. Before leaving call (407) 824–4104 for daily weather information or check one of the many excellent weather sites on the Internet.

What to Pack

Think casual! Park attire is appropriate throughout Disney with the exception of the more stylish resort restaurants (for dress codes, see individual restaurant descriptions). In the warmer months of April through October, bring shorts, light-colored short-sleeved or sleeveless shirts (darker colors really attract the heat), comfortable walking shoes (bring two pairs to switch off), cushy socks, sunglasses, hat, bathing suit and cover-up, water-resistant footwear, and a rain jacket. Women should bring a fanny pack or light backpack; nothing's worse than lugging a heavy purse around all day. For evenings away from the park at one of the more sophisticated dining venues, women should plan on wearing a sundress or casual pants and top with sandals; men will be comfortable in khakis and a short-sleeved casual shirt with loafers or sandals. Only at Victoria and Albert's is a jacket required for men.

The remaining months are anyone's guess. The weather is usually mild, but bring an assortment of casual clothing in the form of shorts and comfortable long pants along with short- and long-sleeved shirts, a sweater, hat, sunglasses, bathing suit and cover-up (pools are heated), rain jacket, light coat, and of course comfortable walking shoes and socks. For evenings away from the parks, women should wear smartly casual transitional clothing, and men casual pants and long-sleeved shirts. Florida is known (particularly November through March) for unexpected cold fronts that will find you in shorts one day and a winter jacket the next, although it never gets uncomfortably hot. Don't get caught off guard or you'll find yourself with an unwanted Mickey Mouse wardrobe. Check the Internet for a weather forecast before packing for your trip.

Water-resistant footwear and fast-drying clothes are desirable at the Animal Kingdom (you'll get quite wet on the Kali River Rapids attraction) and most importantly at Universal's Islands of Adventure, where several rides will give you a thorough soaking. And don't forget plenty of sunscreen, film, and batteries, all of which can be purchased almost anywhere in Disney but at a premium price.

How Long Should I Plan on Staying?

With four major theme parks at Disney, two at Universal Orlando, plus SeaWorld, specialty parks like Discovery Cove, and several water parks, a long weekend will barely give you a taste of the many attractions in the area. Staying seven days or more allows enough time to truly enjoy much of what Orlando has to offer. In one week you'll have time to visit all four of Disney's theme parks, spend a day at Universal, hit one of the water parks, and still have a day left over to relax by the pool and rest your feet. Ten days would really be a treat, allowing a trip to both SeaWorld and Discovery Cove plus a bit of time to stop and smell the roses.

Of course, if you can spare only a long weekend, go for it. You will certainly have some tough decisions to make. With only a few days for touring, go when the parks are not as crowded and plan on visiting the Magic Kingdom, Epcot, and either the Animal Kingdom or Disney–MGM Studios with a trip in mind for another year to pick up all you've missed.

Should I Rent a Car?

Does driving in an unknown place make you uneasy? Do you plan on visiting just Disney, or are SeaWorld and Universal also of interest to you? Will you be staying at a resort serviced by the monorail or at a more isolated one? Would you like to dine at other resorts, or do you see yourself eating at the parks or simply staying put at your hotel? All these factors play a large part in your decision.

The drive from the airport on the Central Florida GreeneWay is a no-brainer, and finding your way around Disney is easy. Traffic is fairly light and there's excellent signage. However, if driving a car in new situations tends to be a nerve-racking experience, use Disney's more-than-adequate transportation system.

If your plans include a stay at the Animal Kingdom Lodge, Old Key West, Wilderness Lodge, the Villas at Disney's Wilderness Lodge, Saratoga Springs, or an off-site property, renting a car provides you with many more options. If you plan to visit Universal Studios or SeaWorld, a car is by far the best choice.

No matter what your plans, a car is usually the best option for traveling to the Animal Kingdom or Disney–MGM Studios (parks not serviced by the monorail), the water parks, or evening restaurant-hopping at the many excellent resort dining spots. However, you may find it simpler to use Disney transportation when traveling to Downtown Disney, where you'll want to spend the evening enjoying Pleasure Island without the worry of driving afterward, or on weekends when parking can be difficult. Think about trying Disney transportation for a day or two and, if it doesn't work for you, then rent a car. Alamo/National has free shuttle service to its Car Care Center location near the Magic Kingdom, and most non-Disney deluxe hotels have car rental desks in their lobbies.

Those who would like to sample some of Disney's excellent resort restaurants will find it time-consuming, not to mention complex, to resort-hop using Disney transportation. It requires a trip to an open park or Downtown Disney and then another bus to the resort and the same thing back again (of course you can always simplify things and take a cab). A stay at one of the Magic Kingdom resorts offers easy monorail access to the Magic Kingdom, other Magic Kingdom resorts, and Epcot. The Epcot Resorts are just a walk or boat launch away from Epcot, the Boardwalk, and Disney–MGM Studios, greatly expanding your restaurant choices.

I consider a car a must at any of the non-Disney properties, where transportation options are quite inconvenient—and don't let them tell you differently. Transportation from off-site properties is inconvenient at best, offering only the bare necessities. The only exception is Universal resorts, extremely convenient to the Universal theme parks and CityWalk; if Universal is all you plan on, a car is really not necessary.

In short, you will probably be using a combination of Disney transportation and a car for added convenience. And if you're like me and hate waiting for public transportation, rent a car to save hours of frustration.

Do remember that if your plans include a rental car, parking will be a factor. Although parking is complimentary to guests of a Walt Disney World resort, those staying off-property will pay $8.00 per day to park at

TIPS FOR WALT DISNEY WORLD FIRST-TIMERS

- Slow down and enjoy the magic. Resist the urge to see every-thing at breakneck speed, and take time to enjoy the many amenities offered at your resort (you certainly paid enough for them). You can't possibly see it all, so think of this as your first trip to Disney, not your last. There will be time to pick up the things you missed on the next go-round.

- Think ahead. Decide your priorities before your vacation begins.

- Get to the parks early! It's amazing, particularly in busy season, how many of the popular rides you can knock off before half the "World" gets out of bed.

- Plan for a rest in the middle of the day if you have children in tow or the parks are open late. Stay at one of the Magic Kingdom or Epcot resorts, allowing an easy return to your room in the middle of the day for a nap or a plunge in the pool.

- If breakfast at Cinderella's Royal Table in the Magic Kingdom is tops on your child's list, you *must*—I repeat *must*—call exactly ninety days prior at 7:00 A.M. Orlando time (eastern standard time) for priority seating or risk missing this highly coveted breakfast. The only time you might get away with sleeping in and booking a bit later in the day is during extremely slow seasons.

- Always come prepared for an afternoon shower during the rainy summer months even if the sky looks perfectly clear in the morn-ing. Rent a locker to store your rain gear, circling back if skies start to look threatening. If you're caught unprepared, just about every store in the parks sells inexpensive rain ponchos.

- If a lounge chair is a priority at the water parks, you'll need to arrive at opening time to secure one. And remember that in the busy summer months, parks are sometimes filled to capacity by midmorning, with new guests kept from entering until late after-noon.

- Use FASTPASS, Disney's nifty time-saving device offered at all four theme parks, saving hours in line (see the FASTPASS section for each park in chapter 4).

- Use advance reservations, especially in the busier times of year (see chapter 8, Dining, for a more detailed explanation), to save hours of waiting and frustration.

- Allow plenty of time to reach the theme parks each morning. It's easy to miss your breakfast priority seating when enough time has not been allocated.

- Be selectively spontaneous. If something catches your eye, even if it's not on your daily list of things to do, be ready to stop and explore or you may miss something wonderful.

- Be attuned to the limitations of your children. If they're tired, take a break; if their feet hurt, get them a stroller (forget that they outgrew one years ago); if a ride scares them, don't force the issue. It will make your day and the day of other park visitors a lot less stressful.

- If your party wants to split up, bring pagers, two-way radios, or cell phones to keep in touch.

- Wear broken-in, comfortable footwear. Better yet, bring two pairs and rotate them. Nothing is worse than getting blisters on your first day and then having to nurse them for the remainder of your vacation.

the Disney theme parks. And instead of being dropped off in front of the theme park entrance, those with a car will need to catch a shuttle from the parking lot. Self parking is complimentary at the Disney resorts, but valet parking will set you back $7.00 per day. That doesn't include the Walt Disney World Swan and Dolphin where it's $7.00 for self-parking and $14.00 for valet. And factor in an even bigger charge off-property where prices vary according to resort.

2

ARRIVAL AT
WALT DISNEY WORLD

Getting to Walt Disney World

By Car

Walt Disney World is located off Interstate 4, about 25 miles southwest of Orlando and west of the Florida Turnpike. From Interstate 95, U.S. Highway 1, or southbound on the Florida Turnpike, take I–4 west and follow the signs to the correct Walt Disney World exit for your resort or theme park destination. Visitors coming from southbound Interstate 75 need to take the turnpike south to I–4 west and follow the signs to Walt Disney World. Those traveling northbound on the turnpike should take the Osceola Parkway that will lead directly to Walt Disney World.

Once inside Walt Disney World, excellent signage will direct you to all destinations; however, you'll need to know what area your resort belongs to in order to find your way. The Contemporary, Grand Floridian, Polynesian, Wilderness Lodge, and Villas at Wilderness Lodge are located in the Magic Kingdom Resort Hotels area. The Boardwalk Inn and Villas, Yacht and Beach Club, Beach Club Villas, and Walt Disney World Swan and Dolphin Hotels are in the Epcot Resort Hotels area. The Animal Kingdom Lodge sits in the Animal Kingdom area. Old Key West and Saratoga Springs are in the Downtown Disney Resort Hotels area.

Airport Transportation

For personalized service book private car or limousine transfers prior to your arrival from **Quicksilver Tours and Transportation** (888–468– 6939 or www.quicksilver-tours.com), **Orlando Airport Transportation Services** (407–658–2284 or www.transportation2 disney.com), or **FL Tours** (888–832–2111 or www.fltours.com). Towncars cost $80 to $100 round-trip and limousines approximately $170 to $220 round-trip (depending on the size of your party). Your driver will meet you as you exit the escalator downstairs at baggage claim. A customary gratuity of 15 to 20 percent should be considered, and reservations are mandatory.

Disney's Magical Express, a motor coach service provided by Mears Transportation, allows guests to check their bags at their hometown airport and bypass baggage claim at the Orlando airport before boarding motor coaches to their Walt Disney World resort. Bags are delivered to the room. When departing, guests avoid airport lines by checking their luggage and receiving a boarding pass before leaving their Disney hotel (available to those passengers of American, Delta, Song, Continental, United, Ted, and JetBlue). Those with flight departures later in the day no longer have to worry about luggage after checkout. They simply check their luggage at the Resort Airline Check-in Desk and then enjoy the last day of their stay. This service is complimentary for now and available only to guests booking a Walt Disney World vacation package (but does not apply to guests of the Walt Disney World Swan and Dolphin).

Mears Transportation offers van and bus service to all Disney hotels. Arrangements can be made in advance by calling (800) 759–5219 or going online at www.mearstransportation.com, or on arrival at the Mears desk on the second level of the airport. Return reservations should be made at least twenty-four hours prior by calling (407) 423–5566. The cost is $29 round-trip per adult and $21 for children (those age three years or younger are free). With three or more people in your party, it will cost about the same for a Towncar, a wiser and certainly more comfortable alternative. Because Mears makes several stops at different resorts, add at least a half hour to your trip. You can always take a taxi, but you'll find it's not the best choice, with cab fares averaging $85 to $100 round-trip.

Arrival Information

1. Animal Kingdom
2. Disney–MGM Studios
3. Epcot
4. Magic Kingdom
5. Universal Orlando
6. SeaWorld of Florida

Car Rental

Alamo Rent A Car, the official car rental company of Walt Disney World, is located both at the airport and at the Car Care Center near the Magic Kingdom, with free shuttle service provided to and from your hotel. For convenience stick with the companies located on airport property—**Alamo, Avis, Budget, Dollar, L&M, and National**—whose cars are parked a quick walk away from the baggage claim area. Off-property car companies include **Enterprise, Hertz, Payless, and Thrifty.** All of them have another location somewhere in the vicinity of Walt Disney World.

For something more luxurious try the **Hertz Prestige Collection** offering Jaguars, Lincoln Navigators, Volvos, and the Land Rover Discovery. Specific models may be reserved, and a complimentary Never-Lost navigational system is included.

Excellent signage and a great toll road from the airport make for an easy twenty-five-minute drive. Take the South Exit out of the airport to toll road State Route 417 South, also known as the Central Florida GreeneWay, and follow the signage to Walt Disney World and your resort or theme park destination. The drive is approximately 22 miles. Another option is the north route out of the airport to toll Highway 528, also known as the Bee Line Expressway, then to I–4. This is the quickest way to Universal Orlando, but it's best to avoid it as a route to Disney during rush-hour traffic. This is the old route before the GreeneWay and only slightly shorter.

Disney Transportation

Disney's complimentary transportation system, designed for the exclusive use of Disney resort guests (although usually no ID is required to ride), is in most cases extremely efficient. A handy transportation map is available on check-in. In addition, taxis can be found at every resort, all four theme parks, and Downtown Disney. For more information call (407) WDW–RIDE or (407) 939–7433.

Bus Transportation

Disney has an extensive and extremely reliable system of over 700 clean, air-conditioned buses traversing the extent of the property. Designed for the exclusive use of Disney's registered guests, buses depart approximately

Disney Transportation Map

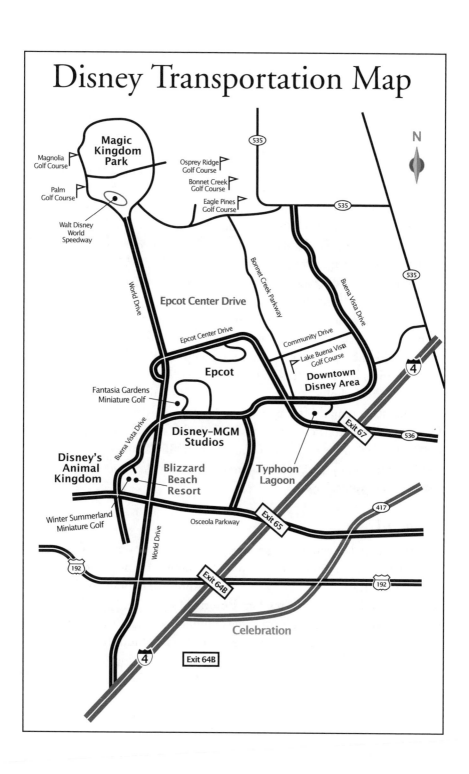

every twenty minutes carrying guests to all four theme parks, both water parks, Downtown Disney, and all resort hotels. Some are direct while others require a change at either the Ticket and Transportation Center (more commonly known as the TTC), Disney's central hub located near the Magic Kingdom, or Downtown Disney. Buses operate as early as 6:30 A.M. for those with breakfast priority seating before park hours until one and a half hours after park closing time. The last buses from Pleasure Island depart until around 3:00 A.M.

One advantage of bus transportation is the convenient drop-off directly in front of the park entrance, translating into no parking hassles and no waiting for a tram. The downside occurs after park closing when quite a line can form; consider leaving just a few minutes before the fireworks are over or hanging out to shop at one of the stores near the exit.

Getting easily from one resort to another is a different story altogether. Those staying at a Magic Kingdom or Epcot resort have many choices within walking distance or a monorail ride away, but those utilizing bus transportation find the only way to accomplish this feat is to take the quickest form of transportation to the nearest theme park and then a bus to the resort of choice. Of course this strategy only works during theme park operating hours. After park hours it's necessary to bus to Downtown Disney and then to the resort. For example, it takes a good hour or more to travel between say the Yacht Club Resort and Wilderness Lodge. If you want to resort-hop, I strongly encourage renting a car or utilizing a taxi for optimum convenience.

Monorail

Twelve monorails, each holding 300 passengers, travel over 13 miles of track at up to 40 mph on three lines: the monorail between Epcot and the Ticket and Transportation Center (TTC), the express monorail to the Magic Kingdom, and the Magic Kingdom Resorts monorail. All use the TTC as their central hub. Monorails traveling counterclockwise around the Seven Seas Lagoon offer a nonstop ride between the TTC and the Magic Kingdom. Monorails running clockwise stop at the Grand Floridian, the Polynesian, the Contemporary, and the TTC. Between Epcot and the Magic Kingdom is a lovely ride with easy access between the parks.

NOTE: If the operator's car is empty of visitors, ask the cast member (Disney's name for park employees) on duty at the monorail stop about the possibility of riding up front. Up to four people at a time are allowed.

TIPS FOR ROMANCE

If you're traveling with children, plan an evening or two on your own at a romantic restaurant or a night on the town at Downtown Disney. Leave the kids at one of Disney's excellent resort child care centers. If your child is age three or younger or is older but not potty trained, call **Kid's Nite Out** at (407) 828–0920 for in-room child care (reservations must be made twenty-four hours in advance). You might also consider springing for two rooms. Disney guarantees connecting rooms for families with children. Here are some suggestions for romance.

- Bring along a bottle of wine to enjoy in your room or on your balcony. The bottled wine selections at the Disney resort shops tend to be a bit sparse; of course room service usually has a nice selection.

- Arrange for a couples massage at the Grand Floridian Spa in a candlelit room.

- Pick up a glass of wine at the kiosk in France or Italy, then stroll Epcot's World Showcase in the evening when all the countries are beautifully lit by twinkling lights.

- Watch the evening fireworks spectacular from one of the resort beaches. Perfect spots can be found at the beaches of the Polynesian, the Grand Floridian, and the Yacht and Beach club.

- Take a Fireworks Cruise from one of the Magic Kingdom or Epcot resorts; bring along a bottle of champagne with two glasses, and enjoy!

Boat Service

Ferryboats found at the TTC are a fun form of transportation for Magic Kingdom visitors. The Magic Kingdom is also accessible by water taxi from the Polynesian, Grand Floridian, Contemporary, and Wilderness Lodge and Villas. Both Epcot and Disney–MGM Studios are accessible by water taxi from the Boardwalk Inn and Villas, Yacht and Beach Club, Beach Club Villas, and the Walt Disney World Swan and Dolphin. Downtown Disney can be reached from the Old Key West and Saratoga Springs resorts by water taxi.

Basic Disney Reference Guide

Alcoholic beverages. You'll find alcohol served at every park and hotel on Disney property, except at the Magic Kingdom. The legal drinking age in Florida is twenty-one; however, most of Disney's lounges allow minors as long as they do not drink alcohol or sit at the bar. Bottles of liquor, wine, and beer can be purchased in at least one shop in every Walt Disney World resort and/or from room service.

ATMs. Bank One automated teller machines (ATMs) are located at each park, in Downtown Disney, at the TTC, and in or near the lobby of each resort.

Business centers. Disney resorts with convention center facilities (Yacht and Beach Club, Boardwalk Inn, Contemporary, Grand Floridian, and Walt Disney World Swan and Dolphin) offer a complete office environment including personal computers, high-speed Internet, fax machines, copiers, and secretarial services.

Car care and gasoline. Hess Express has three stations in Disney World open twenty-four hours: on Floridian Way near the Magic Kingdom; across from Downtown Disney's Pleasure Island; and at the entrance to the Boardwalk across from MGM Studios. For car repair go to the AAA Car Care Center (407–824–0976) adjoining the Hess station near the Magic Kingdom. Open Monday through Friday from 7:00 A.M. to 6:00 P.M. and Saturday 7:00 A.M. to 4:00 P.M. If your car becomes disabled while on Disney property, AAA has complimentary towing to the Car Care Center; after hours call Disney security at (407) 824–4777.

Child care. Disney's Children's Activity Centers include the Cub's Den at Wilderness Lodge, the Sandcastle Club at the Yacht and Beach Club Resort, the Mouseketeer Club at the Grand Floridian, Simba's Cubhouse at the Animal Kingdom Lodge, Camp Dolphin at the Swan and Dolphin Resort, and the Never Land Club at the Polynesian (my favorite), all offering child care services for potty-trained children ages four through twelve. See individual resort descriptions for detailed information. Cost is $10 per hour per child, including a meal, with a minimum charge of $20 for two hours. Reservations should be made at least twenty-four hours in advance by calling (407) WDW–DINE or (407) 939–3463. For Camp Dolphin call (407) 934–4000.

Many off-property resorts have excellent child care facilities. At the Grand Cypress Resort (the Hyatt Regency and the Villas of Grand Cypress) is Camp Hyatt, at Gaylord Palms you'll find La Petite Academy Kids Station, and at the Ritz-Carlton and JW Marriott there's Ritz Kids.

For in-room or drop-off services, Disney recommends Kid's Nite Out. All employees of this service receive a thorough background check. Call (407) 828–0920 at least twenty-four hours in advance.

Dietary requests. Dietary requests such as kosher, no sugar added, low-carb, or low-fat can be accommodated at most Disney full-service restaurants if requested at least twenty-four hours in advance. Special dietary requests regarding allergies to gluten or wheat, shellfish, soy, lactose, peanuts, or other foods will be accommodated at all full-service restaurants as long as Disney is notified at least seventy-two hours in advance. Kosher meals can be found at Cosmic Ray's Starlight Café at the Magic Kingdom, ABC Commissary at Disney–MGM Studios, Liberty Inn at Epcot, and Pizzafari at the Animal Kingdom. Most full-service and many counter-service restaurants offer at least one vegetarian choice, which I have tried to reflect in my entree examples in the restaurant section.

Environmental awareness. Disney's environmental commitment is more than commendable. Efforts include the recycling of over 30 percent of waste; distribution of prepared, unserved food to local missions; collection of food waste for compost production; purchase of recycled products and products with reduced packaging; and use of reclaimed water for irrigation. Recycling containers can be found in every guest room and throughout the parks.

Flowers and such. Flowers, wine, and gourmet food baskets can be delivered anywhere on Disney property between 8:00 A.M. and 8:00 P.M. Call (407) 827–3505.

Groceries. The closest full-service grocery store is twenty-four-hour Goodings, located in the Crossroads Shopping Center of Lake Buena Vista Shopping Center near Downtown Disney. A small selection of groceries is also available at each home-away-from-home resort.

Hair salons. Full-service salons are located at the Grand Floridian, Contemporary, Yacht and Beach Club, and Dolphin as well as at the Hyatt Regency Grand Cypress, Gaylord Palms, Portofino Bay Hotel at Universal, and the JW Marriott/Ritz-Carlton. An old-fashioned barber haircut can be had on Main Street in the Magic Kingdom.

International travelers. Visitors who speak languages other than English may ask at Guest Relations in each theme park for a park guide versed in that language. Guides are available for more than a dozen other languages. Also available at Guest Relations, with a $100 refundable deposit, are complimentary language translation headsets with wireless technology that provide synchronized narration in Spanish, French, German, Japanese, or Portuguese for more than thirty attractions. Interpreters are available by calling the Foreign Language Center at (407) 824–7900. Many restaurants offer menus in several languages. Foreign currency may be exchanged at any Walt Disney World resort.

Internet services. In-room high-speed Internet access is available at the Beach Club Villas, Boardwalk Inn and Villas, Grand Floridian, Contemporary, Old Key West, Saratoga Springs, Yacht and Beach Club, Villas at Wilderness Lodge, and Walt Disney World Swan and Dolphin, with more resorts being added. Additional access can be found at the business centers of all the resorts that offer convention services. High-speed wireless Internet access (WiFi) is available at the Boardwalk, Contemporary, Grand Floridian, and Yacht and Beach Club common areas including the lobbies, convention center hallways, and near the main pool areas. Other resorts support Internet access through a dataport connection on the guest room telephone.

Laundry and dry cleaning. Self-service, coin-operated washers and dryers are located at every Disney resort in addition to same-day dry cleaning and laundry service.

Lockers. Lockers can be found in all four Disney parks as well as both water parks, Downtown Disney, and the Ticket and Transportation Center (TTC).

Lost and found. Lost item claims may be made at each individual park's Lost and Found. The central Lost and Found is located at the TTC, where items not claimed the previous day are sent; call (407) 824–4245.

Mail. The closest post office is at the Shoppes of Buena Vista, 12541 Highway 535; open Monday through Friday from 9:00 A.M. to 4:00 P.M. and Saturday from 9:00 A.M. to noon. Stamps may be purchased and letters mailed at all four theme parks, Downtown Disney, and all Walt Disney World resorts. All shops at Walt Disney World offer worldwide shipping for a fee.

Medical care. All theme parks offer first aid during park hours. Twenty-four-hour, in-room medical care for nonemergencies is handled by Florida Hospital Centra Care In-Room (407–238–2000). Florida Hospital Centra Care Walk-In Medical Center (407–660–8118) has four locations close to Disney, with complimentary transportation available and most insurance plans accepted. Emergency dental services are available by calling (407) 238–2000. Emergency medical needs are met by the Sand Lake Hospital at I–4 exit 74A or at Celebration Health located on Walt Disney World property in the town of Celebration.

Money matters. Walt Disney World accepts cash, traveler's checks, personal checks (at the resorts only, with a $50 limit per day and only if drawn on a U.S. bank, presented along with a valid driver's license and a current major credit card), Disney Dollars (available at Disney Stores, Guest Relations, and Resort Services), and six types of credit cards: American Express, MasterCard, Visa, Discover, Japanese Credit Bureau, and Diners club.

Guests of a Disney-owned resort may charge throughout Disney by using their room key as long as a credit card imprint is given at check-in. ATMs are readily available throughout Walt Disney World, with locations at each resort, each theme park, Downtown Disney, and the TTC.

Parking. Parking at Disney theme parks is free to all registered guests of Walt Disney World resorts and Annual Passport holders. All others pay $8.00 per day. Make sure you make a note of what section and aisle you have parked in; lots are enormous. Save your receipt if you plan on park-hopping; it allows you to park for that day only at any of the other Disney theme parks for no additional fee.

All Disney resorts charge $6.00 per day for valet parking; no charge for self-parking.

Pets. Only service dogs for guests with disabilities are allowed inside Disney's theme parks and resorts. Pet kennels for dogs and cats are available at the TTC, Epcot, Disney–MGM Studios, the Animal Kingdom, and Fort Wilderness Resort and Campground. Proof of vaccination is required.

Day boarding is $6.00. Overnight boarding, available only at the TTC, is $9.00 (including food) for Walt Disney World resort guests and $11.00 for off-site guests. Dogs must be walked daily by their owners. More unusual pets such as birds, ferrets, nonvenomous snakes, and small rodents are admitted as long as they are in their own carriers. Reservations not accepted. Call (407) 824–6568 for more information.

Rider switch. Parents traveling with young children who don't meet height restrictions should consider utilizing the rider switch program. One parent waits with the child while the other rides, then the second parent hands off the child and goes to the head of the line. Just speak to the cast member on duty.

Safety. Walt Disney World is a relatively safe environment, but caution must still be taken. Be alert at all times, particularly at night. Always lock your guest room door, and make sure you verify who is knocking before allowing anyone entry. Use the safe provided in your room to store money and valuables. Park in well-lit areas, lock your car, and be aware of your surroundings when leaving the car. Take extra care when traveling to Orlando and places outside Walt Disney World where security is less stringent.

Security. All bags are checked prior to entering the theme parks; allow yourself extra time if you've booked priority seating. High-security, antiterrorist barricades that can stop speeding trucks have been installed at Walt Disney World, an added level of protection for the theme parks' service entrances. The airspace over Walt Disney World is closed to low-flying aircraft.

Smoking. All Walt Disney World restaurants and public areas at each resort are smoke-free environments. Tobacco products are not sold in the theme parks, where smoking is limited to designated areas; look for the cigarette symbol on the guide maps. Because of the implementation of the Florida Indoor Clean Air Act on July 1, 2003, smoking is no longer allowed at any of Disney's nightclubs or resort lounges. Smoking-optional guest rooms are still available.

Stroller and wheelchair. Strollers, wheelchairs, and electric controlled vehicles (ECVs) may be rented at all major theme parks. Retain your receipt for a replacement at any other Disney theme park for that day only. Wheelchairs are also available at all Disney resorts.

Telephone calls. Orlando has a ten-digit calling system, meaning you must dial the area code of 407 followed by the number when making a local call.

VIP tour services. Those wanting special service should consider Disney's personalized theme park tours. For $125 per hour with a five-hour minimum, a VIP guide will assist you and up to nine others with a customized day at the parks and plenty of Disney trivia along the way. Don't expect to move to the front of the line, but do expect special seating for parades, stage shows, and dining. Reservations must be made at least forty-eight hours in advance by calling (407) 560–4033.

Another excellent option is Michael's VIPs, providing private tours of Walt Disney World and the surrounding Orlando area. Michael's experienced tour guides know the parks inside and out, thus avoiding the long lines. With them you can experience Walt Disney World's "best of the best" rides and attractions, have the best seats at the shows, dine at the best restaurants, and enjoy an unmatched level of service from your personal Disney expert. Michael's VIPs tours run $95 per hour plus an additional 20 percent gratuity for the guide with a minimum of four consecutive hours. There is an additional charge of $45 per planned day for a customized itinerary. Go to www.michaelsvips.com for reservations.

Wheelchair accessibility. All bus routes are serviced by vehicles equipped to accommodate wheelchairs. Watercraft access varies according to the type of craft and water levels. All monorails, many park attractions, and most restrooms are wheelchair-accessible. Special parking areas are available at all four theme parks. Wheelchairs and electric controlled vehicles (ECVs) may be rented in limited quantities at each theme park.

Each resort offers special equipment and facilities for guests with disabilities. Features vary by resort but may include wider bathroom doors, roll-in showers, shower benches, handheld shower heads, accessible vanities, portable commodes, bathroom and bed rails, bed shaker alarm, text typewriter, strobe-light fire alarm, and phone amplifier. Other features include double peepholes in doors, closed-captioned television, and braille on signage and elevators.

Most theme park attractions provide access through the main queue while others have auxiliary entrances for wheelchairs and service animals along with up to five members of your party. Certain attractions require

ANNUAL WALT DISNEY WORLD EVENTS

January: Walt Disney World Marathon the second week of January.

April: Six-week Epcot International Flower and Garden Festival.

May: Epcot International Flower and Garden Festival; Star Wars Weekends at Disney–MGM Studios.

June: Star Wars Weekends at Disney–MGM Studios.

September: Night of Joy at the Magic Kingdom.

October: Six-week Epcot Food and Wine Festival; Mickey's Not So Scary Halloween Party at the Magic Kingdom; FUNAI Classic at Disney's Magnolia and Palm Golf Courses.

November: Epcot Food and Wine Festival; Festival of the Masters at Downtown Disney; ABC Super Soap Weekend at Disney–MGM Studios; Epcot's Holidays Around the World from late November until early January.

December: Mickey's Very Merry Christmas Party at the Magic Kingdom; Osborne Family Spectacle of Lights at Disney–MGM Studios; Pleasure Island's New Year's Eve.

guests to transfer from their wheelchair to a ride system. For detailed information the helpful *Guidebook for Guests with Disabilities* is available at Guest Relations at each park or at the front desk of each Walt Disney World Resort. Handheld receivers are available to read captions at more than twenty park attractions. Each park offers assistive listening devices, video captioning, braille guidebooks, and audiotaped tours, all available for a refundable $25 deposit, and handheld captioning is available with a $100 deposit. Reflective captioning can be found at many theater-type attractions. A sign language interpreter for live shows can be made available with one week's notice on certain days of the week (see each individual park for details). Additional information can be found at www.disneyworld.com or by calling (407) 939–7807 (voice) or (407) 939–8255 (TTY).

For further detailed information consider purchasing *Passporter's Walt Disney World for Your Special Needs,* by Deb Wills and Debra Martin Koma. It's a comprehensive resource for people with mobility, sensory, and other impairments, but it also covers such other diverse topics as pregnancy, travel with infants, needs of seniors, ADD/ADHD, food allergies, special dietary needs, multilingual issues, and plus-size guests.

Disney Weddings

Bride's magazine lists Disney among the top ten U.S. wedding destinations. In fact, Walt Disney World hosts about 2,300 weddings a year. More than 20,000 couples have taken their wedding vows in Disney's storybook atmosphere, and countless more have picked Disney as their choice for a dream honeymoon. Imagine being escorted to your wedding in Cinderella's glass coach with horses and footmen in attendance or perhaps a themed wedding in Epcot's Italy Pavilion surrounded by a replica of St. Mark's Square. Everything can be arranged, from the flowers to the photographer, the waiters to the music. To speak to a wedding planner, call (407) 566–6540. Honeymooners should call (800) 370–6009, or go online at http://disneyweddings.disney.go.com/disneyworldweddings.

Wedding Locations

Although weddings are allowed just about anywhere on Disney property, there are several very popular sites; if you want a theme park wedding, expect the price to skyrocket. On an island surrounded by the Seven Seas Lagoon is the **Wedding Pavilion** at the Grand Floridian Resort, offering a magical view of Cinderella's Castle. The **Rose Garden** fronting Cinderella's Castle at the Magic Kingdom is another top pick, with a medieval-style banquet in the castle afterward. At Epcot, the **Living Seas Lounge** comes with a six-million-gallon aquarium as a backdrop, or choose any of the World Showcase pavilions. **Sea Breeze Point** at Disney's Boardwalk Resort offers a white gazebo overlooking Crescent Lake. Or you may want to consider the wedding gazebo in the Yacht Club Resort's serene rose garden. **Sunset Pointe** at the Polynesian Resort is on a grassy hill overlooking the Seven Seas Lagoon with Cinderella's Castle in the background. **Sunrise Terrace** at the Wilderness Lodge has a fourth-floor balcony overlooking the pine trees and Bay Lake. You can also have your marriage ceremony on Disney Cruise Line's private island, **Castaway Cay.**

Wedding Themes

Choose from a traditional wedding to a variety of Disney-themed weddings. Some theme ideas include an Under the Sea wedding at the Living Seas Pavilion, a Beauty and the Beast Ball Wedding, or a Winter Wonderland Wedding. How about an Animal Kingdom Safari reception? Or a Cinderella ball with the bride arriving in a glass coach pulled by white ponies? What about inviting Mickey to your cake cutting? Just about anything is possible at Walt Disney World.

Wedding Packages

Disney's Intimate Wedding packages or Vow Renewal packages are just how they sound: small and intimate, with a maximum of eight guests (each additional guest up to thirteen is an extra $100 per person) at one of five locations at Walt Disney World. Included are accommodations, park tickets for your entire stay, an on-site wedding coordinator, a wedding officiant, a bouquet for the bride and a boutonniere for the groom, a reception with cake, an organist and a violinist for the ceremony, a limousine, a personalized wedding Web site, a wedding keepsake, two hours of photography, and a marriage certificate. Prices for four-night packages begin at around $3,500. Events with more than fifteen guests are considered Custom Weddings, which begin at $7,500.

Disney Cruise Line's Weddings at Sea begin at around $4,000 for a three-day cruise and include a ceremony on Castaway Cay, marriage license, on-site wedding coordinator, officiant, solo musician, flowers for bride and groom, cake and champagne reception, dinner for two at Palo (the adults-only dining room) on the wedding night, champagne and strawberries in the stateroom, and $100 onboard credit.

Empty Nest Touring

In this final section of the chapter, MousePlanet's Mike Scopa (www .mouseplanet.com) gives his take on empty nesters—that is, parents whose kids have grown up and moved out—in Walt Disney World.

From Magic Kingdom to Mature Kingdom

Sooner or later it happens to the best of us. One day the youngest child leaves home and yet another set of empty nesters is born, a phenomenon taking place every day. So how does this transition from family to empty nester mode impact the planning phase for a Walt Disney World vacation, and how does it impact your wallet? Let's take a look.

As your children grow up and move out, you may still have a hankering to visit Orlando and escape from reality. So how do you approach a visit to Walt Disney World without the kids? What can you expect to be different about a vacation to Orlando sans children?

You'll quickly realize you're looking at a far less expensive vacation than in the past. You'll also approach your vacation in a different manner.

AIRFARE

When traveling as a family, you usually don't have the flexibility that allows you to get the best airfare. With the exception of the summer months, most school vacation weeks aren't usually times when the airlines are offering great prices. Empty nesters are flexible and can schedule their vacation for whatever time of the year they want and take advantage of great prices.

ADMISSION MEDIA

Fewer people mean fewer admission media to buy. You may also change the type of media you would buy. If you realize a huge savings in your overall vacation expense, would you then be able to take two Walt Disney World trips in one year? If so then Annual Passports may be the best admission media for you.

FOOD

A party of two may find the Walt Disney World dining experience to be quite different than it was as a family. Making priority seating is easier for a party of two than a party of four, five, or six. Fewer appetite schedules to coordinate can mean taking advantage of lower lunch prices or a late lunch instead of an early dinner. You can also try out those pricey restaurants you just couldn't afford as a family.

CAR RENTAL

Guess what? With fewer people you have less baggage—er, luggage—and that means you can rent a smaller, less expensive car. So now you can get by with that compact instead of that SUV, van, or "full-size" vehicle.

Is that a smile I see?

Hidden Savings

Imagine all the savings realized when planning an empty nester Walt Disney World vacation. They all add up. We've talked about the obvious ones, but there are some hidden savings as well.

- Many people shop for a vacation wardrobe before vacation, and we certainly don't leave out the children. That clothes budget will definitely go down.

- We all know about those irresistible souvenirs. Does anyone ever go on a Walt Disney World vacation and *not* bring back a souvenir or two . . . or ten? Without the kiddies you won't be spending as much on souvenirs—at least for them.

- How about film? Maybe in today's world of digital photography it's not such a big deal. Without the kids there will be far fewer photos and far less video to take. You won't need to buy as much film and videotape.

- If as a family you could not afford to stay on Disney property, then why not splurge and experience your first empty nest vacation as an on-site guest? Can you afford it now? Probably. If you have stayed on-site in the past, maybe these savings will let you move up in resort class. So an empty nest at home could mean a snazzier nest in Walt Disney World.

Empty Nest Touring Plans?

There are many resources to turn to when you're in need of guidance for a family-touring plan of Walt Disney World. I'm sure there are some that even discuss how best for couples to tour Walt Disney World. What about a plan for empty nesters? More important, instead of a touring plan, why not provide guidelines for empty nesters to design and develop general touring plans that work toward meeting their best interests? Following are some guidelines as to how to best approach a Walt Disney World vacation without the kids.

First of all, if you're looking for a touring plan, you've come to the wrong place. This discussion will not offer you a step-by-step, hour-by-hour tour package of the theme parks. Instead, the objective is to offer you some insight and thoughts on how differently Walt Disney World may appeal to you now that you're an empty nester—and why. The most important goal here is for you to determine for yourself what is best for you and not let me or anyone else position you into a specific touring plan. So wave goodbye to the kids, and let's get started.

There are some aspects of empty nest touring that you should always keep in mind.

Shrinkage. This is obvious. There are only two of you, which means you need to agree on the where, when, and what of only two people. You may not have to spend much time planning ahead and can be more spontaneous than you were as a family

Commando to slug. Without the kids there's less or no pressure to hurry and get to the parks, no rush to get in those early queues for Space Mountain, Test Track, Rock 'n' Roller Coaster, Dinosaur, or other popular thrill attractions. You can now take a leisurely approach to your daily park visits.

Time compression. OK, what's this? With fewer people, you can do more things. In general, a party of two can do more things faster than a family of four. This can range from being seated and served in a restaurant to enjoying *any* attraction.

Dollar stretching. This is a big one. Your vacation dollar now may go a bit further. Fewer family members mean lower costs. You can now do or experience parts of Walt Disney World that before were cost-prohibitive.

A Kinder, Gentler Shopping Experience

Leaving the Magic Kingdom after a long day almost demands a last-minute visit to the Emporium. You know what I mean. Strollers hitting your ankles, lost children screaming for moms, long lines at the registers, and precious few cast members (employees) available to help you because the ratio of guests to cast members at that time seems to be 20,000 to 1.

The empty nester may find that one of the more enjoyable things to do in the Magic Kingdom is to shop leisurely on Main Street. You'll find hardly anyone there during the first two hours of the park's opening, and you will have access to all the well-stocked merchandise and plenty of cast members to help you.

One of the more relaxing things to do in Epcot is to take your time strolling through World Showcase's unique shops. This is not to say that you wouldn't have done so as a family. It's just that number one son and daughter may have been somewhat anxious about spending time in "boring" World Showcase, rushing you through the shops.

As an empty nester, you have the luxury of really catering to your shopping instincts and—oh, by the way—your vacation dollar has been adjusted so maybe now you can afford that $3,000 Buddha statue in Young Feng Shangdian or that $200 sweater in the Crown and Crest.

Disney–MGM Studios is much like the Magic Kingdom in that Hollywood Boulevard is like Main Street, USA. The shops along Hollywood Boulevard are best enjoyed early in the day. No need to rush down to Sunset Boulevard to grab a FASTPASS and then sprint to the Twilight Zone Tower of Terror.

This notion of empty nester shopping is also true of Disney's Animal Kingdom. There are some interesting shops to explore here, and you don't want to rush. The empty nester will enjoy spending time discovering what exactly Chester & Hester's shop has to offer.

Here's a guarantee: By taking this empty nester shopping approach, you'll discover an area in a theme park shop that you've never found before when you toured as a large family. In the past you may have been rushing around in commando mode. Also, you can shop first thing in the morning when 90 percent of the guests are running to attractions.

Discovering Theme Park Transportation

You may now find opportunities to experience in-park transportation that you may have either been too rushed to enjoy in the past or may not have experienced at all.

How about taking the **ferry** from the Ticket and Transportation Center to the Magic Kingdom? Children love the monorail since the ferry doesn't travel through the Contemporary Resort.

Several **Main Street vehicles** will take you from the train station to the Castle hub. A ride in the horseless carriage, trolley, or fire engine is quite enjoyable, especially if you're not traveling with fidgety children who blame you for keeping them from Bre'r Rabbit and Splash Mountain.

Then there's the **Walt Disney Express Railroad.** On a warm day this is a great cooling-off option. You may have enjoyed this train ride with your family in the past and taken it to quickly get from the front of the park to

Frontierland (Splash Mountain), but now you can ride it simply for the sheer enjoyment.

Let's not forget the **Liberty Belle Riverboat.** This excursion is often given a thumbs-down by the younger set. Heck, it's boring—no dips, thrills, or chills. For the empty nester tortured by the sight of Big Thunder Mountain Railroad, this riverboat ride offers another chance to soak up the Magic Kingdom atmosphere in a relaxed mode.

The **Tomorrowland Transit Authority** is usually not a big favorite of the younger set, but it's a chance for adults to take an enjoyable ride around Tomorrowland, get a great view of the park, and see inside Space Mountain.

If you're staying at a monorail resort or even if you intend to leave the Magic Kingdom and head toward Epcot, why not take the **monorail** to the TTC and change to the Epcot-bound monorail? The approach to Epcot offers a breathtaking view of Future World.

While in Epcot, take advantage of the **Friendship Boats** to bring you across the World Showcase Lagoon, a great way to view World Showcase.

In Disney's Animal Kingdom, there's the Kilamanjaro Safari and the **Wildlife Express Train** to Rafiki's Planet Watch.

Attraction Distraction

Ever come home after a Walt Disney World family vacation only to realize that you never got a chance to check out a certain area or an attraction in a theme park? This is called *attraction distraction*. Most of the time this distraction is caused by pressure to do the popular attractions, either before the crowds build or as many times as possible. Empty nesters may be able to avoid attraction distraction and finally check out those nooks and crannies that are waiting to be discovered. Here are just a few of those areas that may have escaped many guests in the past.

- The Town Square Exposition Hall offers you a chance to get away from the crowd and explore some interesting exhibits, early Disney cartoons, and photo opportunities. It's best explored during the first hour of park operation. You may even encounter one of the Seven Dwarfs or Daisy Duck.

- One overlooked attraction is the Swiss Family Robinson Treehouse. When was the last time you took your time and looked at what the Imagineers built?

- Epcot offers so much in the way of relaxing empty nest touring; check out the Stave Church at the Norway pavilion, the miniature train setup near Germany, and the beautiful gardens near the Canada pavilion.

- MGM Studios offers great entertainment in Streetmosphere on Hollywood Boulevard. What about discovering the handprints in front of the Great Movie Ride, One Man's Dream, and of course the back lot and animation tour?

- Disney's Animal Kingdom offers the Maharajah Jungle Trek, Kilimanjaro Safari, and Pangani Forest Exploration Trail, great places that allow a leisurely pace.

Eating for Two

Now is the time to enjoy the pricier restaurants you may not have been able to swing as a family. No picky eaters anymore who don't care to try Moroccan food, eat at a restaurant called Narcoosee's, or even dine with fish looking over their shoulder. Let's not forget that it's easier to secure a priority seating for two than for a larger number. Here's a tip: Enter (407) 939–3463 into your cell phone's memory. It's the number for priority seating. Use it when you want to make arrangements at a restaurant, especially if you're in the theme park where the restaurant is located. This will save time waiting in line.

A Fresh Outlook

Although I've focused on the parks, remember that there are plenty of resorts to visit and much to explore in the Downtown Disney Area. Every Walt Disney World vacation has its own unique personality, and your first empty nest visit will bring with it a new outlook on the Walt Disney World Resort. Who says you either have to be a kid or be with kids to enjoy a Walt Disney World vacation?

3

ACCOMMODATIONS

With more than 25,000 guest rooms, Disney is rich in choices for the deluxe traveler. But which resort is best for you? Let's try to narrow down the field of possibilities by pinpointing your party's personality and preferences.

Those traveling with small children will find themselves spending quite a bit of time at the Magic Kingdom. Strongly consider choosing one of the Magic Kingdom Resorts, where the park is just a short monorail hop away, easily accessible for a quick afternoon nap or a dip in the pool.

Adults traveling without children will probably enjoy being closer to Epcot and Disney–MGM Studios. It's just a short walk or boat ride away to both parks from any of the excellent Epcot resorts. You'll also find a world of possibilities in nearby dining and entertainment. Those who enjoy nature and like a quiet, more isolated resort should opt for the Animal Kingdom Lodge, where hundreds of animals roam just 30 feet from your room balcony, or perhaps Wilderness Lodge, surrounded by pine forest fronting Bay Lake. If the convenience and comfort of a living area and kitchen are appealing, think about one of the home-away-from-home resorts located throughout Walt Disney World. If you plan on spending several days at Universal with a visit to SeaWorld or Discovery Cove, book three or four nights at one of the hotels near Universal and then afterward move to a Disney resort.

Also consider room type preferences. Is a view of the water or pool important? Or would you rather pay less and have a view of the resort's gardens? Will a standard room be all that you need, or should you consider one on the concierge level or maybe even a suite? Of course budget together with how much time will be spent in your room are major considerations and will play a large part in your decision. If hanging out at your resort sounds appealing, the concierge rooms are a smart idea at about $125 to $150 more per day per room. These accommodations, located on a keyed-access floor, come with the use of a private lounge with complimentary continental breakfast, snacks throughout the day, before-dinner hors d'oeuvres and cocktails, and late evening cordials and desserts. These amenities are in addition to private registration and checkout and the assistance of a concierge staff ready to assist you with advance reservations, special dinner shows, or anything else within their power. Definitely a nice plus to your vacation. Suites in each of the deluxe resorts come in virtually all shapes and sizes, some as large as 2,000 or more square feet, certainly the most luxurious option if your pocketbook allows.

Would you rather stay within Walt Disney World, or do you prefer an off-property location? Staying on property certainly has its pluses. In addition to the many benefits (see the sidebar in the next section for more details), consider the ease of transportation. Parents of teens can allow them time on their own without worrying about their every move. And teens will love the freedom of hopping aboard the monorail or a Disney bus to tour the parks without parents. Those with small children will be close enough to head back from the parks for an afternoon nap. I consider only a handful of off-property resorts as deluxe, all of them within ten to fifteen minutes from Walt Disney World. Of course always consider Universal's hotels if your plans include a few days at the Universal parks. One of the chief reasons to consider a stay off-property is if someone (particularly someone who is paying) is Mickey Mouse phobic. For them, Disney theming, though terrific, is a bit of overkill and the thought of spending the entire day in the park and then returning to more of the same is just too much.

Walt Disney World Resorts

Although twenty-two resorts are owned and operated by Disney, only those meeting the standard of superior first class or deluxe have been considered for review in this guidebook. All have attractive guest rooms, land-

BENEFITS OF
STAYING AT DISNEY

- Complimentary and convenient Disney transportation by monorail, bus, and water taxi.

- Complimentary parking at Disney's theme parks.

- Easy access to the parks, making midday breaks and naps possible, plus allowing parties to effortlessly split up to go their independent ways.

- Charge privileges utilizing your resort identification cards (a credit card imprint must be left at the registration desk) for purchases throughout Disney. All purchases are charged to your resort account.

- Guaranteed entry to Disney's theme parks, particularly important during busy holiday periods when filled-to-capacity parks often close to non-Disney resort guests.

- **Extra Magic Hours** whereby each day one of Disney's theme parks opens one hour early exclusively for resort guests or stays open up to three hours later after regular park hours with many but not all attractions open. The schedule is:

  > Sunday: Disney–MGM Studios (evening)
  > Monday: Epcot (morning)
  > Tuesday: Disney–MGM Studios (morning); Animal
  >   Kingdom (evening)
  > Wednesday: Magic Kingdom (evening)
  > Thursday: Epcot (evening)
  > Friday: Magic Kingdom (morning)
  > Saturday: Animal Kingdom (morning)

- Package delivery from anywhere on-property directly to your resort.

- Access to Disney's child care facilities available only to resort guests.

- The magic of Disney twenty-four hours a day.

scaped grounds of sheer artistry, exceptional service, top-notch recreational facilities and services, and, with the exclusion of some of the home-away-from-home properties, at least one excellent restaurant if not two or three. And all, with the exception of the off-site properties, offer Disney's special touch.

Disney Resorts

Although Disney offers a nice range of resorts in every price category, we will consider only the deluxe resorts and the home-away-from-home properties. The moderate properties, though interesting and well themed, do not fit this book's designation of luxury, and of course the value properties do not even come close.

DISNEY'S DELUXE RESORTS

Disney's deluxe properties are graced with impressive lobbies, painstakingly landscaped grounds, first-rate restaurants, elaborately themed pools, and gracious accommodations. These properties include the Grand Floridian, the Polynesian, the Contemporary, the Wilderness Lodge, the Animal Kingdom Lodge, the Boardwalk Inn, the Yacht and Beach Club, and the Walt Disney World Swan and Dolphin.

The Wilderness Lodge as well as the Animal Kingdom Lodge are a slightly different level of deluxe. Standard rooms here are smaller than other deluxe resorts; however, what they lack in room space they more than make up for in atmosphere. Opt for a deluxe room instead of a standard at these properties and you will be more than satisfied.

Those who frequent five-star properties such as the Ritz-Carlton or Four Seasons should not expect quite the same amenities at Disney. Although Disney's resorts are great, don't look for triple-sheeted beds, plush towels, deluxe toiletries, giant marble bathrooms, and butlers. And don't expect pay movies, HBO, and your choice of one hundred channels. The point is to just enjoy the unparalleled theming and exceptionally friendly service in the four-star-rated rooms at "the Most Magical Place on Earth."

For those choosing to stay off-property, deluxe resorts include the Celebration Hotel, the Hyatt Regency Grand Cypress, the Villas of Grand Cypress, and the Gaylord Palms Resort. At Universal are the Hard Rock Hotel, the Portofino Bay Hotel, and the Royal Pacific Resort. The Ritz-

Carlton Hotel and the JW Marriott are between Universal and Disney. All are excellent alternatives to the Disney resorts.

DISNEY'S HOME-AWAY-FROM-HOME PROPERTIES

Old Key West, the Villas at Disney's Wilderness Lodge, the Boardwalk Villas, the Beach Club Villas, and Saratoga Springs are Disney's five deluxe home-away-from-home choices. All are Disney Vacation Club properties leased out to nonmembers when rooms are available, a great way to enjoy Disney with all the conveniences of home, including a full kitchen, a living room, and a bathroom for each bedroom.

I do feel, however, that the home-away-from-home studio accommodations' only advantage is their minikitchen consisting of a microwave, small refrigerator, and sink. A better choice for just about the same price is a guest room at one of the deluxe hotels. The Boardwalk and the Beach Club Villas have easy access to all services and recreation facilities of their adjoining resorts plus the advantage of being close to the many shops and restaurants of the Boardwalk and Epcot. The Villas at Disney's Wilderness Lodge property is just a hop, skip, and jump away from the facilities of the adjoining Wilderness Lodge and a boat ride away from the Magic Kingdom. Although Old Key West and Saratoga Springs are lovely properties, they come with a more remote location and only one dining facility.

CHECK-IN AND CHECKOUT

Check-in time is 3:00 P.M. at all Disney resorts and 4:00 P.M. at all home-away-from-home resorts. If arriving early in the day, go straight to your resort to register and have your luggage stored until check-in time, then head off to a park or spend time exploring the property. In slower seasons it's sometimes possible to check in early.

At check-in you'll receive a bulletin with up-to-date information on resort services, recreation, and special events as well as a *Walt Disney World Update* with park hours, rehabs (attractions closed for renovation), and special events. If you'd like a head start, ask for a copy of the park guide maps. You'll also be handed a *Disney Transportation Guide,* an extremely useful tool for those utilizing Disney's extensive transportation system.

Rerequest any preferences at registration. Be sure to have your room pointed out on a resort map; if the location is undesirable, say so before leaving the desk. And if you've booked the concierge level or a suite, remember to identify yourself as a concierge guest to the bellhop on arrival to be escorted directly to your private check-in.

If you're taking a late plane home on checkout day, store your luggage with either the concierge or valet parking and head out to the parks. If you're staying at more than one Disney property, valet services will transfer your luggage free of charge with luggage arriving by 3:00 P.M.

Disney Discounts

Yes, this book is about a Disney deluxe vacation, but even the biggest spenders like a bargain. And bargains are as easily available at the deluxe resorts as they are at the value ones. Better yet, opportunities to save on everything from dining to entertainment to behind-the-scenes tours abound. With the many discounts available, only in the busiest seasons should anyone pay full price for a Disney resort. Following are some of the many ways to save.

Seasonal discounts. Rooms at Walt Disney World are priced using a four-season system that varies according to resort type. Remember, the busier the season, the more expensive the room. Approximate seasons for deluxe resorts are as follows:

■ Value season: January to mid-February, early July to early October, and late November to right before Christmas

■ Regular season: mid to late April (depending on the Easter holiday) to early July and again early October to late November

■ Peak season: mid-February until mid to late April (depending on the Easter holiday)

■ Holiday season: just before Christmas through December 31

Annual Pass rates. This is one of Disney's best bargains. With the purchase of an Annual Pass, you'll not only receive unlimited park admission for one year but also excellent resort rates. Only one person in the room need be a pass holder to obtain up to a 45 percent discount available throughout most of the year. Also included is a quarterly *Mickey Monitor* newsletter; discounted admission to Blizzard Beach, Typhoon Lagoon, Pleasure Island, and DisneyQuest; as well as discounts on special ticketed events, selected dining, merchandise, car rentals, behind-the-scenes tours, spa treatments, water sports, boat rentals, and golf.

Room discounts aren't typically available until two to three months in advance and are, of course, limited. A good strategy is to hold a room at the regular price just to be safe and continue calling periodically until the pass holder discount becomes available, at which point the reservation agent will lower your rate. With the amount saved, the additional cost of an Annual Pass could more than pay for itself in just one night.

Disney discount codes. Throughout the year Disney has great specials associated with special discount codes often advertised in the Sunday travel section of major newspapers. Perhaps the best way to keep up with them is by going online to www.mousesavers.com, a great Web site that stays on top of the discount game.

AAA discounts. Receive a discounted room price of 10 to 20 percent with a AAA membership.

***Entertainment* publications.** By purchasing either your local or the Orlando version of this discount book at a cost of about $25, members are eligible for 50 percent off discounts to hotels throughout the United States. Participating deluxe hotels in Orlando are the Walt Disney World Swan and Dolphin and Universal's Hard Rock, Royal Pacific, and Portofino Bay Hotels. Order online at www.entertainment.com.

Florida residents. Residents of Florida receive great Disney benefits, particularly during the slower times of the year. Call (407) 824–4321 for special prices on resort rooms and theme park passes.

Making Your Reservations

Don't call for reservations until you narrow the field down to two or three resorts that best suit your needs. Reserve as soon as possible, particularly for travel during major holidays or summer, to ensure that your preferred resort and room type are available. Again, decisions need to be made. Is it best to go with a package deal or book a "room only" reservation and treat your air, resort, and car as separate elements? Is it wiser to make the reservations yourself or call a travel agent? How about booking your trip on the Internet? All good questions. With such a wide array of booking choices on the market, there is no substitute for a good travel agent. This professional can certainly save you a lot of time, headaches, and usually money.

DISNEY AND UNIVERSAL BOOKING NUMBERS

Call a travel agent or Central Reservations at the Walt Disney World Travel Company at (407) 934–7639 or go online at www.disneyworld.com for all on-site Disney resorts. Universal's on-site hotels may be booked online at www.uescape.com or by calling (888) U ESCAPE, (888) 837–2273, (800) 23–LOEWS, or (800) 235–6397.

MAJOR AIRLINES SERVICING ORLANDO

Airlines servicing Orlando include Air Canada, American, America West, Continental, Delta, Frontier Airlines, JetBlue, Northwest, Song, Southwest, Ted, and United. Find the lowest airfare by calling your travel agent or each individual airline servicing your city (a lot of work) or by shopping the Internet, particularly sites such as Expedia, Orbitz, and Travelocity. No one should ever pay full fare for a coach-class seat unless booking at the last minute. Most important, shop, shop, shop! Fares to Orlando tend to be quite a bargain.

BOOKING A PACKAGE OR NOT

Remember when purchasing a package to consider whether all of the included options will be utilized. If not, you'll almost certainly be overpaying. Travel agents have access to tour operators as well as the aforementioned discounted offers and can help you decide what is in your best interest. The following are travel agencies and companies that specialize and market Disney:

- **AAA Vacations:** (888) 937–5523 or www.csaa.com
- **American Airlines Flyaway Vacations:** (800) 321–2121 or www.aa.com
- **American Express Vacations:** (800) 297–6898 or www.travel.americanexpress.com
- **Central Reservations at the Walt Disney World Travel Company:** (407) 934–7639 or www.disneyworld.com
- **Continental Vacations:** (800) 634–5555 or www.covacations.com
- **Delta Dream Vacations:** (800) 872–7786 or www.deltavacations.com/disney.html

- **Luxury Orlando Travel:** That's me! I will personally plan your Disney vacation at www.LuxuryOrlandoTravel.com

- **The Magic for Less Travel:** (888) 330–6201 or www.themagicforless .com

- **MouseEar Vacations:** www.MouseEarVacations.com

- **OLP Travel:** www.ourlaughingplace.com

- **Small World Vacations:** www.wdwvacations.com

- **Universal Orlando Vacations:** (888) 322–5537 or www.universal orlando.com

DISNEY'S VACATION PACKAGE PLANS

Central Reservations at the Walt Disney World Travel Company as well as many of the aforementioned travel agencies and tour operators offer Disney's special package plans. The more elaborate ones are a good buy only if you think you'll use all of the additional features. Beware of purchasing a plan with elements you do not want or need.

Disney also has **air/sea vacations.** Those who love cruising should consider three or four nights on the *Disney Wonder* or seven nights on the *Disney Magic* combined with several days at a Disney resort, the best of both worlds (see the last chapter of this book for more information on the Disney Cruise Line).

Disney's package plans, including Magic Your Way tickets (see sidebar in chapter 4, Theme Parks), are as follows:

Disney's Magic Your Way Package: Resort accommodations and Magic Your Way Base Tickets.

Disney's Magic Your Way Package Plus Dining: Resort accommodations, Magic Your Way Base Tickets, and a Disney dining plan at more than one hundred on-property restaurants including per-person, per-day the following: one table-service meal (appetizer, entree, dessert, and nonalcoholic beverage), one counter-service meal (entree and nonalcoholic beverage or a full combo meal with entree, side dish, and nonalcoholic beverage), and one snack. A table-service meal can be exchanged for a character meal, or two table-service meals can be exchanged for a signature dining experience at places such as California Grill or a dinner show such as Hoop-Dee-Doo Review.

Disney's Magic Your Way Premium Package: Resort accommodations, Magic Your Way Premium Tickets, breakfast, lunch, and dinner per person per day, unlimited selected recreation, admission to Cirque du Soleil, admission to Disney children's activity centers at selected resorts, and unlimited admission to theme park tours.

CONSIDERATIONS WHEN BOOKING YOUR VACATION

When considering a concierge-level room, take into account the schedule you will more than likely keep during your vacation. If you plan on spending most of the day and into the evening at the parks, the additional price for concierge service will not be worth the expense. You'll probably only have time to take advantage of the continental breakfast and perhaps the late-night cordials and dessert, with the remaining offerings wasted. If returning to your resort to dress and relax before dinner or an afternoon swim at the pool sounds more to your liking, the concierge level can't be beat. The continuous food and beverages, the extra attentive service, and that special feeling of staying in a small hotel within a larger complex certainly goes a long way.

Inquire whether any major construction will be in progress at your resort of choice during your visit. If so, book another property. No matter how nicely they try to cover up a pool reconstruction or an all-encompassing face-lift, it most certainly will affect your overall resort experience. Take my word for it. If the reservation agent does not have adequate information on the extent of the renovation, call the front desk of the resort. The people there are normally candid and will advise just how you as a guest will be affected.

At the time of booking, request anything special or important to you, such as a particular view, the desire to be far from the elevator or pool, a smoking or nonsmoking room, or a certain bed type. Remember that these requests are never guaranteed unless you are reserving a suite with an assigned room number (usually only the Presidential or Vice Presidential Suites). The only guarantee Disney will make is connecting rooms for families with children.

Remember to take advantage of any discounts such as Annual Passholder or AAA rates described earlier in this chapter. Consider reserving tee times, child care, special dinner shows, or advance reservations when making your resort reservations.

Magic Kingdom Area Resorts

This is the most enchanting resort area in all of Walt Disney World. Five resorts hug the shoreline of two bodies of water, the Seven Seas Lagoon and Bay Lake, all accessible by either monorail or boat to the Magic Kingdom. Disney's Contemporary, Grand Floridian, and Polynesian Resorts surround the Seven Seas Lagoon and feature magical views of Cinderella's Castle; all three connect to one another as well as to the Magic Kingdom and Epcot (via the Ticket and Transportation Center, or TTC) by monorail. Disney's Wilderness Lodge and the Villas at Disney's Wilderness Lodge are not connected by monorail to the Magic Kingdom; however, they are accessible to the park by boat, with the plus of a pristine setting smack-dab in the middle of a pine forest fronting beautiful Bay Lake.

Those driving for the first time to the Magic Kingdom Resorts may feel confused when the signage seems to be leading straight into the Magic Kingdom parking lot. Drive up to the second turnstile on the right, advise the parking lot attendant that you're checking in, and he or she will wave you past. Stay to your right and follow the signs to your resort.

Disney's Contemporary Resort

1,008 rooms. 4600 North World Drive, Lake Buena Vista 32830; phone (407) 824–1000, fax (407) 824–3539. Check-in 3:00 P.M., checkout 11:00 A.M. For reservations call (407) WDW–MAGIC or (407) 939–6244, or contact your travel agent. $$–$$$$
The fifteen-story, A-frame Contemporary Resort has long been a familiar landmark. What used to be considered modern is now pretty darn austere, with its soaring, open interior and its sharp edges and angles. Love it or hate it, its accessibility to the Magic Kingdom can't be beat. And the sight of the monorail silently gliding through its core is simply magical. The property consists of a high-rise tower, two three-story wings, and a next-door convention center, making this resort a favorite choice for groups. Guest rooms here are borderline deluxe, and I can only recommend staying in one of the tower rooms.

Wacky trees cut in futuristic forms line the entrance leading to the somewhat sterile, marble lobby. Stark but sleek, its small seating area is adorned with angular leather sofas and chairs in shades of purple, teal, and black. To feel the grandeur of the resort, you'll want to head to its centerpiece,

THE BEST OF EVERYTHING

BEST RESORT POOLS

- The Yacht and Beach Club's Stormalong Bay, a three-acre miniature water park
- The Swan and Dolphin's grotto-style lagoon pool
- The Volcano Pool at the Polynesian Resort with its luxuriant waterfall, smoking peak, and perfect views of Cinderella's Castle
- The boulder-strewn wonderland at the Wilderness Lodge with its own erupting geyser
- The lush pool at the Hyatt Regency Grand Cypress cooled by twelve waterfalls
- The JW Marriott's Lazy River, 24,000 square feet of winding delight

BEST DELUXE RESORT

On Disney property it's the Grand Floridian with its upscale Victorian ambience and lagoonside setting facing the Magic Kingdom. Off-property, hands-down it's the Ritz-Carlton Grande Lakes, where you may never even feel the need to go to the parks. At Universal go for the Portofino Bay Hotel, with its unsurpassed atmosphere of an Italian seaside resort.

BEST HOME-AWAY-FROM-HOME PROPERTY

The Villas at Wilderness Lodge with its Bay Lake frontage and national park character, or the Beach Club Villas conveniently located next door to Epcot.

BEST ATMOSPHERE

The Animal Kingdom Lodge, where hundreds of animals roam the savanna and the air is pulsating to the beat of African drums. Running a close second is Universal's Portofino Bay Hotel, where guests are transported to a seaside Italian village.

BEST LOBBY

How to choose? Three make the cut: the Wilderness Lodge, the Grand Floridian, and the Animal Kingdom Lodge, all eye-popping in their grandeur.

BEST ACCESS TO THE PARKS

The Contemporary, Polynesian, and Grand Floridian with monorail access to the Magic Kingdom, Epcot, and the Ticket and Transportation Center. At Universal, the Hard Rock Hotel is just a five-minute walk or boat ride to Universal Studios, Islands of Adventure, and CityWalk.

BEST FOR ROMANCE

The Polynesian Resort, whose lush tiki torch lit grounds and white-sand beaches with views of Cinderella's Castle are simply dreamy, or Universal's Portofino Bay Hotel, where an evening stroll along the bay with Italian arias playing in the distance can't be beat.

BEST FOR NATURE LOVERS

Wilderness Lodge, a nature lover's dream of rushing waterfalls, spouting geysers, and bubbly creeks, all surrounded by stately pine trees and sparkling Bay Lake.

BEST FOR TENNIS

The Contemporary Resort or the Hyatt Regency Grand Cypress.

BEST FOR GOLF

The Hyatt Regency Grand Cypress and the Villas of Grand Cypress have four Jack Nicklaus–signature designed courses. At the Ritz-Carlton Grande Lakes you'll find a Greg Norman–designed course set on the headwaters of the Everglades and an innovative Caddy-Concierge Program.

BEST RESORT LOUNGES

- **California Grill Lounge.** The Contemporary Resort's fifteenth-floor lounge offers unrivaled views of the Magic Kingdom and the Seven Seas Lagoon. It's great for cocktails, sushi, and a view of the Wishes fireworks display. *NOTE:* If you're only coming for drinks it can be difficult to get a seat around fireworks time. You'll need to check in first at the second-floor podium.

- **The Grand Floridian's lobby.** Pick up a cocktail at Mizner's, and then head down to this magnificent oasis to relax while listening to the sounds of a big band or live piano music.

- **Bluezoo's.** This restaurant bar at the Dolphin is by far the coolest place around.

- **Normans Salon.** This sophisticated cocktail lounge is nested within Normans restaurant at the luxurious Ritz-Carlton.

- **Territory Lounge.** Enjoy a drink at this rustic lounge in the Wilderness Lodge.

- **Velvet.** The Hard Rock Hotel is where you'll find this ultrahip cocktail lounge.

- **Bar America.** Portofino Bay's upscale lounge overlooks the romantic piazza.

- **Top of the Palace Lounge.** High atop the Wyndham Palace Resort near Downtown Disney is this sophisticated bar with the best views around.

the fourth-floor Grand Canyon Concourse, whose soaring space boasts eleven-story windows on either end and floors of guest rooms surrounding the vast atrium on two sides. At its heart stands a charming 90-foot mosaic mural of Native American children, which is surrounded by shops, restaurants, a monorail station, and a bar with super views of Bay Lake, all constantly buzzing with traffic. High above it all sits the fifteenth-floor California Grill, one of Disney's best restaurants, with a bird's-eye view of the Magic Kingdom.

ACCOMMODATIONS

Guest rooms. Don your sunglasses before entering or risk being blinded by the blazing colors and zany patterns reminiscent of a *Jetsons* cartoon. The decor runs to the outrageous with purple and yellow walls, kooky contemporary carpet, and multicolored Picasso-style bedspreads making this the most unsettling room in Disney's repertoire. Headboards composed of a wooden backsplash of color running the length of one wall are topped with amoeba-shaped lighting. Furnishings include an austere bureau with loads of drawers, an armless sleeper sofa fronted by a dining-style table, and a green-and-yellow checked easy chair paired with a leather ottoman. The only toned-down space in the 394-square-foot room is the bath, bedecked in rich brown marble and black granite. Divided into two areas, one has a single sink and tub and the other a commode and additional sink. Amenities include a keyed safe, iron and ironing board, coffeemaker, refrigerator, and morning newspaper.

Now for the good news: As of fall 2006, all guestrooms will have undergone a complete—and what I think is a dramatic and fantastic—renovation. I had the chance to look at a model room and was absolutely bowled over by its upscale, elegant decor. Beds are covered in white duvets with red-and-green accents. There are soft sheets, comfy new mattresses, and suede-covered headboards that reach to the ceiling. A sleek, glass desk, contemporary lighting, and a soft, green armless sofa sitting under a copper-lined mirror only add to the beauty of the room. Carpeting and wall coloring is a soft chocolate, and a 32-inch LCD TV, set in a shallow wall unit, is a real bonus. Baths still have the same brown and cream marble floors, but that is where the similarity ends—now the sinks are flat, rectangular wonders set in a stainless steel and frosted-glass vanity. The foyer's two closets are designed with frosted-glass panels set in rich wood with a vanity in the middle that hides a refrigerator and coffeemaker. I can't wait to stay here when the much-needed redo is completed.

Tower rooms, all with balconies, are the ticket here and worth the additional cost with knockout views of either the Magic Kingdom on one side or Bay Lake on the other. The higher the floor, the quieter the room, and the better the view. The lower floors can be noisy due to their suspended position over the Grand Canyon Concourse where the clamor of Chef Mickey's character breakfast begins in the wee hours of the morning.

The quieter, three-story garden wings are certainly an alternative, but not a good one until the rooms are redone. Desperately in need of renovation, these are first in line for the refurbishing. Check with reservations or the resort's front desk before booking.

NOTE: Although tower rooms on the Magic Kingdom side have a marvelous view of the park, they also come with a not-so-marvelous view of the parking lot; however, it's worth it for front-row seats of the nighttime fireworks display.

Concierge rooms. The Contemporary Resort has two concierge levels. Tower Club rooms located on the twelfth floor have access to a limited concierge service. A lounge near the elevators, open to the Grand Concourse, is accessible from 7:00 A.M. to 4:00 P.M. offering a continental breakfast of donuts, pastries, oatmeal, cereal, bagels, fruit, and juice and afternoon snacks of cookies, brownies, Rice Krispies Treats, lemonade, coffee, tea, and sodas. You'll not find alcohol or hot food here. Additional amenities include the services of a concierge desk.

Fourteenth-floor rooms and suites enjoy a much less jarring decor than the rest of the Contemporary's guest rooms, with a soothing palate of soft sand and black. Regular guest rooms here are larger than the rest of the tower's, with leather headboards, deep balconies, larger bathrooms, and spectacular views. Also included is express check-in/checkout, an intimate private lounge with views of the Magic Kingdom and the Grand Floridian, and the services of an excellent concierge staff. Offerings include a continental breakfast and afternoon snacks much like those of the twelfth floor, but come evening the difference between the two becomes more evident with several types of wine, hot and cold hors d'oeuvres, and after-dinner cordials and dessert. Extra amenities include robes and nightly turndown service.

Suites. All of the following suites are located on the fourteenth floor.

The two-bedroom, three-bath Presidential Suite sports 2,061 square feet. Two deep balconies span the length of the suite and afford spectacular Magic Kingdom views. A spacious living room comes with a wet bar and microwave, sofa bed, desk, and six-person dining table. Guests love the huge king-bedded master bedroom with its large sitting area, armoire with TV, and desk, as well as a whirlpool bathtub, separate marble shower with wall jets, double sinks, two closets, and vanity desk. The second bedroom comes with two queen-size beds, a two-person dining table, and full bath.

The two-bedroom, three-bath Vice Presidential Suite at 1,985 square feet has a single-sink full bath just off the large foyer, a roomy living area with a six-person dining table, wet bar and microwave, two easy chairs, sofa bed, desk, armoire with TV, and two balconies spanning the length of the suite with views of Bay Lake and Epcot's Spaceship Earth. There are two queen-size beds in the sizable master bedroom and a king in the second bedroom. The master bathroom does not have a whirlpool tub.

One-bedroom, one-and-a-half-bath Hospitality Suites feature either a lake or Magic Kingdom view, a full-size bath off the foyer, kitchen minus a stove, a six-person dining table, a spacious living area with a sofa bed, and a very deep balcony running the length of the suite. The giant master bedroom has two queen-size beds, large bureau, desk, armoire with TV, bath with vanity table, commode and bidet, and marble shower. With the addition of a king-bedded standard guest room on the opposite side of the living area, it can become a two-bedroom suite.

RESTAURANTS

California Grill. Popular fifteenth-floor restaurant; dinner only. Innovative cuisine accompanied by sweeping views of the Magic Kingdom and the Seven Seas Lagoon. (See full description in Dining chapter.)

Chef Mickey's. Breakfast and dinner with Chef Mickey and friends. (See full description in Dining chapter.)

Concourse Steakhouse. All-day steak house serving breakfast, lunch, and dinner; dine on grilled steaks, pastas, and seafood with the monorail soaring overhead. (See full description in Dining chapter.)

Contemporary Grounds. Lobby counter-service coffee bar open 7:00 A.M. to 9:00 P.M.; hot tea, specialty coffees, hot chocolate, iced coffee, granitas.

Food and Fun Center. 24/7 snack bar and grill; grilled entrees available 7:00 A.M. to 10:00 P.M.; *breakfast:* cereal, bagels, breakfast potatoes, biscuits and gravy, pancakes, egg platters, bacon-egg-and-cheese croissant; *lunch and dinner:* burgers, chicken bacon melt sandwich, grilled chicken breast sandwich, chicken strips, hot dogs, chili, nachos, pizza, cold sandwiches, fruit, salads; wine, beer, nonalcoholic beverages; chocolate or carrot cake, cheesecake, key lime pie, peanut butter bars, cookies, muffins; *children's menu:* hot dog, chicken strips, grilled cheese sandwich, and macaroni and cheese.

Room Service. Available twenty-four hours a day.

LIBATIONS

California Grill Lounge. Fifteenth-floor lounge in the California Grill restaurant with spectacular views of the Magic Kingdom and Seven Seas Lagoon; sophisticated wine and cocktail list, pristine sushi and sashimi, inventive appetizers; check-in at the second floor podium.

Outer Rim. Fourth-floor lounge with sweeping views of Bay Lake; open noon to midnight: specialty drinks, martinis, wine, beer; buffalo chicken wings, cheese and fruit, chips and salsa, peel-and-eat shrimp, fried mozzarella, jalapeño poppers.

Sand Bar and Grill. Pool bar; specialty drinks, beer; burgers, hot dogs, chicken bacon melt, turkey or deli subs, tuna salad sandwich, chef's salad, nachos; ice-cream bars, smoothies, brownies, cookies.

RECREATION AND ACTIVITIES

Arcade. Located in the Food and Fun Center on the lobby level; open 24/7; largest Disney resort arcade.

Beach. Small white-sand beach located near marina.

Boating. Boat on miles of Bay Lake and the adjoining Seven Seas Lagoon; Sea Raycers, pontoons, Boston Whaler Montauks, sailboats; specialty cruises: call (407) WDW–PLAY or (407) 939–7529 for reservations.

Children's playground. Located near North Garden Wing.

Electrical Water Pageant. On the Seven Seas Lagoon nightly at 10:05 P.M.; best viewed from bay-view tower room balconies, pool, or the beach. Delightful 1,000-foot string of illuminated barges featuring King Neptune and his court of whales, sea serpents, and other deep-sea creatures. May be canceled due to inclement weather.

Fishing. Guided two-hour fishing excursions for as many as five people include boat, guide, and gear; one-hour kids' fishing excursion for ages 6–12, catch-and-release only (call 407–WDW–BASS or 407–939–2277 for reservations).

Swimming. Two heated pools and two hot tubs with little theming; largest pool (6,500 square feet) has 17-foot-high waterslide; smaller pool rests at end of dock surrounded by marvelous lake vistas.

Tennis. Disney Racquet Club located near North Wing. Walt Disney World's best tennis facility, with six lighted hydrogrid clay courts, pro shop, lessons, clinics; call (407) WDW–PLAY or (407) 939–7529 for more information.

Volleyball. Sand volleyball court located on the beach.

Waterskiing and parasailing. Only Disney resort offering waterskiing, wakeboarding, Jet Skiing, and parasailing. See chapter 6, Sporting Diversions, for full details.

SERVICES

Business center. Located at the Contemporary Resort Convention Center, with personal computers, Internet service, fax machine, and copier.

Hair salon. American Beauty Salon & Barber located on third floor; open 9:00 A.M. to 6:00 P.M.; hairstyling, color, facials, manicures, pedicures.

Health club. Olympiad Health Club located on third floor; open 6:00 A.M. to 9:00 P.M.; Life Circuit machines, treadmills, fitness bicycles, Cybex machines, free weights; dry sauna, tanning facilities; personal training and massage by appointment; complimentary for resort guests.

SHOPPING

BVG. Disney-logo apparel and sleepwear for adults; confections and chocolates; Disney scrapbooking material and home decor.

Concourse Sundries and Spirits. Snacks, sundries; film; small selection of wine and liquor; newspapers, books; luggage.

Fantasia. Disney merchandise store.

TRANSPORTATION

Board the monorail, take the boat launch from the marina to the Magic Kingdom, or walk for about ten minutes along the short path. The monorail goes to the Ticket and Transportation Center, where you can then transfer to the Epcot monorail. Buses run to Disney–MGM Studios, Animal Kingdom, Blizzard Beach, Downtown Disney, and Typhoon Lagoon. The Blue Flag Launch, operating between 7:30 A.M. and 10:00 P.M., departs from the marina and goes to the Magic Kingdom, Wilderness Lodge, and Fort Wilderness. The monorail goes to the Polynesian and Grand Floridian Resorts.

To reach other Disney resorts during park operating hours, take the monorail to the Magic Kingdom and from there pick up a bus to your resort destination. After park hours, take the bus to Downtown Disney and transfer to your resort destination.

Disney's Grand Floridian Resort & Spa

867 rooms. 4401 Floridian Way, Lake Buena Vista 32830; phone (407) 824–3000, fax (407) 824–3186. Check-in 3:00 P.M., checkout 11:00 A.M. For reservations call (407) WDW–MAGIC or (407) 939–6244, or contact your travel agent. $$$–$$$$

Spreading along the shore of the Seven Seas Lagoon with views of the Magic Kingdom, this world-class, exclusive resort is Disney's flagship, one that certainly lives up to its exalted reputation. Its red-gabled roofs and Victorian elegance transport you to the time of Florida's nineteenth-century grand seaside "palace hotels." Impeccably maintained and perfectly manicured grounds are strung with fragrant, blossom-filled lanes that meander among the gracious four- and five-story buildings fabricated with gleaming white clapboard siding, red shingled roofs, fairy-tale turrets, and intricate latticework; a favorite sight is the housekeepers in Victorian period costumes strolling the grounds twirling lacy parasols.

Guests' preferred gathering spot is the exquisitely soaring, five-story Grand Lobby topped with stained-glass cupolas and massive filigree chandeliers. Strewn with potted palms, cushy seating, and extravagant flower arrangements, it's at its liveliest in the late afternoon and evening hours when entertainment rotates between a relaxing piano player and a dynamic eight-piece big band. Because the resort possesses a popular wedding chapel, don't be surprised to see white-gowned brides frequently roaming the lobby; if you're in luck, a Cinderella coach with footmen and white ponies will be on hand to whisk away the newly wedded couple.

Aquatic enticements include a sugar-soft sand beach dotted with brightly striped, canopied lounge chairs, a large swimming pool in the central courtyard, a beachside Florida springs–style pool, and a marina sporting a wide assortment of watercraft including a 45-foot yacht. A full-service spa and health club, tennis courts, five restaurants, three lounges, and upscale shopping round out the list of exceptional offerings.

ACCOMMODATIONS

Guest rooms. These gracious guest rooms are the most comfortable in Disney's repertoire. Decorated in a cheery, Victorian floral motif, each holds one king-size or two queen-size beds (most are queens), a full-size sofa, two chairs and a table, an armoire-concealed television, and a minibar. At over 400 square feet, they are among the largest in "the World." Marbled baths have fluffy towels, separate twin sinks, an extra phone, luxe toiletries (no Mickey Mouse soaps for this resort), makeup mirrors, and hair dryer. The closet contains an electronic safe and robes, and all rooms have daily newspaper delivery, coffeemaker, and nightly turndown service. Most rooms come with generous balconies and vary only in the view of either the gardens or the lagoon. Refrigerators are on request and are complimentary.

If you're smart, you'll book one of the lagoon-view rooms facing either the Magic Kingdom or the Polynesian Resort (choice of views is on request only and not guaranteed). Garden views overlook the flowering grounds, the sparkling courtyard pool, or the marina. The top-floor dormer guest rooms have vaulted ceilings along with very private balconies that require standing for a view; although their high ceilings give them a more open feel, most do not offer daybeds and are actually a bit smaller than a normal guest room.

Lodge Tower rooms are located in turreted corners of many of the buildings. Similar to a standard room with balcony, they offer the bonus of an additional sitting area with an extra phone and TV.

NOTE: For a lagoon-view room with the best vistas of the Magic Kingdom, ask for one in the Boca Chica building. (Magic Kingdom views are also available in Sago Cay and Conch Key.) Rooms in Sago Cay have maximum peacefulness in a setting far from the pool; however, they also require a longer walk to the main building. Sugar Loaf and Big Pine are closest to the main building and the monorail, but because they are near the courtyard pool, they tend to be a bit noisier.

Concierge rooms. Accommodations on the concierge level vary from standard guest rooms to larger deluxe rooms (rooms in the main building offering a spacious sitting area within the guest room with sofa, coffee table, entertainment center, wet bar, writing desk, two chairs and a table, and two queen-size beds) to one- and two-bedroom suites, all with a variety of views including marina, lagoon, and garden. Located in both the upper floors of the main building (the Royal Palm Club) and the Sugar Loaf building (the Lodge Concierge), they provide extra amenities such as VCRs, curbside check-in, private checkout, and the feel of being a special guest in a much smaller hotel.

The Royal Palm Club, located on the fourth floor of the main building, is the more upscale of the two concierge lounges, offering views of the Seven Seas Lagoon and the resort's lovely courtyard. Serving all rooms and suites on floors 3, 4, and 5 of the main building, you'll find a concierge staff on duty near the main elevator of the third floor. A continental breakfast; midday offerings of dip, fruit, cookies, and lemonade; and late-afternoon tea with scones, tarts, fruit, tea, and lemonade are served in the spacious lounge overlooking the Grand Lobby. Early evening brings wine and champagne along with appetizing hors d'oeuvres from the resort's notable restaurants such as cheese, pâté, stuffed chicken rolls, prosciutto and melon, marinated vegetables, and salad. Kids look forward to their own spread of chicken "fingers" or corn dogs. After-dinner desserts like miniature eclairs, cream puffs, chocolate-covered strawberries, and strawberry shortcake with real whipped cream are served with a nice selection of liqueurs. And everyone enjoys the self-service cappuccino machine.

There are two types of Honeymoon Rooms found in the main building: second-floor, standard-type rooms facing the Magic Kingdom and equipped with a Jacuzzi, or turreted rooms with a separate sitting area but no balcony and no views of the Magic Kingdom. All have king-size beds, and all are part of the Royal Palm Club. Room types are on request only.

The Lodge Concierge, found in the lobby of the Sugar Loaf building, offers the services of a concierge desk and the same food as the Royal Palm Club; there's also a cappuccino machine. But don't expect a lagoon view in this building—you'll find only garden, marina, or pool views here. Of course the room prices are lower than those in the Royal Palm Club.

Suites. The Grand Floridian's twenty-five suites are over the top and can be had in all shapes and sizes. In the main building are four Signature Suites: the Grand Suite, Walt Disney Suite, Roy O. Disney Suite, and Victorian Suite.

From its fifth-floor perch, the blue and cream-colored Grand Suite at 2,220 square feet features five balconies with sweeping views of the Seven Seas Lagoon, Cinderella's Castle, Space Mountain, the Contemporary, the Polynesian, even Spaceship Earth in the distance. Its turreted living room has blond hardwood flooring and a wall of mirrors. Furnishings include two sofas, two coffee tables, two easy chairs, a dining table for four, a desk, Bose stereo system, a corner marble wet bar with refrigerator and microwave, and an upright piano. Off one side of the large foyer is the master bedroom with a draped king-size bed, desk, and entertainment center; the master bathroom has double sinks in a marble vanity with mini-TV, whirlpool tub, shower, and a separate toilet and bidet. Off the other side of the foyer is a half bath as well as a second bedroom with two daybeds, an entertainment center, and a single-sink bath.

The 1,690-square-foot Walt Disney Suite is a favorite filled with Walt memorabilia including railroad models and family pictures; you almost feel you're in Walt's apartment, expecting him to return any minute. Enter through a lovely marble foyer with half bath to a cozy living room with wet bar, desk, entertainment center, chaise lounge, sofa, easy chairs, coffee table, and four-person dining table. The lovely master bedroom has a delightful four-poster king-size bed, two desks, a sofa, an entertainment center, a huge walk-in closet with a bureau, and a marble bathroom with two sinks, whirlpool tub, and separate shower. The second bedroom has twin beds in a swan theme, two easy chairs, an entertainment center, and another bathroom. Balconies face the courtyard pool, the beach, and the lagoon with views of the Polynesian resort. Just below the Walt Disney Suite is the Roy O. Disney Suite, comparable in shape and size, with memorabilia representing Walt's brother Roy, including a wall of family photographs.

The intimate Victorian Suite at 1,083 square feet, on the top floor of the main building, is bedecked in soft green and rose hues with floral accents. The living area holds a small sofa, coffee table, entertainment center, wet bar with refrigerator, and four-person dining table. From its three balconies are views of the top of Cinderella's Castle and Space Mountain, the Polynesian, and the Seven Seas Lagoon. The bedroom comes with a four-poster king-size bed, desk, oversize easy chair and ottoman, and entertainment center. The master bath has a huge closet with a sitting area, double-sink bath with mini-TV, and oversize tub. Off the small foyer is a half bath.

The Cypress Suite, located on the second floor of the Conch Key building, has 1,048 square feet with two bedrooms, three bathrooms, and a parlor with sofa bed, easy chair, coffee table, writing desk, small table with two chairs, entertainment center, full bath, and wet bar with a refrigerator and ice machine. The master bedroom comes with a king-size bed, entertainment center, writing desk, and small table with two chairs. The second bedroom is a regular guest room with two queen-size beds. Views from the four balconies are of the lagoon and Cinderella's Castle as well as the marina.

A nice getaway is the Cape Coral Suite located in the remote Sago Cay building at the edge of the property. Situated on the ground floor, it boasts 1,792 square feet with two bedrooms, two bathrooms, and a lovely waterfront patio with perfect views of Cinderella's castle and the Magic Kingdom fireworks.

You'll also find a wide assortment of one- and two-bedroom suites ranging in size from 678 to 1,792 square feet, all outfitted with at least one wet bar, a parlor, and from one-and-a-half to three baths. Most have more than one balcony.

RESTAURANTS

Citricos. Innovative New American cuisine and a world-class wine list; dinner only. (See full description in Dining chapter.)

Garden View Tea Room. Lobby tearoom open 2:00–6:00 P.M.; advance reservations available; English-style tea served in high style; teas, crumpets, scones, tarts, trifle, pound cake; pâté, fruit and cheese, tea sandwiches; champagne; come after 3:00 P.M. when tea is accompanied by live entertainment from the Grand Lobby.

Gasparilla Grill and Games. Snack bar open 24/7; grill items served 6:30 A.M. to 11:30 P.M.; eat inside adjacent to the arcade or outside overlooking the marina; *breakfast:* bagel with cream cheese, biscuits, English muffins, scrambled eggs, hash brown casserole, grits, oatmeal, sausage, bacon, pancakes, waffles, cereal, muffins, donuts, Danish pastries, croissants, cinnamon buns; *lunch and dinner:* chili, chicken noodle soup, chicken strips, grilled chicken sandwich, pizza, burgers, Reuben, hot dogs, Southwest chicken sandwich, roast beef sandwich, Italian meat sandwich, jerk chicken sandwich, tabbouleh wrap, grilled chicken or shrimp Caesar salad; *children's menu:* miniburgers, hot dogs, chicken strips; *anytime items:* slushes, salads, cold sandwiches, fruit, frozen yogurt, soft-serve ice cream, cookies, pastries.

Grand Floridian Café. Casual cafe serving breakfast, lunch, and dinner in a garden-view setting. (See full description in Dining chapter.)

Narcoossee's. Fresh seafood with a lovely waterside setting; dinner only; views of the Magic Kingdom fireworks. (See full description in Dining chapter.)

1900 Park Fare. Breakfast and dinner character buffet; Victorian charm and the sound of Big Bertha, an antique French organ. (See full description in Dining chapter.)

Victoria and Albert's. Disney's grandest dining establishment; dinner only; the only AAA Five-Diamond awarded restaurant in Central Florida. (See full description in Dining chapter.)

Private dining. Twenty-four-hour room service; in-room dinner served butler-style; dining aboard the *Grand I* yacht or in one of the many secluded and romantic venues located throughout the property.

LIBATIONS

Beachside Pool Bar. Cocktails, beer, frozen drinks, nonalcoholic beverages; spinach dip, shrimp cocktail, cobb salad, Caesar salad, fruit plate; turkey club, Reuben, BLT, burgers, deli sandwiches of chicken, tuna salad, or shrimp salad; *children's menu:* miniburgers, fried chicken, little hot dogs, grilled cheese, PB&J sandwich.

Citricos Lounge. Small bar found within Citricos restaurant; international wines, martinis, cocktails, espresso; appetizers; desserts.

Courtyard Pool Bar. Specialty drinks, beer, wine, nonalcoholic beverages; soft pretzels, cold sandwiches.

Mizner's Lounge. Second-story lobby lounge with picturesque views of the resort courtyard and pool; cocktails, port, cognac, brandy, coffee; appetizers and light meals from Citricos restaurant; open 5:30–11:00 P.M.

Narcoossee's Lounge. Small bar inside Narcoossee's restaurant; specialty drinks, wine, espresso; appetizers; desserts; step outside to the boat dock for views of the Magic Kingdom fireworks and the Electrical Water Pageant.

RECREATION AND ACTIVITIES

Arcade. Very small arcade located inside Gasparilla Grill.

Beach. In front of the Florida Natural Springs Pool; lovely crescent of white-sand beach with canopy-covered lounge chairs; no swimming allowed in lagoon.

Boating. Rentals at the Captain's Shipyard Marina; Sea Raycers, pontoon boats, Boston Whaler Montauks; 13-foot catamaran; specialty cruises. 45-foot Sea Ray yacht available for charter; call (407) 824–2439. Jet Skiing; parasailing; wakeboarding; tubing; waterskiing also available.

Children's activities. Some of the very best children's activities are here at the Grand Floridian; "Grand Kid Adventures in Cooking" offered Tuesday and Friday, 10:00–11:45 A.M. ($30); two-hour supervised sail to a deserted island in search of buried treasure on Monday, Wednesday, Thursday, and Saturday, 9:30–11:30 A.M. ($30); "Wonderland Tea Party" Monday through Friday, 1:15–2:30 P.M., hosted by characters from *Alice in Wonderland* ($30); "Perfectly Princess Tea Party" Sunday, Monday, Wednesday, Thursday, and Friday, 10:30 A.M. to noon, at which little princesses ages three through eleven along with a parent receive the royal treatment in the Garden View Lounge, including a meet and greet with Princess Aurora, a My Disney Girl Princess Aurora doll, a tiara, and tea for two along with storytelling, sing-alongs, and a princess parade ($200 for one adult and one child; dressing in royal finery encouraged). Reservations for all activities can be made up to ninety days prior by calling (407) WDW–DINE or (407) 939–3463.

Electrical Water Pageant. On the Seven Seas Lagoon nightly at 9:15; best viewed from the beach or the boat dock near Narcoossee's; may be canceled due to inclement weather. Delightful 1,000-foot string of illuminated barges features King Neptune and his court of whales, sea serpents, and other deep-sea creatures.

Fishing. Two-hour guided bass fishing excursion includes guide, boat, and gear for as many as five guests; one-hour kids' fishing trip for ages 6–12, catch-and-release only (call 407–WDW–BASS or 407–939–2277 for reservations).

Jogging. A 1-mile trail along the beach to the Polynesian Resort and back; maps available at the bell stand and valet desk and from concierge.

Swimming. Florida natural springs–style pool fronts the beach with waterfall, sunbathing deck, changing rooms, kiddie pool, waterslide, and pool bar; twenty-four-hour free-form pool cools the central courtyard along with a children's wading pool and whirlpool; both pools heated.

Tennis. The Wingfield Tennis Courts feature two Har-Tru lighted clay courts; lessons available; call (407) WDW–PLAY or (407) 939–7529 for information or reservations.

Volleyball. Sand volleyball court located on the beach.

Waterskiing and parasailing. Offered from the Contemporary Resort with an extra charge for drive time; see chapter 6, Sporting Diversions, for details.

SERVICES

Business center. Fax, Internet, copying, shipping and receiving; open 7:00 A.M. to 5:00 P.M. daily.

Child care. Mouseketeer Club; Disney movies, art activities, video games; open 4:30 P.M. to midnight daily for potty-trained children ages 4–12; only for guests of the Grand Floridian or those dining at the resort. Call (407) WDW–DINE or (407) 939–3463 for reservations.

Hair salon. Ivy Trellis Salon open daily 9:00 A.M. to 6:00 P.M.

Spa and health club. Grand Floridian Spa and Health Club; 9,000 square-foot facility; *spa*: massage, shiatsu, reflexology, facials, water therapies and soaks, hand and foot treatments, body treatments and wraps; *health club* (complimentary to guests): Life Fitness treadmills, elliptical cross trainers, stair-climbers, Precor recumbent cycles, Cybex strength equipment, Smith machine, free weights; personal training available by appointment; locker rooms equipped with whirlpools, Turkish bath, and Finnish saunas. Treatment hours 8:00 A.M. to 8:00 P.M.; health club open 6:00 A.M. to 9:00 P.M.; call (407) 824–2332.

SHOPPING

Bally. Leather jackets; computer briefcases; shoes; luggage; belts; handbags; neckties.

Commander Porter's. Men's Disney-logo clothing and resort wear including Tommy Bahama and Ralph Lauren; golf accessories.

M. Mouse Mercantile. Disney merchandise store.

Sandy Cove. Disney wedding merchandise and housewares; chocolates; Grand Floridian logo robes and towels; *Alice in Wonderland* clothing; sundries; newspapers.

Summer Lace. Women's designer resort clothing including Lilly Pulitzer, Ralph Lauren, Tommy Bahama, Eileen Fisher; swimwear.

TRANSPORTATION

Transportation choices to the Magic Kingdom include both monorail and water taxi. Take the monorail to the Ticket and Transportation Center (TTC) and transfer to the Epcot monorail. There is a direct bus to Disney–MGM Studios, Animal Kingdom, Downtown Disney, Typhoon Lagoon, and Blizzard Beach. Use monorail service to reach the Contemporary Resort. Walk (ten minutes) or take the water taxi or monorail to the Polynesian Resort.

To reach other Disney resorts during park operating hours, take the monorail to the Magic Kingdom and from there pick up a bus to your resort destination. After park hours take a bus to Downtown Disney and then transfer to your resort destination.

Disney's Polynesian Resort

853 rooms. 1600 Seven Seas Drive, Lake Buena Vista 32830; phone (407) 824–2000, fax (407) 824–3174. Check-in 3:00 P.M., checkout 11:00 A.M. For reservations call (407) WDW–MAGIC or (407) 939–6244, or contact your travel agent. $$$–$$$$

Along with a warm aloha and a lei greeting, guests are invited to enter the soothing South Seas environment of the Great Ceremonial House, a green oasis sheltering the front desk, shops, and restaurants. Vines encase the rugged lava rock cataracts that cool the two-story lobby resting below towering palm trees. The centerpiece garden has a profusion of flowering orchids, bromeliads, ginger, and anthurium scattered throughout banana trees, elephant's ears, and rubber plants. High-backed rattan chairs sit on floors of polished flagstone while overhead brilliantly colored macaws perch in the branches of the surrounding foliage. Two-story picture windows draw the eye outdoors to the lush landscape surrounding the Volcano Pool and the Seven Seas Lagoon beyond. Some find this resort a bit hokey and old-fashioned, but it has a loyal following—and I love it.

Located on the monorail system and within walking distance of the Ticket and Transportation Center, the Polynesian is the most convenient of Disney's resorts, with direct access to both the Magic Kingdom and Epcot. Lodging is in eleven tangerine- and mahogany-tinted longhouses scattered throughout the luxuriant grounds composed of more than seventy species of dense vegetation. Ducks and ibis roam the thick grassy lawns, and rabbits hop along meandering pathways lined with volcanic rock. In the evenings the resort is torchlit, and soft Hawaiian melodies set a romantic mood. Three white-sand beaches dotted with hammocks and lounge chairs are a spectacular place to sun or to relax while viewing the Magic Kingdom fireworks.

ACCOMMODATIONS

Guest rooms. The largest standard rooms in Disney are here at the Polynesian. Those in the Tokelau, Tahiti, and Rapa Nui longhouses are downright enormous. And what's more, between now and summer 2006, the Polynesian will undergo a dramatic room redo sure to please. Staying with a South Seas–style, the new look is more sophisticated and sleek. Tall bamboo and rattan headboards sit above lovely queen beds covered in a batik spread in shades of rich orange and brown; new mattresses and soft sheets and pillows are also part of the package. An upholstered, rattan easy chair with ottoman sits in the corner, and carpeting is a fun, batik print in chocolate and beige hues. A daybed sits below a hand-carved mirror. A beautiful bureau offers six drawers and a desk at one end, and built into the wall above it is a 32-inch flat-screen TV. The foyer's two closets, designed of soft, blond wood, have a vanity in the middle that hides a refrigerator and coffeemaker.

Until the new rooms are in place, you may receive a guest room with the older design. Two queen beds, attractively canopied in bamboo and covered with a batik print in shades of teal, terra cotta, and black, along with the rattan furnishings evoke an island atmosphere. Many rooms also offer a daybed that sits below a banana leaf mirror; curtains sport the same banana-leaf motif. Smallish baths are without Disney's typical split-bath configuration and double sinks, but all are handsomely festooned with rich, green marble and a fun, primitive Polynesian decor; baths in the Tokelau, Tahiti, and Rapa Nui longhouses are a bit larger. Amenities include iron and ironing board, dual-line phones, keyed safe, coffeemaker, refrigerator, and daily newspaper.

NOTE: Your best chance of receiving the perfect room (of which there are many) is to educate yourself before check-in and request exactly what you would like, both at reservation time and again at the front desk before being handed your key. The following information may sound excessive, but it could make the difference between a perfect vacation and a disappointing one. The longhouses of Tokelau, Tahiti, and Rapa Nui feature the largest rooms, all of which come with patios or balconies and a convenient location near the Ticket and Transportation Center. Older longhouses, closer to the Great Ceremonial House, lack second-floor balconies.

The two-story Niue and Tonga longhouses, with the Tonga being an all-suite building, are small and intimate; the Tonga has second-floor balconies, the Niue does not. Water-view rooms in the Tahiti building front a lovely beach with great views across the lagoon but are also located very close to the Ticket and Transportation Center, so there is noise from the ferryboat during park hours. One side of the Samoa and the Niue buildings faces the rambunctious Volcano Pool, a plus or minus depending on your personality. One side of the Aotearoa, Tonga, and Rarotonga longhouses faces the monorail, and one side of the Rapa Nui faces the parking lot, although these are actually considered "garden" views.

If staying in the Fiji, Tuvalu, Tonga, and Aotearoa, you had better enjoy the beat of drums, because the Polynesian Luau is held nearby. The worst view is from the so-called garden-view side of the Tuvalu longhouse that stares at one end of the Fiji building only a few feet away.

Concierge rooms. Nestled up against the beach is the Hawaii concierge building offering the services of a top-notch concierge staff as well as private check-in and checkout. The bi-level Royal Polynesian Lounge is among the best in Disney's repertoire, affording a fantastic view of Cinderella's Castle and the Magic Kingdom fireworks. Accommodations come with either a lagoon or garden view, but second-floor rooms do not have balconies. Additional amenities include robes and nightly turndown service.

Open from 7:00 A.M. to 10:00 P.M., the concierge service has complimentary food and beverages, beginning with a continental breakfast of juice, coffee, tea, fresh fruit, hot oatmeal, Danish pastries, bagels, and cereal. From noon to 4:00 P.M., guava juice, lemonade, coffee, and ice tea are served along with snacks such as cookies, gummy worms, and goldfish crackers. Evenings choices include appetizers of fresh strawberries, cheese and crackers, fruit, crudités and dip, PB&J sandwiches, two hot appetizers the likes of barbecue ribs and chicken wings, as well as wine and beer. After-dinner are cordials and desserts of miniature eclairs, cream puffs, tarts, and cakes. There's also a self-service espresso and cappuccino machine.

Suites. All suites are located in the small and intimate two-story Tonga longhouse. Their only drawback is the inconvenient walk to the Hawaii longhouse concierge lounge for food offerings, because the only meal served in the Tonga building is a continental breakfast. The great news is that all suites were renovated in 2005, with almost every piece of furniture replaced. Baths have new stone vanity tops, tub and shower surround, tile floors, and accessories. Flooring has been updated with a combination of tile and carpet throughout all suites. There are new wall coverings, lighting, artwork, and accessories as well as new patio tile and furnishings. And great, flat panel TVs throughout.

For the ultimate vacation, try the King Kamehameha, a two-story wonder with two bedrooms, two and a half baths, a parlor, and a kitchen. The upstairs master offers a balcony, an enormous two-part bath with a sink, bidet, commode, whirlpool tub, mini-TV, and walk-in closet on one side— and a bath, shower, sink, and commode on the other. The second bedroom and bath are similar to a standard guest room with balcony. Downstairs is a great parlor with TV, VCR, stereo, four-person dining table, three small sofas, rattan chairs, coffee table, overhead paddle fans, a half bath, and a full kitchen (minus a stove). A balcony spanning the length of the suite overlooks the marina and Cinderella's Castle in the distance.

The two-bedroom, three-bath Ambassador Suites have a master with a four-poster king bed, entertainment armoire, chaise lounge, desk, table and two chairs, large bath, and balcony. The lovely living room has two small couches, a large TV, chaise lounge, dining table for four, pull-down bed, large garden-view balcony the length of the room, wet bar, full bath, and separate full kitchen (minus a stove). The second bedroom is the same size as a standard guest room with a balcony.

Each of the marina-view, one-bedroom, one-bath Princess Suites offers two queen-size beds as well as a daybed in a separate parlor.

RESTAURANTS

Captain Cook's Snack Company. Snack bar located in the Great Ceremonial House with indoor and outdoor seating; open 24/7 but grill closes at 11:00 P.M.; *breakfast:* French toast sticks, scrambled egg and cheese sandwich, scrambled eggs, bacon, sausage, breakfast potatoes, cereal, fruit, pastries, specialty coffees; *lunch and dinner:* burgers, hot dogs, pizza, chicken sandwich, pork sandwich, chicken strips, salads, assorted cold sandwiches; apple pie, brownies, carrot or chocolate cake, muffins, croissants, cookies; *children's menu:* hot dog, chicken strips, macaroni and cheese.

Kona Café. Causal dining for breakfast, lunch, and dinner; American cuisine with delicate hints of Asia; famous for breakfast Tonga Toast, batter-fried, banana-stuffed sourdough bread rolled in cinnamon sugar. (See full description in Dining chapter.)

Kona Island. Coffee and pastry stand near the monorail platform; open 6:30–11:00 A.M. Kona coffee, latte, cappuccino, café au lait, espresso, iced mochas; assorted pastries.

Ohana. Breakfast and dinner only; all-you-care-to-eat Polynesian feast prepared on an 18-foot semicircular fire pit; Mickey Mouse hosts a family-style breakfast. (See full description in Dining chapter.)

Spirit of Aloha Dinner Show. Polynesian luau with modern song and dance from *Lilo and Stitch;* after dinner is more traditional Polynesian entertainment; roasted chicken, pork ribs, shrimp fried rice, sautéed vegetables, pineapple upside-down cake; unlimited drinks, including beer and wine. Held at the Luau Cove Tuesday through Saturday, 5:15 P.M. and 8:00 P.M.; subject to cancellation in inclement weather; call (407) WDW–DINE or (407) 939–3463 for reservations.

Room Service. Available 6:30 A.M. to midnight.

LIBATIONS

Barefoot Pool Bar. Volcano Pool thatch-roofed bar; tropical alcoholic and nonalcoholic drinks, beer.

Tambu Lounge. Located upstairs in the Great Ceremonial House over-looking the pool with the picturesque Seven Seas Lagoon in the distance; tropical drinks served in hollowed-out pineapples and coconuts, wine, beer; appetizers including chips and salsa, egg rolls, chicken wings, cheese plate, shrimp cocktail, flatbread; open 1:00 P.M. to midnight, with appe-tizers served 5:00–10:00 P.M.

RECREATION AND ACTIVITIES

Arcade. Moana Mickey's Fun Hut; open 24/7; three rooms of game fun with the latest in video equipment.

Beaches. Three idyllic beaches with perfect vistas of Seven Seas Lagoon and Magic Kingdom; swimming prohibited in the lagoon; lounge chairs, beach hammocks, swings; prime viewing for the Magic Kingdom fireworks; *best views:* beach in front of Tahiti longhouse; *closest to Volcano Pool:* beach in front of Hawaii longhouse; *most secluded:* beach on the Grand Floridian side of the property.

Bicycles. Two- and four-seater surrey bicycles for rent at the marina.

Boating. Boat rentals available at the Mikala Canoe Club; Sea Raycers, pontoons, sailboats; fireworks boating excursion with driver (call 407–WDW–PLAY or 407–939–7529 for reservations).

Children's activities and playground. Arts and crafts and Disney movies daily in the Never Land Club, noon to 4:00 P.M., and in the Great Cere-monial House, noon to 2:00 P.M.; pool games, arcade challenges, hula lessons.

Electrical Water Pageant. On the Seven Seas Lagoon nightly at 9:00; best viewed from the beach, Ohana restaurant, or a lagoon-view room; may be canceled due to inclement weather. Delightful 1,000-foot string of illu-

minated barges features King Neptune and his court of whales, sea serpents, and other deep-sea creatures.

Fishing. Guided two-hour fishing excursions for as many as five people
include boat, guide, and gear; guided one-hour kids' fishing excursion for
ages 6–12, catch-and-release only (call 407–WDW–BASS or 407–
939–2277 for reservations).

Jogging. A 1.5-mile scenic jogging path circles the resort; ask for a map at
Guest Services.

Swimming. Nanea Volcano Pool features a smoking volcano slide, underwater music, sparkling waterfall, and kiddie pool, all with a superb view
of the Seven Seas Lagoon; no whirlpool; quieter East Pool is often filled
with ducks in the morning; both pools are heated.

Volleyball. Sand court located on beach in front of Volcano Pool.

Waterskiing and parasailing. Offered from the Contemporary Resort wih
an extra charge for drive time; see chapter 6, Sporting Diversions, for
details.

SERVICES

Child care. At the Never Land Club, Peter Pan–themed facility with a
replica of Wendy's bedroom; arcade games, arts and crafts, Disney classic
movies on a giant screen. Open 4:00 P.M. to midnight, for potty-trained
children ages 4–12 of registered guests of any Disney-owned property.
Cost includes buffet dinner; call (407) 939–3463 for reservations.

Spa and health club. Grand Floridian Spa located between the
Grand Floridian and the Polynesian; see previous entry on Grand
Floridian Resort.

SHOPPING

News From Polynesia. Polynesian Resort logo goods; beach towels, grass
skirts, straw hats, leis; Hawaiian-print clothing for all ages; tropical-
inspired gifts for the home; newspapers, magazines, books, sundries.

Polynesian Princess. Men and women's Tommy Bahama resort wear;
swimwear; jewelry; sunglasses.

Robin Crusoe's. Tommy Bahama, Billabong, and Quiksilver men's resort
wear.

Samoa Snacks. Liquor, beer, wine (a nice selection), sodas; snacks; sundries.

Trader Jack's. Disney merchandise.

Wyland Gallery. Environmental marine art.

TRANSPORTATION

Transportation choices to the Magic Kingdom include both monorail and water taxi. To reach Epcot, walk to the Ticket and Transportation Center (TTC)—you'll find excellent signage throughout the resort—and take a direct monorail. There is a direct bus to Disney–MGM Studios, Animal Kingdom, Downtown Disney, Typhoon Lagoon, and Blizzard Beach. Take the monorail or water taxi or follow the walking path to the Grand Floridian Resort (about a ten-minute walk). Monorail service will get you to the Contemporary Resort.

To reach other Disney resorts during park operating hours, take the monorail to the Magic Kingdom and from there pick up a bus to your resort destination. After park hours, take a bus to Downtown Disney and then transfer to your resort destination.

Disney's Wilderness Lodge

728 rooms. 901 Timberline Drive, Lake Buena Vista 32830; phone (407) 824–3200, fax (407) 824–3232. Check-in 3:00 P.M., checkout 11:00 A.M. For reservations call (407) WDW–MAGIC or (407) 939–6244, or contact your travel agent. $$–$$$

Teddy Roosevelt would exclaim "bully" to Disney's dramatic depiction of an early 1900s national park lodge, an atmosphere that simply can't be beat. I challenge you to keep your jaw from dropping open on your first encounter with its awesome eight-story lobby. A marvel of timber, sheer walls of lodgepole pine logs and rugged rock surround the huge, open expanse filled with oversize leather chairs and Native American crafts of beaded moccasins, feathered headdresses, textiles, and drums. Relax in old-fashioned rockers fronting the massive, 82-foot-tall fireplace composed of rockwork replicating the diverse strata of the Grand Canyon. Two authentic 55-foot Pacific Northwest totem poles overlook rustic stone and hardwood floors topped with Native American rugs, tepee chandeliers, and a bevy of "park ranger" staff who roam the lodge attending to guests. Quiet and seductive nooks and crannies on the floors above the lobby offer hours of privacy, and rows of back porch rockers facing the resort grounds look out to a serene scene of natural beauty.

Seven floors of guest rooms are found above the lobby and in two six-story wings composed of quarry stone, chunky logs, and green tin rooftops surrounded by a breathtaking scene of roaring waterfalls, rushing creeks, and towering pines. What begins in the lobby as a bubbling hot spring turns into Silver Creek that widens to become a sparkling waterfall emptying into the boulder-lined, hot springs–style swimming pool, one of Disney's best. The chirping of crickets is heard beneath the bridges and along the meandering pathways lined with natural grasses, junipers, sotols, and wildflowers. On the shore of Bay Lake, the resort's very own re-created geyser, surrounded by a steaming expanse of geothermal activity, erupts hourly from early morning to late night. After dark when the waterfall is lit, it's even more spectacular.

ACCOMMODATIONS

Guest rooms. Those who have experienced other deluxe Disney resorts may be surprised at the smallish guest rooms here, measuring only 340 square feet. Though pleasant, they don't leave room for a sitting area. Bedding is either two queen-size beds, a king-size bed (wheelchair-accessible rooms), or a queen-size bed and a set of bunk beds (an extremely popular choice with the kids). You'll find it's a bit like staying in a nicely decorated young boy's room from the 1950s. Earthy shades of green and brown abound in the decor of plaid curtains and Native American motif bedspreads while prints of the American West and old territory maps bedeck the honey-colored walls.

Furnishings that are beginning to show some wear and tear (I would hope a room refurbishing is in the planning stages) include a woodland scene–painted pine armoire, a bureau in the entry hall, and a small table and two chairs. Bathrooms are a few feet smaller than other deluxe resorts, with a separate vanity holding double sinks and a hair dryer; the adjoining bathtub-commode area is embellished with white-and-gold tiles and wallpaper imprinted with old-fashioned scenes of a Native American village. Room view choices include a standard view with a look at either the parking lot or rooftops; a lodge view of either the forested area facing the Magic Kingdom (views of the park and the fireworks are mostly obscured by the trees except from some rooms on the top floors) or the adjoining Villas at Wilderness Lodge and woods; or a picturesque courtyard view of either the pool or Bay Lake. Room amenities include a small safe, iron and ironing board, coffeemaker, refrigerator, and daily newspaper. Sixth-floor rooms in the outer wings closer to the lake come with dormer balconies that require standing for a view.

Concierge rooms. Concierge rooms on the seventh floor include standard rooms with a variety of views, four Honeymoon Suites, and the Vice Presidential and Presidential Suites. Expect a quick check-in at the downstairs lobby and then more detailed information given by the concierge staff in a small seating area by the seventh-floor elevators. Guests receive the services of a private concierge staff and access to an informal lounge, the Old Faithful Club, set up around the balcony overlooking the lobby with six tables for dining (not really enough). Included is a continental breakfast of bagels, strudel, muffins, fruit, cereal, instant oatmeal, and juice. Each afternoon you'll find very light snacks (just pretzels and gummy worms) and beverages throughout the day (ask the staff to fetch sodas and beer for you if they aren't sitting out). Evenings bring a spread of cheese and crackers, two hot appetizers such as lime shrimp or Italian sausage, along with wine and beer. After dinner you'll find cordials with desserts of brownies, Magic Bars, and cookies. Extra amenities include robes and nightly turndown service. All concierge rooms have dormer balconies that require standing for a view.

Although they're the same size as a standard room, the Honeymoon Suites surrounding the lobby feel larger because they come with only one king-size bed, leaving more room to walk around. Their claim to fame is a large chocolate-brown marble whirlpool tub perfect for romance. Rooms also hold an entertainment center, table with two chairs, and clothes bureau. Remember, they come with dormer balconies, so you must stand for a view—two of the suites offer a not-so-great look at the rooftops and the Villas at Wilderness Lodge in the distance, while the other two enjoy a view of the Seven Seas Lagoon, the Grand Floridian, the Contemporary, and the top of the Magic Kingdom fireworks.

Suites. If a larger room is more to your liking, consider a Deluxe Suite sleeping six. At 500 square feet, these suites offer a comfortable but not huge balconied parlor area holding a queen-size sofa bed, two easy chairs, coffee table, two-person table and chairs, TV, wet bar, coffeemaker, and small refrigerator. The bedroom, separated by curtained French doors from the parlor, has two queen-size beds, entertainment armoire, and a dormer balcony. Robes are included. The double-sinked bathroom with separate commode and shower area can be accessed from either the bedroom or the foyer. The Deluxe Suites come with some sort of a view of the water (some rooms are nicely obstructed with trees), but alas with no concierge service. With the addition of standard room with two double beds on the other side of the parlor, they become a two-bedroom suite that can accommodate ten people.

The 885-square-foot Vice Presidential Suite (also known as the Yosemite) is outfitted cowboy-style with rawhide curtains, branding-iron towel bars, wood-paneled walls, and lodgepole trim. It features one bedroom with a king-size bed, one-and-a-half baths, and separate parlor with two sofas, minikitchen, desk, four-person dining table, and wet bar. The oversize bathroom has a whirlpool tub and separate shower. The huge wraparound balcony affords a great view of the courtyard and Bay Lake.

On the opposite side of the courtyard is the 1,000-square-foot Presidential Suite (also known as the Yellowstone), a Teddy Roosevelt delight with hardwood flooring, an elk-horn chandelier, and balconies running the length of the corner suite overlooking Bay Lake and the pool. The living area holds a sofa bed, coffee table, two easy chairs, and wet bar with sink, refrigerator, microwave, coffeemaker, and dishes. A rustic dining table, separated from the living room by a full-length buffet, seats eight. Off the foyer is a half bath as well as a cozy office with a balcony overlooking the courtyard. The bedroom is outfitted with twig-style furnishings and a leather easy chair and ottoman. A chocolate and black marble bathroom comes with two sink areas, commode and bidet in a separate room, vanity, separate shower, and a fantastic whirlpool tub. An option of a connecting standard room would make this a two-bedroom, two-and-a-half bath suite.

RESTAURANTS

Artist Point. Outstanding Pacific Northwest cuisine and wine with views of Bay Lake and courtyard waterfall; dinner only. (See full description in Dining chapter.)

Roaring Forks Snacks. Cozy atmosphere indoors and picturesque outdoor area near pool; *breakfast:* sausage biscuit, breakfast sandwich, scrambled egg plate, bacon, hash browns, breakfast pizza, oatmeal, cereal, yogurt, fruit, assorted pastries, bagels, croissants; *lunch and dinner:* smoked turkey sandwich, pizza, Philly steak sandwich, grilled chicken breast sandwich, hot dogs, burgers, chicken strips, pizza, tuna salad sandwich, chicken wrap sandwich, PB&J sandwich, chili, nachos, salads, ice cream, desserts; open 6:00 A.M. to midnight; grill items available 7:00 A.M. to 11:00 P.M.

Whispering Canyon Café. Open breakfast, lunch, and dinner for Western-style fun and hearty food; smoked meats served skillet-style. (See full description in Dining chapter.)

Room Service. Available 7:00 to 11:00 A.M. and 4:00 P.M. to midnight.

LIBATIONS

Territory Lounge. Rustic atmosphere of lodgepole pine posts, old territorial maps, prints of the American West, vintage surveyor equipment, and carved wooden bears; Pacific Northwest wine, beer, martinis, specialty drinks and coffees, port, single-malt scotches, all "guaranteed to prevent snakebite"; light meals of potato skins, nachos, cheese plate, chicken wings, and pizza; open 4:30–11:30 P.M.

Trout Pass. Log cabin pool bar; specialty drinks, beer, wine, nonalcoholic smoothies, other beverages; nachos, giant soft pretzels, popcorn, chips; ice cream; open noon to dusk.

RECREATION AND ACTIVITIES

Services and recreational activities here are shared with the adjacent Villas at Wilderness Lodge.

Arcade. Buttons and Bells Game Arcade with state-of-the-art video games for all levels.

Beach. The smallish Bay Lake Beach is nestled against tall pine trees.

Bicycles. Rentable at the marina for exploration of wilderness trails connecting to Fort Wilderness; bicycles, two- and four-seat surrey bikes.

Boating. Rentals available for the enjoyment of Bay Lake and the Seven Seas Lagoon at Teton Boat Rentals; Sea Raycers, Boston Whaler Montauks, pontoon boats, sailboats; Magic Kingdom fireworks cruise (call 407–WDW–PLAY or 407–939–7529 for reservations).

Children's activities and playground. Children's playground located on the beach; family arts and crafts in the Cub's Den, 2:30–4:00 P.M. (children must be accompanied by a parent); duck races, pool activities, beach games; next-door Fort Wilderness, just a boat ride away, offers nightly carriage and wagon rides (extra fee) and a complimentary sing-along campfire, marshmallow roast, and Disney movie program hosted by Chip 'n Dale.

Electrical Water Pageant. On the Seven Seas Lagoon nightly at 9:35; best viewed from the beach, boat dock, or a Bay Lake–facing room; may be canceled due to inclement weather. Delightful 1,000-foot string of illuminated barges features King Neptune and his court of whales, sea serpents, and other deep-sea creatures.

Fishing. Two-hour fishing excursions for as many as five guests includes boat, fishing equipment, and guide; one-hour kids' fishing trip for ages 6–12; catch-and-release only (call 407–WDW–BASS or 407–939–2277 for reservations).

Jogging. Jogging paths connect to Disney's Fort Wilderness, where several trails through a forest of pines and along Bay Lake make for pleasant exercise routes.

Swimming. A top attraction at Wilderness Lodge is its boulder-lined, free-form pool featuring waterfalls, rocky overlooks, waterslide, and nearby geyser; kiddie pool, two whirlpools.

Tours. Meet in the lobby for a "Wonders of the Lodge" ranger-led tour of the resort. Check your resort guide for day and time; no reservations necessary.

Volleyball. Sand volleyball court located on Bay Lake Beach; equipment at Teton Boat Rentals.

SERVICES

Child care. Simba's Cubhouse features computer games, Northwestern arts and crafts, and Disney movies. Open 4:30 P.M. to midnight for potty-trained cubs ages 4–12; also open to registered guests of any Disney-owned property; cost includes dinner; call (407) WDW–DINE or (407) 939–3463 for reservations.

Health club. Sturdy Branches Health Club located at the adjoining Villas at Wilderness Lodge; Cybex equipment, Smith machine, treadmills, stair-climbers, free weights, upright and recumbent exercise bicycles; personal training and Swedish massage available by appointment; complimentary to resort guests; open 6:00 A.M. to 9:00 P.M.

SHOPPING

Wilderness Lodge Mercantile. Daniel Boone–style shopping, including coonskin caps; Mickey and friends miniature totem poles; Wilderness Lodge logo clothing; forest ranger hats; Disney merchandise; sundries; books, magazines; small selection of food staples and snacks; basic wines and liquors.

TRANSPORTATION

Since the monorail doesn't reach this neck of the woods, Wilderness Lodge is definitely less accessible than other Magic Kingdom resorts. Take the boat leaving from the Northwest Dock and Ferry (a separate area from the marina) to the Magic Kingdom, Contemporary Resort, and Fort Wilderness. Or take a bus to the TTC and then the monorail to the Magic Kingdom. There is a direct bus to Epcot, Disney–MGM Studios, Animal Kingdom, Downtown Disney, Typhoon Lagoon, and Blizzard Beach.

To reach other Disney resorts during park operating hours, take the boat to the Magic Kingdom and pick up a bus or monorail from there to your resort destination. After park hours take a bus to Downtown Disney and then transfer to the resort.

The Villas at Disney's Wilderness Lodge

136 units. 801 Timberline Drive, Lake Buena Vista 32830; phone (407) 938–4300, fax (407) 824–3232. Check-in 4:00 P.M., checkout 11:00 A.M. For reservations call (407) WDW–MAGIC or (407) 939–6244, or contact your travel agent. $$–$$$$$
Sharing the same lobby, check-in desk, and amenities with the adjoining Wilderness Lodge (a short, covered walkway connects the two), this Disney Vacation Club property is a tribute to the Western railroad hotels built in the early 1900s. Rooms not occupied by members are available to the many visitors who wish to stay on Disney property but who would also like the convenience of a kitchen and the extra breathing space of a living area.

This is my favorite Disney Vacation Club property. The overall effect is one of coziness and intimacy. Its four-story buildings, tucked away in the pine trees, are tinted with soothing earth tones of soft brown and green. Inside the lobby, guests step into a rustic four-story atrium of log construction adorned with detailed wood carvings and paintings of the Pacific Northwest. A rock and timber living room made snug with fireplace, leather easy chairs, and window seats features railroad memorabilia, some belonging to Walt Disney. Outdoors a small springs-style pool is surrounded by towering pine trees and natural vegetation. For additional information on the Villas' restaurants, libations, recreation, services, shopping, and transportation, see the appropriate sections in the previous entry on the Wilderness Lodge.

ACCOMMODATIONS

Villa choices come in studios as well as one- and two-bedroom units (three-bedroom units are not offered at this property), each with a balcony or patio. Autumn colors in splashes of rich red and forest green intermingle with rustic pine furnishings. Sofas in Native American print fabrics mix well with curtains and chairs sporting a whimsical gingham design. Woodland scene prints decorate the cream, gold, and crimson walls. The carpet is imprinted with a pinecone motif. The small but efficient full kitchens are done in a cream-colored granite with forest green cabinetry. Beds feature headboards carved with woodland scenes and down-home quilt bedspreads in a leaf-and-pinecone print. Views from all units are of either the pool or the woods, with some of the units on the higher floors enjoying a glimpse of Bay Lake.

The 356-square-foot studios sleep a maximum of four people plus one child age two or younger. They include either two queen-size beds or one queen-size bed and a double sofa bed, armoire with TV, small dining table with two chairs, patio or balcony, microwave, small refrigerator, coffeemaker, and wet bar. Bathrooms have a single sink with a separate, small bath-commode area decorated with colorfully splashed tile. A small closet holds an iron and ironing board. Just slightly larger than the next-door Wilderness Lodge guest rooms, their advantage is the addition of a sofa bed and minikitchen but at a higher nightly rate.

The One-Bedroom Villas, at 727 square feet, sleep a maximum of four plus one child age two or younger. Each unit has a small living area with a queen-size sofa bed, easy chair, entertainment center containing a TV/VCR, two-person dining table, two-chair eating bar, and balcony or patio. The kitchen, open to the living area, contains a small refrigerator plus stove, dishwasher, coffeemaker, toaster, microwave, and all utensils, dishes, and pots and pans to make a complete meal. The spacious bedroom holds a king-size bed, armoire with TV, small table, and rattan chair. The bedroom adjoins a two-room bath, one room holding a whirlpool tub, vanity sink, and hair dryer and the other containing a commode (in a separate enclosure), shower, and additional pedestal sink. There's also a large closet with portable crib, iron and ironing board, and keyed safe. A nice feature is the stacked washer-dryer. I loved my unit (number 2523)—it had a view of the pine trees and the Hidden Springs Pool in the distance with no adjoining balconies to disturb the peace and quiet.

Two-Bedroom Villas sleep a maximum of eight people plus one child age two or younger and offer 1,080 square feet of room. This unit is exactly the same as the one-bedroom unit, with the addition of a studio bedroom, which adds up to two bedrooms, two baths, living area, kitchen, three TVs, and two balconies or porches.

NOTE: One caveat is to avoid units at the extreme far end of the property, which come with a not-so-great side view of the service area.

RECREATION AND ACTIVITIES

Swimming. The scent of pine perfumes the air at the peaceful Hidden Springs pool, a free-form pool with geyser bubbles; no lifeguard on duty.

SERVICES

Health club. Sturdy Branches Health Club; Cybex equipment, Smith machine, treadmills, stair-climbers, free weights, upright and recumbent exercise bicycles; personal training and Swedish massage available by appointment; complimentary to resort guests; open 6:00 A.M. to 9:00 P.M.

Epcot Area Resorts

Those who plan to spend a lot of time at Epcot and Disney–MGM Studios should strongly consider selecting one of the resorts in this terrific area. Options include Disney's Beach Club Resort, Disney's Beach Club Villas, Disney's Boardwalk Inn, Disney's Boardwalk Villas, Disney's Yacht Club Resort, the Walt Disney World Swan, and the Walt Disney World Dolphin. All, with the exception of the Beach Club Villas, front Crescent Lake and all are within walking distance or a boat ride to Epcot, Disney–MGM Studios, and the Boardwalk. With such easy access to so many resorts and Epcot just a few minutes away, you'll find more restaurant and entertainment choices than you can count.

Disney's Beach Club Resort

583 rooms. 1800 Epcot Resorts Boulevard, Lake Buena Vista 32830; phone (407) 934–8000, fax (407) 934–3850. Check-in 3:00 P.M., check-out 11:00 A.M. For reservations call (407) WDW–MAGIC or (407) 939–6244, or contact your travel agent. $$–$$$$
At this delightful resort, five-story, blue and white, Cape Cod–style buildings fronting a white-sand beach bordered with sea grass bring to mind late-nineteenth-century Martha's Vineyard. Inviting white rockers on the front porch; airy, high ceilings and bare floors in the pink-and-cream-colored lobby; and a sunny solarium overlooking the resort's lovely gardens add up to a charmer of a place.

The casually elegant grounds surrounding Disney's Beach Club Resort are planted with a variety of crape myrtles, gardenias, and roses, but the resort's highlight is the fantastic Stormalong Bay, a winding wonderland of a small-scale water park shared with the Yacht Club. Since this is the closest resort to Epcot, it offers supereasy access to the International Gateway entrance, a convenience that can't be beat.

ACCOMMODATIONS

Guest rooms. Captivating 380-square-foot guest rooms are bedecked with sea blue and sand-colored checked carpeting, striped curtains, character beach scene bedspreads, and metal seafoam-tinted headboards. Sitting on a large white wooden bureau is the television, with an additional bureau found in the foyer, and in the corner is a small combination table and desk with two chairs. Many rooms also come with a full-size sofa bed upholstered in a whimsical multistripe topped with beach print pillows. The lively decor continues in the bathroom where the lighthouse and sailing ship motif wallpaper and shower curtain adorn a separate tub and commode area of pale gold ceramic tile. Outside is a gray and white marble vanity with two sinks, makeup mirror, and hair dryer. Amenities include a small keyed safe, iron and ironing board, coffeemaker, refrigerator, and daily newspaper.

Water-view Deluxe Rooms, at 533 square feet, offer two queen-size beds in an extralarge bedroom as well as a separate sitting room with daybed and reading chairs.

The only aspect of the resort that disappoints is the scarcity of full-size room balconies, most of which measure only 1 by 3 feet, standing room only. If a balcony is important to you, strongly request a full balcony (although there are very few) or a first-floor patio; it might be simpler to book the adjoining Yacht Club instead.

NOTE: Request a room facing Epcot for a view of Illuminations, and remember that standard-view rooms could have a view of the parking lot. Water-view rooms aren't always of Crescent Lake; many times they face Stormalong Bay, a somewhat noisy location.

Concierge rooms. Fifth-floor concierge-level rooms include the amenities of a small but cozy lounge (one that tends to be a bit crowded when the occupancy level is high) with complimentary food and beverages throughout the day. Expect a continental breakfast of muffins, pastries, bagels, doughnuts, fruit, juice, and cereal, along with afternoon snacks of beverages, cookies, crudités, pretzels, popcorn, salsa and chips, and fruit. Early evening brings wine with hot and cold hors d'oeuvres the likes of cheese and crackers, crudités with dip, fruit, stuffed mushrooms, miniature corn dogs, vegetarian sandwiches, and puff pastry chicken cups. After dinner you'll find desserts such as cheesecake, carrot cake, flan, cookies, cream puffs, and petits fours along with liqueurs. There's even a self-service espresso and cappuccino machine. Additional amenities include the services of a friendly concierge staff, private check-in and checkout, nightly turndown service, and robes.

Suites. All suites regardless of floor location are part of the concierge level. For the ultimate in comfort choose the 2,200-square-foot Presidential Newport Suite, where a marble foyer leads to an enormous formal living room with two seating areas, fireplace, wet bar, dining table for eight, full kitchen (minus a stove), and half bath. In the colossal master bedroom are two queen-size beds topped with attractive rattan headboards, a desk, two easy chairs and ottomans, a relaxing chaise, an armoire, and loads of windows with everything outfitted in shades of sea foam green and pink and white stripes. The sensuous marble master bathroom holds a lavish whirlpool tub, separate toilet area with a bidet, separate walk-in shower, little TV, and large walk-in closet. The second bedroom is actually the size of a one-bedroom suite with a separate sitting area. Three extended balconies almost encircle the entire suite, affording views of the pool and lagoon.

The fifth-floor Vice Presidential Nantucket Suite at 996 square feet is a one-bedroom, one-and-a-half-bath gem with a sizable parlor holding a sofa, coffee table, easy chairs, wet bar with microwave and small refrigerator, four-person dining table, desk, armoire, and balcony overlooking a quiet garden courtyard. The bedroom has a small standing-room-only balcony facing Stormalong Bay and a beautiful marble bathroom with whirlpool tub, separate shower, double sinks, and little TV. A standard guest room can be added to make this a two-bedroom, two-and-a-half-bath suite.

RESTAURANTS

Beach Club Marketplace. Located within the Atlantic Wear and Wardrobe Emporium; counter service available all day; breakfast: omelet sandwich on a croissant, white chocolate bread pudding, made-to-order yogurt parfait, fresh-baked pastries, muffins, bagels, croissants; lunch and dinner: roast beef and brie on ciabatta roll, turkey and mozzarella on sourdough baguette, smoked ham and Black Diamond cheddar sandwich, grilled vegetable wrap, grilled chicken Caesar salad, New England clam chowder; dessert: chocolate or lemon mousse, fruit tart, key lime tart, Rice Krispies treat, marshmallow kebab, chocolate chip cookies, cupcakes, gelato; espresso, cappuccino, wine; children's menu: ham and cheese wrap, PB&J.

Beaches and Cream. Disney's best milk shake and ice-cream stop; burgers and sandwiches; open for lunch and dinner. (See full description in Dining chapter.)

Cape May Café. Open for breakfast and dinner; breakfast buffet with Goofy and friends; evening New England–style clambake buffet. (See full description in Dining chapter.)

Room service. Available 24/7.

LIBATIONS

Hurricane Hanna's Grill. Poolside bar and grill; full bar, cocktails, beer, alcoholic and nonalcoholic frozen drinks; grilled chicken sandwich, chicken strips, cheeseburgers, hot dogs, wrap sandwich, chicken or tuna salad; *children's menu:* chicken strips, PB&J sandwich, kid-size cheeseburgers.

Martha's Vineyard. Cocktail lounge adjoining Cape May Café; wine and champagne by the glass or bottle, along with wine flight tastings; large selection of beers; *light meals:* peel-and-eat shrimp, barbecue ribs, "wing dings," nachos, clam chowder, bucket of clams and mussels.

RECREATION AND ACTIVITIES

Arcade. Lafferty Place Arcade located next to Beaches and Cream soda shop.

Beaches. An enticing white-sand beach dotted with lounge chairs fronting Crescent Lake with views of the Boardwalk and the Epcot fireworks.

Boating. Rentals at Bayside Marina for touring Crescent Lake and the adjacent waterways; Sea Raycers, Boston Whaler Montauks, pontoon boats.

Illuminations cruise on a pontoon boat or the *Breathless,* a 24-foot mahogany replica of a 1930s Chris Craft Runabout (make reservations exactly ninety days ahead or risk losing out)—the viewing point from under the International Bridge is unrivaled; also available are thirty-minute spins around Crescent Lake. Call (407) WDW–PLAY or (407) 939–7529 for reservations.

Children's playground and activities. Playground located near Stormalong Bay; pool games, water volleyball, treasure hunts, tug-of-war; *Albatross* Treasure Cruise sets sail in search of treasure each Wednesday at 9:30 A.M. for a two-hour cruise ($28); lunch included.

Croquet. Croquet court located at Beach Club Resort; complimentary equipment available at Ship Shape Health club.

Fishing. See Recreation and Activities section for Disney's Yacht Club Resort.

Jogging. Joggers utilize the 0.75-mile circular Boardwalk as their track.

Swimming. Stormalong Bay is an eye-popping, free-form, miniature water park complex that meanders between the Beach Club and the Yacht Club. The most divine pool at Disney, its three acres of winding, watery delight offer sandy-bottom pools, a 230-foot-long "shipwreck" waterslide, a snorkeling lagoon, a tidal whirlpool, bubbling hot tubs, a kiddie pool with its own slide next to the beach, and enough length to float lazily in inner tubes to your heart's content. Inner tubes are available for rent; swimming is not allowed in Crescent Lake. A quiet pool and whirlpool are located at the Epcot end of the resort at the Beach Club, with another at the Dolphin end of the Yacht Club. All pools are heated.

Tennis. See Recreation and Activities section in subsequent entry for Disney's Yacht Club Resort.

Tours. See Recreation and Activities for Disney's Yacht Club Resort.

Volleyball. Sand court located at Beach Club Resort; ball available at Ship Shape Health club.

SERVICES

Business center. See Services section of subsequent entry for Disney's Yacht Club Resort.

Child care. The Sandcastle Club features video and board games, arts and crafts, Disney movies, play kitchen; open 4:30 P.M. to midnight, for potty-trained children ages 4–12; cost includes dinner; open only to registered guests of the Yacht Club, Beach Club, Beach Club Villas, and Boardwalk Inn and Villas; call (407) WDW–DINE or (407) 939–3463 for reservations.

Hair salon. Periwig Beauty and Barber Salon; haircuts, perms, color, manicures, pedicures; open 9:00 A.M. to 6:00 P.M.

Health club. Ship Shape Health Club; Cybex machines, Life Fitness treadmills, bicycles, elliptical machines, Stairmaster stair-climbers, free weights; whirlpool, steam room, and sauna; massage available by appointment, including in-room; complimentary to resort guests; open 6:00–9:00 P.M.

SHOPPING

Atlantic Wear and Wardrobe Emporium. Resort wear including Tommy Bahama; swimwear; Disney logo clothing and character merchandise; sundries; framed Beach Club watercolor prints; small assortment of groceries.

TRANSPORTATION

There is a watercraft taxi to Disney–MGM Studios from the Bayside Marina at the Yacht Club. Although boat transportation is available to Epcot, it's quicker to walk to the park than to walk to the marina to catch the boat. The Boardwalk is a 0.75-mile stroll around the lagoon. Bus service is available to the Magic Kingdom, Animal Kingdom, Typhoon Lagoon, Blizzard Beach, and Downtown Disney.

To reach other Disney resorts outside of the Epcot area, you must first bus to Downtown Disney and then transfer to your resort destination.

Disney's Beach Club Villas

205 units. 1900 Epcot Resorts Boulevard, Lake Buena Vista 32830; phone (407) 934–2175, fax (407) 934–3850. Check-in 4:00 P.M.; check-out 11:00 A.M. For reservations call (407) WDW–MAGIC or (407) 939–6244, or contact your travel agent. $$–$$$$$

This Robert A.M. Stern–designed home-away-from-home property reflects the architecture of the oceanfront houses found in Cape May, New Jersey, in the early part of the twentieth century. Adjoining Disney's Beach Club Resort and within a very short walking distance to Epcot, it shares all facilities with both that resort and Disney's Yacht Club Resort, including the wonderful Stormalong Bay pool. Cape Cod–style villas are washed in a soothing teal bordered with sparkling white latticework trim. All units have either a garden view (although many so-called garden-view units overlook Epcot Resorts Boulevard) or a pool view, each with a balcony or patio. Check-in is located at the Beach Club Resort. See the previous entry for Disney's Beach Club Resort and the subsequent entry for Disney's Yacht Club Resort for information on restaurants, libations, recreation, services, shopping, and transportation. The Beach Club Villas has its own quiet pool, Dunes Cove, with whirlpool, lockers, and restrooms.

ACCOMMODATIONS

Villa choices include studios as well as one- and two-bedroom units (three-bedroom units are not offered at this property), each with a nice balcony or patio. Ocean blue and sea green furnishings and fabrics intermingle with pickled blue-on-white furniture, rattan chairs, and sea horse, seashell, and dolphin decorative tiles. Seaside framed prints decorate the walls colored in soft peach, and the carpeting is imprinted with a vine motif. Kitchens come with granite countertops, and bedrooms feature cream-colored scrolled metal headboards and morning glory print spreads.

The 356-square-foot studios sleep a maximum of four people plus one child age two or younger. They include a queen-size bed, double sofa bed, armoire with TV, small table and two cushioned rattan chairs, patio or balcony, microwave, minifridge, coffeemaker, and wet bar. Bathrooms have a single sink with hair dryer and a separate, small bath-commode area. A small closet holds an iron and ironing board. The decor is a bit different in the studios, with a coral reef patterned bedspread and curtains, soft blue wooden headboards, and a pastel plaid sofa bed. Just slightly larger than the next-door Beach Club guest rooms, their advantage is the addition of a sofa bed and minikitchen but at a higher nightly rate.

The One-Bedroom Villa, at 727 square feet, sleeps a maximum of four plus one child age two or younger. Each unit has a small living area with a queen-size sofa bed, reading chair, entertainment center containing a TV with DVD player, a five-person booth-style dining table, and a balcony or patio. The small but adequate kitchen, open to the living area, contains a refrigerator, stove, dishwasher, coffeemaker, toaster, microwave, and all utensils, dishes, and pots and pans to prepare a complete meal. The spacious bedroom holds a king-size bed, armoire with TV, desk, and sea green easy chair as well as an additional patio or balcony. It adjoins a two-room bathroom. One room has a whirlpool tub, vanity sink, and walk-in closet with a laptop-size safe, iron, and ironing board. The other contains a commode (within an enclosure), shower, and an additional freestanding sink. A nice feature is the stacked washer-dryer.

Two-Bedroom Villas sleep a maximum of eight people plus one child age two or younger and have 1,080 square feet of room. This unit is exactly the same as the one-bedroom unit with the addition of a studio bedroom, which adds up to two bedrooms, two baths, living area, kitchen, three TVs, and three balconies or porches.

Disney's Boardwalk Inn

372 rooms. 2101 Epcot Resorts Boulevard, Lake Buena Vista 32830; phone (407) 939–5100, fax (407) 939–5150. Check-in 3:00 P.M.; check-out 11:00 A.M. For reservations call (407) WDW–MAGIC or (407) 939–6244, or contact your travel agent. $$–$$$

The Boardwalk Inn's intimate charm captures the feeling of a 1930s mid-Atlantic seacoast retreat. In the lobby is a nostalgic living room scene of chintz-covered, oversize chairs, invitingly plump sofas, floral rugs, and potted palms set atop gleaming hardwood floors and plush area rugs. Walls are a soothing sea green with cream-colored trim, and looming overhead is the barrel-shaped, chandeliered ceiling embellished with delicate lattice-work. Views from the lofty windows are of a lush courtyard green fronting a festive, old-fashioned boardwalk. Step outside to the wide veranda lined with wicker rocking chairs, a perfect early evening spot from which to bathe in the pink glow of sunset as the Boardwalk slowly comes alive.

The resort's gleaming white four-story buildings, dotted with latticework and crowned with sea green roofs and striped awnings, surround interior courtyards fragrant with blooming roses. Adjoining the inn and sharing all amenities is the Boardwalk Villas, a home-away-from-home property. Both front the picturesque Boardwalk overlooking Crescent Lake and are just a short walk away from Epcot's International Gateway entrance.

ACCOMMODATIONS

Guest rooms. Well-appointed accommodations average 390 whimsical square feet, all with French doors leading to full-size balconies or patios. Cheerfully furbished in a floral decor mixed with leaf-patterned wallpaper, vintage-postcard-printed curtains, and rose-studded carpeting, most offer two queen-size beds with white iron headboards (a few come with king-size beds), small table and two chairs, a soft-blue armoire with TV, and ample closet space. Daybeds just large enough for a small child come in many of the rooms. A second clothes bureau is near the bathroom, which has two areas: one with a marble-topped vanity with double sinks, hair dryer, and makeup mirror, and the other with a separate tub and toilet. Amenities include a keyed wall safe, iron and ironing board, coffeemaker, refrigerator, and daily newspaper.

Standard-view rooms could mean either a view of the front of the resort and perhaps a bit of the parking lot or a delightful one of the peaceful, interior courtyard and with any luck the Illuminations fireworks. Water-view rooms are pleasing, but those closest to the Boardwalk or overlooking the pool could be a bit noisy. Keep in mind that ground-floor rooms have open patios that afford little privacy, with vistas sometimes blocked by too-tall hedging.

Concierge rooms. Consider upgrading to one of the 65 concierge-level rooms where the Innkeeper's Club, a relaxing lounge on the fourth floor with a splendid view of the fireworks, features a complimentary continental breakfast of bagels, pastries, cereal, juice, coffee, and tea. Midday refreshments are chips and salsa, popcorn, pretzels, nuts, hummus, dips, and beverages. Early evening comes with hot and cold hors d'oeuvres of crudités, cheese and crackers, fruit, and puff pastry appetizers along with wine. After dinner are cordials and desserts such as chocolate-covered strawberries, tarts, cookies, brownies, and cheesecake. There's even a self-service cappuccino machine. All this along with concierge services, nightly turndown, private check-in and checkout, and robes.

As well as standard-size rooms, the concierge level offers a 644-square-foot Deluxe Concierge Room with two queen-size beds and a nice seating area outfitted with a queen-size sofa bed, rattan chair, and extra armoire with TV/VCR.

Suites. A gated, white picket fence encircles the serene, two-storied Garden Suites (915 to 1,100 square feet), most with a private front yard complete with rose garden, arbor, mailbox, birdhouse, and porch. Downstairs is a living area with an entertainment center with TV, queen-size sofa bed, coffee table, easy chair, two-person dining table, wet bar with coffeemaker and small refrigerator, and half bath. Upstairs is a loft bedroom with four-poster bed, entertainment center with TV, and a bathroom with double sink, whirlpool tub, separate shower, and tiny TV. Three of the fourteen Garden Suites have a large, upstairs balcony instead of a front yard, so be sure to request your preference.

One-bedroom suites feature a parlor with a half bath, clothes bureau, sofa bed, easy chair, armoire with TV, four-person dining table, coffee table, fax machine, wet bar with refrigerator, microwave, sink, and coffee-maker, as well as a balcony. Off the parlor is a very nice master bedroom separated by curtained French doors with a king-size four-poster bed, balcony, and dressing area and closet. The bath has a marble shower, whirlpool tub, separate commode, double sink, and little TV. This suite can be made into a two-bedroom, two-and-a-half-bath suite with the addition of a connecting standard room.

The Vice Presidential Sonora Suite's lovely living room is perfect for entertaining, with plush floral furnishings in a soft green, blue, and rose palatte combined with an armoire with TV/VCR and stereo, two easy chairs, sofa, coffee table, eight-person dining table, wet bar, buffet, kitchen minus a stove, half bath, and balcony. On one side of the living area is a standard guest room with an upgraded bedspread and carpeting in rose motif; on the other side a somewhat feminine master bedroom features a four-poster king-size bed, armoire with TV, and easy chair. The marble master bathroom comes with double sink, separate shower, whirlpool tub, little TV, and separate commode area. In my opinion, the master bedroom in the less expensive One-Bedroom Suite is really nicer and larger than this one. But I do like the story behind the suite's name: Sonora Carver was a woman who had a diving-horse act in the 1920s at the Atlantic City Board-walk, plunging 40 feet on a horse and landing in a tank of water.

From balconies that run the length of the two-bedroom, two-and-a-half-bath Presidential Steeplechase Suite are sweeping views of the Boardwalk and Crescent Lake. This 2,170-square-foot wonder comes with a massive, poshly furnished living room with two seating areas and an eight-person dining table. The lavish master bedroom boasts a gorgeous canopied four-poster bed, and the marble bathroom has a whirlpool tub and separate shower.

RESTAURANTS

See Restaurants and Snacks section for Disney's Boardwalk in chapter 5, Beyond the Theme Parks.

Room service. Available 24/7.

LIBATIONS

Belle Vue Lounge. Sentimental music the likes of Benny Goodman plays from vintage radios in this comfy bar; additional balcony seating overlooks the Boardwalk; cocktails, specialty drinks, single-malt scotches, wine, beer, Grand Marnier; opens at 5:00 P.M.

Leaping Horse Libations. Luna Park pool bar; assorted sandwiches, hot dogs, green salad, nachos, fruit cup; *children's menu*: PB&J sandwich; smoothies, nonalcoholic beverages, beer, specialty drinks.

RECREATION AND ACTIVITIES

Arcade. Sideshow Arcade just off the Village Green with the newest in video and computer games as well as the old reliable pinball machines.

Bicycle and surrey rentals. In front of the Village Green; two-, four-, and six-seater surreys available for rent 10:00 A.M. to 10:00 P.M., weather per-mitting; single and tandem bicycles for rent at Community Hall.

Children's activities and playground. Playground next to Luna Park Pool; Luna Park poolside activities; arts and crafts in Community Hall.

Ferris W. Eahlers Community Hall. Video games, air hockey, table tennis, foosball; arts and crafts; life jackets, noodles (foam flotation toys), bikes, books, DVDs, and videos for rent; open 8:00 A.M. to 10:00 P.M.

Fireworks cruise. View the Illuminations display from the privacy of a pontoon boat; call (407) WDW–PLAY or (407) 939–7529 for reservations.

Fishing. Guided two-hour fishing excursions each morning for as many as five people including boat, guide, and gear; twice-daily guided one-hour kids' fishing trip for ages 5–12 departs from Community Hall, catch-and-release only (call 407–WDW–BASS or 407–939–2277 for reservations at least twenty-four hours in advance).

Jogging. Either the circular 0.75-mile Boardwalk or the path encircling the canal leading to Disney–MGM Studios can serve as a jogging track.

Swimming. 190,000-gallon Luna Park Pool with 200-foot-long "Keister Coaster" waterslide; kiddie pool and whirlpool; smaller Inn Pool and whirlpool in Rose Courtyard on Epcot side of inn; quiet Villa Pool and whirlpool next to Community Hall; all pools heated and open 24/7; no lifeguard on duty.

Tennis. Two hard-surface, lighted courts at Boardwalk Villas; complimentary to registered guests; make reservations at Community Hall.

SERVICES

Business center. Located at the Boardwalk Conference Center; personal computers, Internet, fax machine, copier, package mailing, secretarial service.

Muscles and Bustles Health club. Cybex strength training equipment, Life Fitness treadmills, elliptical trainers, bicycles, stair-climbers; free weights; co-ed sauna and steam room; massage available, including in-room; complimentary to resort guests; open 6:00 A.M. to 7:00 P.M.

TRANSPORTATION

A water taxi to Epcot and Disney–MGM Studios departs from the Board-walk dock. It's a five- to ten-minute walk to Epcot's International Gateway and about a fifteen-minute walk to Disney–MGM Studios along the walkway found behind the resort. Bus service is available to the Magic Kingdom, Animal Kingdom, Typhoon Lagoon, Blizzard Beach, and Downtown Disney.

To reach other Disney resorts outside of the Epcot area, you must first take a bus to Downtown Disney and then transfer to your resort destination.

Disney's Boardwalk Villas

520 units. 2101 Epcot Resorts Boulevard, Lake Buena Vista 32830; phone (407) 939–5100, fax (407) 939–5150. Check-in 4:00 P.M., check-out 11:00 A.M. For reservations call (407) WDW–MAGIC or (407) 939–6244, or contact your travel agent. $$–$$$$$
Sharing the same lobby, check-in desk, pools, and all amenities as the adjacent Boardwalk Inn is this Disney Vacation Club property. It's probably my least favorite decor at a DVC property, but the location can't be beat. Villas not occupied by members are available to the many visitors who wish to stay on Disney property but would also like the convenience of a kitchen and the extra breathing space of a living area. The pastel, three-story buildings are decked out with yellow-striped awnings and lush lawns, while inside you'll find a summer seaside cottage atmosphere in hallways painted with white picket fences and wooden decking motif carpeting. See the previous entry for Disney's Boardwalk Inn for information on restaurants, libations, recreation, services, shopping, and transportation.

ACCOMMODATIONS

Villa choices come in studios, one-bedroom, two-bedroom, and three-bedroom Grand Villas, each with balcony or patio. All are decorated in a variety of pastel shades, with bedrooms sporting country-style quilted spreads, wicker headboards, and blue and rose carpeting.

Studios at 359 square feet are one-room accommodations with a queen-size bed and double sofa bed, small table with two chairs, a mini-kitchen with microwave, sink, and under-the-counter refrigerator, and balcony or patio. The bathroom has a single-sink vanity outside the tub and toilet area.

One-bedroom units at 712 square feet have a small living area that accommodates a chintz-covered sofa bed, several chairs, an entertainment center containing a TV/VCR, and a small balcony or patio. The cheerful kitchen is open to the living room with a breakfast bar and stools and contains a small but adequate refrigerator plus stove, dishwasher, coffeemaker, toaster, microwave, and all utensils, dishes, pots and pans to prepare a complete meal. A two-person dining table sits out in the living area. In the bedroom is a king-size bed and armoire with TV adjoining a two-part, white-tiled bathroom with whirlpool tub, sink, and closet in one area and shower, freestanding sink, and toilet in the other. The bathroom closet contains a safe, iron, and ironing board. Added pluses are a stacked washer-dryer and portable crib. Request a villa that comes with an additional balcony or patio off the master bedroom (most do).

Two-bedroom units at 1,072 square feet are essentially one-bedroom villas joined with a studio.

Grand Villas, at a whopping 2,142 square feet, are three-bedroom, three-bath accommodations offering a somewhat austere but supersize living area with almost rugless parquet floors (certainly not the villa's most impressive feature) and two seating areas, one with a chintz-covered sofa bed and armoire with TV, the other facing the balcony in the middle of the room with a wicker sofa. Off to one side is a ten-person dining table and full-size kitchen. The best aspect of a Grand Villa is its spectacular balcony running the length of the living room overlooking the Boardwalk and Crescent Lake with views extending to Spaceship Earth in the distance. The master bedroom, by itself on one side of the living area, is like the bedroom you'll find in a one-bedroom unit, including a balcony. Two other bedrooms are found on the opposite side of the living area, each with two queen-size beds, an armoire with TV, and bathroom with a single sink and separate toilet-bathtub area. Both share a common balcony. A giant laundry room comes with a full-size washer and dryer, utility sink, and iron and ironing board.

NOTE: If you're having trouble choosing between a studio here or a room at the Boardwalk Inn, opt for the more spacious resort room for the same price; the only plus in booking a studio is its minikitchen.

Disney's Yacht Club Resort

630 rooms. 1700 Epcot Resorts Boulevard, Lake Buena Vista 32830; phone (407) 934–7000, fax (407) 934–3450. Check-in 3:00 P.M.; check-out 11:00 A.M. For reservations call (407) WDW–MAGIC or (407) 939–6244, or contact your travel agent. $$–$$$$
The theme here is one of a sophisticated, exclusive yacht club where a navy blue blazer should be in order for a stay. Four- and five-story oyster gray clapboard buildings with balconies shaded by red and white striped awnings front Crescent Lake and a sliver of groomed beach that stretches over to the adjoining Disney's Beach Club Resort. The resort's prime location, within walking distance of Epcot's International Gateway entrance as well as the Boardwalk and just a short boat ride away from Disney–

MGM Studios, is near perfect. The polished, sleek lobby of ship-shiny hardwoods, potted palms, roped nautical railings, leather sofas, and over-stuffed, striped easy chairs creates an environment reminiscent of a classy eastern seaboard hotel of the 1880s. The antique globe in the center of the room along with detailed ship models and oceans of gleaming brass complete the picture. The resort shares Stormalong Bay, a fantasyland pool complex, and all recreational areas and facilities with its sister property, the Beach Club.

ACCOMMODATIONS

Guest rooms. Enter your casually elegant room through a yacht-style door. Inside, the room has two queen-size beds covered with ship-themed spreads and topped with a gleaming white headboard in a ship's wheel motif, brass sconce lamps, gold and blue striped drapes with admiral star sheers, and lots of maritime accents. Rooms are fairly spacious at 380 square feet, with cheery all-white furnishings including a writing table, a bureau on top of which sits the TV, and an additional bureau near the bathroom. French doors lead to a private balcony or patio with a variety of views. Some rooms come with a daybed, and all have an easy chair and ottoman. The marble bath vanity holds double sink, hair dryer, makeup mirror, and TV speaker below porthole-style mirrors. There is a separate tub and toilet area. Amenities include an iron and ironing board, coffeemaker, refrigerator, keyed safe, and daily newspaper.

NOTE: Standard rooms come with a view of either the gardens or the less desirable front of the resort with perhaps a slice of the parking lot. Try for the standard rooms on the back side near the quiet pool that look out to a grassy area with a fountain and duck pond. Water views face Crescent Lake, Stormalong Bay, or sometimes both; ask for one facing Epcot for a view of the fireworks. If a lot of walking is not your idea of a vacation, request a room close to the lobby; the resort is quite spread out, and long treks to your room are not uncommon.

Concierge rooms. Concierge rooms and suites located on the fifth floor are privy to the classy Regatta Club, one of only two Disney concierge lounges with a balcony, but alas with a view of the front of the resort instead of Crescent Lake. Rooms here can be booked in either a standard or water view—most standard rooms overlook the gardens, but a few have a view of the parking lot, while water-view rooms face the pool and offer a full-frontal view of Crescent Lake. In the mornings there's a continental breakfast of coffee with a self-service cappuccino machine, tea, juice, bagels, croissants, pastries, fruit, cereal, oatmeal, and grits. Midday snack consists of edamame, chips and salsa, pretzels, and nonalcoholic beverages. Early evening brings wine and hors d'oeuvres such as hummus, olives, vegetable crudités, and cookies along with two hot items such as crab cakes (kids feast on PB&J sandwiches). After dinner you'll find a selection of cordials along with cookies, cream puffs, and brownies. Extra amenities include robes, turndown service, private check-in and checkout, and the services of an excellent concierge staff.

Suites. A variety of plush suites are available, the smallest being the 654-square-foot Junior Suite with two queen-size beds, an armoire, and small table and chairs in the extralarge balconied bedroom, and a daybed, coffee table, and chair in a small sitting area separated by French doors.

Turret Two-Bedroom Suites offer 1,160 square feet, including two queen-size beds and a bath in each bedroom; off the master is a six-sided turreted living area with sofa, chairs, entertainment armoire, four-person dining room, and small balcony with standing room only.

The Vice Presidential Suite (or the Commodore Suite) is 1,375 square feet. Enter through a large marble foyer to two bedrooms, two-and-a-half baths, three balconies (one standing room only) with both pool and lake views, and a living room with sofa, chairs, entertainment center with TV, DVD player, stereo, and wet bar with small refrigerator. The incredible marble master bath has a whirlpool tub, separate shower, and TV.

Almost identical at 2,017 square feet are the two-bedroom, two-and-a-half-bath Presidential and Admiral Suites. Both are richly decorated and come with a marble foyer, two living areas (one turreted), a fireplace, a separate eight-person dining room, a small kitchen, and three balconies. The master bedroom has a whirlpool tub in its luxurious marble bathroom.

The largest suite at 2,374 square feet and the best on property is the first-floor, two-bedroom, two-and-a-half-bath Captain's Deck Suite. A marble octagonal foyer leads to a nautically decorated parlor (the size of three regular guest rooms) in rich sea blue and rose shades along with silky striped easy chairs, all reminiscent of a superbly decorated yacht. The suite features an open sitting area, living area, large business desk, dining room with seating for ten, full kitchen (minus a stove), and huge garden patio (with a not-so-great view of the valet parking lot through the shrubbery). Each of the bedrooms has its own private patio, and the plush master bedroom offers a canopy king-size bed with a teal and rose checked bedspread, bureau, entertainment center, easy chair and ottoman, walk-in closet, and luxuriously large marble bathroom with vanity area, TV, huge shower, and separate whirlpool tub. The second bedroom is similar to a regular guest room. All suites regardless of floor location receive concierge service and amenities.

RESTAURANTS

Yacht Club Galley. Casual all-day eatery open for breakfast, lunch, and dinner. (See full description in Dining chapter.)

Yachtsman Steakhouse. Oak grilled steaks and seafood; dinner only. (See full description in Dining chapter.)

Room service. Served 24/7; limited menu after 10:00 P.M.

LIBATIONS

Ale and Compass Lounge. Lobby bar serving specialty drinks, wine, beer, cordials; continental breakfast served 6:00–10:30 A.M.; *light meals:* clam chowder, house-made garlic potato chips with smoked jalapeño dip, chili and cheese, baked garlic shrimp, chicken quesadilla, buffalo chicken wings, buffalo tenders, shrimp cocktail.

Crew's Cup Lounge. Cozy seaport-style lounge adjoining Yachtsman Steakhouse; beers from around the world, wine and champagne by the glass, specialty cocktails; *light meals:* shrimp cocktail, three-cheese spinach dip, chipotle barbecue shrimp, spinach salad, Caesar salad, buffalo chicken tenders, oysters Rockefeller; open noon to midnight.

Hurricane Hanna's Grill. Poolside bar and grill; full bar, cocktails, beer, alcoholic and nonalcoholic frozen drinks; grilled chicken sandwich, chicken strips, cheeseburgers, hot dogs, wrap sandwich, chicken or tuna salad; *children's menu:* chicken strips, PB&J, minicheeseburgers.

RECREATION AND ACTIVITIES

The Yacht Club shares all recreational activities with the adjacent Disney's Beach Club Resort. See also the Recreation and Activities section in the earlier entry for the Beach Club.

Fishing. Two-hour guided fishing excursions on Crescent Lake depart both morning and afternoon from the Yacht Club marina for a maximum of five guests, including gear and beverages; one-hour fishing excursion for kids ages 6–12; strictly catch-and-release (call 407–WDW–BASS or 407–939–2277 for reservations; twenty-four-hour notice required).

Tennis. One lighted hard-surface court available for complimentary use; complimentary equipment available at Ship Shape Health Club.

Tours. Complimentary walking Garden Tour of the Beach and Yacht Club's beautifully landscaped grounds led from the Yacht Club by a member of Disney's horticulture team each Monday, Wednesday, and Friday at 8:30 A.M. and again at noon.

SERVICES

The Yacht Club shares all services with the adjacent Disney's Beach Club Resort. See also the Services section in the earlier entry for the Beach Club.

Business center. Located at the Yacht Club Convention Center; personal computers, Internet, fax machine, copier, secretarial services; open 7:00 A.M. to 6:00 P.M. Monday through Friday and 8:00 A.M. to 4:00 P.M. Saturday and Sunday.

SHOPPING

Fittings and Fairings Clothing and Notions. Disney character merchandise and housewares; Disney and Yacht Club logo clothing for all ages; Tommy Bahama men and women's resort wear; swimwear; golf clothing and accessories; sundries; magazines, books, newspapers.

TRANSPORTATION

Take a water taxi to Epcot and Disney–MGM Studios from the Bayside Marina. It's a ten-minute walk to Epcot's International Gateway entrance and five minutes to the Boardwalk. Take a bus to the Magic Kingdom, Animal Kingdom, Typhoon Lagoon, Blizzard Beach, and Downtown Disney.

To reach other Disney resorts outside the Epcot area, you must first take a bus to Downtown Disney and then transfer to your resort destination.

Walt Disney World Dolphin

1,509 rooms. 1500 Epcot Resorts Boulevard, Lake Buena Vista 32830; phone (407) 934–4000, fax (407) 934–4099. Check-in 3:00 P.M.; check-out 11:00 A.M. For reservations call (407) WDW–MAGIC, (407) 939–6244, or (888) 828–8850, or contact your travel agent. Reservations and information also available online at www.swandolphin.com. $$–$$$

Operated by Sheraton Hotels but situated within the grounds of Walt Disney World, this pyramid-shaped, Michael Graves–designed resort can certainly be described as whimsical. All eyes are immediately drawn to the pair of five-story dolphins high atop the twenty-seven stories of the structure and then are immediately lured to the exterior fountain composed of giant clamshells cascading down nine stories to the resort entrance. Shades of rich coral and turquoise create a cacophony of color throughout the resort and into the lobby draped with a gaily striped cabana-style tent, underneath which sits a fanciful fountain of dolphins. Outside you'll find a super Grotto Pool fronting the white-sand beach of Crescent Lake.

Extensive meeting facilities, ballrooms, and exhibit halls make this property a popular choice for conventioneers, so come prepared for large groups roaming the public areas both here and at the next-door Swan, which shares all recreational and service facilities with the Dolphin.

Although this is not a Disney-owned resort, guests receive the same amenities as at other Disney resorts, including Extra Magic Hours, Disney transportation to all attractions, complimentary parking at Disney's theme parks, package delivery, and guaranteed park admission. However, charging privileges to your resort account do not extend outside of the Dolphin or Swan. Dollar for dollar, the Disney-owned deluxe resorts are a better choice—unless, of course, you want to escape the Mouse trap and prefer a convenient hotel that offers a break from everything Mickey at the end of your day.

ACCOMMODATIONS

Guest rooms. At both the Dolphin and the Swan, you'll find newly redecorated guest rooms embodying a contemporary style and replacing the former, whimsical look. The walls are covered with a soft peach, beige, and blue palette. Sleek, bleached wood furnishings with frosted blue accents fill the rooms. Sweet Sleeper Beds feature pillow-top mattresses, triple-sheeted linens, down blankets and pillows, and snow-white duvets topped with cheery blue-striped bolsters. The 360-square-foot rooms come with either two double beds with an easy chair or a king-size bed with a sofa. Bathrooms have one sink in a corner marble vanity outside the separate tub-shower and toilet area. In the foyer is a vanity with hair dryer and coffeemaker. Amenities include an iron and ironing board, two dual-line telephones, minibar, keyed safe, high-speed Internet connection, and cable TV with pay movies. A nice option is a room with a balcony (for which an extra charge is assessed).

NOTE: A small percentage of the rooms offer a view of the Epcot fireworks. Request one at time of booking and again at check-in.

Concierge rooms. Club Level rooms, located on the twelfth and fourteenth floors, come with the benefit of a large twelfth-floor private lounge with views of the Illuminations fireworks display plus a complimentary continental breakfast in the morning as well as fruit, cheese, and honor bar wine and beer from 5:00 to 7:00 P.M. Extra amenities include the services of a concierge desk, robes, and nightly turndown service. The lack of a private check-in desk, afternoon snacks, hot hors d'oeuvres in the evening, and evening desserts and cordials as well as the additional charge for alcoholic beverages make the concierge level here not really worth the extra cash outlay.

Suites. Junior Suites offer quite a bit more room than a regular guest room and a second bathroom as well. In the bedroom is a king-size bed, queen-size sofa bed, desk, and bureau with TV. The separate parlor area holds a queen-size Murphy bed, queen-size sofa bed, reading chair, entertainment center, and desk.

Executive Suites are even larger. The parlor includes a king-size Murphy bed, sofa, easy chairs, coffee table, bureau with TV, full bath with two sinks, and wet bar. One or two guest rooms (one with a king-size bed and the other with two doubles) can be added on either side of the living area.

The Dolphin has four presidential suites, each with a different theme. The Caesar and Pharaoh Suites, on the nineteenth floor, are each 2,451 square feet and similar in layout. They boast a massive living area with two separate seating areas, an eight-person dining table, a wet bar, an extra full bath, and a kitchen with a small refrigerator. Both bedrooms (one with a king-size bed, the other with two double beds) are similar to the regular guest rooms but with a totally different and upgraded decor. Alas, there is no balcony. On the twentieth floor are two other presidential suites, both larger two-story units. The Emperor's Suite is nicely done in Asian decor with walls hung with Japanese kimonos. The Los Presidentes Suite is similar in size and layout but decorated in an attractive Southwest theme. Each is 2,589 square feet with three bedrooms, four baths, grand piano, kitchen, wet bar, four sitting areas, and eight-person dining table. Two bedrooms come with king-size beds and the third with two double beds.

RESTAURANTS

Dolphin Fountain. Old-fashioned 1950s soda shop atmosphere; hot dogs, burgers, vegetarian burgers, BLT sandwich, fried chicken sandwich; ice cream, banana split, ice-cream-topped strawberry shortcake, floats, sundaes, malts, homemade pies; open 11:00 A.M. to 11:00 P.M.

Fresh Mediterranean Market. Innovative and delicious twist on a buffet meal; open for breakfast and lunch. (See full description in Dining chapter.)

Shula's Steakhouse. Best steak on Disney property; dinner only; clubby, luxurious atmosphere. (See full description in the Dining chapter.)

Todd English's Bluezoo. Fresh seafood in a stunning setting; dinner only. (See full description in Dining chapter.)

Tubbi's Buffeteria and Convenience Store. Twenty-four-hour cafeteria (grill open until 1:00 A.M.) with adjoining convenience store; *breakfast:* fresh fruit, omelets, muffins, bagels, oatmeal, grits, cereal, Krispy Kreme donuts, Starbucks coffee; *lunch and dinner:* chef's salad, burgers, chicken sandwich, Philly cheesesteak, grilled New York strip steak, fried chicken, pizza, vegetarian burgers, daily blue plate special; cold sandwiches, salads; *children's menu:* hamburgers, hot dogs, PB&J sandwich.

Room service. Available 24/7.

LIBATIONS

Bluezoo Bar. Chic lounge adjoining Todd English's Bluezoo restaurant; open 3:30–11:00 P.M. daily; full bar, specialty cocktails and martinis; light meals and raw bar.

Cabana Bar and Grill. Full bar, alcoholic and nonalcoholic frozen tropical drinks; pool grill; roasted veggie wrap, tuna sandwich, Cuban sandwich, seafood gyro, Philly cheesesteak sandwich, hot dogs, pizza, burgers, sandwiches, fruit plate; tuna niçoise, and Caesar salads.

Lobby Lounge. *Morning:* coffee and pastries; *afternoon and evening:* cocktail service.

Shula's Steakhouse Lounge. Cigar bar adjoining Shula's Steakhouse; clubby and sophisticated; cocktails, wine, champagne, port, single-malt scotches; appetizers.

RECREATION AND ACTIVITIES

Arcade. Downstairs near health club.

Basketball. Courts on each side of Grotto Pool.

Boating. Swan paddleboats near Grotto Pool.

Children's playground. In pool area.

Jogging. Four miles of jogging trails surround the resort; ask at health club or concierge desk for map.

Swimming. Rambling, three-acre Grotto Pool with waterfall and waterslide located between the Dolphin and the Swan; children's pool, four whirlpools, Spring Pool, two lap pools; Grotto and Spring pools are heated.

Tennis. Four lighted tennis courts located just across Epcot Resorts Boulevard.

Volleyball. Sand courts on beach.

SERVICES

Business center. Packaging and shipping, printing, computer and laptop workstations, copying, fax, office supplies; open 24/7 and staffed 7:00 A.M. to 6:30 P.M. Monday through Saturday.

Car rental. Alamo/National Car Rental desk located just off lobby.

Child care. Camp Dolphin with arts and crafts, trip to the game room, Disney movies. Open 5:30 P.M. to midnight, for potty-trained children ages 4–12; cost includes dinner; open to all Walt Disney World guests; complimentary two hours for children of Bluezoo and Shula's diners; call (407) 934–4000 for reservations.

Hair salon. Haircuts, color, styling, manicures, pedicures; open 9:00 A.M. to 6:00 P.M. daily.

Health studio. Free weights, Life Fitness cycles, treadmills, elliptical trainers; locker rooms, dry saunas; open 6:00 A.M. to 9:00 P.M.; massage available by appointment. New Mandara Spa scheduled to open summer 2005.

SHOPPING

Daisy's Garden. Disney merchandise store.

Galleria Sottil. Fine-art gallery featuring Louis Sottil's nature paintings.

Indulgences Gourmet. Chocolates, fudge, cookies.

Statements of Fashion. Men's and women's resort wear; swimwear; purses and straw hats; accessories.

TRANSPORTATION

The resort has a boat launch to Epcot's International Gateway and Disney–MGM Studios and bus service to the Magic Kingdom, Animal Kingdom, Downtown Disney, Typhoon Lagoon, and Blizzard Beach. If you prefer to walk, it's a pleasant ten- to fifteen-minute walk to Epcot's International Gateway entrance (one that is sometimes quicker than the boat service) or a fifteen- to twenty-minute walk to Disney–MGM Studios.

Walt Disney World Swan

758 rooms. 1200 Epcot Resorts Boulevard, Lake Buena Vista 32830; phone (407) 934–3000, fax (407) 934–4099. Check-in 3:00 P.M., check-out 11:00 A.M. For reservations call (407) WDW–MAGIC, (407) 939–6244, or (888) 828–8850, or contact your travel agent. Reservations and information also available online at www.swandolphin.com. $$–$$$

Designed by Michael Graves and operated by the Westin, the Swan, composed of a twelve-story main building and two seven-story wings, is a bit more subdued than the Dolphin. Linked by an awning-covered walkway (the place to catch the boat launch to Epcot and Disney–MGM Studios), it shares the same glorious three-acre grotto pool. The low-ceilinged, minuscule lobby adorned with a sparkling swan fountain is so understated that you'll feel you've somehow missed it. But if the colossal style of the Dolphin is simply not your scene, the smaller-scale Swan is the place for you.

Although not a Disney-owned resort, guests receive the same amenities as at other Disney properties, just as at the Dolphin, including Extra Magic Hours, Disney transportation to all attractions, complimentary parking at Disney's theme parks, package delivery, and guaranteed park admission. However, charging privileges to your resort account do not extend outside of the Swan or Dolphin.

ACCOMMODATIONS

Guest rooms. From a hallway painted with beach murals and through a cabana-striped door, as at the Dolphin you'll find guest rooms embodying a contemporary style. The palette is soft peach, beige, and blue with sleek, bleached wood furnishings with frosted soft blue accents, slate foyers, leaf-motif rust-colored carpeting, and lofty headboards. Heavenly Beds are the thing here, featuring pillow-top mattresses along with triple-sheeted linens, down blankets and pillows, and snow-white duvets topped with cheery blue-striped bolsters. The 360-square-foot rooms come with either a king-size bed and pullout sofa bed or two double beds, plus a lounge chair and ottoman. The bathrooms have two sinks, one outside the bath area with a hair dryer and coffeemaker and one inside with the tub-shower and toilet. Amenities include an iron and ironing board, minibar, a pair of two-line telephones, high-speed Internet connection, and cable TV with pay movies. Views from the upper floors can be impressive, with panoramas of either Disney Studios or Epcot and the Grotto Pool. A nice option is a room with a balcony, for which an extra charge is assessed.

NOTE: A small percentage of guest rooms offer a view of the Epcot fireworks. Request one at the time of booking and again at check-in.

Concierge rooms. Concierge rooms are located on the eleventh and twelfth floors (none with balconies) with access to the roomy twelfth-floor Royal Beach Club lounge. Here guests will find the services of a concierge staff, a complimentary continental breakfast, and evening offerings of fruit, cheese, crudités with dipping sauce, and nonalcoholic beverages from 5:00 to 7:00 P.M. Wine and beer are available at an additional charge. Other amenities include robes and nightly turndown service. As with the Dolphin, the lack of private check-in desk, afternoon snacks, hot hors d'oeuvres in the evening, and evening desserts and cordials together with the additional charge for alcoholic beverages makes the concierge level here not really worth the extra cash outlay.

Suites. At 500 square feet, Swan Studios offer quite a bit more square footage than a regular guest room. The bedroom contains a king-size bed, queen-size sofa bed, easy chair, and bureau with TV, opening up to a bonus room with four-person dining table and desk. Some suites have balconies (on request only).

Executive Suites feature a regular guest room (with no balcony) connected to a parlor in which you'll find a wet bar, two desks, four-person dining table, an austere modern sofa, two armless easy chairs, an extra full bath, and a balcony (avoid the corner rooms, where your balcony looks directly at the next room's balcony). This type of suite also can be reserved as a two-bedroom with another standard guest room opening into the other side of the parlor.

There are four presidential suites, each with a different decor and theme. On the twelfth floor is the large Japanese Governor's Suite furnished in shades of deep blue and terra-cotta. It comes with two bedrooms (the master with a king-size bed and the second bedroom with two queen-size beds), three full baths, large parlor with a grand piano, dining room with seating for eight, and full kitchen. The same layout but a different decor is in the Italian Governor's Suite. On the eleventh floor is the Oasis Suite, offering a somewhat Egyptian decor and a view of Crescent Lake. Here you'll find a master bedroom with a king-size bed and a large sitting area, an additional guest room, three full baths, huge living area with a grand piano, dining table for eight, and kitchen. The Southwest Presidential Suite is similar and is located on the twelfth floor; it has a Native American and rustic Western decor.

RESTAURANTS

Garden Grove Café and Gulliver's Grill. Serving breakfast, lunch, and dinner; setting reminiscent of a giant soaring birdcage; *breakfast:* a la carte menu items and buffet, Saturday and Sunday character breakfast; *lunch:* hot and cold sandwiches, low-carb options, salads, and pizza; *dinner:* buffet (Italian Tuesday, Thursday, and Sunday; American Southern food Monday, Wednesday, and Saturday; Key West fare on Friday) and a la carte choices of pizza, low-carb, seafood, steak, and pasta with characters each evening.

Palio. Disney's best Italian restaurant; open for dinner only. (See full description in Dining chapter.)

Splash Grill. Lap pool grill with full-service bar; open seasonally for lunch only; roasted veggie wrap, tuna sandwich, Cuban sandwich, seafood gyro, Philly cheesesteak sandwich, hot dogs, pizza, burgers, sandwiches, fruit plate; tuna niçoise, and Caesar salads; ice cream, bulk candy.

Room service. Available 24/7.

LIBATIONS

Kimonos. Sushi and sake bar; superfun karaoke nightly beginning at 9:00 P.M.

Lobby Court Lounge. *Morning:* Krispy Kreme donuts, specialty coffees, fruit, yogurt, brioche, bagels, pastries; *evening:* cocktail service with live piano music only in busier seasons.

RECREATION AND ACTIVITIES

The Swan shares all recreational activities with the Dolphin. See the Recreation and Activities section in the previous entry for additional information.

Arcade. A small arcade is located near Splash Grill.

SERVICES

Business center. Packaging and shipping, printing, computer and laptop workstations, copying, fax, office supplies; open 24/7 and staffed 7:00 A.M. to 6:30 P.M. Monday through Saturday.

Child care. Available at adjacent Dolphin Resort (see Services section of previous Dolphin entry).

Hair salon. Available at adjoining Dolphin Resort (see Services section of previous Dolphin entry).

Health club. Swan Health Studio; very small workout room with Life Fitness exercise machines, free weights, elliptical trainers, treadmills; locker rooms with dry saunas; massage available by appointment; open daily 6:00 A.M. to 9:00 P.M.

SHOPPING

Disney Cabanas. Men's and women's resort clothing; Disney merchandise; sundries.

TRANSPORTATION

See Transportation section of previous entry for Walt Disney World Dolphin.

Animal Kingdom Area Resorts

Disney's only deluxe resort in the Animal Kingdom area is the extraordinary Animal Kingdom Lodge. Although its solitude adds to the allure, that isolation also makes this property a less convenient choice than resorts in the Magic Kingdom or Epcot area. Those choosing this property should consider renting a car to take full advantage of all that Walt Disney World has to offer in the way of resort restaurants and entertainment. Nearby is, of course, the Animal Kingdom as well as Blizzard Beach, Winter Summerland miniature golf, and Disney's Wide World of Sports.

Disney's Animal Kingdom Lodge

1,293 rooms. 2901 Osceola Parkway, Bay Lake 32830; phone (407) 938–3000, fax (407) 938–7102. Check-in 3:00 P.M., checkout 11:00 A.M. For reservations call (407) WDW–MAGIC or (407) 939–6244, or contact your travel agent. $$–$$$

Disney's version of a safari lodge is truly a stunner, a faithful celebration of African wildlife, culture, and cuisine. Its authentic architecture combined with grasslands filled with hundreds of roaming exotic animals is simply a stroke of genius. The six-story, horseshoe-shaped structure topped with extravagant thatch rooftops is rustically surrounded by eucalyptus fencing and thirty-three acres of glorious savanna. Though often compared to the Wilderness Lodge in design and pricing, the Animal Kingdom Lodge is a step above in terms of sophistication.

The imposing, five-story thatch-roofed lobby is a wonder. Just as at Disney's Wilderness Lodge (both designed by architect Peter Dominick), the first impression is nothing but *wow!* Resplendent overhead chandeliers formed by Masai shields and spears tower over the boulder-lined lobby. Safari-chic seating areas, the most striking of any Disney resort, are extraordinary, with hand-carved coffee tables, handsome handwoven rugs, richly tinted rattan and cane chairs, and relaxing leather sofas adorned with brilliant textile throw pillows. A rope suspension bridge spans the lobby and draws the eye to balconies carved with graceful antelopes and a 46-foot picture window framed with the branches of an intricate ironwork tree. The centerpiece of the lobby is the one-of-a-kind sacred Ijele, a 16-foot, dazzling mask created by the Igbo people of Nigeria.

Out back sits a massive yellow flame tree poised atop Arusha Rock, an outcropping with panoramic views of the savanna. Nearby, a fire pit surrounded by rocking chairs is the site of nightly storytelling by the African staff. Lobby and restaurant greeters together with the savanna guides are all cultural representatives from Africa, more than delighted to answer questions or share information and tales of their homeland.

Located within a five-minute drive to the Animal Kingdom theme park (but with no walking path to the park), the animals you'll see here are exclusively the lodge's and not part of the theme park's menagerie. The design is one that encourages observation of the animals from both common lookouts as well as from 75 percent of the rooms. Several viewing platforms are staffed by guides helpful in identifying wildlife as well as communicating interesting information about the animals. Each savanna holds different species, and patience is sometimes required to spot them. But more times than not, you'll find the savanna brimming with an abundance of prime viewing opportunities including zebras, giraffes, gazelles, ankole (African cattle), wildebeests, exotic birds, and more.

If you can somehow find the time, take a tour of the resort's outstanding collection of museum-quality African art, including intricate masks, amazing beadwork, artifacts dating as far back as 8,500 B.C., and much, much more.

ACCOMMODATIONS

Guest rooms. Don't even consider booking a room without a savanna view, well worth every penny for a front-row seat from which to view the animals. And remember to bring your binoculars from home! Through a shield-covered door is an attractively designed, honey-colored room outfitted with handcrafted and carved furnishings, torch-shaped lamps, tribal baskets, and ethnic prints. Textiles in earth tones of gold, yellow, and brown cover the beds, and intricately engraved headboards are draped in a gauzy fabric reminiscent of mosquito netting. Baths have a separate granite-topped vanity area boasting a double sink, hair dryer, and a full-length mirror. Bathroom walls are covered with maps of Africa, and the vanity is topped with a wonderful hand-carved mirror.

Amenities include an iron and ironing board, safe, refrigerator, coffeemaker, and daily newspaper. All rooms have balconies, with 75 percent of them offering savanna views. The regular guest rooms at 344 square feet are a bit cramped, so I highly suggest an upgrade to a deluxe room with that extra 40 square feet of space needed for comfortable living quarters. Room bedding choices include one king, two queens, or a queen-size and bunk beds. Views are: standard, overlooking the front of the resort and the parking lot; savanna, overlooking one of three savannas; and pool, overlooking the pool area.

NOTE: At the Animal Kingdom Lodge are three savannas, each with their own charm; however, you might want to request Arusha, the inner savanna (the only one with zebras). Outer ones sometimes sport a not-so-great view of the highway, a sliver of the resort pool, or a stockade that just might kill any illusion you have of being in deepest Africa.

Concierge rooms. The concierge-level rooms, located on the non-keyed-access fifth floor and a much smaller number on the keyed-access sixth floor, as well as all suites, come with the use of the thatch-roofed, sixth-floor Kilimanjaro Club overlooking the lobby. This is one of my favorite concierge lounges; it has great food and a wonderful ambience. Extra amenities include the services of a concierge staff, curbside check-in, and turndown service. In the morning there's a continental breakfast of juice, Danish pastry, muffins, bagels, croissants, fresh fruit, yogurt, and cereal. Later you'll find afternoon beverages and snacks of pretzels, goldfish, crackers, and gummy bears. In the evening you can enjoy South African wine and beer as well as cold hors d'oeuvres and two hot items from the on-site restaurant Boma, including such goodies as veggie flatbread, Moroccan meatballs, noodle salad with tofu, black-eyed pea salad, scallops with sun-dried tomato chutney, assorted cheeses, hummus, beef satay, skewered nut-crusted salmon, and barbecue pork. Kids enjoy PB&J sandwiches and chicken nuggets. After-dinner treats include cookies, chocolates, minitarts, Rice Krispies Treats, cordials, and sometimes zebra domes (ganache-covered chocolate-coffee mousse) from Boma. Lemonade, iced tea, and sodas are available throughout the day. You'll even find a self-service espresso and cappuccino machine.

A special early morning excursion, the Sunrise Safari Breakfast Adventure, is available to concierge guests only on Thursday and Sunday at 6:30 A.M. It includes a forty-five-minute, before-park-hours ride through the

Animal Kingdom's Kilimanjaro Safaris followed by a buffet breakfast at Tusker House. The price is $50 per person and advance reservations can be made ninety days prior through the concierge desk by calling (407) 938–4755.

Another concierge option is the three-hour Wanyama Sunset Safari, an evening game drive around the resort's savannas in an open-air safari van followed by a preset, multicourse meal with wine pairings at the resort restaurant Jiko. It's available on Sunday, Monday, and Tuesday at 4:00 P.M. for $150 per person including dinner, tax, and gratuity. Reservations are taken at (407) 938–4755 as early as ninety days in advance. Only eight guests per evening are allowed on the safari, so book it early.

NOTE: My only hesitation in booking a concierge-level room would be the disappointment in not receiving a room with a view of the savanna. Most rooms have a savanna view, but some come with a view of the pool; you won't know until check-in which type you'll be receiving.

Suites. One-bedroom suites at 777 square feet feature a separate parlor with a queen-size sofa bed, easy chair, coffee table, entertainment center, four-person dining table, wet bar with small refrigerator and microwave, writing desk, half bath, and balcony with savanna view. In the bedroom are two queen-size beds, entertainment center, vanity desk, and balcony. The bath has a double sink, both a tub and a large shower, and a separate room for the toilet.

Two-bedroom suites have the same living room layout, but the master bedroom has a king-size bed, easy chair and ottoman, and a separate vanity area. A standard-size second bedroom with two queen-size beds sits off the foyer.

For something really special book the two-bedroom, two-and-a-half-bath Royal Assante Suite with over 2,115 square feet of exotic luxury. Enter the rounded foyer where you'll find a circular living room with a domed thatch roof, hardwood floors, exquisite African furnishings and artwork, queen-size sofa bed, easy chairs, dining table for eight, granite kitchen, armoire with extralarge TV, fireplace, writing desk, and half bath. There's also a separate office. The master bedroom features a stylishly rustic four-poster king-size bed with mosquito net draping, plenty of built-in cabinets and bureau space with TV and DVD player, desk, easy chair and ottoman, oversize whirlpool tub, granite vanity area with double sink, TV, huge separate shower, and walk-in closet; there's even a treadmill on the balcony.

And from the wraparound balconies you'll get sweeping views of the savanna. The second bedroom is a standard room with two queen-size beds.

The two-bedroom, two-and-a-half-bath Royal Kuba Vice Presidential Suite at 1,619 square feet is also a gem. Similar to the Royal Assante Suite, it comes with smaller rooms, no separate office, a stair-climber instead of treadmill, and a less extensive balcony (around the living area the small circular balcony allows standing room only).

RESTAURANTS

An interesting array of dining choices, many with an African flair, will please even the most timid eaters. Wine connoisseurs will love the fact that the Animal Kingdom Lodge has the largest offerings of South African wines in the United States. One thing the hotel lacks is a full-service restaurant open for lunch, the only Disney deluxe resort without such a venue.

Boma. Lively African and American buffet open for breakfast and dinner. (See full description in Dining chapter.)

Jiko. One of Disney's loveliest restaurants; dinner only; international food with an African flair and an extensive South African wine list. (See full description in Dining chapter.)

The Mara. Self-service snack bar; open 6:00 A.M. to 11:30 P.M.; *breakfast:* scrambled eggs, waffles, brioche French toast, egg and bacon croissant sandwich, breakfast pizza, fruit smoothies, oatmeal, pastries, muffins, specialty coffees; *lunch and dinner:* pizza, fish sandwich, fish and chips, chicken strips, grilled chicken sandwich, fried shrimp, burgers, rotisserie chicken, fresh fruit, cold sandwiches, pita wraps, salads; South African bottled wine and beer; *children's menu:* hot dogs, chicken strips; zebra domes (ganache-covered chocolate-coffee mousse), chocolate mousse crunch, cheesecake, paw print brownies, carrot cake, apple strudel, freshly baked cookies.

Room service. Available 6:00 A.M. to midnight.

LIBATIONS

Capetown Lounge and Wine Bar. Jiko's very small but eye-catching bar; largest South African wine list in the United States.

Uzima Springs. Thatch-roofed pool bar; frozen margaritas, daiquiris, piña coladas, beer, wine, nonalcoholic smoothies.

Victoria Falls. Lounge overlooking Boma (Sigh! Too bad it doesn't overlook the savanna); open 4:00 P.M. to midnight; African bush lodge atmosphere; exotic, African-inspired cocktails, South African wine, port, and beer, Kenyan AA coffee; fruit and cheese platter, nut mix, sampler dessert plate.

RECREATION AND ACTIVITIES

Arcade. Pumbaa's Fun and Games arcade located near the pool.

Children's playground and activities. Hakuna Matata playground near pool with a nice view of the flamingo area and the savanna; flamingo feedings, cookie decorating, junior researcher afternoon program at Flamingo Pond, afternoon games, and African crafts at pool.

Storytelling. African folktales shared each evening at 7:30 around the outdoor Arusha Firepit.

Swimming. Uzima Pool, the lodge's 11,000-square-foot version of a watering hole, highlighted by a 67-foot waterslide; cement is darkened to create the effect of swimming out in the bush, minus the crocodiles; two secluded whirlpools; heated kiddie pool.

Tours. Daily architecture and art collection tours; culinary tour of Africa in Jiko restaurant; cultural talks and horticulture activity at Arusha Rock.

SERVICES

Child care. Simba's Cubhouse with classic Disney movies, storytelling, arts and crafts, arcade and computer games. Open 4:30 P.M. to midnight, for potty-trained children ages 4–12; cost includes dinner and snacks; open to all registered guests of Walt Disney World resorts; call (407) WDW–DINE or (407) 939–3463 for reservations.

Health club. Zahanati Massage and Fitness Center; free weights, Cybex equipment, Life Fitness treadmills, stair-climbers, exercise bicycles; steam room and sauna in each locker room (complimentary to resort guests); personal training; facials, massage, and body treatments with in-room service available for an additional fee; open 6:00 A.M. to 9:00 P.M.

SHOPPING

Zawadi Marketplace. African wood carvings; hand painted ostrich eggs;

Disney and Animal Kingdom Lodge logo clothing; wooden masks; Zimbabwe tableware; Animal Kingdom Lodge logo stock; African coffee-table books and cookbooks; sundries; cigars, wine, liquor; *real find:* traditional Zulu baskets.

TRANSPORTATION

Bus transportation is available to all four Disney theme parks, Downtown Disney, Typhoon Lagoon, and Blizzard Beach. To reach other Disney resorts, you must first take a bus to Downtown Disney and then transfer to your resort destination.

Downtown Disney Area Resorts

Another exciting area is the one encompassing Downtown Disney with its profusion of restaurants, shopping, and nightlife as well as DisneyQuest, AMC Theaters, and Cirque du Soleil. Resorts nearby are Disney's Old Key West and Saratoga Springs. The Lake Buena Vista Golf Course winds through these two properties. Another close attraction is Typhoon Lagoon.

Disney's Old Key West Resort

761 units. 1510 North Cove Road, Lake Buena Vista 32830; phone (407) 827–7700, fax (407) 827–7710. Check-in 4:00 P.M.; checkout 11:00 A.M. For reservations call (407) WDW–MAGIC or (407) 939–6244, or contact your travel agent. $$–$$$$$

For a taste of a Key West–style village and the convenience of home-away-from-home condominium-style accommodations, look no more. This was the first Disney Vacation Club property, and villas not occupied by members are available to the many visitors who want the plus of a kitchen and the extra breathing space of a living area. Clustered around the registration building is a small marina area consisting of the main swimming pool, restaurant, store, bar, small health club, and activity center. A red-and-white-striped lighthouse leads the way to the resort's 156 acres filled with two- and three-story pastel structures, each with a shiny tin roof, white gingerbread trim, and striped awnings. Peace and quiet prevails amid the tropical landscaping of palms, flowering hibiscus, and brilliantly colored bird-of-paradise. Numerous waterways and lagoons together with the Lake Buena Vista Golf Course (described more fully in Sporting Diversions chapter) that meanders throughout the property make for soothing views from many of the villa's patios and balconies.

ACCOMMODATIONS

Villas here are the largest of all the home-away-from-home properties, offering plenty of room to sprawl. Washed in green and mauve pastels, they come with soft blond and pickled wood furnishings, plaid sofas, and floral bedspreads. An abundance of windows and plenty of softly turning ceiling fans make for airy, bright rooms. Each unit has a patio or balcony with varying views of the golf course, waterways, woodlands, or a combination of all three. Bathrooms are large and feature shiny white tiles, pickled green wood trim, and whirlpool tubs (except in the studio units). A portable crib is stored in the closet in each unit along with an iron and ironing board.

The 376-square-foot studio accommodates up to four adults plus one child age two or younger. It holds two queen-size beds, a small table with two chairs, an armoire with TV, and a minikitchen with a small refrigerator, coffeemaker, sink, and microwave. There are no safes in these units, but safety deposit boxes are available at the front desk free of charge. The nice-size bathrooms feature two sinks, one inside the bathtub-toilet area and one outside.

One-Bedroom Villas are 942 square feet, sleeping up to four adults and one child age two or younger. They have a separate living area, full-size kitchen, and spacious bedroom. The large living room is appointed with a sofa bed, love seat, coffee table, and easy chair in addition to a four-person dining table and TV/VCR. The green-tiled kitchen, open to the living area, includes a microwave, coffeemaker, dishwasher, toaster, sink, and full-size refrigerator and is stocked with dishes, flatware, pots and pans, even placemats and cloth napkins. A comfortable patio or balcony is perfect for dining al fresco and opens into the living area as well as the master bedroom. The roomy master bedroom holds a king-size bed, television, armoire, bureau, cozy sitting chair and ottoman. It connects to a two-room bathroom with large whirlpool tub, separate shower, and two sinks. You'll find a wall safe in the master bathroom closet and a laundry room with full-size washer and dryer.

Spacious at 1,333 square feet, the Two-Bedroom Villas sleep up to eight adults and one child age two or younger. They're exactly the same as the one-bedroom units, with the addition of a large extra bedroom with two queen-size beds, an armoire with TV, a small table and chairs, and a second bath.

Gigantic three-bedroom, four-bath Grand Villas sleep up to twelve people plus one child age two or younger and offer a whopping 2,202 square feet of space. These two-story units are luxuriously roomy with the addition of hardwood floors in the living area, vaulted ceilings, rattan game table, stereo system, and six-person dining table. A laundry room is situated off the full-size kitchen. The master bedroom is located downstairs with the usual whirlpool tub, two sinks, and shower with separate toilet. Two other bedrooms, each with bathroom, are found upstairs, with two queen-size beds in one and two double beds in the other. An additional bathroom is located in the downstairs hallway.

NOTE: There are no elevators at this property; if stairs are a problem, request a ground-floor room. Try to avoid units facing Bonnet Creek Parkway and Buena Vista Drive.

RESTAURANTS

Good's Food to Go. Snack bar open 7:30 A.M. to 10:00 P.M.; *breakfast:* croissant sandwich, scrambled eggs, bagels with cream cheese, pastries, cinnamon roll, muffins, cereal, fruit; *lunch and dinner:* cheeseburgers, hot dogs, veggie wrap, conch fritters, chef's salad, fruit plate, sandwiches of turkey, tuna, and chicken salad; brownies, cookies, Rice Krispies Treats, ice cream; *children's meals:* hot dog, grilled chicken breast.

Olivia's Café. Dine in a casual Key West setting; breakfast, lunch, and dinner. (See full description in Dining chapter.)

Pizza delivery. Available 4:00 P.M. to midnight.

LIBATIONS

Gurgling Suitcase. Tiny beach-style bar adjacent to marina and main pool; specialty drinks, beer, cocktails, wine, sodas.

RECREATION AND ACTIVITIES

Arcade. Electric Eel Arcade located next to marina.

Bicycles. Mongoose bicycles, two- and four-seater surrey bikes, and hydrobikes (pedal boats that sit atop pontoons) available for rent on the grounds of the resort at Hank's Rent 'n' Return.

Boating. Pontoons, Boston Whaler Montauks, paddleboats, and Sea Racers available for rent at Hank's Rent 'n' Return.

Children's activities and playground. Sandcastle-themed playground near main pool; additional playground located near quiet pool on Turtle Pond Road; daily activities at Conch Flats Community Hall, such as arts and crafts, movies, and pool parties; once-a-week complimentary "unbirthday" party for children ages 2–12 (reservations required).

Conch Flats Community Hall. Arts and crafts, family bingo, board games, foosball, table tennis, large-screen TV; DVD rentals.

Fishing. Guided two- and four-hour fishing excursions morning and afternoon for as many as five people, including boat, guide, and gear; twice daily guided one-hour kids' fishing trip for ages 5–12 along the Sassagoula River; catch-and-release only (call 407–WDW–BASS or 407–939–2277 for reservations at least twenty-four hours in advance).

Golf. Lake Buena Vista Golf Course winding through the grounds; pro shop at nearby Sarasota Springs Resort. (See full description in Sporting Diversions chapter.)

Jogging. A 3-mile path winds through the property.

Swimming. Free-form main pool surrounded by palms and tropical plants; nearby whirlpool, sauna, and sandcastle-themed kiddie pool; three additional quiet pools spread around property; all pools are heated.

Tennis. Three tennis courts; two near main pool are lighted; equipment for rent at Hank's Rent 'n' Return.

Other activities. Shuffleboard, volleyball, basketball, table tennis; equipment available (compliments of the resort) at Hank's Rent 'n' Return.

SERVICES

Health club. R.E.S.T. Exercise Room open 6:30 A.M. to midnight; free weights, Life Fitness treadmills, elliptical trainers, bicycles, strength training equipment.

SHOPPING

Conch Flats General Store. Groceries, wine, beer, liquor; sundries; newspapers, books; Disney merchandise; Old Key West logo attire.

TRANSPORTATION

Bus transportation is provided to all four Disney theme parks plus Blizzard Beach, Typhoon Lagoon, and Downtown Disney, with five bus stops scattered throughout the resort. To reach other Disney resorts, you must first take a bus to Downtown Disney and then transfer to your resort destination. The D.V.C. Ferry departs every hour from 11:00 A.M. to 4:00 P.M. and every half hour from 4:00 to 11:00 P.M. to Saratoga Springs Resort and Downtown Disney (weather permitting). A car is a definite plus here due to the large size of the property and the limited number of dining options.

Disney's Saratoga Springs Resort & Spa

1,262 units after all buildings are completed. 1960 Broadway, Lake Buena Vista 32830; phone (407) 827–1100, fax (407) 827–1151. Check-in 4:00 P.M., checkout 11:00 A.M. For reservations call (407) WDW–MAGIC or (407) 939–6244, or contact your travel agent. $$–$$$$$

Located across Lake Buena Vista from Downtown Disney, this newest of Disney's home-away-from-home resorts evokes upstate New York country retreats of the late 1800s. With a captivating pastel palette of green, orange, and buttercup yellow buildings spread over 65 acres, it's a delightful resort choice. Check-in is at the octagonal Carriage House, and just outside is the High Rock Spring pool surrounded by the spa and fitness center, the resort's only dining facility, the Artist's Palette, and a comfortable lounge called the Turf Club. The first two phases of the resort have been completed, with two more scheduled to open by 2007, so expect to see plenty of ongoing construction until then.

ACCOMMODATIONS

Villa choices come in studios as well as one-, two-, and three-bedroom units, each with a nice balcony or patio. Soft mossy green and yellow fabrics intermingle with warm wood furniture, and fun photos of Saratoga decorate the soft pastel walls. Kitchens come with green granite countertops, and bathrooms have tile flooring in shades of soft green and yellow. Bedrooms feature two-poster headboards and lovely spreads with a yellow, coral, and green floral motif. Views are of either the gardens, a quiet pool, the resort's waterway, or Lake Buena Vista; unfortunately, there's one other category of units in the Paddock area that face Buena Vista Drive.

The 355-square-foot Studios sleep a maximum of four people plus one child age two or younger and include a queen-size bed, double sofa bed, armoire with TV, small table and two chairs, patio or balcony, microwave, under-the-counter refrigerator, coffeemaker, and wet bar. Baths have a single sink, hair dryer, and full-length mirror with a small, separate bath-commode area. A closet holds an iron, ironing board, and crib. Expect to find slightly different decor in the studios with a green and rose quilt-style bedspread. Also included is a double sofa bed, ottoman, entertainment center, and patio or balcony.

One-Bedroom Villas, at 714 square feet, sleep a maximum of four plus one child age two or younger. Each unit has a small living area with a queen-size sofa bed, a reading chair, an entertainment center containing a TV with DVD player, a booth-style dining table, a bar with two stools, and a balcony or patio. A small but adequate kitchen, open to the living area, contains a refrigerator, stove, dishwasher, coffeemaker, toaster, microwave, and all utensils, dishes, and pots and pans to prepare a complete meal. The spacious bedroom, painted in soft green and yellow, holds a king-size bed, armoire with TV, and easy chair. It adjoins a two-room bathroom. One room features a whirlpool tub, vanity sink, and walk-in closet with a laptop-size safe, iron, and ironing board, while the other contains a commode (within an enclosure), a shower, and an additional free-standing sink. A nice feature is the stacked washer-dryer.

Two-Bedroom Villas sleep a maximum of eight people plus one child age two or younger and offer 1,075 square feet of room. This unit is exactly the same as the one-bedroom with the addition of a studio with two queen-size beds or one queen-size bed and a double sofa bed, which adds up to two bedrooms, two baths, living area, kitchen, three TVs, and two balconies or porches.

Three-bedroom Grand Villas are quite impressive. In fact, they're the nicest three-bedroom home-away-from-home units on Disney property. Enter the two-story unit into a lofty living room with floor-to-ceiling windows, sofa, easy chairs, chaise, and entertainment center. Off the living area are a kitchen, dining room with balcony, and bathroom with single sink and shower only. The master bedroom offers a king-size bed, armoire with TV, desk, and easy chair. The master bathroom has a whirlpool tub, separate shower, and single sink on a golden granite vanity. Upstairs are two bedrooms, each with two queen-size beds and each with a single-sink bathroom and separate toilet-bath area. Between the two bedrooms is a stacked washer-dryer. The unit's only drawback is the small single balcony off the dining area; a villa this large should come with at least two good-size balconies.

NOTE: Request a unit in the Congress Park area facing Downtown Disney. Many of the units in the Paddock area face Buena Vista Drive.

RESTAURANTS

The Artist's Palette. Cooked-to-order counter service restaurant serving breakfast, lunch, and dinner; *breakfast:* French toast casserole, breakfast flatbread, scrambled eggs, bacon, sausage, oatmeal, grits, breakfast croissant sandwiches, waffles; *lunch and dinner:* sandwiches of smoked turkey and brie, grilled vegetable, roast beef and bleu cheese, or smoked turkey Caesar; barbecued pork, grilled vegetable, or chicken, spinach, and artichoke flatbreads; salads of spinach and blue cheese or Caesar with grilled chicken or shrimp; daily chef's special; cold sandwiches and salads; bakery featuring cinnamon rolls, muffins, turnovers, croissants, cheesecake, bagels, and donuts; open 7:30 A.M. to 11:00 P.M.; grill closes at 10:00 P.M.

LIBATIONS

On the Rocks Pool Bar. Specialty drinks, beer, wine, smoothies, soft drinks, iced tea.

Turf Club. Masculine bar next to the Artist's Palette; pool table, TV, chess and checkers; martinis, specialty drinks, beer, wine; *appetizers:* homemade chips with blue cheese dressing, buffalo-style boneless barbecue chicken strips, hummus, fruit and cheese platter.

RECREATION AND ACTIVITIES

Arcade. Win, Place, or Show Arcade located next to the pool.

Bicycles. Bicycles and surrey bikes available on-site at Horsing Around Rentals.

Children's activities and playground. Children's playground near the quiet pool in Congress Park area; arts and crafts, pool games.

Community Hall. Arts and crafts.

Golf. Lake Buena Vista Golf Course Pro Shop located at the resort with the course adjacent to the property. (See full description in Sporting Diversions chapter.)

Swimming. High Rock Spring Pool, emulating the rock features at the Saratoga Spa State Park, features zero-depth entry, interactive wet area for children, twisting and turning waterslide, waterfall, and two whirlpools; additional quiet pools at the Congress Park and the Springs area of the resort.

Tennis. Two complimentary lighted clay courts, located near the Carriage House; equipment available at Horsing Around Rentals.

Other activities. Shuffleboard and basketball courts located near the tennis courts; equipment available at Horsing Around Rentals.

SERVICES

Fitness center. Located within the Saratoga Springs Spa; exclusive line of Life Fitness and Hammer Strength equipment including elliptical machines, treadmills, bicycles, free weights (complimentary to resort guests); personal training and in-room massage available by appointment; open 6:00 A.M. to 9:00 P.M. daily.

Spa. The Spa at Disney's Saratoga Springs Resort, retail store offering Jurlique products; open 8:00 A.M. to 8:00 P.M. daily. (See full description in Spas section of chapter 5, Beyond the Theme Parks.)

SHOPPING

Artist's Palette. Store within the Artist's Palette restaurant; wine; groceries; Disney merchandise; Saratoga Springs logo clothing; sundries.

TRANSPORTATION

Bus transportation is provided to all four Disney theme parks plus Blizzard Beach, Typhoon Lagoon, and Downtown Disney, with three bus stops scattered throughout the resort. To reach other Disney resorts, you must first take a bus to Downtown Disney and then transfer to your resort destination. The D.V.C. ferry departs every hour from 11:15 A.M. to 4:15 P.M. and every half hour from 4:15 to 11:15 P.M. to Old Key West and Downtown Disney (weather permitting). A car is a definite plus here due to the large size of the property and the limited dining options.

CHRISTMAS AT WALT DISNEY WORLD

Christmas is a special time at Walt Disney World, when it's adorned with over 1,200 Christmas trees, 10 miles of garland, 8 million lights, and 300,000 yards of ribbon. If you'd like to bring your Christmas spirit up a few notches, just head to one of the following locations:

- The Magic Kingdom features a huge Christmas tree in Town Square, garland and lights draped down Main Street, and a special Christmas parade. And don't forget about Mickey's Very Merry Christmas Party, an after-park-hours ticketed event.

- Epcot's Liberty Inn has Santa's Bakeshop, a life-size gingerbread house selling Christmas cookies and beverages. World Showcase features Christmas story-telling from around the world, and each night Mickey and his friends hold a Christmas tree lighting ceremony. Best of all is the Candlelight Processional, staged three times each evening from late November through December 30, with a massed choir, fifty-piece orchestra, and celebrity narrators who tell the story of Christmas.

- Disney–MGM Studios is one of the most popular places around, with its fan-tastic Osborne Family Spectacle of Lights, millions of colorful, twinkling Christmas lights on the Streets of America.

- The Animal Kingdom hosts Mickey's Jingle Jungle Parade complete with Santa, Goofy, and falling snow. Carolers greet guests around the 65-foot-tall Christmas tree at the park's entrance, and children have the opportunity to meet Disney characters dressed in holiday finery at Camp Minnie-Mickey.

- At Disney's Boardwalk Inn is a 15-by-20-foot chocolate, sugar, and gingerbread display with a carousel, a miniature village, Santa on a roller coaster, and a 5-foot-tall Ferris wheel.

- The Grand Floridian lobby's life-size, 300-square-foot gingerbread house is a wonder, along with a 45-foot-tall Christmas tree with 45,000 lights, roasted chestnuts, and carolers.

- Animal Kingdom Lodge features an entirely edible miniature African village of sugar, chocolate, and gingerbread.

- The Beach Club display is a life-size gingerbread and chocolate carousel.

- The Polynesian decorates with a South Seas gingerbread village surrounded by volcanoes and palm trees.

- The Yacht Club presents a miniature train running through a village and a mountain made of sweets.

Other Notable Resorts Near Disney

Those who want a resort with easy access to the theme parks (but without Mickey Mouse at every turn) should consider one of the luxury resorts within a five-to-ten-minute drive from Disney. These include the Celebration Hotel, the Gaylord Palms Resort, the Hyatt Regency Grand Cypress, and the Villas of Grand Cypress. Each resort is a great alternative offering its own brand of comfort, dining opportunities, and excitement.

Celebration Hotel

115 rooms. 700 Bloom Street, Celebration 34747; phone (407) 566–6000, fax (407) 566–6001. Check-in 3:00 P.M.; checkout 11:00 A.M. For reservations call (888) 499–3800 or your travel agent, or go online at www.celebrationhotel.com. $–$$$

Billed as "Orlando's only luxury boutique hotel," this charmingly intimate property lives up to its name. Only minutes from Walt Disney World, its Old World Florida style is enchanting and appealing, a perfect alternative to the hustle and bustle of the Disney resorts. Within its four-story pastel veneer are comfortable guest rooms outside whose windows are vistas of a picture-perfect lake and the charming town of Celebration.

The cozy living room–like lobby is dotted with small seating areas of period furnishings reminiscent of early twentieth-century Florida hotels. Cushy sofas and easy chairs made plump with pillows are surrounded by potted palms and the soft warmth of polished wood floors topped with thick area rugs and gently turning rattan paddle fans. Off the lobby is a gracious brick terrace with restful rocking chairs and a peaceful view of Celebration Lake, and lying just outside the front door is the town of Celebration with its fun boutiques and excellent dining choices. Guests have privileges at the nearby Celebration Golf Course as well as at the 60,000-square-foot Celebration Fitness Center and Day Spa, with complimentary transportation in the hotel's 1947 black Cadillac.

ACCOMMODATIONS

Hallways laid with rich carpeting the color of café au lait are painted in an eye-pleasing pistachio, and near the elevators are super sitting areas of dark leather sofas and rattan chairs. Guest rooms show nothing but good taste with understated golden bedspreads, walls of soft butternut yellow, subtle tropical drapes, and rich cherrywood furnishings. All have armoires with TV and minibar, oversize writing desks, and tall windows with charming views of either the lake or the town of Celebration. Comfortable beds are dressed in luxe linens and soft downy pillows. Other amenities include high-speed Internet access, three phones with dataports, on-demand movies, video games, safe, iron, ironing board, coffeemaker, morning newspaper, and turndown service. Ample bathrooms have a single sink, Yardley bath products, thick towels, makeup mirror, and hair dryer. Sixty percent of the rooms have lake views, although only a few come with small balconies.

Deluxe Rooms at 320 square feet are snug but cozy with a king-size bed, reading chair and desk, armoire with TV, and some with a dormer window area. Superior Rooms at 380 square feet are more comfortable, with either two queen-size beds or a king-size, a large desk, and two pillowed rattan easy chairs. The 420-square-foot Junior Suites are oversize rooms with either two queen-size or one king-size bed, and an entertainment center opening up to a sitting area holding a double sofa bed, coffee table, desk, wet bar, and small refrigerator; French doors lead to a small balcony with standing room only. Strangely enough, however, the bathroom has less counter and sink space than in the Superior Rooms. Wonderful 700-square-foot Luxury Suites feature a living area with a queen-size sofa bed, two rattan chairs, coffee table, desk, entertainment center with TV, and wet bar with small refrigerator and microwave. The separate bedroom has a king-size four-poster bed, entertainment center, and French doors leading to a standing-room-only balcony. Again, the counter and sink area is smaller than in a Superior Room.

RESTAURANTS

Plantation Dining. Open daily for breakfast and dinner, 7:00–10:30 A.M. and 6:00–10:00 P.M.; plantation-style setting serving New Florida cuisine; breakfast buffet.

Room Service. Available breakfast and dinner hours from the Plantation Room.

LIBATIONS

Lobby Bar. Full bar, open 5:00 P.M. to midnight; live piano entertainment Friday and Saturday evenings.

RECREATION AND ACTIVITIES

Jogging. Celebration's nature trails begin just outside the hotel.

Swimming. Small heated pool overlooking the lake; whirlpool.

SERVICES

Child care. Babysitting provided by a licensed and bonded agency can be arranged through the concierge.

Health club. Small fitness center with lakeside views; treadmills, elliptical machines, weight stations.

TRANSPORTATION

Complimentary transportation is available to Walt Disney World theme parks (must be arranged ninety minutes prior). For a change of pace, make use of the 1947 black Cadillac that transports guests to the town of Celebration, including the Celebration Golf Club and the Celebration Fitness Center and Day Spa just minutes away. A rental car here is almost a must.

Gaylord Palms Resort

1,406 rooms. 6000 West Osceola Parkway, Kissimmee 34746; phone (407) 586–0000, fax (407) 586–1999. Check-in 3:00 P.M.; checkout 11:00 A.M. For reservations call (407) 586–2000 or your travel agent, or go online at www.gaylordpalms.com. $–$$$

The Gaylord Palm's resort's claim to fame is its fascinating, 4-acre glass-domed atrium. Conveniently located at Interstate 4 and Osceola Parkway, it's only a five-minute drive to Walt Disney World and just fifteen minutes to Universal Studios. Beneath the stunning Grand Atrium sit the Emerald Bay and St. Augustine areas, where visitors will find a replica of a Spanish fort, lush vegetation, towering palms, rushing waterfalls, a street of shopping opportunities, and Gator Springs with its juvenile alligators and native turtles. In the festive, five-story Key West wing, a 60-foot sailboat is moored in a blue lagoon surrounded by piers, palm trees, and sand sculptures; there are daily sunset celebrations. Everyone's favorite locale is the intimate Everglades, where elevated boardwalks cross over a foggy swamp filled with lofty cypress trees, croaking frogs, and flashing lightning bugs. All of this under one giant dome.

Because this is a major convention hotel with over 400,000 square feet of meeting facilities and ballrooms, I suggest steering clear of here when any large conferences are occurring. The best times for leisure travelers are the summer months or around Christmas and New Year's, when more than two million pounds of ice are carved into a wintry wonderland at the resort's ICE! extravaganza.

ACCOMMODATIONS

Guest rooms. Tastefully decorated guest rooms offer 410 square feet with one king-size or two queen-size beds, a desk with two chairs, and armoire with TV and minifridge stocked with complimentary water and orange juice. Amenities in each room include an iron, ironing board, coffeemaker, CD player alarm clock, a pair of two-line telephones (one of them cordless), in-room movies, guest room doorbells with electronic "do not disturb" indicators, and laptop-size safes wired for recharging. One super feature is the complimentary, in-room computing system with high-speed Internet, message center, and online guest services including housekeeping, valet, and bell services. Bathrooms include granite countertops, double sink, makeup and full-length mirrors, and hair dryers. Most rooms have oversize showers in place of bathtubs. Inner rooms facing the atrium offer French doors leading to a pleasant balcony or patio, but be prepared to hear the noise from below; ask for a higher floor, avoid a room over one of the restaurants, or simply consider one of the Florida-view rooms that face the exterior but come without balconies and may have a view of the highway. A $10 per night per room resort fee covers Internet service, daily newspaper, two bottles of juice and water daily, use of the fitness facility, and local phone calls up to twenty minutes.

The casual beach decor in the Key West area is a winning combination of whitewashed cottage furnishings, energetic cabana-striped bedspreads, turtle motif sheers, and lime-colored carpeting. Everglade rooms have light wood furnishings, moss green bedspreads, forest green carpeting, and cheery dragonfly motif curtains and wallpaper. Florida's Spanish influence is seen in the St. Augustine guest rooms located in the Grand Atrium. They feature a neutral color scheme of black and taupe, walnut furnishings, explorer map pillows and bed skirt fabric, carpeting reminiscent of Spanish tile, and tapestry and mosaic touches. Rooms in Emerald Bay are the most expensive. They have marble foyers, butternut-colored walls, dark walnut furnishings, and whimsical gold-and-blue monkey motif bed-spreads. Guests love the palm-imprinted wallpaper and elegant touches such as elevated beds and crown molding.

Suites. There are plenty of choices in upscale accommodations with 106 suites on-property. All are one bedroom, one bath, but many come with the option of adding standard rooms on either side to make a two- or three-bedroom suite.

The resort's nine Presidential Suites are some of the most comfortable and exquisite in Orlando, each with a different look, but all beautifully decorated in updated decor and lavish fabrics. In the foyer you'll find a half bath and a great office, then proceed to ooh and aah as you enter the living area with marble flooring, wet bar, baby grand piano, sofa, easy chairs, coffee table, and entertainment center. There's also a formal dining room seating ten adjoined by a kitchen and breakfast room. The master bedroom features a comfortable sitting room with large plasma TV, four-poster king-size bed with a second plasma TV, and large marble bathroom with whirlpool tub, separate shower, double sink, little TV, and toilet area. Several balconies run the length of the suite overlooking the atrium.

Junior Suites with king-size bed have a separate living area from the bedroom that includes a sofa bed, coffee table, entertainment center, desk, and easy chair.

Deluxe Suites, located in the Emerald Bay area, offer a separate bedroom with king-size bed, TV, and bureau. The living room has a six-person dining table, wet bar, sofa bed, easy chairs, coffee table, entertainment center, and desk.

RESTAURANTS

Ben and Jerry's. Hand-scooped Ben and Jerry's ice cream, sundaes, banana splits, milk shakes; fruit smoothies.

Old Hickory Steakhouse. Dine above the swamps of the romantic Everglades on steaks and seafood; dinner only. (See full description in Dining chapter.)

Planet Java. Twenty-four-hour coffee shop; specialty coffees, wine, beer, sodas, juice; pastries, bagels, muffins, cookies; salads, fruit, sandwiches.

Sunset Sam's Fish Camp. Delightfully fun Key West–style seafood restaurant open for lunch and dinner; 60-foot sailboat bar overlooking the lagoon with island-style entertainment nightly, colossal drinks, and raw bar; conch and clam chowder, fish sandwich, crab cakes, seafood pasta, potato-crusted snapper, fisherman's stew.

Villa de Flora. Mediterranean buffet with chef stations in an Old World–style mansion atmosphere; open for breakfast, lunch, and dinner.

Room service. Available 24/7; try the five-course candlelight dinner.

LIBATIONS

Auggie's Jammin' Pianos. Sing along with comedic dueling pianos playing old favorites; open 5:00 P.M. to 1:00 A.M.; piano music begins at 9:00 P.M.

Lobby Lounge. Cocktails, wine, and champagne on the elegant terrace surrounding the lobby; live piano music.

Old Hickory Steakhouse Bar. Attractive candlelit bar adjoining the Old Hickory Steakhouse overlooking the misty swamps of the Everglades; martinis, port, sherry, wine, beer, single-malt scotch, specialty drinks, cognac; *appetizers:* shrimp or crab cocktail, smoked salmon, steak tartare, artisanal cheese plates, tenderloin of alligator lasagna, oysters Rockefeller, jumbo lump crab cakes, warm pear Gorgonzola tart, foie gras.

H₂0 Sports Bar and Grill. Pool bar with indoor and outdoor seating and ten TV screens for sporting events; *light meals:* fruit with yogurt and granola, Caesar salad, honey-chipotle buffalo wings, chicken and corn fritters, pizza, fish and chips, burgers, chicken club sandwich, shrimp quesadillas, crab and avocado salad, Ben & Jerry's ice cream.

Sunset Sam's Fish Camp Bar. Sixty-foot sailboat bar anchored in lagoon in front of Sunset Sam's Fish Camp Restaurant; oversize island-style drinks on the *S.S. Gaylord;* raw bar; evening sunset celebration Jimmy Buffett–style with steel band, stilt walkers, and balloon animals for the kids.

RECREATION AND ACTIVITIES

Arcade. Located in the shopping area.

Children's playground. Sand beach playground next to the Marine Pool.

Golf. At nearby Falcon's Fire Golf Club, an 18-hole Rees Jones signature designed course, just 2 miles away; complimentary transportation for registered guests.

Swimming. Marine Pool with zero-depth entry, delightful octopus slide, whirlpool, kiddie pool; adjoining sandy beach and children's playground; adults-only South Beach Pool with two whirlpools, private tented cabanas, and poolside massages.

SERVICES

Business center. Located within the convention center with copying, faxing, printing, mailing, packing, shipping, computer stations, laptop connections, office supplies, and equipment rentals; open daily 7:00 A.M. to 8:00 P.M.

Car rental. Hertz Car Rental counter in the lobby.

Child care. La Petite Kids Station with arts and crafts, video games, karaoke, indoor climbing, playacting; open Monday through Thursday 9:00 A.M. to 10:00 P.M. and Friday and Saturday 9:00 A.M. to 11:00 P.M., for potty-trained children ages 3–14; cost includes snacks; call (407) 586–2505 for reservations.

Hair salon. Canyon Ranch SpaClub Salon; hair and nail treatments, makeup consultation, makeovers; open 9:00 A.M. to 8:00 P.M.; call (407) 586–2160 for appointments.

Health club. Canyon Ranch SpaClub, 4,000-square-foot fitness facility complimentary to guests; Life Fitness exercise machines, treadmills, elliptical cross trainers, upright and recumbent bicycles, free weights, Smith press system; fee-based classes including yoga, Pilates, kickboxing, meditation, total body fitness, tai chi; open 6:00 A.M. to 9:30 P.M.

Spa. Canyon Ranch SpaClub, a marvelous 20,000-square-foot facility with twenty-five treatment rooms; spa boutique; open 8:00 A.M. to 9:00 P.M.; call (407) 586–2051 for reservations; information and reservations online at www.canyonranch.com. (See full description in Spas section of chapter 5, Beyond the Theme Parks.)

SHOPPING

Detail. Brighton merchandise; women's resort wear and swimwear; island-motif housewares; jewelry; cosmetics.

Disney Gateway. Disney theme park tickets and merchandise.

Godiva Chocolatier. Godiva deluxe chocolates.

Island Style. Key West–style housewares; handblown glass; handpainted furniture, lamps, and light fixtures.

Marketplace News and Sundries. Gaylord Palm and Florida logo attire for all ages; Florida souvenirs; sundries; magazines, books.

Mel Fisher's Treasures. Authentic shipwreck treasures; gold doubloons and silver reals (or pieces of eight) in jewelry settings.

Orlando Harley-Davidson Gear Shop. Harley-Davidson apparel and stock.

PGA Tour Shop. Golf apparel and merchandise; resort wear for men.

St. Augustine News and Sundries. Newspapers, books, magazines; Gaylord Palms logo caps and apparel; snacks; sundries.

TRANSPORTATION

Complimentary shuttle service is available to all four Walt Disney World parks, departing every hour on the hour during park operating hours. Twice-a-day shuttles go to SeaWorld, Universal Orlando, and Wet 'n' Wild. A car is needed here for added convenience.

Hyatt Regency Grand Cypress

750 rooms. 1 Grand Cypress Boulevard, Orlando 32836; phone (407) 239–1234, fax (407) 239–3800. Check-in 4:00 P.M., checkout noon. For reservations call (800) 233–1234 or your travel agent, or go online at www.hyattgrandcypress.com. $$–$$$

Located less than a mile from Walt Disney World and around the corner from Downtown Disney, the Grand Cypress Resort is composed of both the Hyatt Regency Grand Cypress and the Villas of Grand Cypress, which share a sprawling property and a wealth of recreational facilities. Don't be put off by the slightly dated pyramid exterior—all doubts evaporate as you enter the Hyatt Regency's luxuriant, eighteen-story atrium lobby, a soothing tropical atmosphere of verdant palm trees, flowering foliage, and trickling streams that complement a notable art collection. The warm welcome continues with a glass of champagne punch and a congenial staff ready and waiting to assist.

Opulent grounds quickly lure guests outside to a 1,500-acre wonderland of lush landscaping featuring over 20,000 shrubs, 50,000 annuals, a private lake, and a fantasyland pool. Stroll along meandering pathways through exotic tropical foliage intermingling with moss-covered boulders, trickling waterfalls, sculpture gardens, and soothing ponds. Or relax lake-side in swaying hammocks while swans glide gracefully across the waters of Lake Windsong.

With 65,000 square feet of meeting space, be prepared for plenty of conventioneers. Here, however, ballrooms are in a separate downstairs area out of the way of public spaces, giving the resort a much more inviting feel than most convention hotels.

ACCOMMODATIONS

Guest rooms. Glass elevators rise to comfortable guest rooms cheerfully outfitted with leafy wallpaper and bedspreads, jungle green carpeting, and tropical motif curtains and upholstered headboards. Rich green marble tops the side tables and the large desk, and a pale wood armoire holds the TV, minibar, and safe. Beds are extravagantly made with luxe linens and plush pillows. Bathrooms contain only a single sink but come with Bath and Body Works toiletries, a lighted makeup mirror, hair dryer, and scale. Each 360-square-foot room has a small balcony (standing room only), robes, weekday newspaper delivery, iron, ironing board, coffeemaker, and on-demand movies. The only difference between a standard and a deluxe room is simply in the view. A $13 per room per day resort fee covers access to high-speed Internet in guest rooms, local and toll-free telephone service charges, health club, shuttle to theme parks, Pitch 'n' Putt Golf, golf driving range, bicycles, tennis court time, and watersports.

NOTE: Book a premium room and request an upper floor to receive not only a view of the unbelievable pool but outward to a stunning vista of the surrounding area including literally all of Walt Disney World. Light sleep-ers will want a room away from the atrium in order to avoid the music waft-ing up from the lobby bar. Other views include a garden view, pool view, and lake view.

Concierge rooms. For about $130 more per night, consider upgrading to the Regency Club located on the privately accessed eleventh and seventeenth floors. What you get for the extra cash outlay are robes in the room and an eleventh-floor lounge with private concierge staff, complimentary continental breakfast of pastries, fruit, bagels, and cereal, and afternoon beverages, cookies, and snacks. Hot and cold hors d'oeuvres, wine, and beer are available from 5:00 to 8:30 P.M. Dessert and liqueurs are served from 8:30 to 10:00 P.M. in an adults-only atmosphere. Most guests seeking a quieter spot head to the tables set up outside the lounge, offering great vistas of the pool, the surrounding area, and the Epcot and Magic Kingdom fireworks.

Suites. Executive Parlors have one or two standard guest rooms connecting to a living area with full-size sofa bed, easy chair, four-person table, and an extra full bath. Kid Suites are the same size as Executive Parlors but have the living area set up as a kid's bedroom, including a L-shaped trundle bed, kid-size table and chairs, children's bath amenities, and swim noodles. VIP Suites come with one or two standard bedrooms on either side of a parlor holding a sofa bed, desk, six-person dining table, full bath, and small balcony with standing room only.

The one-bedroom, two-bath Hospitality Suites offer a standard guest room with king-size bed connected to a living area with a six-person marble dining and meeting table, large wet bar, and additional full bath. Ask for a twelfth-floor Hospitality Suite which comes with one of the largest terraces I've ever seen, perfect for a reception. None of these suites has Regency Club access.

Five Penthouse Suites, each with a different color scheme and decor, are found on the seventeenth floor. Two of them are considered Owners Suites with a bi-level configuration—upstairs is a loft bedroom with king-size bed, desk, and armoire with TV as well as a bathroom with lovely whirlpool tub, separate shower, double sink, vanity, and upgraded toiletries. The downstairs living area boasts a six-person dining table, sizable sitting area, baby grand piano, large wet bar with refrigerator, half bath, and giant-size patio with spectacular views. These two suites not only have access to the Regency Club but private butler service as well. An option is the addition of a downstairs connecting standard bedroom with two double beds.

Now for something really different, consider the intimate President's House, located on the shores of Lake Windsong, with two bedrooms, a den, an exercise room, a full kitchen, a washer and dryer, and a screened-in porch.

RESTAURANTS

Cascade. Casual dining spot centered around a 35-foot cascading mermaid fountain and views of the lush Hyatt grounds through its almost solid wall of windows; open for breakfast, lunch, and dinner; Sunday breakfast buffet.

Hemingways. Steak and seafood in a Key West atmosphere; dinner only. (See full description in Dining chapter.)

La Coquina. Orlando's best Sunday champagne brunch overlooking Lake Windsong; Chef's Table dining in the kitchen Wednesday through Saturday; open only seasonally, October through June; call (407) 239–3853 for reservations.

Palm Café and General Store. Snack bar near pool; *breakfast:* Krispy Kreme doughnuts, French toast, omelets, pancakes, waffles, oatmeal, fruit; *lunch and dinner:* salads, pizza, sandwiches, burgers, fried chicken, nachos, hot dogs; indoor and outdoor seating; adjoining General Store sells ice cream, beer, soda, chips, candy, cookies.

White Horse Sports Bar and Grill. Upscale sports lounge open daily 6:00–11:00 P.M.; tempura-fried Florida gator tail, lamb chops, barbecue grilled salmon, steak au poivre, lobster tail.

Room service. Available 24/7.

LIBATIONS

Hurricane Lounge. Atmospheric cocktail lounge adjoining Hemingways restaurant; full bar with food from next-door Hemingways; open nightly from 5:00–11:00 P.M.

Papillon. Pool bar; specialty cocktails, beer, cold drinks; light meals such as tossed salad, wrap sandwich, pizza sub, hot dogs, burgers, and grilled chicken sandwiches served 11:00 A.M. to 3:00 P.M.

Trellises. Hopping atrium lobby bar with live entertainment nightly; outside seating available; open 4:00 P.M. to midnight.

RECREATION AND ACTIVITIES

Arcade. Located behind the grotto pool's waterfall; video entertainment and pinball machines.

Basketball. Court located near Racquet Club; balls available from Racquet Club attendant.

Beaches. A 1,000-foot beach on the shores of 21-acre Lake Windsong; hammocks and lounge chairs.

Boating. Paddleboats, sailboats, and canoes for rent at Towel Hut next to pool for recreation on Lake Windsong; complimentary for guests.

Bicycles. For rent at the Towel Hut next to pool; two bike paths, one 3.2 miles and the other 4.7 miles; complimentary for guests.

Children's playground. Located just outside of Camp Hyatt.

Fire pit. Lit on the shore of Lake Windsong Friday and Saturday evenings; blazing fire, storytelling, roasted s'mores on Saturday.

Fishing. Fishing permitted on Lake Windsong for guests only; catch-and-release.

Golf. Golf desk in lobby available 8:00 A.M. to 4:00 P.M. See subsequent entry for Villas of Grand Cypress for more information.

Horseback riding. See subsequent entry for Villas of Grand Cypress for more information.

Jogging. Three jogging courses ranging from 1.3 miles to 4.7 miles meandering through the property; map available at bell stand.

Nature area. Cypress swamp maintained in conjunction with the Florida Audubon Society; 45 acres; 1 mile of raised boardwalks with three side trails.

Pitch 'n' Putt Golf. On Lake Windsong; no tee time required; 9-hole, par-3 course; complimentary for guests.

Swimming. Sensational 800,000-gallon, half-acre pool with twelve waterfalls, meandering grottos, three whirlpools, suspension bridge, and 45-foot waterslide; only the smaller of the two pools is heated; open 24/7; no lifeguard; dive-in family movies every Saturday night in the summer months, weather permitting.

Tennis. Twelve tennis courts: eight clay (Har-Tru) and four hard (Deco-Turf II), five of which are lighted (call the Racquet Club at 407–239–1944 to reserve a court); complimentary to guests. Two outdoor racquetball courts; pro shop; instructional packages for all levels, round robins, game matching, racquet stringing, rentals, ball machines, videotape analysis.

Volleyball. Sand court located at beach; water volleyball in grotto pool.

SERVICES

Business center. Open Monday through Friday, 7:00 A.M. to 7:00 P.M., and

Saturday and Sunday 8:00 A.M. to 4:00 P.M.; computer, Internet, fax, and copier workstations available 24/7.

Child care. Camp Hyatt for outside children's activities; open daily from Memorial Day to Labor Day 9:00 A.M. to 4:00 P.M., and weekends only the remainder of the year for children ages 5–12; twenty-four-hour notice required; call (407) 239–1234 for reservations.

Another facility, the Childcare Center, offers arts and crafts, an outside play area, sand sculpting, volleyball, movies, Pitch 'n' Putt Golf, magic shows, nature walks, and tennis; open Sunday through Thursday from 8:00 A.M. to 10:00 P.M., and Friday and Saturday from 8:00 A.M. to 11:00 P.M., for potty-trained children ages 3–12; arrangements can be made for a private in-room sitter with a 24-hour advance notice.

Hair salon. Grand Cypress Salon open daily; full range of salon services for men and women.

Health club. Located behind grotto waterfall; Keiser and Gravitron exercise equipment, treadmills, Lifecycles, stair-climbers, cross trainers, free weights; morning aerobics classes on Monday, Wednesday, and Saturday; men's and women's locker rooms, each with sauna and steam room (complimentary to guests); personal training and massage available by appointment; open 6:00 A.M. to 10:00 P.M.

Helipad. Helipad on property available 8:30 A.M. to 10:00 P.M. daily; landing clearance must be arranged at least eight hours in advance.

SHOPPING

Racquet Club Pro Shop. Tennis attire, footwear, accessories, equipment.

Lamonte. Women's and men's casual resort wear; Grand Cypress Resort logo clothing; sundries; snacks; books, magazines.

TRANSPORTATION

Complimentary shuttle service within the resort is available from 6:30 A.M. to 1:00 A.M., including service to the Villas of Grand Cypress and all recreational facilities. A complimentary hourly shuttle departs to Disney's four theme parks, Universal Orlando, and SeaWorld. However, I would advise a rental car.

Villas of Grand Cypress

146 rooms. 1 North Jacaranda, Orlando 32836; phone (407) 239–4700, fax (407) 239–7219. Check-in 4:00 P.M.; checkout noon. For reservations call (800) 835–7377 or your travel agent, or go online at www .grandcypress.com. $$–$$$$$

Part of the Grand Cypress Resort, the Villas of Grand Cypress shares a golf club, racquet club, equestrian center, and all facilities with its Hyatt Regency sister property. Mediterranean-style villas worthy of AAA four-diamond and Mobil four-star ratings overlook lovely undulating greens, romantic lakes, and flowering foliage. Check-in is a breeze; the guard at the gate calls ahead, and after a speedy registration in the small lobby along with complimentary soda, beer, and bottled water, the staff is ready and waiting to swiftly escort you to your stylish villa. All the villas are clustered in a series of nicely landscaped culs-de-sac encircled in natural grasses, flowering bougainvilleas, climbing jasmine, and swaying palm trees. This is a property not only for ardent golfers (although it is a golfer's paradise) but for discerning vacationers who wish to be near Walt Disney World but at the end of the day come home to plenty of comfort and not a trace of Mickey Mouse.

ACCOMMODATIONS

The spacious villas are tasteful and pleasant enough to be your own. You'll find four types of decor according to the type of unit: A-units have a light blue and cream color scheme (club, two-, three-, and four-bedroom villas); B-units are my favorite, with rich colors of cherry red, yellow, and green (two-, three-, and four-bedroom villas); C-units are done in pale green tones with buttercup walls, D-units come in a somewhat boring neutral look (one- or two-bedroom villas with wood-burning fireplaces).

Villas are so roomy that you'll be tempted to stay in for the day just to revel in the comfort. Plush bedding and enormous bathrooms with whirlpool tubs are par for the course. Even though the Club Suite Villa is more luxurious than any standard room in Disney's repertoire, I suggest spending the $100 more per night to upgrade to the One-Bedroom Villa, worth every additional penny. For larger families, units are available with two, three, or four bedrooms. Each has twice-daily housekeeping in addition to nightly turndown service, safe, iron and ironing board, and robes. Included in the room rate are two morning newspapers, in-room wireless high-speed Internet service, and the use of the Villas' bicycles, health club, sauna, and driving range as well as boating, Pitch 'n' Putt, and tennis courts at the Hyatt Regency. Although there are no on-demand movies, you'll find cable TV and a nice selection of complimentary videos available for room delivery. All rooms have a view of the golf course, with half of them also offering a water view; be sure to request one with both.

The smallest room type available is the Club Suite Villa with 425 square feet of comfort. Similar to a Junior Suite, it features a step-down sitting room with a queen-size sofa bed open to the bedroom. No kitchen in these units, only wet bars and coffeemakers. Large bathrooms come with a large whirlpool tub and separate shower. Outside each unit is a private patio.

One-, Two-, Three-, and Four-Bedroom Villas all come with a full kitchen complete with stove, sink, full-size refrigerator, coffeemaker, dishwasher, microwave, blender, toaster, and plenty of dishes, pots and pans, and utensils needed to prepare meals. Living rooms are spacious and have striking furnishings including a queen-size sofa bed, two easy chairs, and coffee table in addition to a TV, VCR, and stereo. The separate formal dining room is a true indulgence, and an abundance of attractively draped windows and French doors make for a bright, airy space. Wonderful bathrooms have a large whirlpool tub, huge separate shower, single sink, makeup mirror, deluxe toiletries, and hair dryer.

One-Bedroom Villas at 1,200 square feet have a luxurious separate living room with fireplace, wet bar, and queen-size sofa bed, formal dining room, full kitchen, and three terraces. The master bedroom is similar to that of the Club Villa Suite, with a step-down sitting area off the bedroom as well as a second wet bar. The 1,750-square-foot Two-Bedroom Villas come in both one- and two-story units boasting two bedrooms (one with a sitting area exactly like the Club Villa Suite), two master-type bathrooms, three patios, full kitchen, beautiful living room (some with fireplace), wet bar, queen-size sofa bed, and formal dining room. Three-Bedroom Villas (2,400 square feet), some one-story and some two-story, offer three master bathrooms together with the same amenities as the Two-Bedroom Villa. Two-story, Four-Bedroom Villas with just under 3,000 square feet contain two bedrooms with seating areas, four baths, and the same amenities as the other villas.

RESTAURANTS

Black Swan. AAA Four-diamond restaurant; dinner only. (See full description in chapter 8, Dining.)

Club Restaurant. Casual dining spot in the Golf Club serving breakfast, lunch, and dinner; great view of the greens.

Poolside snack bar. Snacks and sandwiches; wine, beer, cocktails, soda; open 11:00 A.M. to 5:00 P.M.

Room service. Available 7:00 A.M. to 11:00 P.M.

LIBATIONS

Club Sports Bar. Casual bar in the Golf Club.

RECREATION AND ACTIVITIES

The Villas share facilities with the Hyatt Regency Grand Cypress, but at a mile and a half away, getting there requires a car or shuttle ride. See the Recreation and Activities section in the previous entry for the Hyatt Regency for more information.

Bicycles. Complimentary bicycles available at the pool area.

Golf. Four Jack Nicklaus–designed golf courses; Golf Club with two restaurants; pro shop; Golf Academy offers lessons under the guidance of PGA and LPGA certified professionals utilizing CompuSport video teaching technology. Call 800–835–7377 or 407–239–9999 for more information and reservations. (See full description in the Golf section of chapter 6, Sporting Diversions.)

Horseback riding. Equestrian Center located within the grounds of the Villas of Grand Cypress but about a mile down Jacaranda (the road fronting the property); first facility in United States approved by the British Horse Society; riding instruction in both western and English for all skill levels, junior lessons for ages 2–9, pony rides; forty-four-stall barn, lighted and covered riding area, outdoor lighted jumping and dressage rings, cross-country course; locker rooms; Tack and Gift Shop selling equestrian equipment, attire, gifts.

Swimming. Small, beautifully landscaped free-form, heated pool; whirlpool with waterfall; locker-style restrooms with sauna.

SERVICES

See also the Services section for the previous entry, Hyatt Regency Grand Cypress, for more information.

Child care. Private in-room babysitters arranged with twenty-four-hour notice, or take advantage of the Hyatt Regency's Childcare Center.

Private spa services. Range of spa and salon services performed in the privacy of your villa, with a two-hour notice required; Swedish massage, body polish, aromatic cellulite body wrap; personal tai chi and yoga instruction.

SHOPPING

Golf Shop. Golf apparel, accessories, equipment.

Tack Shop. Riding equipment; equestrian gifts.

TRANSPORTATION

Complimentary shuttle service from Hyatt Regency Grand Cypress also goes to the Villas. An hourly shuttle departs from the Grand Cypress and stops at Disney's four theme parks, Universal Orlando, and SeaWorld. However, I recommend renting a car.

Universal Orlando Resorts

With the opening of first the Portofino Bay Hotel, later the Hard Rock Hotel, and in summer 2002 the Royal Pacific Resort, Universal has established itself as a complete and self-contained vacation destination, offering some of the most deluxe resorts in all of Orlando. All are within walking distance or a short boat ride to Universal's theme parks, CityWalk, and each other; all are operated by Loews Hotels; and all are worlds apart in personality.

If rock music and contemporary guest rooms are your thing, the Hard Rock Hotel should definitely be your choice, but if gracious accommodations with a European ambience are more your style, it should be Portofino all the way. Or perhaps a tropical island ambience at the Royal Pacific is more to your liking.

A weakness of all Universal hotels is the lack of room balconies. Disney has continued to indulge vacationers with a place from which to enjoy the glorious Florida weather, but Universal hasn't mastered this lesson. One can only hope they'll realize the error of their ways as they add more hotels to their repertoire.

Those with pets will appreciate Loews hotels. Their exceptional Loews Loves Pets policy allows pets in the room, even a menu of special dog and cat bedding, pet toys and treats, and gourmet food.

Why Stay at a Universal Hotel?

On-site guests receive exceptional entitlements, such as:

- Bypassing the regular lines at both parks each day of your stay. Simply present your room key to the ride attendant and be directed to the Express Entrance with a wait of fifteen minutes or less, this is heaven in busy season.

- Advance reservations for dining at all full-service restaurants in both parks and at most full-service restaurants at CityWalk—excluding Emeril's, which takes its own reservations (407–224–2424).

- Charging purchases to your room.

- Package delivery directly to your hotel room from select retail shops.

- Complimentary transportation by water taxi or shuttle bus to both parks and CityWalk and by shuttle bus to SeaWorld.

- Length-of-stay passes providing unlimited access to both parks and admission to CityWalk beginning at check-in and ending at midnight on the day of checkout.

- Preferred seating at select shows at both parks.

Booking a Universal Vacation

Consider staying several nights at one of Universal's fantastic resorts for convenient access to the Universal theme parks, CityWalk, SeaWorld, and Discovery Cove, combined with a stay at Disney for one great vacation.

PACKAGES

Call (800) 711–0080 or (888) 837–2273 for Universal resort packages, or your travel agent. Book online at www.uescape.com. And always price the

Universal hotels separately by calling Loews Hotels at (800) 23–LOEWS, or (800) 235–6397.

DISCOUNTS

At the time this book went to press, all three Universal hotels were accepting the Entertainment Card offering 50 percent off the published rate of many hotels nationwide. It isn't necessary to purchase the Orlando book to obtain the discount; buy your book locally in your hometown or purchase one online at www.entertainment.com. Another way to save big is to check out Universal's Hot Deals at www.usevacations.com. Universal annual passholders and AAA members also receive seasonal discounts.

Hard Rock Hotel

650 rooms. 5800 Universal Boulevard, Orlando 32819; phone (407) 503–ROCK or (407) 503–7625, fax (407) 503–ROLL or (407) 503–7655. Check-in 4:00 P.M.; checkout 11:00 A.M. For reservations call (888) U–ESCAPE, (888) 837–2273, (800) 23–LOEWS, (800) 235–6397, or your travel agent, or go online at www.loewshotels.com or www .universalorlando.com. $$–$$$

Hard Rock's motto is "love all, serve all," and serve they certainly do at the single coolest place in Florida to hang out in California-hip style. Luxury reigns, from the ultraslick marble lobby to the marvelous pool complex to the stylish guest rooms. Designed to look as if it were the estate of a rock star, the California mission–style resort features a cream-colored stucco exterior, clay red-tiled roofs, shaded porches supported by arched beams, wrought-iron balconies, and imposing towers. And Hard Rock's prime location within a short walk or boat ride to Universal's theme parks is certainly a major plus.

The groovy, sunken lobby will bowl you over with its panoramic views through enormous picture windows of the sparkling pool and palm-studded grounds along with distant vistas of Universal Studios. Relax in lavish seating areas of chocolate-brown leather chairs and cushy, velvet sofas scattered among towering potted palms and massive vases overflowing with opulent, fresh flowers. Glassed display coffee tables showcasing guitars from music legends are strewn throughout, while the walls are lined with an Elvis jumpsuit, a Jimi Hendrix guitar, shoes of famous rockers, and scads of gold records—more than $1 million worth of rock 'n' roll music memorabilia. It's a mix of pure style and star worship.

Service is friendly and energetic, although it sometimes seems as if no one over the age of thirty is employed here. Staff are allowed plenty of freedom, and they take full advantage, so come prepared for spiked and off-color hair and plenty of pierced body parts. It's a great place, in spite of the fact that it's impossible to escape the loud rock music blasting away in every public space; more than 900 speakers are scattered throughout the property, all running seven days a week, twenty-four hours a day. Of course, the younger crowd loves it. But rest assured, from the moment you enter the hallways leading to your guest room, only beautiful silence is heard.

ACCOMMODATIONS

Guest rooms. Modern without being stark, the comfortable guest rooms offer a clean, contemporary motif, one that is certainly good-looking. Standard Rooms, adequate in size at 375 square feet, come with closet and minibar in the entrance hall and either two queen-size beds or a king-size bed. The overall tone is stylish and sophisticated with a soothing palette of soft green, cream, and blue. White swag curtains frame the windows, and the walls hold framed black-and-white photos of rock 'n' roll legends. Beds are laid with soft green satin spreads, luxe linens, and cushy pillows. Novel lighting casts a soft glow throughout. My only complaint is carpeting that's beginning to show a bit of wear and tear in some of the rooms. Each room features an entertainment center with CD player (guests receive a special Hard Rock compilation CD on arrival), two dual-line telephones, safe, minibar, iron and ironing board, coffeemaker, and large writing table with two cream-colored leather chairs. A single sink vanity in green granite comes with plush towels, hair dryer, and makeup mirror, while the separate bath-toilet area contains a second sink. Added benefits include high-speed Internet and dataport access, newspaper delivery Monday through Friday, and cable TV with HBO and on-demand movies. Views are of the gardens; a pool view comes at an additional charge.

Deluxe Rooms at 500 square feet (the rooms with king-size beds are smaller) feature a sitting area as well as a window seat and desk, offering that extra bit of space needed to spread out.

 Concierge rooms. The very contemporary Hard Rock Club, located on the seventh floor facing the front of the hotel, features the services of a concierge desk along with complimentary continental breakfast of fruit, pastries, and juice. Nonalcoholic beverages are available throughout the day. Each evening brings a rock 'n' roll star themed appetizer spread along with beer and wine. In addition to the use of a rock 'n' roll book and CD library, you'll receive daily turndown service, DVD players in your room, half-price pool cabanas, and complimentary health club facilities.

Suites. Lil' Rock Suites at 800 square feet are absolutely the greatest with two rooms: one for adults and one just perfect for kids. A tiled entry hall with a large, curtained closet and minibar leads to the parents' bedroom, featuring a king-size bed and sitting area with love seat, chair, ottoman, coffee table, large bureau, TV, and stereo with CD player. The children's room contains two twin beds or bunk beds, a kid-size table and chairs, and armoire with TV. A convenient bathroom has two areas: one with a sink and toilet and the other with a double sink in the vanity and a shower.

King Suites at 650 square feet are especially nice, with a living area featuring a full-size sofa bed, easy chair with ottoman, and coffee table in addition to a four-person dining table. In an alcove is a king-size bed with white duvet bed covering, a bureau, a TV, and a second closet.

The 2,000-square-foot Graceland Suite is fit for a king. The giant living area has modern furnishings in neutral tones, hardwood floors topped with an area rug, a soft gold chenille sofa, easy chairs, a coffee table, an entertainment center with stereo and DVD player, a baby grand piano, silken drapes, a circular dining table for eight, a kitchen, and a half bath. An office sits off to one side. The bedroom features a flat-screen TV, two-sided fireplace, king-size bed sporting a brown leather headboard and ultrasuede bedspread, corner sofa, and stereo. And then there's the bathroom. My goodness! Within the chocolate-brown granite, double-head shower (large enough for ten people) is a whirlpool tub that sits by a picture window overlooking the pool and parks. Other amenities include vanity, walk-in closet, double sink, and separate bidet and toilet area. A standard guest room can be added to the suite if desired.

RESTAURANTS

Emack & Bolio's/Starbucks. Ice cream and coffee spot; hand-scooped ice cream, smoothies, floats, ice-cream sodas; pastries, muffins, doughnuts, bagels; Starbucks specialty coffees; open 6:30 A.M. to 11:00 P.M.

The Kitchen. A spin on restaurant dining, with visiting rock stars often performing cooking demonstrations; open for breakfast, lunch, and dinner.

The Palm. Famous New York–based steak house featuring prime, aged cuts of beef and jumbo Nova Scotia lobster; dinner only. (See full description in Dining chapter.)

Room service. Available 24/7.

LIBATIONS

Hard Rock Beachclub. Poolside bar and grill; full bar, tropical drinks, smoothies; mozzarella sticks, artichoke spinach dip, chicken "fingers," wings, quesadillas, nachos, Caesar-cobb salad, apple walnut salad, pizza, battered codfish, popcorn shrimp, Florentine panini, ancho chile chicken sandwich, burgers.

Lobby Lounge. Sophisticated lobby lounge; drinks, appetizers, desserts.

Velvet Bar. Hip cocktail lounge; great specialty martinis and drinks; champagne and wine by the glass; open 4:00 P.M. to 2:00 A.M.

RECREATION AND ACTIVITIES

Arcade. Power Station offering high-tech games and pinball machines.

Jogging. Lovely pathways connecting all three Universal hotels with City-Walk; maps available at the concierge desk.

Swimming. Luxurious pool with zero-depth entry and underwater sound system; two whirlpools, kiddie pool, and 260-foot pool slide surrounded by sand beach, massive boulders, lofty palm trees, and flowering, tropical plants; poolside tented white cabanas available for full- and half-day rentals equipped with lounge chairs, television, phone, fax, videos, refrigerator, and ceiling fan; adjoining outside game area featuring shuffleboard, table tennis, and lawn checkers; roaming waiters serve food and drinks from the Beachclub; Friday night dive-in movies.

Volleyball. Sand court next to pool.

SERVICES

Business center. Printing, fax, copying, Internet, shipping and receiving; open 7:00 A.M. to 6:00 P.M. Monday through Friday.

Child care. Camp Lil' Rock; games, computers, movies, Nintendo, arts and crafts, field trips. Open Sunday through Thursday, 5:00–11:30 P.M., and Friday and Saturday, 5:00 P.M. to midnight, for children ages 4–14.

Health club. Workout Room; Cybex and Precor cardiovascular equipment, Cybex strength training equipment, free weights; men's and women's locker rooms, each with steam room and sauna; open 6:00 A.M. to 9:00 P.M.

Spa. Complimentary transportation provided to Mandara Spa located at the nearby Portofino Bay Hotel; in-room or in-cabana massage can be scheduled.

SHOPPING

Hard Rock Hotel Store. Hard Rock Hotel logo clothing; swimsuits; Hard Rock Barbie; Oakley sunglasses; sundries; newspapers, magazines.

TRANSPORTATION

Custom-designed Hummer and purple Chrysler PT Cruiser limos are available for hire. A three-minute water taxi or a lovingly landscaped walkway transports you to Universal Studios, Islands of Adventure, and City-Walk. Complimentary shuttle bus service is provided to Universal, with infrequent service to SeaWorld.

Portofino Bay Hotel

750 rooms. 5601 Universal Boulevard, Orlando 32819; phone (407) 503–1000, fax (407) 503–1010. Check-in 4:00 P.M.; checkout 11:00 A.M. For reservations call (888) U–ESCAPE, (888) 837–2273, (800) 23–LOEWS, (800) 235–6397, or your travel agent, or go online at www.loewshotels.com or www.universalorlando.com. $$–$$$

It's *La Dolce Vita* in a Mediterranean seaside setting at this exclusive hotel. The folks at Universal have outdone themselves in designing this resort to resemble the harbor and idyllic seaside town of Portofino, the jet-setter's paradise on the Italian Riviera. The scenery is pure postcard, with colorful fishing boats bobbing in the seductively curving bay, gentle waves lapping the shoreline, and sun-bleached buildings with shuttered windows and trompe l'oeil decorative facades. A charming, waterside piazza, loaded with appetizing restaurants, offers plenty of outdoor seating areas and a scattering of interesting shops. The ambience of a quaint Italian village is

overwhelming as you wander the cobbled streets encountering tiny piaz-
zas, back alleyways, sparkling fountains, lofty bell towers, and flickering
iron streetlamps. And I mustn't forget the lobby, resplendent with marble
floors, tiled murals, sparkling Venetian glass chandeliers, and refined furnishings.

ACCOMMODATIONS

Guest rooms. Standard rooms here at 462 square feet offer either a garden or a bay view. From the tiled foyer enter a lovely, comfortable room
decorated in neutral colors. Four-poster beds with handpainted headboards sit high off the ground, topped with simple soft gold duvet-covered
comforters, fine sheets, and down pillows. Italian-style furnishings include
a sea green and cream easy chair, large granite writing table and two
chairs, and a somewhat strange-looking painted armoire holding a fully
stocked minibar and TV. Some rooms have French doors leading to deep
balconies with wrought-iron table and chairs (available only on request at
check-in). Large bathrooms boast a granite-topped, double-sink vanity
over which hangs a mirror lined in colorful Italian tile. Amenities include
robes, a laptop-size wall safe, iron and ironing board, fluffy towels, hair
dryer, scale, coffeemaker, makeup and full-length mirrors, high-speed
Internet access, VCR, three phones, on-demand movies, and a morning
newspaper.

Deluxe Rooms, located on the fifth and sixth floors, are 490 square feet
and come with a larger sitting area, stereo and CD player, plus a larger
bathroom with separate shower in addition to the bathtub.

NOTE: Pay the extra $30 per night for a standard room with a bay view,
and beg for a balcony at check-in.

Concierge rooms. Most concierge rooms are located on the fifth
and sixth floor, but if you prefer another location, your request can
usually be accommodated. Extra amenities include free access to the fitness center, a CD and DVD library, turndown service, and an efficient
concierge staff. At the concierge lounge overlooking the piazza and lagoon,
you'll find a continental breakfast of fresh fruit, granola, cereal, yogurt, pastries, muffins, and croissants. An afternoon service from 3:00 to 4:00
offers biscotti, tiramisu, and cannoli, and early evening brings a cold
antipasto buffet of assorted Italian meats, cheeses, and roasted vegetables
along with beer and wine. After dinner look for milk and cookies.

Suites. Portofino Bay's Kid's Suites are similar to the Hard Rock Hotel's but smaller at 675 square feet, with a separate bedroom done in kid-oriented decor.

Off the foyer of the Villa Parlors is a study as well as a bathroom with single sink and shower. There are either one or two bedrooms, and the parlor holds two balconies, sofa, two easy chairs, entertainment center, large granite coffee table, service kitchen, and eight-person dining table.

The two-bedroom, two-bath Portofino Parlor at 930 square feet features a living room with sofa bed, or consider the two-bedroom, two-bath Villa Parlor at 1,360 square feet with a parlor over twice the size of the Portofino Parlor and the addition of a dining room and a second full bath.

The Governatore Suite at 2,700 square feet offers two bedrooms and three full baths with a living area holding two sofas, big-screen TV, dining table for ten, and an office area. Extra pluses are a large balcony and a luxurious whirlpool tub in the master bathroom.

The fantastic Presidente Suite is much like the Governatore's Suite only with a whopping 3,220 square feet of lavishness. The decor is done in soft neutrals intermixed with splashes of red. It comes with an extended balcony, a huge living room with a fireplace, a butler's pantry, a dining table for twelve, and a posh marble master bathroom with whirlpool tub and separate shower.

RESTAURANTS

Bice. Portofino Bay's new trendsetting Italian restaurant; dinner only; menu items range from a belgian endive salad in a light dijon mustard dressing with gorgonzola cheese and toasted walnuts as an appetizer, to spaghetti with Maine lobster, cherry tomatoes, and braised green onions as an entree, to toasted hazelnut and coffee semifredo for dessert; call (407) 503–1415 for reservations.

Gelateria/Caffe Espresso. Specialty coffees; pastries, bagels, muffins, cereal, and juice in the morning; the best gelato around; banana splits, sundaes, smoothies, soft-serve ice cream, milk shakes; open 6:00–11:00 A.M. and 4:00–11:00 P.M.

Mama Della's Ristorante. Old-World, hearty Italian food; dinner only; festive atmosphere of Mama Della's home; outdoor seating available on piazza. (See full description in Dining chapter.)

Sal's Market and Deli. Delightfully authentic Italian deli; antipasto, excellent brick-oven pizza, panini, salads; cheesecake, cannoli, tiramisu; specialty coffees, wines by the bottle or glass; additional seating on piazza; open 11:00 A.M.–11:00 P.M. daily.

Splendido Pizzaria. Brick-oven pizzas, salads, burgers, hot dogs, grilled chicken sandwich saltimbocca, fried calamari, buffalo chicken tender sandwich, wrap sandwich; specialty drinks and smoothies; adjacent to Beach Pool.

Trattoria Del Porto. Family-style restaurant serving breakfast and lunch daily, dinner Thursday through Sunday; character dinner on Friday night; delicious banana pancakes and frittatas at breakfast; outdoor seating available on piazza.

Room service. Available 24/7.

LIBATIONS

Bar America. One of the most elegant bars around; martinis, fine wines, grappa, single-malt scotches; *appetizers:* smoked salmon, shrimp cocktail, flatbread pizza, cheese and fruit platter; *dessert:* ricotta lemon cheesecake, white chocolate lasagna, tiramisu; open 4:00 P.M. to midnight.

Splendido Poolside. Beach Pool bar; cocktails; smoothies, sweets, ice cream.

Thirsty Fish Bar. Family-friendly bar on the piazza; late-night Happy Hour from 10:00 P.M. to 1:30 A.M.; open Monday through Friday, 6:00 P.M. to 2:00 A.M.; Saturday noon to 2:00 A.M., Sunday noon to midnight.

RECREATION AND ACTIVITIES

Arcade. Located adjacent to Beach Pool.

Children's playground. Located by children's pool.

Jogging. Lovely pathways connecting all three Universal hotels with City-Walk; maps available at the concierge desk.

Swimming. Mediterranean-style Beach Pool with Roman aqueduct–style waterslide, waterfall, kiddie pool, and two whirlpools; secluded Hillside Pool at end of East Wing; Villa Pool encircled by tall cypress trees and swank cabanas with TV/VCR, lounge chairs, table, and pool floats; cabanas complimentary with a Mandara Spa in-cabana massage.

SERVICES

Business center. Computer rentals, packaging and shipping, fax and copy service; open Monday through Friday, 7:00 A.M. to 7:00 P.M., and Saturday, 9:00 A.M. to 3:00 P.M.

Car rental. Hertz Rent-A-Car desk located just off main lobby.

Child care. Campo Portofino; arts and crafts, video games, movies. Open Sunday through Thursday, 5:00–11:30 P.M., and Saturday and Sunday, 5:00–midnight for children ages 4–14; reserve twenty-four hours in advance.

Health club. Cybex cardio equipment and machines, free weights, coed whirlpool, steam room, sauna, and locker facilities.

Spa. Mandara Spa; massage, facials, body and hydrotherapy treatments; manicures, pedicures, salon services, scalp and hair treatments. (See full description in Spas section of chapter 5, Beyond the Theme Parks.)

SHOPPING

Alta Moda. Resort wear; accessories.

Galleria Portofino. Fine arts gallery.

L'Ancora. Gift items; tropical sportswear; swimwear; Portofino Bay logo clothing; sundries; snacks.

Le Memorie di Portofino. Portofino Bay logo merchandise; fragrances; Italian ceramic pottery; gift items; sundries; magazines.

Universal Studios Store. Universal Studios merchandise.

TRANSPORTATION

A walking path near the hotel's west wing connects Portofino Bay with the Hard Rock Hotel, Universal Studios, Islands of Adventure, CityWalk, and the Royal Pacific Resort, or take the lovely, convenient boat ride leaving from the dock located bayside. Complimentary shuttle bus service is provided to Universal, with infrequent service to SeaWorld.

Royal Pacific Resort

1,000 rooms. 6300 Hollywood Way, Orlando 32819; phone (407) 503–3000, fax (407) 503–3010. Check-in 4:00 P.M.; checkout 11:00 A.M. For reservations call (888) U–ESCAPE, (888) 837–2273, (800) 23–LOEWS, (800) 235–6397, or your travel agent, or go online at www.loewshotels.com or www.universalorlando.com. $$

The Golden Age of travel in the 1930s South Pacific is the setting of this exotic resort. From a bamboo footbridge suspended above a rushing stream, you'll enter the stunning lobby filled with hundreds of flowering orchids, lofty potted palms, exotic wood carvings, and Asian-style batik and rattan furnishings. In the middle of the lobby, a picturesque glassed court-yard is centered around a sparkling reflecting pool surrounded by hand-carved Balinese stone maidens and elephants. A soothing lobby lounge is the perfect spot for drinks and appetizers, and out back beyond the resort's famous pool is a lovely lagoon where a vintage floatplane is beached. It's simply a tropical paradise.

ACCOMMODATIONS

Guest rooms. I was at first hesitant to include this resort because the rooms don't quite live up to a deluxe standard. But with such reasonable room rates (this is Universal's least expensive resort) and lovely public areas, I thought otherwise. The somewhat dark guest room decor in shades of burgundy and gold takes its inspiration from Bali, with dark wood fur-nishings, rattan lamps, vintage South Seas travel posters, and carved wood room dividers. Furnishings are attractive, not of the highest quality but cer-tainly adequate. A TV sits on top of a bureau holding a minibar, and all rooms come with a small table and two chairs. Rooms with a king-size bed offer the addition of a small sofa bed; rooms with two queen-size beds, an easy chair. In the gold and black granite vanity area is a single sink with makeup and full length mirrors, hair dryer, and scale; a separate toilet and tub area is decorated with gold ceramic tile. Amenities include high-speed Internet access, safe, iron and ironing board, and coffeemaker. The bed linen thread count here is lower than at other Universal hotels, but then again so is the room price.

NOTE: There are only two types of views here: standard and pool. Stan-dard views overlook the highway or the front of the hotel and parking lot. Pool views are a hundred times better, facing the resort's beautiful pool and the Universal parks in the distance. Alas, none of the rooms, including suites, have balconies.

Concierge rooms. Concierge rooms on the seventh floor as well as all suites come with access to the spacious, upscale Royal Club (albeit with a view of the highway), well worth the extra charge. Begin your day with a continental breakfast of hot cinnamon rolls, pastries, breakfast breads, bagels, yogurt, fruit, juice, and cereal. Beverages and light snacks are offered throughout the day. In the evening you'll find a small but great selection of offerings—the likes of Asian noodle salad with seared ahi, guacamole and salsa with chips, and crudités with dip—along with wine and beer. After dinner there are wonderful full-size desserts such as coconut cream and key lime pie, pineapple upside-down cake, cheesecake, brownies, and cookies, along with coffee and nonalcoholic beverages. Also included are the services of a very nice concierge staff, complimentary fitness room privileges, and robes.

Suites. Executive Suites offer a living area the size of a regular guest room with a sofa bed, rattan easy chair, entertainment center, and desk. The separate bedroom has a king-size bed, table with two chairs, easy chair and ottoman, bureau, and TV. The bathroom is off the foyer of the living area.

Hospitality Parlors come with a large living area holding a sofa, entertainment center with stereo and DVD player, rattan easy chairs, large desk, butler's pantry, bathroom with single sink and shower only, and eight-person dining table. Attached is a standard guest room with two queen-size beds.

The resort's Presidential Suite, otherwise known as the Captain's Suite, is smaller than comparable suites at other resorts, but what it lacks in size it more than makes up for with its wonderful island style. Along with a nice view of the pool and parks, the living room has lovely bamboo and rattan furniture with gold and purple accents, a six-person dining table, kitchen, half bath, and entertainment center with a large flat-screen TV, stereo, and DVD player. There's a great office with a plasma TV, full-size desk, fax machine, and easy chair with ottoman. The delightful bedroom comes with sea grass furnishings, a chocolate-brown and black tropical motif decor, and walls of sea grass wallpaper and hand-carved wood. You'll also find an entertainment center, king-size bed, and easy chair. The bathroom features a small plasma TV, walk-in closet, above-counter double sink, whirlpool tub, shower, vanity, and separate toilet/bidet area. One or two standard guest rooms can connect to this suite if desired.

RESTAURANTS

Bula Bar and Grille. Poolside eatery and bar; appetizers, wrap sandwiches, fish sandwich, burgers; specialty tropical drinks, beer, wine.

Emeril's Tchoup Chop. Contemporary Asian/Polynesian cuisine in a stunning setting; lunch and dinner. (See full description in Dining chapter.)

Island Dining Room. Casual family dining for breakfast, lunch, and dinner; breakfast buffet and a la carte menu; nightly entertainment in the form of hula dancing, magic performer, Universal characters, and face painting.

Jake's American Bar. Fun, atmospheric bar with food from 2:00 to 11:00 P.M. and drinks until 2:00 A.M.; karaoke Sunday and Thursday, live music Friday and Saturday night; specialty and tropical drinks, full bar; potato cheese soup, peel-and-eat shrimp, chicken quesadilla, pupu platter, baby back ribs, smoked chicken pizza, cobb and Caesar salads, club sandwich, salmon penne pasta, fish and chips, burgers, roasted chicken.

Wantilan Luau. Saturday luau at 6:00 P.M.; fruit, green salad, ahi poke salad, macadamia-crusted goat cheese, kimchee, pit-roasted suckling pig, catch of the day, teriyaki chicken, guava barbecue beef short ribs, grilled pineapple jasmine rice, vegetable medley, white chocolate macadamia nut pie, tropical-fruit cake, chocolate banana cake, mai tai, beer, wine, non-alcoholic beverages; *children's meal:* PB&J sandwich, chicken "fingers," pizza, macaroni and cheese. Call (407) 503–3463 for reservations.

Room service. Available 24/7.

LIBATIONS

Bula Bar and Grille. Poolside eatery and bar; specialty drinks, beer, tropical smoothies, frozen favorites; shrimp cocktail, nachos, crab and spinach dip, chicken "fingers," Caesar salad, grilled snapper salad, fruit salad, grouper wrap, smoked turkey sandwich, burger, hot dog, steak sandwich, quesadilla.

Orchid Court Lounge. Sophisticated lobby lounge; wine, martinis, tropical drinks, sake, port, beer; *appetizers and desserts:* shrimp cocktail, crab and corn cakes, soba noodle salad, sushi sampler, cheese and berries, dark chocolate souffle, créme brûlée, mango cheesecake; specialty coffees, pastries, bagels, fruit, and juice in the morning hours; open 6:00 A.M. to midnight.

RECREATION AND ACTIVITIES

Arcade. Game Room adjacent to the pool; high-tech games, pinball machines, and old-school machines.

Beach. A pleasant beach with lounge chairs facing the lagoon; beach volleyball.

Children's playground. Located by the children's pool.

Jogging. Lovely pathways connecting all three Universal hotels with City-Walk; maps available at the concierge desk.

Swimming. One of Royal Pacific's best assets is its tropical, 12,000-square-foot Lagoon Pool with zero-depth entry; two whirlpools, kiddie pool; 4,000-square-foot "ocean liner" interactive water play area with water cannons, lifeboats, water curtains, and squirters; sandy beach area; water volleyball, shuffleboard, table tennis; rustic poolside cabanas with TV, phone, ceiling fan, lounge chairs, and refrigerator rentable for half or full day; torch-lighting ceremony every Friday and Saturday.

Volleyball. Sand court on the beach.

SERVICES

Business center. Fax, printing, copying, Internet, shipping and receiving, office supplies; open Monday through Friday, 7:00 A.M. to 7:00 P.M., and Saturday 9:00 A.M. to 3:00 P.M.; closed Sunday.

Car rental. Hertz Rent-A-Car desk located just off main lobby.

Child care. The Mariner's Club; movies, computer, video games. Open Sunday through Thursday 5:00 A.M. to 11:30 P.M.; Friday and Saturday 5:00 A.M. to midnight for children ages 4–14. Reservations should be made twenty-four hours in advance by calling (407) 503–3235. Be sure to verify hours of availability, as they may change seasonally.

Health club. The Gymnasium; Cybex equipment, Smith machine, free weights; men's and women's locker rooms, each with steam and sauna, coed whirlpool; in-cabana poolside massage available on weekends; open 6:00 A.M. to 8:00 P.M.

SHOPPING

Toko Gifts. Lobby gift shop; Universal and Royal Pacific logo merchandise; sundries; sunglasses; magazines.

Treasures of Bali. Universal apparel; animal wood carvings; straw hats; beach towels; sundries; island print clothing for all ages; swimsuits; snacks; magazines.

TRANSPORTATION

A walking path connects the resort to Islands of Adventure, Universal Studios, and CityWalk, or take the convenient boat ride. Complimentary shuttle bus service is provided to Universal, with infrequent service to Sea-World.

Other Notable Resorts Near Universal

The 500-acre Grande Lakes Orlando Resort cements the idea of luxury in the Orlando area. Sister properties that share all their marvelous facilities with each other, the JW Marriott and the Ritz-Carlton are connected by a convention center and the most glorious spa in central Florida. Although its location just off John Young Parkway seems out of the way, Walt Disney World is only fifteen minutes away, Universal ten minutes, and Sea-World and Discovery Cove just down the road.

JW Marriott Orlando Grande Lakes

1,000 rooms. 4040 Central Florida Parkway, Orlando 32837; phone (407) 206–2300, fax (407) 206–2301. Check-in 3:00 P.M.; checkout 11:00 A.M. For reservations call (800) 576–5750 or your travel agent, or go online at www.grandelakes.com. $$–$$$
A bubbling fountain centers the JW Marriott's elegant, Spanish-Moorish-style lobby. Miles of marble continue throughout the public areas and into the guest rooms. But fair warning! This is a major convention hotel, and you'll certainly feel the effects if your travel plans coincide with a large group. Double-check when making reservations to see whether a convention is planned during your stay, and if so, think about planning another date when this otherwise lovely spot is not teeming with conventioneers.

Perhaps the resort's best feature is its Lazy River Pool, similar to the Yacht and Beach Club's Stormalong Bay. The JW Marriott shares all facilities with the Ritz-Carlton, which translates into access to the fabulous spa and fitness center, the Ritz-Carlton Golf Club, and the Ritz's luxurious pool and grounds. What a deal! It's like getting double the pleasure for your money.

ACCOMMODATIONS

Guest rooms. The 420-square-foot guest rooms are stylish as well as comfortable with buttercup yellow walls, warm furnishings, and delicate floral and check motif fabrics in soft gold, green, and blue. Beds are triple-sheeted and the feather pillows are soft, and by the end of the year, all beds will feature higher-thread-count sheets and luxurious, new mattresses. Inside a spacious armoire are a great 29-inch flat-screen TV, minibar, and laptop-size safe with power source. Other amenities include daily newspaper delivery, robes, high-speed Internet access, three telephones (one of them mobile), and on-demand movies. Lovely marbled bathrooms come with a tub and separate shower. There are two types of guest rooms: (1) those with king-size bed, a small sofa bed, coffee table, and easy chair, and (2) ones with two queen-size beds and an easy chair. Both are furnished with an ample work desk. Seventy percent of rooms come with a balcony (on request only), but don't expect full-size ones—it's standing room only for guests.

NOTE: Lakefront Rooms come with a view of the pool or lake with the golf course in the distance. But beware the so-called Garden View Rooms that actually have a view of the highway and parking lot.

Suites. Doors lead into the living area as well as the bedroom and bathroom from the foyer of the 840-square-foot Executive Suites. Separated from the living room with a curtained French door is a standard guest room with king-size bed, balcony, and bathroom but minus the sofa, chair, and desk, while the living area features a sofa bed, easy chair, armoire with TV, minibar, safe, desk, and another standing-room-only balcony. With the addition of a standard guest room on the other side of the living room, these suites can become two-bedroom suites.

The 2,100-square-foot Presidential Suite is a beauty, embellished with lovely rose and moss green hues. The bedroom has a king-size bed, easy chair, and entertainment center with a huge sitting area and a bathroom with double sink, whirlpool tub, and separate shower. The enormous living room holds two sofas, easy chairs, a coffee table, an entertainment center, an eight-person dining table, a kitchen, and a half bath off the foyer. The suite has three small balconies with standing room only.

RESTAURANTS

Citron. Billed as an "American brasserie"; a la carte breakfast menu as well as a super buffet with made-to-order omelets, fruit, pastries, potatoes, roasted vegetables, smoked salmon, scrambled eggs, Irish rolled oatmeal, waffles, French toast, assorted cheeses and meats; *lunch and dinner:* soup, seared ahi niçoise salad, veggie stack, Cuban panini, lemon grouper sandwich, American Kobe beef burgers, pizza, chicken potpie, veggie penne pasta.

Primo. Executive Chef Melissa Kelly, a James Beard award winner, oversees this superb restaurant; dinner only; on balmy nights opt for the lovely outdoor terrace. (See full description in Dining chapter.)

Starbucks. Espresso, cappuccino, soft drinks; pastries.

LIBATIONS

Lobby Lounge. Sushi-raw bar and cocktails; open noon to midnight with live entertainment from 7:00 to 9:00 P.M.

Quench Bar and Grill. Pool bar; wine, beer, tropical drinks; cayenne Gulf shrimp, honey dijon chicken salad, grouper sandwich, mesquite turkey swiss sandwich, turkey club wrap, chicken Caesar salad, grilled chicken sandwich, burgers, shrimp wrap; *children's menu:* miniburger, chicken strips, hot dog, grilled cheese, PB&J sandwich.

RECREATION AND ACTIVITIES

For additional recreation and activities, see the subsequent entry for the Ritz-Carlton Orlando Grande Lakes, which shares all facilities with the JW Marriott.

Arcade. Located on lower level near pool.

Bicycles. Surrey and single-passenger bicycles available for rent.

Children's activities and playground. Playground located outside game room; arts and crafts, pool games, arcade challenges, sand art, campfire s'mores.

Jogging. A 1.3-mile path around the resort.

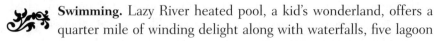 **Swimming.** Lazy River heated pool, a kid's wonderland, offers a quarter mile of winding delight along with waterfalls, five lagoon

pools, and whirlpool; tube and float rentals; dive-in movies Saturday evenings, weather permitting.

Tennis. Three lighted courts located in front of the hotel open 7:00 A.M. to 10:00 P.M.

Volleyball. Complimentary sand court located lakefront near the pool.

SERVICES

For additional services see the subsequent entry for the Ritz-Carlton Orlando Grande Lakes, which shares all facilities with the JW Marriott.

Business center. Computer workstations, fax, copier, office supplies, posters and signage, printing, high-speed Internet; open 24/7 with attendant on duty 7:00 A.M. to 7:00 P.M.

Car rental. A Hertz Rent-A-Car desk in the lobby area.

SHOPPING

John Craig. Fine Italian attire for men.

Landau. Affordable jewelry.

Mimi's Boutique. Fine attire for women including Lilly Pulitzer, Zanella, and Nanette Lepore.

Montage. Sundries; newspapers, books, magazines; snacks; wine; Brighton products; JW Marriott logo clothing; gift items.

TRANSPORTATION

Regular shuttle service is available to all four Walt Disney World theme parks, Universal Orlando, and SeaWorld for $12 to $14 per person round-trip. A car rental here is a must for convenience.

Ritz-Carlton Orlando Grande Lakes

584 rooms. 4012 Central Florida Parkway, Orlando 32837; phone (407) 206–2400, fax (407) 206–2401. Check-in 3:00 P.M.; checkout 11:00 A.M. For reservations call (800) 241–3333 or your travel agent, or go online at www.grandelakes.com. $$–$$$$

Welcome to paradise! Hands down, this resort is my choice for the very best, and I mean the *very best* off-property resort. The only five-star deluxe hotel in Orlando, it's a stylish refuge in the middle of a sea of theme parks, the height of sophistication and elegance, a destination in itself. It simply redefines the Orlando experience. If you feel like heading to the theme parks, great. If not, don't worry! You really won't feel you've missed much, so engrossed you'll be in the resort's luxurious spa, its full-service fitness center, the ornate pools, a Greg Norman–designed eighteen-hole golf course with a unique Caddy-Concierge Program, and Normans, the resort's signature restaurant.

You know you've come to the right place as you enter the limestone and marble lobby, a study of understated luxury. Throughout the public areas are sofas and easy chairs covered in exquisite, yet soothing fabrics of sea blue, mossy green, buttercup yellow, and delicate rose hues, with floors covered in Oriental rugs and walls adorned with original oil paintings. The level of service is unsurpassed in all of Orlando. You'll understand what I mean when every staff member, from the housekeepers to the top eche-lon, always passes with a greeting.

The grounds are sumptuous, perfectly manicured with rose gardens and palm trees, bocce ball courts, and a palazzo-style pool overlooking the resort's lake and golf course.

And who can resist the Mediterranean-style spa, located between the Grande Lake's two hotels, by far the most deluxe and undoubtedly the largest in the Orlando area. Its forty luxurious treatment rooms are quite a wonder, along with a 4,000-square-foot private lap pool, the first Carita Institute and Salon in the United States, a spa cafe, and a 6,000-square-foot workout facility. Just a walk through is enough to soothe your fragile nerves. Soft, gentle music wafts down the halls, with each darkened treat-ment room more extravagant than the last. And in the fitness area, each treadmill, elliptical rider, and stair-climber is outfitted with its own TV monitor and headphones as well as in-machine fans that cool you through-out your routine. How fantastic is that!

ACCOMMODATIONS

Guest rooms. In these ultraplush, 490-square-foot beauties, you'll find so-soft feather beds topped with delicate sea green duvets, triple-sheeted Frette linens, and down pillows. A Floridian leaf motif dust ruffle and drapery complete the sophisticated picture. Furnishings include a buttercup yellow easy chair with ottoman (only in rooms with king-size bed), golden blond desk and armoire. Creamy white marble bathrooms with subtle leafy green wallpaper have double sinks, a tub as well as a roomy shower, and a separate room for the toilet. Each guest room has a 5-foot-long balcony, and, as you might expect, is well equipped with Internet access, a 29-inch flat-screen TV, on-demand movies, a safe large enough for a laptop computer, minibar, CD player, multiline telephones, and iron and ironing board. Extra amenities include complimentary shoe shines, twice-daily housekeeping service, and a daily *New York Times*. Upon returning to your room in the evenings, you'll find the bed turned down, slippers on the floor beside it, and the radio softly playing in the background. Views are either of the front of the hotel and the highway in the distance (the so-called garden view), the lake and golf course (lake view), or the pool, lake, and golf course (lake front).

 Concierge rooms. Guests of the twelfth and fourteenth floors as well as all suites bask in the lap of luxury at the Ritz-Carlton Club, a keyed-access fourteenth-floor lounge with spectacular views of the surrounding area. There's even a large balcony, a perfect spot from which to watch the sunset. A "Your wish is my command" policy is in full force here regarding the unbelievably accommodating staff, who go so far as to shake up a James Bond–style martini just for the asking. With such diverse food and beverage choices, you could just about skip restaurant meals. Breakfast is a full spread of incredible hot and cold pastries, four types of freshly squeezed juice, fruit, meats, cheeses, cereal, yogurt, hard-boiled eggs, even smoked salmon. Lunch brings a make-your-own sandwich bar, salads, fruit, desserts, four types of ice tea, and wine. Late afternoon there's a lovely tea of assorted cookies, pastries, scones, fruit, sandwiches, hot and cold teas, wine, and champagne. Before-dinner options consist of an excellent selection of wine, champagne, and liquor as well as caprese salad, fresh stone crabs, shrimp salad, cheeses, pâté, and more. And be sure not to miss the after-dinner cordials, more wine and champagne, and desserts to die for, including *pots de crème*, fruit and chocolate fondue, meringue tarts, and madeleines. This is one concierge lounge where your money is more than well spent and all for around $100 more per night than the regular rooms. Consider booking a Key to Luxury Package that includes a deluxe guest room on the club level, the use of a Mercedes-Benz for the duration of your stay, a full tank of gas each morning, and valet parking.

Suites. The Ritz-Carlton offers sixty-six suites, each more fantastic than the last. The 960-square-foot Executive Suite doesn't even feel like a hotel room; it's more like a very stylish apartment—spacious, gorgeous, and wonderfully luxurious with Frette linens, down pillows and comforters, feather beds, and elegant fabrics (of course, all of these items are standard in each of the resort's exquisite guest rooms). The large separate bedroom holds a king-size bed, desk, easy chair with ottoman, and walk-in closet. The impressive marble bathrooms, of which there are two (one is a half bath), and the spacious living room are a welcome indulgence. In the living area is an entertainment center with TV, sofa, coffee table, easy chairs, and wet bar. Perhaps the most difficult decision is choosing which of the suite's two balconies you want to loaf on. All come with Bose speakers, Bose wave radios, and CD and DVD players (a selection of DVDs is available from the resort's library). Executive Suites can become two-bedroom suites with the addition of a standard guest room on the opposite side of the living room.

Kids Suites are basically an Executive Suite with a additional connecting guest room outfitted especially for children. Absolutely precious is the regatta decor, which includes twin beds, kid-size table and chairs, a padded window seat in place of balcony doors, a TV with DVD player, and an assortment of fun toys and games. Bathrooms come with a step stool and SpongeBob bath accessories.

The opulent, penthouse-level Ritz-Carlton and Presidential Suites are exactly the same configuration at 2,400 square feet but with different color schemes. The Ritz-Carlton Suite is decorated in soft lemon colors, and the Presidential Suite is adorned in a richer rose hue, both with possibly the most divine fabrics in all of Orlando. Enter from a large marble foyer into a living room furnished with two sofas, easy chairs, coffee table, armoire with TV, and six-person dining table. You'll also find a half bath, a service kitchen, and three balconies running the length of the suite overlooking the resort's pool and golf course with fantastic views outward to the surrounding area. The master bedroom contains a huge sitting area with another TV, a walk-in closet with vanity table, and an immense white marble bathroom with a whirlpool tub, double sink, separate shower, and separate toilet area.

RESTAURANTS

Bleu. Atypical pool grill serving wonderful updated appetizers, sandwiches, salads, and desserts; gourmet pizzas, Maine lobster quesadilla, coconut shrimp, a great Florida blue crab salad, blackened snapper sandwich with smoked pepper remoulade; views of the lake and golf course from a covered or open-air patio; frozen drinks and cocktails great for sunset viewing; also services the pool area.

Fairways Pub. Dining at the golf clubhouse; Maine crab and corn chowder, fried calamari, Caesar salad with blackened shrimp, jumbo lump crab cakes, citrus poached chicken salad wrap, roasted Atlantic salmon, Florida grouper, dry rubbed and smoked Black Angus strip loin served on a sourdough hoagie roll with Muenster cheese, fried onions, and chipotle pepper mayonnaise; open 11:00 A.M. to 5:00 P.M. with cocktails until dusk.

Normans. The resort's premier restaurant, featuring the New World cuisine of Norman Van Aken; dinner only; jackets preferred for men. (See full description in Dining chapter.)

Vitale Spa Café. The spa's eatery offering healthy appetizers, sandwiches, salads, smoothies, juices, and low-fat desserts.

Vineyard Grill. Casual restaurant serving breakfast (a la carte and buffet), lunch (grilled salmon and cobb salads, Black Angus sirloin burgers, chicken BLT, filet mignon sandwich, pan-roasted red snapper with lump crab), and dinner (surf and turf, citrus maple glazed salmon, pomegranate glazed grilled swordfish, Colorado lamb chops, grilled veal chop); Sunday brunch.

Room service. Available 24/7.

LIBATIONS

Lobby Lounge. Lovely and relaxing lobby lounge serving cocktails and light meals; live entertainment 7:00–11:00 P.M.; shrimp cocktail, onion soup, crab cakes, imported cheeses, smoked turkey club, chicken quesadilla, sirloin burger.

Normans Salon. Sophisticated cocktail lounge within Normans restaurant; premium wine and champagne, martinis, beer, brandies; full restaurant menu available.

RECREATION AND ACTIVITIES

For additional recreation and activities see the previous entry for the JW Marriott Orlando Grande Lakes, which shares all facilities with the Ritz-Carlton.

Bicycles. Available near the pool area.

Bocce court and shuffleboard. Located near pool.

Children's activities and playground. Children's check-in desk in the lobby; playground located near pool; arts and crafts, Frisbee toss, scavenger hunts, pool relay races; Ritz Kids Junior Golf on Saturday for $30.

 Fishing. Fly fishing available on private charter boat from Shingle Creek, the headwaters of the Everglades; make arrangements at golf club.

Golf. Greg Norman–designed course set on the headwaters of the Florida Everglades; 11,000-square-foot clubhouse with retail store and restaurant; innovative Gold Caddy-Concierge Program; Golf FORE Kids etiquette class (see full description in the Golf section of chapter 6, Sporting Diversions, for details).

Segway experiences. Thirty-minute, one- and two-hour lessons on a Segway Human Transporter, a motorized, self-balancing, personal transportation device.

 Swimming. Stunning Romanesque-style main pool; private outdoor lap pool and whirlpool on the third floor of the spa building surrounded by a luxurious garden open only to spa guests.

SERVICES

For additional services see the previous entry for the JW Marriott Orlando Grande Lakes, which shares all facilities with the Ritz-Carlton.

Business center. Fax, photocopying, shipping, high-speed Internet access, personal computers, and laser printers; located on the lower level next to the convention area; 24/7 access with attendants on duty Monday through Friday 7:00 A.M. to 7:00 P.M. and Saturday 7:00 A.M. to 5:00 P.M.

Child care. Ritz Kids for children ages 5–12 offers a variety of programs including culinary creations, arts and crafts, swimming, nature walks, fitness challenges, and more; open daily 9:00 A.M. to 10:00 P.M.; youth program also available for older children; nanny service by licensed and bonded professionals can be arranged with the concierge with a twenty-four-hour advance notice.

 Fitness center. Complimentary to resort guests; 6,000-square-foot facility; dry saunas, steam rooms, and specialty showers; weight resistance training equipment, free weights, and Movement Studio cardiovascular equipment, each with its own personal fan, headset, and monitor; fitness classes ($15); open daily 5:00 A.M. to 11:00 P.M.

Hair and nail salon. Carita Salon, located within the spa building, for cut, styling, shampoo and conditioning, blow-drying and sets, scalp and hair reconstructive treatments, coloring and highlighting, mustache and beard trims, manicures, pedicures, tips and acrylics, sculptured nails, silk and fiberglass wraps; open 8:00 A.M. to 8:00 P.M.

Spa. The most luxurious spa in the Orlando area; 40,000-square-foot facility with 40 treatment rooms; men's and women's areas offering locker rooms, relaxation lounges, dry sauna, aromatic steam rooms, showers, and verandas; retail store; private spa pool available only to spa guests; open 8:00 A.M. to 9:00 P.M. daily; call (407) 393–4200 for reservations and information. (See full description in Spas section of chapter 5, Beyond the Theme Parks.)

SHOPPING

Golf Shop. Sophisticated sportswear and golf equipment; Tommy Bahama, Lilly Pulitzer, and Ralph Lauren golf and resort wear; Ritz-Carlton logo clothing.

Ritz-Carlton Signature Shop. Men and women's resort clothing; Ritz-Carlton logo clothing; beach hats; swimsuits; sleepwear; lingerie.

Spa Tranquility Boutique. Beauty and nail care products.

TRANSPORTATION

Regular shuttle service is available to all four Walt Disney World theme parks, Universal Orlando, and SeaWorld for $12 to $14 per person round-trip. A car rental here is a must for convenience.

4

THE VERY BEST OF THE WALT DISNEY WORLD THEME PARKS

Newcomers often think Walt Disney World is comparable in size to California's Disneyland, with the Magic Kingdom being first and foremost in their minds. Most never envision a complex twice the size of Manhattan with four theme parks spread out over 30,000 acres. Yes, the Magic Kingdom, completed in 1971, was the first theme park at Walt Disney World. But three more parks followed in succession, beginning with Epcot a decade later. Twice the size of the Magic Kingdom, it was a totally different concept—an education in technology and innovation, other lands and cultures. Disney–MGM Studios followed in 1989, and with it came the glamour and glitz of show business. Then came the Animal Kingdom in 1998, conveying the theme of unity and harmony among all living creatures. Each park is unique and wonderful and offers its own brand of enjoyment. And who knows what we can look forward to in the future?

General Information

First we'll go over what you need to know about getting into and around the parks. Then we'll examine the best of each park. Walt Disney World features such a wealth of attractions that most people don't have enough time on a vacation to experience them all. That's why we've narrowed down the field for you and have chosen to feature the attractions that are, in my expert opinion, the very best each park has to offer. You'll find important information on only the best attractions and dining, the most anticipated special events, and the most memorable entertainment, plus loads of tips for making your vacation an exceptional one.

Disney Theme Park Admission

Disney totally revamped its theme park passes in January 2005. There are now more than thirty options available, beginning with a basic pass. Choose the number of days you wish to purchase and then start considering the many choices available to you. Purchase tickets by calling (407) WDW–MAGIC or (407) 939–6244; by going online at www.disney world.com; by visiting a Disney retail store, or by consulting a Disney specialist travel agent. No matter which ticket plan you opt for, children age two or younger get in free. The following are your ticket options.

Magic Your Way Base Ticket. Choose the number of days you'll need, allowing entrance to one theme park each day. Base tickets are offered for as many as ten days. Tickets expire fourteen days after first use. Notice how much you save with each extra day added. Base Ticket prices as of press time are featured in the chart later in this section.

Park Hopper. Allows park-hopping privileges for a flat rate of $35 regardless of the number of days.

Magic Plus Pack. Choice of admission to Typhoon Lagoon, Blizzard Beach, DisneyQuest, Downtown Disney's Pleasure Island, or Disney's Wide World of Sports. For a flat rate of $45, you get a set number of visits according to the length of ticket you buy (two visits for a one- to three-day ticket, three visits for a four- or five-day ticket, four visits for a six-day ticket, and five visits for tickets of seven days or more).

Magic Your Way Premium Ticket. Combines the benefits of the Magic Plus Pack and the Park Hopper for a flat rate of $80.

PRICE PER PERSON PER DAY

	Adult	Child (ages 3–9)
1-Day Ticket	$59.75	$48.00
2-Day Ticket	$59.50	$48.00
3-Day Ticket	$57.00	$45.67
4-Day Ticket	$46.25	$37.00
5-Day Ticket	$38.60	$31.00
6-Day Ticket	$32.67	$26.17
7-Day Ticket	$28.43	$22.86
8-Day Ticket	$25.25	$20.25
9-Day Ticket	$22.78	$18.22
10-Day Ticket	$20.80	$16.70

No Expiration Option. Allows the freedom to return to Walt Disney World anytime in the future and take advantage of unused days on your Magic Your Way Tickets, which would normally expire fourteen days after first use ($10 for two- or three-day tickets, $15 for a four-day, $35 for a five-day, $45 for a six-day, $55 for a seven-day, and $100 for an eight-, nine-, or ten-day ticket).

Advance Purchase Options. Receive a slight savings on tickets of five days or more when you purchase a Magic Your Way Ticket with Park Hopper, a Magic Your Way Ticket with Magic Plus Pack, or a Magic Your Way Premium Ticket before leaving home.

Theme Park Annual Pass. Unlimited access to all four Disney theme parks as well as complimentary parking and an array of discounts for 365 days. If you plan to return within a year, this is the way to go. You may even consider this type of pass for shorter stays simply to receive the great savings available to Annual Pass holders; only one person in your party must have an annual pass to obtain the discount. If you make an annual trip to Disney, you should plan your return trip a few weeks shy of the expiration date of your pass and your park admission will already be paid. At press time Annual Pass rates were $395 for adults (age ten and up) and $336 for children ages three through nine.

Theme Park Premium Annual Pass. Same as the Annual Pass but also includes Blizzard Beach, Typhoon Lagoon, Wide World of Sports, and DisneyQuest. At press time Premium Annual Pass rates were $515 for adults (age ten and up) and $438 for children ages three through nine.

FASTPASS

FASTPASS is a free computerized service offered to all visitors as a way of reducing time spent waiting in line. Here's how it works. As you approach a FASTPASS attraction, you'll see two time clocks on display: one estimating the wait time in the normal line, the other the return time for the FASTPASS being issued at the moment. If the normal wait time is less than thirty minutes, by all means get in line. If not, just insert your park pass in one of the machines located at each individual FASTPASS attraction and receive a ticket printed with a designated one-hour window in which you may return and enter a special line with little or no waiting.

In most cases, only one FASTPASS at a time can be issued. To find out when you can receive another FASTPASS ticket, look on your current FASTPASS. Each person must have a FASTPASS to enter the line and must show it to the cast member (Disney's name for park employees) at the beginning of the line and the cast member waiting at the boarding area. There is usually no need to use FASTPASS for the first hour or so after the park opens. Note that on the most popular attractions, particularly in the busier seasons, those seeking a FASTPASS late in the afternoon may find there are none left for the remainder of the day.

Touring Advice

Much ado is made of exactly how to approach each park and in what direction and order to tour. I think a bit of planning is necessary, and I have outlined a suggested touring plan for each theme park in the appendix. However, it does take the fun out of your vacation if you're tied down to a crazy, high-speed timetable. During slow times of the year, determine which attractions are the most desirable in each park, and simply see each one as you encounter them.

In the busier seasons get to the park entrance a half hour early, at which time the gates are usually open along with a few stores and breakfast stops. Be in place at rope drop and head immediately to the most popular rides in the park. In the Magic Kingdom this means Splash or Space Mountain; in Epcot it's Test Track and Soarin'; at Disney–MGM Studios the biggies are the Tower of Terror and Rock 'n' Roller Coaster; and at the Animal Kingdom move quickly to the Kilimanjaro Safaris or Expedition Everest (scheduled to open in 2006). When you're finished with these attractions, pick one or two of the more popular rides and knock them off. After that you'll have lost your edge on the latecomers, so simply explore each attraction as you come to it, utilizing FASTPASS when necessary.

At the very least plan a loose itinerary for each day and make priority seating for any full-service restaurants. Find out before leaving home the park hours for the days of your vacation and what special events might be happening during your stay by going online at www.disneyworld.com or calling (407) 824–4321. The worst thing you can do is wake up each morning and then decide what you want to do that day; that's best left for free days when you plan to just relax by the pool (speaking of free days, try to schedule one at some point in the middle of your trip to ease sore feet, unwind, and just enjoy). Failure to plan at least a bit could mean losing out on that great restaurant your friends told you about or missing a special show like Cirque du Soleil because it's totally booked. Of course, don't plan so stringently that there's no spontaneity in your day, no time to smell the roses. This is Disney after all.

The best advice I can give is to come during the slower times of the year (see chapter 1, Planning Your Trip, for details) by avoiding holiday weekends (except for maybe Labor Day and Veterans Day) and summer. Of course, that may not be possible for those tied down to school schedules. I shouldn't admit it, but I took my children out of school during slower seasons, worrying about the extra homework later. It was well worth it!

Ride-Share Program

Disney extends this option to parents with small children at all attractions with a height restriction. Just advise the cast member on duty upon entering the line. Your entire party will wait in line as usual until you reach the loading area. Then one adult rides while the other stays behind with the child. When the first adult returns, the second adult rides without delay while the other waits with the child. Attractions offering this program include the following.

Magic Kingdom: Big Thunder Mountain, Space Mountain, Splash Mountain, Stitch's Great Escape.

Epcot: Body Wars, Mission: SPACE, Test Track, Soarin'.

Disney–MGM Studios: Rock 'n' Roller Coaster, Star Tours, Tower of Terror.

Animal Kingdom: Dinosaur, Kali River Rapids, Expedition Everest (scheduled to open in 2006).

The Magic Kingdom

Most people's image of Disney is encompassed in a mere 107 acres of pure enchantment. Walt Disney World's first theme park is a kid's fantasy of marvelous, themed lands created to charge the imagination of young and old alike. Around every corner is a vision bound to take the breath away, one that's guaranteed to draw you back time and time again. Cinderella's Castle, the park's visual magnet, hits you square in the face as you walk under the train station and into a world of make-believe with all the glory of Main Street spread out before you and that fairytale castle at the end. Get ready for the time of your life!

Park Basics

GETTING THERE

Those driving to Walt Disney World should take Interstate 4 to exit 64 and then follow the signs to the Magic Kingdom.

USING WALT DISNEY WORLD TRANSPORTATION

From the Grand Floridian, Polynesian, and Contemporary Resorts: Board the monorail and disembark at the park's entrance, or take the boat launch to the Magic Kingdom's dock. You can also walk a short path from the Contemporary.

From the Wilderness Lodge and Villas: Take the Wilderness Lodge boat to the Magic Kingdom dock.

From other Disney Resorts, Disney–MGM Studios, and the Animal Kingdom: Board the bus marked MAGIC KINGDOM.

Magic Kingdom

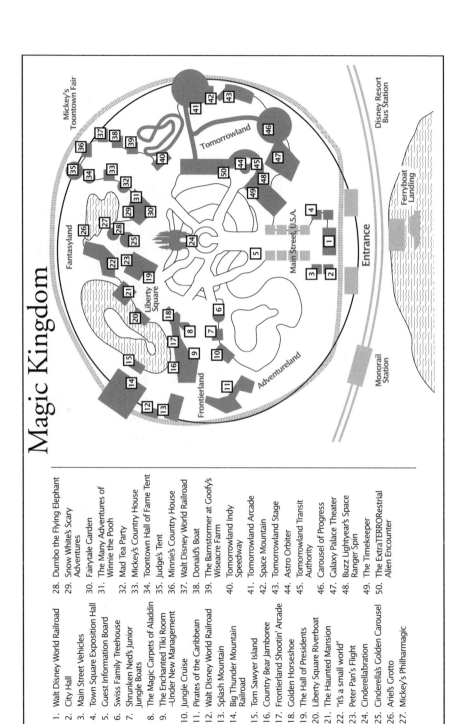

1. Walt Disney World Railroad
2. City Hall
3. Main Street Vehicles
4. Town Square Exposition Hall
5. Guest Information Board
6. Swiss Family Treehouse
7. Shrunken Ned's Junior Jungle Boats
8. The Magic Carpets of Aladdin
9. The Enchanted Tiki Room –Under New Management
10. Jungle Cruise
11. Pirates of the Caribbean
12. Walt Disney World Railroad
13. Splash Mountain
14. Big Thunder Mountain Railroad
15. Tom Sawyer Island
16. Country Bear Jamboree
17. Frontierland Shootin' Arcade
18. Golden Horseshoe
19. The Hall of Presidents
20. Liberty Square Riverboat
21. The Haunted Mansion
22. "it's a small world"
23. Peter Pan's Flight
24. Cinderellabration
25. Cinderella's Golden Carousel
26. Ariel's Grotto
27. Mickey's Philharmagic
28. Dumbo the Flying Elephant
29. Snow White's Scary Adventures
30. Fairytale Garden
31. The Many Adventures of Winnie the Pooh
32. Mad Tea Party
33. Mickey's Country House
34. Toontown Hall of Fame Tent
35. Judge's Tent
36. Minnie's Country House
37. Walt Disney World Railroad
38. Donald's Boat
39. The Barnstormer at Goofy's Wiseacre Farm
40. Tomorrowland Indy Speedway
41. Tomorrowland Arcade
42. Space Mountain
43. Tomorrowland Stage
44. Astro Orbiter
45. Tomorrowland Transit Authority
46. Carousel of Progress
47. Galaxy Palace Theater
48. Buzz Lightyear's Space Ranger Spin
49. The Timekeeper
50. The ExtraTERRORestrial Alien Encounter

From Epcot: Take the monorail to the Ticket and Transportation Center (TTC), and then transfer to either the ferry or the direct monorail to the Magic Kingdom.

PARKING

Cost is $8.00 per day; free to Walt Disney Resort guests and Annual Pass holders. Keep your receipt, good for parking at the Animal Kingdom, Epcot, and Disney–MGM Studios for that day only.

Because of the beautiful obstacle of the Seven Seas Lagoon, parking at the Magic Kingdom is a bit different than the other three Disney theme parks. Park in the lot, make a note of the section and aisle, and board the tram to the Transportation and Ticket Center. From there, take the ferry or monorail to the park entrance. If the monorail line is long, take the quicker ferry. If riding the monorail, make sure you board the one departing for the Magic Kingdom, not Epcot.

OPERATING HOURS

Open 9:00 A.M. to 6:00 or 7:00 P.M. with extended hours during holidays and busy seasons. Call (407) 824–4321 or log on to www.disneyworld.com for updated park hours along with parade and fireworks information.

Main Street is normally open a half hour before official park opening time. Get a jump on the crowds by arriving at least one hour early, allowing plenty of time to park, ride the monorail or ferry, buy tickets, purchase a snack or cup of coffee, and be one of the first to hit the big attractions. I recommend heading straight to Splash or Space Mountain.

FASTPASS ATTRACTIONS

- Big Thunder Mountain Railroad
- Buzz Lightyear's Space Ranger Spin
- Haunted Mansion
- Jungle Cruise
- Many Adventures of Winnie the Pooh
- Mickey's PhilharMagic
- Peter Pan's Flight

- Space Mountain

- Splash Mountain

- Stitch's Great Escape!

See the introduction to this chapter for FASTPASS details.

PARK SERVICES

ATMs. Three cash-dispensing ATMs are located in the park: next to the locker rentals under the Main Street Railroad Station, near the Frontier Shootin' Arcade, and in Tomorrowland Arcade. An additional machine is located at the TTC.

Baby care center. An infant facility found next to the Crystal Palace at the castle end of Main Street is outfitted with changing tables, high chairs, and a room for nursing mothers. Disposable diapers, bottles, formula, and baby supplies can be purchased. All restrooms throughout the park are outfitted with changing tables.

Cameras and film processing. The Camera Center, located in the Main Street Exposition Hall, sells cameras, film, videotapes, batteries, and memory cards. You can also download your digital pictures at the Picture Maker Digital Station for a fee.

First aid. The First Aid Center is located at the end of Main Street next to Crystal Palace.

Guest Relations. City Hall, just inside the park entrance on the left, houses Guest Relations, where a knowledgeable staff is ready to assist with priority seating, lost children, purchase of annual passes and upgrades, stamps, messages for separated parties, information for guests with disabilities, language translation headsets, foreign currency exchange, sign language services, fax services, international phone cards, VIP tour information, behind-the-scenes programs, resort reservations, and character greeting information. A smaller Guest Relations is located on the right before entering the park.

Guests with disabilities. A guidebook for guests with disabilities is available at Guest Relations. Guests with mobility disabilities should park adjacent to the Entrance Complex (ask at the Auto Plaza for directions). Wheelchairs and ECVs are available for rent. Most restaurants and shops

BEST HOTELS FOR MAGIC KINGDOM VISITORS

If you plan on spending a large majority of your time at the Magic Kingdom, choose one of the monorail-serviced hotels (Contemporary, Grand Floridian, or Polynesian). Their convenience just can't be beat. Boat transportation is also available from all three resorts. Although the Wilderness Lodge and Villas are not serviced by the monorail, there is boat service to the Magic Kingdom.

in the Magic Kingdom are accessible to guests with disabilities, although some counter-service locations have narrow queues with railings (ask a host or hostess for assistance). Companion-assisted restrooms are located at First Aid, the lower level of Cinderella's Royal Table, Pirates of the Caribbean, Splash Mountain, Mickey's Toontown Fair, near the Tomorrowland Stage, and at the TTC East Gate.

Over half of the attractions provide access through the main queue while others have auxiliary entrances for wheelchairs and service animals along with as many as five members of your party. Certain attractions require guests to transfer from their wheelchair to a ride system. Parade routes and some shows have designated viewing areas on a first-come, first-served basis.

Braille guidebooks, assistive listening devices, and audiotape guides are available at City Hall for a $25 refundable deposit. Handheld captioning receivers for twelve attractions are available for a $100 refundable deposit. Reflective captioning is provided at many theater-type attractions and video captioning at five attractions. With a seven-day notice, a sign language interpreter will be provided at live shows on Monday and Thursday. For more information call (407) 824–4321 or (407) 827–5141 (TTY).

Lockers. Lockers are located at the TTC as well as under the Main Street Railroad Station. The cost is $7.00 per day, including a $2.00 refundable key deposit. If you're park-hopping, keep your receipt for a locker at the three other Disney theme parks for no extra charge.

Lost and Found. Located at City Hall near the entrance or call (407) 824–4245.

Lost children. Locate lost children at the Baby Care Center next to the Crystal Palace at the castle end of Main Street. Go to City Hall after operating hours.

Package pickup. Located next door to City Hall close to the train station. Allow three hours for delivery. Disney resort guests may send packages directly to their hotel for next-day arrival.

Pet kennel. A kennel is located next to the TTC for a daily rate of $6.00. For information call (407) 824–6568. Proof of vaccination is required.

Strollers and wheelchairs. Rentals are located on the right as you enter the turnstiles. Single strollers are $8.00 per day, double strollers $15.00, and wheelchairs $8.00 inclusive of a $1.00 refundable deposit. Electric convenience vehicles are $40.00, inclusive of a $10.00 refundable deposit. If you're park-hopping, keep your receipt for a same-day replacement at the three other Disney theme parks and Downtown Disney Marketplace.

The Lay of the Land

The compact Magic Kingdom consists of seven bewitching lands accessed by five bridges leading from a central hub in front of Cinderella's Castle. Travel down Main Street to reach the hub from the front entrance. Moving counterclockwise around the hub you first encounter the bridge to Tomorrowland, then the bridge to Mickey's Toontown Fair. The third bridge takes you to Fantasyland, the fourth crosses under the castle to Liberty Square and Frontierland, and the fifth brings you to Adventureland.

The Very Best Attractions in the Magic Kingdom

SPACE MOUNTAIN

Located in Tomorrowland, a 180-foot, conical-shaped "mountain" is one of the most popular attractions in the park, a cosmic roller coaster shooting through the darkest depths of the solar system. Load into six-person shuttle transporters and blast into orbit, plunging through a dark interior of sparkling comets, shooting stars, and glowing planets. Look closely to spot the other coaster ripping around on the second track. The somewhat slow (28 mph) ride holds only small drops and no loops or twists: it's just

CHARACTER GREETING SPOTS IN THE MAGIC KINGDOM

The pointing Mickey gloves on your guidemap will help you find the following locations:

- An assortment of Disney characters in Main Street Square during the morning hours.
- *Alice in Wonderland* characters near the Mad Tea Party attraction in Fantasyland.
- Ariel's Grotto in Fantasyland where the mermaid herself is on hand for photos and autographs.
- *Toy Story 2* characters Woody, Jessie, and Bullseye in Liberty Square's Diamond Horseshoe.
- Mickey Mouse in the Judge's Tent at Mickey's Toontown Fair.
- A bevy of characters including Disney princesses at Toontown Hall of Fame.
- Mickey's pals at Minnie's Gazebo behind her Country House.
- An assortment of characters at the Toontown train station.
- Buzz Lightyear and Stitch in Tomorrowland.
- Jasmine and Aladdin near Aloha Isle (the Dole Whip booth) in Adventureland.
- Peter Pan characters near Pirates of the Caribbean.
- A variety of characters in front of the Castle Forecourt Stage intermittently throughout the day.

the darkness that makes it such a thrill. **Minimum height 44 inches (3 feet, 8 inches). Not recommended for expectant mothers, those with back or neck problems, or those prone to motion sickness. FASTPASS. 2½-minute ride.**

NOTE: This is the second most popular ride in the park (Splash Mountain being the first), and lines can sometimes be extremely long. Come first thing in the morning or before park closing. And hang onto your valuables or risk losing them in the deep, dark vastness of space.

THE MANY ADVENTURES OF WINNIE THE POOH

Board giant "hunny" pots to travel through the Hundred Acre Wood with Pooh and his friends Piglet, Tigger, Eeyore, Owl, Kanga, and Roo. In Fantasyland, giant storybook pages relay the tale of a blustery day while sailing and bouncing through a Pooh dream sequence, rain and more rain, and at last a celebration. "Hooray!" Adults and children alike will be lulled into the delights of A. A. Milne's captivating stories accompanied by delightful music. **FASTPASS. 3½-minute ride.**

NOTE: *Expect long lines and remember to use FASTPASS if necessary.*

MICKEY'S PHILHARMAGIC

This 3-D attraction located in Fantasyland is a delightful winner! Even though Mickey's name is featured in the title, the mischievous Donald Duck steals the show as he takes visitors along on a wild ride through Disney animated movies, interacting with the largest cast of Disney characters ever in a single 3-D movie. You'll see Ariel, Aladdin, Jasmine, Lumiere, Simba, Peter Pan, Tinker Bell and more, all accompanied by popular Disney music and fun in-theater effects of squirting water and delicious aromas. Shown on the largest seamless projections screen in the world (150 feet long and 28 feet high), it's an attraction kids as well as kids-at-heart will absolutely adore. **FASTPASS. Ten-minute show.**

PETER PAN'S FLIGHT

This is one of the most endearing attractions in Fantasyland, sure to steal your heart. Though old-fashioned and certainly not a thrill a minute, you'll find it hard to resist "flying" with Peter Pan, Wendy, and the boys to Never Never Land. On gently soaring pirate ships, your adventure begins in the Darling nursery, "and off we go," flying over the twinkling lights of London

QUIET SPOTS IN THE MAGIC KINGDOM

If you're looking to escape the hustle and bustle of the park for a few moments, there are a few quiet spots.

Out the back door of Ye Olde Christmas Shop is a shady area with benches and views of the moat surrounding Cinderella's Castle.

The pathway leading from behind Cinderella's Castle to Liberty Square along the moat has benches with views of the castle.

A picturesque veranda overlooks the river on the side of Aloha Terrace.

A shady area with benches can be found next to the river before crossing the bridge into Adventureland.

On the pathway between Tomorrowland and the front of Cinderella's Castle is a quiet seating area with Cinderella's wishing well.

with Big Ben and the London Bridge standing out against a starry, moonlit night (definitely the best part of the ride). Next stop Never Never Land, where far below are glistening waterfalls, glowing volcanoes, sunning mermaids, an Indian Village, the Lost Boys, and Captain Hook's ship. All the while the movie's theme song tells us "you can fly." The sight of Wendy walking the plank is hair-raising, but of course Peter Pan saves the day. This ride is a real charmer; perfect for all ages. **FASTPASS. 3-minute ride.**

HAUNTED MANSION

Eerie sounds, toppled fountains, unkempt grounds, and not even a hint of a smile on the faces of the creepy cast member servants cause a definite sense of foreboding on approach to this Tudor-style, redbrick mansion in Liberty Square. Enter a gargoyle-guarded Stretch Room where your "ghost host" asks all to gather tightly in the "dead" center of the room and warns that "there is no turning back." Then board a "doom buggy," your conveyance through this dusty, ghostly retreat where many terrific special effects and hair-raising sounds up the ante. You may have to ride several times to spy even half of the terrific details. If this sounds frightening, it's not. It's nothing but fun and only the smallest of children might become alarmed. **FASTPASS. 9-minute ride.**

NOTE: If the line seems abnormally long, it's probably because of the arrival of the *Liberty Belle* riverboat or the conclusion of the Hall of Presidents show; try again at a later time. And if you're prone to allergies, don't worry; the "dust" used here is an artificial, nonallergenic material.

BIG THUNDER MOUNTAIN RAILROAD

In Frontierland, inside the 200-foot, rocky outcropping resembling the scenery in Monument Valley is a zippy coaster ride offering visitors a peek at the mining country of the Old West. Disney rounded up an amazing assortment of old mining equipment to give a taste of the gold rush to this blast of an attraction. Board a fifteen car "runaway" mining train led by a puffing and chugging engine for a wild journey through creepy bat caves, steaming geysers, bubbling mud pots, hazardous rockslides, rumbling earthquakes, and collapsing mine shafts. The details whip by so quickly, you'll have difficulty absorbing them all. For those who like speed but not big drops, this is your coaster; there are plenty of curves and small dips, but all in all you'll find it fairly tame and loads of rip-roarin' fun. **Not recommended for expectant mothers or those with back or neck problems. Minimum height 40 inches (3 feet, 4 inches). Children age six or younger must be accompanied by an adult. FASTPASS. 4-minute ride.**

SPLASH MOUNTAIN

This is one ride guaranteed to put a smile on your face. Who can resist the charms of Brer Rabbit, Brer Fox, Brer Bear, and the rest of the gang, even if it culminates in one heck of a plunge? Float through Audio-Animatronics scenes from Disney's classic film *Song of the South* in a hollowed-out log, splashing and dropping through Brer Rabbit's Laughin' Place. Drift 'round the briar patch while toe-tapping music plays among the cabbages and carrots, jugs of moonshine, chirpin' birds, and croakin' frogs as you relax and bob your head to the beat. Inside the mountain Brer Fox and Brer Bear cause plenty of commotion along the way as Brer Rabbit outwits them at every turn. As you float through bayous, marshes, and caverns, all a delight to the eye with loads of colorful detail and too-cute cavorting characters,

THE MAGIC KINGDOM'S BEST BEHIND-THE-SCENES TOURS

Fifteen percent discounts on tours are available to Annual Pass holders, Disney Vacation Club members, and AAA cardholders. Call (407) WDW–TOUR or (407) 939–8687 for reservations.

Backstage Magic. This seven-hour tour encompasses all four parks. Check out the Utilidors (subterranean tunnels) at the Magic Kingdom and learn about the behind-the-scenes artistic and technical creations at each park. $199 including lunch. Park admission not required. Begins at 9:00 A.M. Monday through Friday. Guests must be age sixteen or older.

Disney's Behind the Magic of Our Steam Trains. Join the Disney crew early in the morning for three hours as they prepare the trains for operation. Check out the engine cab, see the roundhouse where the trains are stored overnight, and learn about Walt Disney's fascination with steam trains. $40 plus park admission. Begins at 7:30 A.M. Monday, Tuesday, Thursday, and Saturday. Guests must be age ten or older.

Disney's Family Magic Tour. A two-hour interactive tour through the Magic Kingdom. $25 plus park admission. Starts at 10:00 A.M. daily. Guests must be age three or older.

Keys to the Kingdom. One of the best behind-the-scenes tours offered in all of Disney. Meet at City Hall for a 4½-hour trip around the park to learn the hidden secrets and history of the Magic Kingdom. Visit three attractions, the Production Center where floats line up for the daily parade, and the Utilidors, the tunnels below the park. $58 plus park admission, including lunch. Tours depart daily at 8:30, 9:00, and 9:30 A.M. Guests must be age sixteen or older.

Mickey's Magical Milestones. This two-hour spin around the park visits attractions and special locations associated with Mickey Mouse's famous career. $25 plus park admission. Begins at 9:00 A.M. Monday, Wednesday, and Friday. Guests must be age ten or older.

the addictive theme song "Time to Be Moving Along" plays. When the ride creeps upward, heed the doomsday warnings of a gloomy pair of buzzards ("It's turning back time" and "We'll show *you* a laughing place") just before the final doozy of a splashdown over a five-story waterfall and into an oversize briar patch. It's pretty tough to keep your eyes open (at least for firsttimers), but try to grab a peek of the park from the top. And don't think you missed the cherished "Zip-A-Dee-Doo-Da" tune; you'll hear it on the way out. **Not recommended for expectant mothers or those with back or neck problems. Minimum height 40 inches (3 feet, 4 inches). FASTPASS. 11-minute ride.**

NOTE: If you'd like to avoid a soaking, ask the attendant for a seat in the last row and sit on the left-hand side of the log (although this really doesn't guarantee a completely dry ride). The drop's really not as bad as it looks, so don't let it keep you from experiencing one of the best rides Disney has to offer. Parents who want to stay behind with the little ones will want to utilize the playground area just to the right of the attraction's FASTPASS distribution area.

PIRATES OF THE CARIBBEAN

The tune "Yo Ho, Yo Ho, a Pirate's Life for Me" will ring in your ears for hours after leaving this likable ride. Float through dripping caves and into a darkened bombardment of a Caribbean town at the merciless hands of scurvy pirates. Hundreds of shouting, singing, and grunting Audio-Animatronics buccaneers chase women (some women chase the men), pillage and burn the town, and party through the night. It may sound a bit rough, but it's quite a charmer and executed in nothing but good humor. **10-minute ride.**

NOTE: As you enter this attraction, look up at the zany, one-eyed, talking parrot perched over the doorway.

The Very Best Dining in the Magic Kingdom

MAIN STREET U.S.A. DINING

Crystal Palace. Breakfast, lunch, and dinner buffet with Winnie the Pooh characters. (See full description in the Magic Kingdom Dining section of the Dining chapter.)

Tony's Town Square Restaurant. New York–style Italian restaurant; lunch and dinner. (See full description in the Magic Kingdom Dining section of the Dining chapter.)

TOMORROWLAND DINING

Tomorrowland Terrace Noodle Station. A giant step above counter service meals, the Noodle Station offers what the folks at Disney call *fast casual*, prepared-to-order food. Available dishes include shrimp, chicken, or tofu noodle bowls, a variety of stir-fries, Asian-inspired salads, and iced green teas infused with flavors of blackberry, jasmine, or peach (all organic), and a wide variety of hot teas. The children's menu includes noodle soup and teriyaki stir fry.

FANTASYLAND DINING

Cinderella's Royal Table. Dine high above Fantasyland in the towers of Cinderella's Castle; breakfast character buffet, and a la carte lunch and dinner. (See full description in the Magic Kingdom Dining section of the Dining chapter.)

LIBERTY SQUARE DINING

Liberty Tree Tavern. Colonial tavern serving good old American fare; lunch a la carte; colonial-dressed characters host evening all-you-care-to-eat meal. (See full description in the Magic Kingdom Dining section of the Dining chapter.)

FRONTIERLAND DINING

Pecos Bill Café. Best counter-service spot in the Magic Kingdom; unbelievably good char-grilled burgers and such in an Old West atmosphere; quarter-pound cheeseburgers, half-pound bacon double cheeseburgers, chicken wraps, BBQ pork sandwiches, grilled chicken salad, chili, chili cheese fries, great topping bar with hot skillets of onions and mushrooms; chocolate cream pie; *children's menu:* hot dog, chicken strips.

Special Entertainment

Cinderellabration. It's a bippity-boppity-boo time at this new musical stage show, performed several times daily in front of Cinderella's Castle. It's Cinderella's coronation day, and along to celebrate is her Fairy Godmother and members of the royal court accompanied by singing, dancing,

BEST PLACES FROM WHICH TO VIEW THE WISHES FIREWORKS SHOW

- Bridge to Tomorrowland, for a prime view of Tinker Bell on her flight from the top of the castle.
- In the hub directly in front of the castle near Walt and Mickey's statue.
- The California Grill's fifteenth-floor observation deck at the Contemporary Resort (advance reservations required).
- The romantic beach at the Polynesian Resort.
- The marina or Narcoossee's Restaurant at the Grand Floridian Resort.
- The balcony of a tower guest room on the Magic Kingdom side of the Contemporary Resort.
- A lagoon-view room at the Polynesian Resort.
- A Magic Kingdom lagoon-view room at the Grand Floridian Resort.

and plenty of pageantry. Snow White, Aurora, Belle, and Jasmine bring along their princes to join in the celebration, which ends in a quick fireworks display. **Check your guidemap for showtimes. 19-minute show.**

Share a Dream Come True Parade. This wonderful afternoon parade is a huge hit with guests of all ages. Giant floats topped with rotating globes filled with Disney's favorites—the likes of Mickey Mouse, Pinocchio, Aladdin, and more—are accompanied by more than one hundred walking characters and a medley of classic Disney songs. Don't miss it! **15-minute parade.**

NOTE: Those not interested in the parade will find this to be a great time to ride the big-name attractions when all the crowds are elsewhere.

SpectroMagic. A glittering sorcerer Mickey leads this parade of dazzling Disney characters aglow with fiber optics, holographic images, and twinkling lights (more than 600,000 of them), all accompanied by Disney classic songs.

Wishes. What a way to end your day at this magical park! Jiminy Cricket narrates the story of how wishes come true, accompanied by Disney songs, character voices, and unbelievable pyrotechnics. While the castle constantly changes colors, you'll be wowed by 557 firing cues and 683 individual pieces of fireworks launched from 11 locations. The new display is several times the size of and five minutes longer than the previous Fantasy in the Sky show. Thankfully, Tinker Bell's flight from the castle into Tomorrowland is still a part of the show. **12-minute show.**

NOTE: Although it can be seen throughout the entire park, the best spot from which to view the show is near the Walt Disney and Mickey statue in front of the castle.

Special Events

Night of Joy. On two consecutive nights in early September, some of the biggest names in contemporary Christian music perform at the Magic Kingdom. Acts include such names as Steven Curtis Chapman, Casting Crowns, Audio Adrenaline, Donnie McClurkin, and more. Call (407) W–DISNEY, or (407) 924–7639 for ticketing information and pricing.

Mickey's Not-So-Scary Halloween. On selected nights throughout the month of October, Halloween is celebrated at a kid-friendly, after-hours party featuring trick or treat and costumed characters. The park's most popular attractions are open as well as mask-making stations, a Halloween riverboat ride, storytelling, family photos, Mickey's Boo to You Parade, and a special fireworks display. Call (407) W–DISNEY, or (407) 924–7639 for ticketing information and pricing.

Mickey's Very Merry Christmas Party. "Snow" falls on the decorated streets of the Magic Kingdom on select nights in December. The park's most popular attractions are open, along with enchanting parades, special Christmas shows, character greetings, holiday family portraits, cocoa and cookies, and a presentation of the Wishes fireworks with a holiday twist. Call (407) W–DISNEY, or (407) 924–7639 for ticketing information and pricing.

Epcot

Although its founder died in 1966, the Walt Disney Company brought Walt Disney's dream of an experimental prototype community of tomorrow to reality in 1982, only in a much broader fashion—an atypical theme park dedicated to the resourcefulness and imagination of the American free enterprise system, a continual showcase of imagination, instruction, research, and invention, an education in technology and innovation, other lands and cultures.

Comprising 260 acres (over twice the size of the Magic Kingdom) and divided into two parts, Future World and World Showcase, it takes almost two full days and a good pair of walking shoes to truly explore the park's full scope.

At Future World visitors encounter shining glass pyramids, choreographed fountains, shimmering steel, and unconventional landscaping. Towering above it all is Epcot's symbol, Spaceship Earth, topped with a massive, white-gloved Mickey hand sporting a sparkling magic wand. Here visitors learn about communications, energy, health, agriculture, transportation, the oceans, space, even their imagination. If it sounds a bit like school, don't worry. Disney always manages to add its special style to the learning process, transforming it into sheer fun.

At World Showcase you'll see authentic-looking replicas of famous landmarks and buildings, typical streets overflowing with marvelous architectural detail, shops presenting the best of the world's merchandise, exotic food and wine, and captivating entertainment. Without leaving the country, or the park for that matter, behold the Eiffel Tower, stroll a Japanese garden, witness Venice's St. Mark's Square, or visit a Mexican *mercado* (market). Definitely plan to spend an evening here, when all the countries are lit with shimmering lights and the true romance of this wonderful area of the park shines through.

Strolling in a counterclockwise direction around the 1.3-mile World Showcase walkway you'll encounter each country in this order: Canada, United Kingdom, France, Morocco, Japan, America, Italy, Germany, China, Norway, and finally Mexico. Those weary of walking can utilize the very slow Friendship water taxis that ply the World Showcase Lagoon, located at strategic points: two on each side of Showcase Plaza, one in front of Morocco, and another in front of Germany.

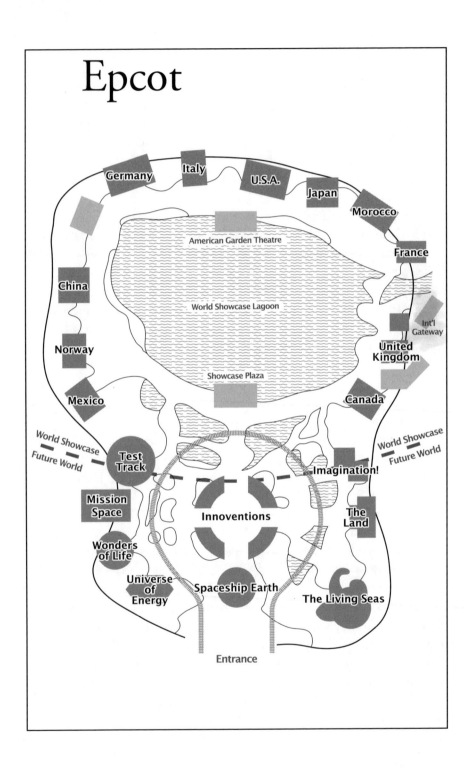

Epcot

Germany
Italy
U.S.A.
Japan
Morocco
France

American Garden Theatre

China

World Showcase Lagoon

Int'l Gateway

Norway

United Kingdom

Showcase Plaza

Mexico

Canada

World Showcase
Future World

World Showcase
Future World

Test Track

Imagination!

Mission Space

Innoventions

The Land

Wonders of Life

Universe of Energy

Spaceship Earth

The Living Seas

Entrance

While there are plenty of attractions and activities for the little ones, Epcot's appeal is mainly to older children and adults. The draw: a huge variety of dining choices, loads of exciting entertainment, magnificent gardens, around-the-world shopping, and attractions that simultaneously entertain and educate. The grounds alone are worth the price of admission, a fact well known to horticulturists worldwide. Most important, just enjoy!

Park Basics

GETTING THERE

Those driving to Walt Disney World should take exit 67 off Interstate 4 and follow the signs to Epcot's main entrance.

USING WALT DISNEY WORLD TRANSPORTATION

From the Grand Floridian, Polynesian, and Contemporary Resorts and the Magic Kingdom: Board the monorail, disembark at the Ticket and Transportation Center (TTC), and then transfer to the Epcot monorail.

From the Yacht and Beach Club, Beach Club Villas, Boardwalk Inn and Villas, and Walt Disney World Dolphin and Swan: Walk or take a boat to the International Gateway entrance in World Showcase. Although World Showcase isn't open until 11:00 A.M., entrance is allowed anytime after Future World opens. Park passes may also be purchased here.

From all other Disney resorts, Disney–MGM Studios, and Animal Kingdom: Board the bus marked EPCOT. Boat transportation is also provided between Disney–MGM Studios and Epcot's International Gateway.

PARKING

Cost is $8.00 per day; free to Walt Disney Resort guests and Annual Pass holders. Keep your receipt, good for parking at the Magic Kingdom, Disney–MGM Studios, and Animal Kingdom on that day only.

Parking is conveniently located in front of the park. Trams circulate throughout the parking area for easy transportation to the entry gate. Be sure to make a note of your aisle and section.

OPERATING HOURS

Future World open 9:00 A.M. to 7:00 P.M. (*Honey, I Shrunk the Audience*; Test Track; Mission: SPACE; Soarin'; and Spaceship Earth are usually open until 9:00 P.M.) and World Showcase 11:00 A.M. to 9:00 P.M. Call (407) 824–4321 or log on to www.disneyworld.com for updated park hours.

Entrance Plaza and Spaceship Earth normally open a half hour before official park opening time. To get a jump on the crowds, arrive at least thirty minutes early to allow time to park, buy tickets, purchase a snack or cup of coffee, and be one of the first to hit the big attractions. I recommend heading straight to Test Track or Soarin'.

ENTRY GATES

Epcot has two entrances: the main gate in front of Spaceship Earth and the International Gateway Entrance in World Showcase between the United Kingdom and France. Visitors staying at the Epcot resorts should use the International Gateway that opens at the same time as Future World. Park passes may be purchased at both entrances.

FASTPASS ATTRACTIONS

- Mission: SPACE

- *Honey, I Shrunk the Audience*

- Living with the Land

- Soarin'

- Test Track

- Maelstrom

See the introductory section of this chapter for FASTPASS details.

PARK SERVICES

ATMs. There are three: next to the stroller rentals at Entrance Plaza, on the center walkway between Future World and World Showcase, and at the America pavilion in World Showcase.

Baby care center. An infant facility is located in the Odyssey Center between Test Track and the Mexico Pavilion on the east side of the park, outfitted with changing tables, high chairs, and a room for nursing mothers. Disposable diapers, bottles, formula, and baby supplies can be purchased. All restrooms throughout the park have changing tables.

Cameras and film processing. The Camera Center on your right as you enter the park sells cameras, film, camcorder tapes, memory cards, and batteries. Download your images from a digital media card to a CD here.

First aid. For minor medical problems head to the First Aid Center in the Odyssey Center located between Test Track and the Mexico Pavilion on the east side of the park.

Guest Relations. On the east side of Spaceship Earth is Guest Relations, where a knowledgeable staff is ready to assist with priority seating, lost children, lost and found, purchase of annual passes and upgrades, information for guests with disabilities, taped narration for visitors with sight impairment, assisted listening devices, foreign currency exchange, language translation headsets, sign language services, VIP tour information, behind-the-scenes programs, character greeting information, and resort reservations.

Information Central. Check the up-to-the-minute tip board between Innovations East and West near the Fountain of Nations for wait times and special event information.

Lockers. Locker rentals, $7.00 per day inclusive of a $2.00 refundable key deposit, are available next door to the Camera Center in Entrance Plaza and just outside the International Gateway entrance. If you're park-hopping, keep your receipt for another locker at the three other Disney theme parks for no extra charge.

Lost and Found. Located at Guest Relations, or call (407) 824–4245.

Lost children. Locate lost children at the Baby Care Center or Guest Relations.

Package pickup. Purchases may be sent to the Gift Stop located just outside the main entrance as well the International Gateway next to stroller rentals for pickup at the end of the day; allow three hours for delivery. Disney resort guests may send packages directly to their hotel for next-day arrival.

Pet kennel. A kennel is located on the left before entering the park. Daily rate is $6.00. For information call (407) 824–6568. Proof of vaccination required.

Stroller and wheelchair rentals. Rentals are located on the left as you enter the park's main entrance and at International Gateway. Single strollers are $8.00 per day, double strollers $15.00, and wheelchairs $8.00 inclusive of a $1.00 refundable deposit. Electric convenience vehicles are $40.00 inclusive of a $10.00 refundable deposit. If you're park-hopping, keep your receipt for a same-day replacement at the three other Disney theme parks and Downtown Disney Marketplace.

Wheelchair Accessibility. A guidebook for guests with disabilities is available at Guest Relations. Guests with mobility disabilities can park adjacent to the Entrance Complex (ask at the Auto Plaza for directions). Wheelchairs and ECVs are available for rent. Most restaurants and shops at Epcot are accessible to guests with disabilities, although some counter-service locations have narrow queues with railings (ask a host or hostess for assistance). Companion-assisted restrooms are located at First Aid, near Spaceship Earth, in Future World East opposite Test Track, in Future World West opposite the Land, and in World Showcase near the pavilions for Norway, Germany, Morocco, and Canada.

Most attractions in Future World and the ride at Norway in World Showcase provide access through the main queue, while others have auxiliary entrances for wheelchairs and service animals (service animals are not permitted on Soarin', Body Wars, Mission: SPACE, and Test Track) along with as many as five members of your party. Certain attractions require guests to transfer from their wheelchair to a ride system.

Braille guidebooks, audiotape guides and portable tape players, assistive listening devices, and video captioning devices are available at Guest Relations with a $25 refundable deposit. Wireless handheld captioning receivers are also available with a $100 refundable deposit. Many theater-type attractions have reflective or video captioning. With a seven-day notice, a sign language interpreter will be provided at live shows on Tuesday and Friday. Call (407) 824–4321 with any questions.

The Lay of the Land

Epcot looks a bit like a figure 8, with Future World being the northern region (shown on the guidemap at the bottom; think "upside down") and World Showcase the southern region. Future World is composed of two concentric rings, with Spaceship Earth and Innoventions forming the inner circle and seven pavilions the outer. The Universe of Energy, Wonders of Life, Mission: SPACE, and Test Track are located on the east side of Spaceship Earth, and Imagination, the Land, and the Living Seas are on the west side. Walkways connect Future World to World Showcase, which is made up of eleven pavilions fronted by a 1.3-mile promenade surrounding the forty-acre World Showcase Lagoon.

The Very Best Attractions in Epcot

SPACESHIP EARTH

Visible for miles, this symbol of Epcot comprises over 2 million cubic feet of expanse, a silver geosphere 180 feet tall and 164 feet in diameter composed of 954 glowing panels of various shapes and sizes. Inside you'll find an attraction chronicling the story of human communications beginning with the dawn of recorded time. The slow journey to the top takes visitors through marvelous, Audio-Animatronics scenes representing humankind's quest for more efficient means of communication—see Cro-Magnon storytellers, Egyptian papyrus scroll readers, ancient Greek actors, Roman couriers, Islamic scholars, even Michelangelo painting the Sistine Chapel.

Following in swift succession come the new tools and technologies of the teletype, telephone, radio, moving pictures, and television. Finally there's today's communication supernetwork conveying information at the speed of light. The most captivating scene is found at the top of the sphere where, in the middle of a sky thick with stars, the earth sits suspended in space. **15-minute ride.**

NOTE: Lines move quickly and efficiently on this continually loading ride. Because this is the first attraction visitors encounter, lines can get lengthy in the morning. If the wait looks reasonable, go for it; if not, come back in the afternoon when most people are touring World Showcase. This attraction is usually up and running a half hour before official park opening time.

FOUNTAIN OF NATIONS

This dancing fountain, located in Innovations Plaza, is one of the best shows in the park and, most important, one that doesn't require a wait in line. Every fifteen minutes it explodes with jets of water, choreographed in rhythmic movement to stirring, magnificent music. It's quite a sight to see—and even better after dark with added lighting effects.

UNIVERSE OF ENERGY

Ellen's Energy Adventure. Journey to the time of the dinosaurs in this show featuring the images of comedian Ellen DeGeneres and Bill Nye the Science Guy. During the preshow, Ellen dreams she's a contestant on the *Jeopardy* TV game show, failing miserably because of her lack of knowledge about energy. She asks Bill Nye to take her back billions of years to the "big bang," where the birth of the universe all began.

In a traveling theater, visitors move through a dark, misty forest brimming with swamps and volcanic activity, towering prehistoric trees and plant life. The air is steamy and damp, and the smell of sulfur and sounds of the night only add to the thrill. Towering overhead are roaring, lifelike Audio-Animatronics dinosaurs, the most astounding aspect of this attraction.

At the final theater are wide aerial shots of the world's ever-expanding energy requirements, the latest technologies of solar and wind energy, and new ways of finding more oil and clean-burning natural gas. Of course Ellen, now an energy expert, returns to beat her competitors on *Jeopardy*. If all this sounds too much like school, never fear; Ellen's wisecracking along the way keeps the informative aspect of this attraction entertaining. One of Future World's best attractions, it's worth your time, if only to see the dinosaurs. **45-minute show beginning every 17 minutes.**

NOTE: This attraction holds almost 600 people at a time; even though lines seem long, everyone almost always gets in. Enter the door to the theater on the left and make a beeline to the front row of the far-left section for the best unobstructed views. Sensitive young children may be bothered by the darkness and the huge, roaring dinosaurs.

MISSION: SPACE

The year is 2036. You're off to Mars in an X-2 Deep Space Shuttle with a team of four—Commander, Pilot, Navigator, and Engineer. As the engines rumble, seats tilt back in preparation for countdown. Then liftoff. Wow! Experience the heart-palpitating, G-force thrill of rocketing into outer space through clouds of exhaust. As you peer out the window into a computer-generated imagery of space, panic sets in. But after the first thirty seconds or so, you'll settle down for the ride of your life with a brief sense of weightlessness, a slingshot maneuver around the moon, and one heck of a landing on Mars. What a rush!

EPCOT'S BEST BEHIND-THE-SCENES TOURS (FUTURE WORLD)

Fifteen percent discounts on tours are available to Annual Pass holders, Disney Vacation Club members, and AAA cardholders. Call (407) WDW–TOUR or (407) 939–8687 for reservations.

Dolphins in Depth. A look at dolphin behavior and training with a chance to enter the water and get up close to these astonishing creatures. The three-hour program includes a souvenir photo and T-shirt. $150. Starts at 9:45 A.M. Monday through Friday. Be sure to bring a bathing suit. No swimming required. Theme park admission is neither required nor included. Guests must be age thirteen or older to participate; those ages thirteen through seventeen must have a parent or guardian participating in the tour.

Epcot Dive Quest. This two-and-a-half-hour program includes a forty-minute dive in the six-million-gallon aquarium at the Living Seas. $140. Theme park admission is neither required nor included. Offered daily at 4:30 and 5:30 P.M. to all certified divers; those ages ten through fifteen must dive with a parent or guardian, and those ages sixteen through eighteen must have a signed consent from a parent or guardian. Dive equipment provided.

Seas Aqua Tour. A two-and-a-half-hour program in the backstage area of the Living Seas with a chance to explore the aquarium for thirty minutes using a supplied air snorkel system. $100; includes gear, T-shirt, and group photo. Daily at 12:30 P.M. Theme park admission is neither required nor included. Bring a bathing suit. Available to guests ages eight and older, those ages eight through sixteen must be accompanied by a parent or legal guardian.

The Undiscovered Future World. On this four-and-a-half-hour tour, visitors learn about the vision and history of Epcot, hear in-depth information on each pavilion (even a few peeks backstage), and take a look at the Epcot marina where the Illuminations fireworks show is put together. $49 plus park admission. Starts at 9:00 A.M. Monday, Wednesday, and Friday. Guests must be age sixteen or older.

Afterward head to the Advanced Training Lab, an interactive center featuring the popular Mission: SPACE Race with two teams of twenty competing to be the first to complete a successful mission; Expedition Mars, a test of skill in guiding astronauts around the Red Planet; and Space Base, an interactive children's play area. Lines are longest for Postcards From Space, a space-based video email program. **Minimum height 44 inches (3 feet, 8 inches). An adult must accompany children age six or younger. This is a highly turbulent motion simulator ride and not recommended for expectant mothers or those with high blood pressure; back, heart, or neck problems; motion sickness; or other medical conditions. FAST- PASS. Singles Line. Four-minute ride with a short preshow.**

NOTE: If you're willing to ride without other members of your party, the single-riders' line is a much quicker alternative; simply ask for directions at the entrance.

TEST TRACK

In a six-passenger vehicle, riders move through a series of rigorous tests normally used on prototype cars. Begin your journey with a hill climb, then a rough road test, two brake tests (one with and one without antilock brakes), subjection to extremes of hot and cold temperatures, and finally the long-awaited handling run. Move through hairpin turns before barreling outside onto a high-speed banking loop at over 60 mph. It's quite a ride, not really scary but fast and absolutely loads of fun! **Minimum height 40 inches (3 feet, 4 inches). An adult must accompany children age six or younger. Not recommended for expectant mothers or those with back, heart, or neck problems. Closed in inclement weather. FASTPASS. Singles Line. Five-minute ride with a short preshow.**

NOTE: This ride is notorious for breakdowns, so prepare for long waits, some of which don't necessarily come with a ride at the end. If you want to utilize FASTPASS (which is a great idea), don't wait until the end of the day; passes are sometimes gone by the afternoon. If you're willing to ride without other members of your party, the single-riders' line is a much quicker alternative; simply ask for directions at the entrance.

HONEY, I SHRUNK THE AUDIENCE

Don't miss this full-of-surprises 3-D film. Professor Wayne Szalinski of *Honey, I Shrunk the Kids* fame manages to cause plenty of chaos with a series of mishaps involving his quirky inventions. Thanks to his out-of-con-

EPCOT'S BEST BEHIND-THE-SCENES TOURS (WORLD SHOWCASE)

Fifteen percent discounts on tours are available to Annual Pass holders, Disney Vacation Club members, and AAA cardholders. Call (407) WDW–TOUR or (407) 939–8687, for reservations.

Around the World at Epcot. Tour World Showcase for two hours while maneuvering on a Segway Human Transporter, a motorized, self-balancing, personal transportation device. $80. Twice daily at 8:30 and 9:30 A.M. Participants must be at least age sixteen and there is a maximum weight limit of 250 pounds. Young people ages sixteen and seventeen must have a parent or guardian sign a waiver.

Gardens of the World. Learn the secrets behind the World Showcase gardens on this three-hour tour led by a Disney horticulturist. $59 plus park admission. Starts at 9:00 A.M. Tuesday and Thursday. Participants must be age sixteen or older.

Hidden Treasures of World Showcase. Explore the art and architecture of the World Showcase pavilion on this three-hour tour. $59 plus park admission. Starts at 9:00 A.M. Tuesday and Thursday. Participants must be age sixteen or older.

trol machines and great Disney special effects, guests involuntarily become the casualties of hundreds of scampering mice, a colossal dog, and a very large python loose in a very small theater. Get out your handkerchief for the final surprise. **FASTPASS. Continuous shows every 20 minutes.**

NOTE: Although the dark theater combined with the slapping of numerous mouse tails and a snake in the face will probably scare small children, older kids and adults will love it.

LIVING WITH THE LAND

Explore the past, present, and future of farming on a boat tour through three diverse ecosystems: a stormy rain forest; a harsh, arid desert landscape; and the rolling American prairie; complete with an early nineteenth-century family farm. Then proceed to immense greenhouses where more efficient and environmentally friendly ways of producing food are researched and developed. You'll see plants grown hydroponically (without soil; check out the trees with nine-pound lemons); there's even a fish farm. Work is also done here in conjunction with NASA to learn how to grow crops for future space colonies. A remarkably absorbing attraction for all ages. **FASTPASS. 13-minute ride.**

NOTE: At lunchtime the overflow from the food court produces extremely long waits. Also be sure to check out Epcot's talking water fountains. There are three (that I know of): next to the restrooms between the Land and Imagination, outside the MouseGear shop, and near the play fountain on the walkway between Future World and World Showcase. You try to figure it out!

SOARIN'

Hang glide over California in Epcot's newest attraction, one that's guaranteed to leave you speechless. After rising 40 feet inside a giant, 80-foot projection screen dome, you're completely surrounded with phenomenal, bird's-eye views of the Golden State. Soar over the Golden Gate Bridge, towering Redwood forests, hot air balloons drifting over the Napa Valley wine country, golf courses in Palm Springs, the majesty of Yosemite, and more; ending high above Disneyland just in time for a fireworks display. Smell the aroma of the orange groves and pine trees and feel the wind in your face, all while listening to a stirring musical score. This is one fantastic ride! **Minimum height 40 inches (3 feet, 4 inches). Not recommended for expectant mothers or those with motion sickness, or heart, back, or neck problems. FASTPASS. 10-minute ride.**

O CANADA

You'll be chomping at the bit to book a trip north after seeing this awe-inspiring film, a dazzling portrayal of the Canadian people and their spectacular land. Facilitated by the wonder of 360-degree Circle-Vision photography, feel as if you're in the center of the action as you sled along the St. Lawrence River in romantic Quebec City, sail the Bluenose along the coast of Nova Scotia, walk the cobblestone streets of Montreal, or ride the Trans-Canadian railroad. Soar above the majestic mountains of Banff,

EPCOT'S MOST ROMANTIC PLACES

- Hidden garden behind the Tea Caddy Shop in the United Kingdom
- The charming Bistro de Paris Restaurant
- Mexico's candlelit San Angel Inn Restaurant
- An Illuminations fireworks cruise
- Butchart-style gardens in Canada
- Garden on the canal side of France
- Benches overlooking the carp-filled reflecting pool in China

stroll the Butchart Gardens in Victoria, and leave with just a small sense of the grandeur of Canada. **Shows every 20 minutes.**

IMPRESSIONS DE FRANCE

You'll be enthralled by the captivating images of France in this impressive film with dazzling clips of the Loire chalets, mouthwatering pastry shops, grape fields in harvest, the island of Mont-Saint-Michel, the gardens of Versailles, and the spectacular French Alps, all accompanied by stirring French classical music. If you're a lover of visual beauty, don't miss this opportunity to witness the grandeur of France in the World Showcase. **18-minute show every 30 minutes.**

THE AMERICAN ADVENTURE SHOW

Momentous film, inspiring music, and lifelike, talking, gesturing, and walking Audio-Animatronics characters weave the impressive tale of the United States of America, with Ben Franklin and Mark Twain serving as hosts; the grand finale film montage is a real tearjerker. Some adore this show while others sleep right through it; personally, I'm one of its greatest fans. **Shows every 35 minutes.**

NOTE: It's fairly easy to get a seat in this huge theater. Try to catch the Voices of Liberty performance in the waiting area and just watch your patriotism shoot up a few notches.

REFLECTIONS OF CHINA

Wonders of China has been replaced by this newer adaptation, a fresher and improved version of a remarkable 360-degree film presentation. Although Poet Li Bai is still the narrator and many of the old scenes remain, the addition of modern Shanghai, Hong Kong, and Macau give it new life. With the help of Circle-Vision, walk atop the Great Wall, enter the Forbidden City, stand in the middle of Tiananmen Square, and cruise down the mighty Yangtze River. Stunning views of rice terraces, Inner Mongolia's nomadic people, the misty Huangshan Mountains, the Gobi desert, the extraordinary Terra Cotta Warriors, and the haunting landscape of Guey Ling only serve to make you want more. Come prepared to stand throughout the presentation. **12-minute show.**

MAELSTROM

A favorite of World Showcase visitors is this watery boat ride through both real and mythical scenes of Norway's history. In your dragon-headed longboat, drift past a tenth-century Viking village and then on to a dark, mysterious forest where a hairy, three-headed troll casts a spell on your vessel, causing it to drop backward down a soggy cataract. Sail past glacier-bound polar bears, narrowly miss a plunge off the edge of a waterfall, and finally drop into a stormy North Sea. Your voyage ends with a pleasant, short film on Norway. **FASTPASS. 10-minute ride and show, including the film.**

NOTE: Drops are very small and of no consequence on this tame ride. If you would rather not see the film, walk into the theater and then immediately out the doors on the opposite side.

The Very Best Dining in Epcot

Coral Reef Restaurant. Dine on delicious seafood in front of the Living Sea's massive aquarium; lunch and dinner. (See full description in the Epcot Dining section of the Dining chapter.)

Bistro de Paris. Second-floor dining room featuring French food in an upscale atmosphere; lunch and dinner. (See full description in the Epcot Dining section of the Dining chapter.)

BEERS FROM AROUND THE WORLD

Create your own beer festival while walking from country to country in World Showcase:

- Maudite and La Fin du Monde in Canada
- Harp, Bass, Guinness, and Tennants in the United Kingdom
- Fischer La Belle in France
- Casablanca in Morocco
- Kirin in Japan
- Samuel Adams and Budweiser in America
- Peroni in Italy
- Lowenbrau, Franziskaner Weisse, and Spaten Optimator in Germany
- Tsing Tao in China
- Carlsberg in Norway
- Dos Equis in Mexico

Chefs de France. Lively French bistro serving lunch and dinner. (See full description in the Epcot Dining section of the Dining chapter.)

Restaurant Marrakesh. Exotic Moroccan cuisine; lunch and dinner; picture-perfect surroundings with belly dancer entertainment. (See full description in the Epcot Dining section of the Dining chapter.)

Tangierine Café. Excellent counter-service cafe, shawarma sandwiches and platters (marinated, rotisserie-roasted sliced chicken and lamb); meatball platter; Mediterranean wraps of lamb, chicken, or tabbouleh; vegetarian plate (couscous, hummus, and tabbouleh); freshly baked Moroccan pastries; Moroccan wine, Casablanca beer, Moroccan mint tea, mimosas, strawberry or tangerine daiquiris, specialty coffees; *children's menu:* hamburgers, pizza, chicken tenders.

SPECIALTY DRINKS AT WORLD SHOWCASE

- French wine and champagne from a kiosk in France
- Tangerine daiquiris and mimosas at Tangierine Café
- Sake martinis at Matsu No Ma Lounge in Japan
- Wine tasting at Vinoteca Castello in Italy
- German wines at Valckenberg Weinkeller
- Viking coffee spiked with Bailey's Irish Cream at Kringla Bakery in Norway
- Margaritas at Cantina de San Angel in Mexico

San Angel Inn. Unquestionably Epcot's most romantic restaurant; lunch and dinner; spicy, traditional Mexican dishes in a candlelit riverside setting. (See full description in the Epcot Dining section of the Dining chapter.)

Sunshine Seasons. Here you'll find prepared-to-order, fast-casual food options at several different counters.

The Grill: rotisserie chicken flatbread with wild greens tabbouleh, grilled salmon and mashed potatoes with kalamata olive pesto (excellent!), rotisserie beef flatbread with wild greens tabbouleh; *children's menu:* chicken leg with mashed potatoes.

Asian Noodles: chicken chili garlic noodle bowl, grilled vegetable and beef with jasmine rice, vegetable and tofu noodle bowl with lime ginger broth; *children's menu:* sweet and sour chicken.

Sandwiches: Black Forest ham and salami grinder, turkey and muenster cheese on focaccia with chipotle mayonnaise, grilled vegetable Cuban sandwich (all of these delicious sandwiches are served on artisan breads); *children's menu:* minisub sandwich.

Soup and Salad: grilled chicken and rocket (arugula) salad with pumpkin seed vinaigrette (yum!), seared tuna on mixed greens with sesame rice wine dressing, roasted beet and goat cheese salad with cilantro lime dressing, freshly made soups include crawfish chowder, vegetable minestrone, and broccoli and Tillamook cheese; *children's menu:* macaroni and cheese.

The Bakery: Rice Krispies treats, croissants, cheesecake, strawberry short-cake, lemon meringue tartlets, fruit tartlets, muffins, and more.

Special Entertainment

Illuminations: Reflections of Earth. Each evening at closing time, crowds begin to gather around the World Showcase Lagoon to witness Walt Disney World's most spectacular nighttime extravaganza. The story of planet Earth is told in a combination of unbelievable pyrotechnic displays, amazing lasers, stirring music, and fanciful water movement. Each show takes 480 worker-hours to set up, but it's worth every penny. **13-minute show.**

NOTE: To avoid smoke from the fireworks, check which direction the flame in the torches are pointed and avoid that side of the lagoon. Illuminations does not cancel during inclement weather.

Special Events

Epcot Flower and Garden Festival. For seven weeks each spring, Epcot is covered in more than 30 million blooms with over 100 extravagant topiaries, a Rose Walk between Future World and World Showcase, a floating wonderland in East Lake, and an array of amazing gardens throughout World Showcase. Special appearances by nationally recognized gardeners, how-to presentations by Disney horticulturists, kid-friendly activities and play areas, and a nightly Flower Power concert series add to the festivities. Entrance is included in the price of park admission.

Epcot Summer Series. Top-notch entertainment at the America Gardens Theater for ten weeks in the summer. Past years have featured such names as Riverdance and the fifty-six-member troupe Blast. Entrance is included in the price of park admission.

International Food and Wine Festival. This six-week fall festival is the most heavily visited food festival in the world, attracting more than one million visitors. Booths representing the cuisine of more than thirty countries line the World Showcase walkway, each one selling reasonably priced, appetizer-size food along with wine and beer. Events include complimentary daily cooking demonstrations by some of the countries' top chefs, a

BEST PLACES FROM WHICH TO VIEW ILLUMINATIONS FIREWORKS

Staking out a good spot for viewing the Illuminations fireworks show seems to be an obsession with some, meaning that the nonobsessed will have to be content to watch the show from behind someone else's head. If a prime spot is important to you, find a place at least thirty minutes prior to showtime in slow season and up to an hour in busier times. If you'd like to snag a table at one of the following seated areas, you'll certainly need to think ahead. Here are my suggestions for the best views:

- Outdoor lagoon-facing table at the Rose and Crown (make advance reservations for one hour prior to showtime and request a lagoonside table).

- Cantina de San Angel in Mexico (unless you find a lagoonside table, the fireworks will be partially obstructed by the table umbrellas).

- From an Illuminations Cruise boat (for details see Special Excursions section of chapter 5, Beyond the Theme Parks).

- Bridge between United Kingdom and France (great view, but one of the most popular spots).

- Promenade in front of Canada.

- Between Mexico and Norway.

- In front of Italy by the gondola dock (this area is sometimes reserved for private parties).

- Lagoonside at Showcase Plaza, where all must agree to stay seated for the entire show.

Junior Chef program, complimentary beer- and wine-tasting seminars, and Eat to the Beat nightly concerts with such past performers as Three Dog Night, the Commodores, and the Beach Boys. Avoid the weekends if you can, when the locals come out in full force. Entrance is included in the price of park admission.

Special themed dinners and wine seminars that sell out months in advance include:

Food and Wine Pairings. Daily one-and-a-half-hour wine and appetizer seminars held at various Epcot restaurants where VIP winemakers present three wines paired with food samplings ($35).

Brewers Dinners. Sample international and domestic beers along with unique menu selections ($55).

Sweet Sundays. Some of the country's top pastry chefs demonstrate the preparation of three sweet delights; the evening ends in a sampling ($55).

Lunch and Learn. Celebrity chefs the likes of Rick Bayless and Todd English prepare a four-course lunch and pour wine at a Disney resort restaurant ($75).

Epcot Wine Schools. Daylong wine seminar hosted by a prestigious wine authority. Included is a wine pairing lunch and a certificate of completion ($125).

Party for the Senses. Weekly Saturday evening extravaganza with tasting stations prepared by more than twenty celebrity chefs along with fifty wines and beers at this party of all parties. Entertainment provided by Cirque du Soleil ($95).

Signature Dinners. Five-course meal with wine pairings held at Disney's finest resort restaurants, hosted by a celebrity chef and featured vineyards ($125).

Vertical Wine Tastings. Sample ten vintages from one producer and listen to a speaker ($95–$150).

Exquisite Evening at Epcot. A team of celebrity and Walt Disney World chefs prepare a five-course meal along with wine and live entertainment. The evening concludes with a private viewing of Illuminations ($185; park admission fee not required).

Holidays Around the World. Christmas is a special time at Epcot, with loads of decorations, a nightly tree-lighting ceremony with Mickey and friends, storytelling around World Showcase, a special Illuminations holiday finale, and the Lights of Winter, thousands of miniature lights in the center walkway linking Future World with World Showcase, choreographed to holiday music.

The Candlelight Processional, a thrice-nightly event staged from late November until the end of December at the America Gardens Theater, features a celebrity narrator, a mass choir, and a fifty-piece orchestra who together retell the story of Christmas. Entrance is included in the price of park admission. To guarantee seats for this performance, book a Candlelight Processional Dinner Package that includes dinner at a select World Showcase restaurant and reserved general seating for the show (call 407–WDW–DINE or 407–939–3463, for reservations).

Disney–MGM Studios

"Welcome to the glamour and glitz of show business." Although Disney's version of the heyday of Hollywood is certainly a rose-colored one, its entertainment value can't be beat. On the boulevards of Hollywood and Sunset, legendary Los Angeles buildings, re-created in romanticized and appealing art deco forms, literally scream excitement. It's as if the whole park is on the brink of breaking into a zany show at any minute.

The park is actually a working film and television studio with three production soundstages and a back lot. Visitors are allowed a sample of the mystery at the Backlot Tour attraction, where they're invited to watch the artistic and technical processes involved in the creation of movies and television.

This is a small park, one that can be seen in a full day. Since many of the shows are scheduled, check your guidemap on arrival for showtimes and plan your day accordingly.

Park Basics

GETTING THERE
Those driving to Walt Disney World should take exit 64 off Interstate 4 and follow the signs to Disney–MGM Studios.

Disney–MGM Studios

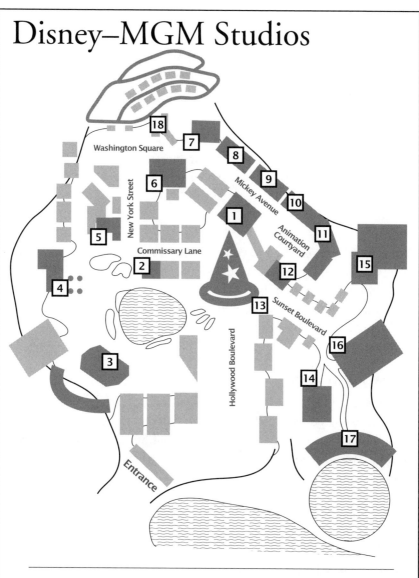

Washington Square

New York Street

Mickey Avenue

Animation Courtyard

Commissary Lane

Hollywood Boulevard

Sunset Boulevard

Entrance

1. The Great Movie Ride
2. Sounds Dangerous – Starring Drew Carey
3. Indiana Jones Epic Stunt Spectacular
4. Star Tours
5. Jim Henson's Muppet ★ Vision 3-D
6. *Honey, I Shrunk the Kids* Movie Set Adventure
7. The Disney – MGM Studios Backlot Tour
8. Who Wants to Be a Millionaire—Play It!
9. Walt Disney: One Man's Dream
10. Voyage of The Little Mermaid
11. The Magic of Disney Animation
12. Playhouse Disney – Live on Stage!
13. Guest Information Board at Hollywood Junction
14. Beauty and the Beast – Live on Stage
15. Rock 'n' Roller Coaster
16. The Twilight Zone Tower of Terror
17. Fantasmic!
18. Lights, Motors, Action! Extreme Stunt Show

USING WALT DISNEY WORLD TRANSPORTATION

From the Yacht and Beach Club, the Boardwalk Inn and Villas, the Beach Club Villas, and the Walt Disney World Swan and Dolphin: Take the boat or walk the path located behind the Boardwalk Inn and the Swan.

From all other Disney resorts, Epcot, and Animal Kingdom: Board the bus marked DISNEY–MGM STUDIOS. Boat transportation is also provided from Epcot's International Gateway.

From the Magic Kingdom: Take the monorail to the Ticket and Transportation Center (TTC), where you can then board the bus marked DISNEY–MGM STUDIOS.

PARKING

Cost is $8.00 per day; free to Walt Disney Resort guests and Annual Pass holders. Keep your receipt, good for parking at Epcot, Magic Kingdom, and Animal Kingdom on that day only.

Parking is conveniently located in front of the park. Trams circulate throughout the parking area for easy transportation to the entry gate. Make a note of what aisle and section you've parked in.

OPERATING HOURS

Open from 9:00 A.M. until an hour or so after dark. Call (407) 824–4321 or log on to www.disneyworld.com for updated park hours.

Hollywood Boulevard is usually open a half hour prior to official opening time. Arrive at least thirty minutes early, allowing time to park, buy tickets, purchase a snack or cup of coffee, and be one of the first to hit the big attractions. I recommend heading straight to the Tower of Terror or Rock 'n' Roller Coaster.

FASTPASS ATTRACTIONS

- Indiana Jones Epic Stunt Spectacular
- Lights, Motors, Action! Extreme Stunt Show
- Rock 'n' Roller Coaster
- Star Tours
- Twilight Zone Tower of Terror

■ Voyage of the Little Mermaid

See the introduction to this chapter for FASTPASS details.

PARK SERVICES

ATMs. For quick cash, two ATMs are located at the park: just outside the entrance and inside the Toy Story Pizza Planet Arcade.

Baby care center. At the Guest Relations center is an infant facility outfitted with changing tables, high chairs, a companion restroom and chairs for nursing mothers. Disposable diapers, bottles, formula, and baby supplies can be purchased. All restrooms throughout the park are outfitted with changing tables.

Cameras and film processing. Stop at the Darkroom located on Hollywood Boulevard for cameras, film, camcorder tapes, memory cards, and batteries. Download your images from a digital media card to a CD here.

First aid. For minor medical problems head to the First Aid Center located next to Guest Relations.

Guest Relations. Located just inside the park on the left is Guest Relations, where a knowledgeable staff is ready to assist with ticket upgrades, priority seating, messages for separated parties, information for guests with disabilities, taped narration for visitors with sight impairment, assisted listening devices, foreign currency exchange, language translation headsets, VIP tour information, behind-the-scenes programs, and resort reservations.

Guests with disabilities. A guidebook for guests with disabilities is available at Guest Relations. Guests with mobility disabilities should park adjacent to the Entrance Complex (ask at the Auto Plaza for directions). Wheelchairs and ECVs are available for rent. Most restaurants and shops at Disney–MGM Studios are accessible to guests with disabilities, although some counter-service locations have narrow queues with railings (ask a host or hostess for assistance). Companion-assisted restrooms are located at First Aid, opposite the Twilight Zone Tower of Terror, opposite Star Tours, at FANTASMIC!, at Rock 'n' Roller Coaster, and next to *Who Wants to Be a Millionaire*.

Most attractions provide access through the main queue, while others have auxiliary entrances for wheelchairs and service animals along with as many as five members of your party. Certain attractions require guests to transfer from their wheelchair to a ride system. Braille guidebooks, assistive listening devices, video captioning, and audiotape guides are available at Guest Relations for a $25 refundable deposit. Many theater-type attractions have reflective or video captioning. A handheld captioning receiver is available at Guest Relations with a $100 refundable deposit. With seven-day notice, a sign language interpreter will be provided at live shows on Sunday and Wednesday. Call (407) 824–4321 with any questions.

Lockers. Lockers are located at Oscar's Service Station on the right as you enter the park, available for $7.00 per day, including a $2.00 refundable key deposit. If you're park-hopping, keep your receipt for another locker at no additional charge at the three other Disney theme parks.

Lost and Found. Located next to Oscar's Gas Station or call (407) 824–4245.

Lost children. Locate lost children at Guest Relations.

Package pickup. Purchases may be sent to the package pickup window located next to Oscar's Gas Station near the Main Entrance for pickup at the end of the day. Allow three hours for delivery. Disney resort guests may send packages directly to their hotel for next-day arrival.

Pet kennel. A kennel is located just outside the park entrance. Daily rate is $6.00. For information call (407) 824–6568. Proof of vaccination is required.

Strollers and wheelchairs. Rentals are located at Oscar's Gas Station on the right as you enter the park. Single strollers are $8.00 per day, double strollers $15.00, and wheelchairs $8.00 inclusive of a $1.00 refundable deposit. Electric convenience vehicles are $40.00, inclusive of a $10.00 refundable deposit. If you're park-hopping, keep your receipt for a same-day replacement at the three other Disney theme parks and Downtown Disney Marketplace.

The Lay of the Land

Disney–MGM Studios' main street, Hollywood Boulevard, leads directly to the park's central plaza, where you'll find a 122-foot Sorcerer Mickey hat. If you're facing the hat from Hollywood Boulevard, to the right are two walkways: one branching to Sunset Boulevard and the other to Animation

Courtyard. On the left is the Echo Lake area of the park that leads to the Streets of America section. Mickey Avenue, the park's working area, sits behind the Chinese theater and may be accessed via Animation Courtyard or Streets of America. It's a bit more confusing than the Magic Kingdom but fairly easy to maneuver.

The Very Best Attractions in Disney–MGM Studios

ROCK 'N' ROLLER COASTER

You've nabbed a special invitation to an Aerosmith concert, but it's clear across town and you're late! Disney's wildest coaster ride takes place inside a twenty-four passenger "stretch limo" speeding down a Los Angeles freeway amid blasting Aerosmith music. Zooming past, through, and around neon Hollywood landmarks, you'll loop and corkscrew in the dark. And that's after you've accelerated to a speed of 60 mph in just under three seconds. Hold onto your hat (or anything else you might treasure), because this is pure Disney fun. **Minimum height 48 inches (4 feet). Not recommended for expectant mothers; those with back, heart, or neck problems; or those prone to motion sickness. FASTPASS. 10-minute ride.**

NOTE: Head straight to this attraction when the park opens; you'll find it's one popular ride and certainly the biggest thrill at any Disney theme park. Then immediately go next door to the Twilight Zone Tower of Terror. If you'd like to sit in the Rock 'n' Roller Coaster's front seat, just ask, but be prepared for a wait, because every other daredevil around has the same idea. The chicken-hearted can take comfort in knowing that although there are three inversions on the ride, there are no steep drops.

TWILIGHT ZONE TOWER OF TERROR

On this free-falling adventure, you'll certainly feel you've entered the twilight zone or at the very least a brand new dimension of fright. The waiting line snakes through the crumbling grounds of the deserted, thirteen-story Hollywood Tower Hotel, with its rusty grillwork, cracking fountains, and overgrown, unkempt foliage, before proceeding through the spooky, abandoned lobby dusty with forgotten luggage and dead flower arrangements. Step into the gloomy hotel library for a message from *Twilight Zone* TV show host Rod Serling (on a black-and-white television, of course), who relays the tale of a stormy night in 1939 when an elevator full

CHARACTER GREETING SPOTS AT DISNEY–MGM STUDIOS

The pointing Mickey gloves on your guidemap will help you find the following locations:

- *Toy Story* 2 friends Woody, Buzz Lightyear, and Jessie near Mama Melrose's Ristorante at Al's Toy Barn.

- *Monsters Inc* characters on Commissary Lane.

- An assortment of Disney characters throughout the day around the Sorcerer Mickey Hat.

- Miss Piggy and Kermit outside the exit of MuppetVision.

- Sorcerer Mickey in the Soundstage 1 lobby on Mickey Avenue.

- Donald and Daisy Duck, JoJo and Goliath on Mickey Avenue.

- An assortment of characters intermittently throughout the day in Entrance Plaza.

- *The Incredibles* characters inside the Magic of Disney Animation.

- The Green Army Men from *Toy Story* several times a day in front of the Sorcerer Mickey Hat.

of guests was struck by lightning and then disappeared. A bellhop invites you into a seemingly old, rusty service elevator that ascends and moves horizontally through several remarkable special effects but then, in the pitch-black space and without warning, plummets thirteen stories to the bottom. Up you go again, and down, and up, and down, during which you'll be treated to dazzling views of the park. If you can stand the thrill, don't miss this one—just be sure to ride it with an empty stomach. **Minimum height 40 inches (3 feet, 4 inches). Not recommended for expectant mothers; those with back, heart, or neck problems; or those prone to motion sickness. FASTPASS. 10-minute ride.**

NOTE: If you chicken out, there's an escape route immediately before entering the elevator; just ask a bellhop for directions.

INDIANA JONES EPIC STUNT SPECTACULAR

In this open-air theater is a fun stunt show that allows the audience to observe the choreography of safely performed stunts and special effects—and maybe even co-star. Indiana Jones is at it again, fleeing from a 12-foot rolling ball before heading to Cairo for a street scene with audience volunteers who play along with the professionals performing a variety of flips, drops, bullwhip-cracking, and fistfights. The show's grand finale finds Indiana making a dangerous escape through a wall of flames, a barrage of gunfire, a large dousing of water, and one massive explosion; be prepared to feel the heat. **Check your guidemap for showtimes. FASTPASS. 30-minute show.**

MUPPET★VISION 3-D

Another hoot of a 3-D movie and then some! Put on your special glasses and sit back to watch your host, Kermit the Frog, and the bumbling, fumbling Muppets. Miss Piggy's production is quite something, accompanied by a barrage of flying cream pies, fiber-optic fireworks, blasting cannons, floating bubbles, and squirting water. The grand finale is a major disaster, seemingly damaging the theater in another example of Disney wizardry. And who can forget Statler and Waldorf, the grumpy old geezers perched in their box seat in the balcony offering comical snide commentary throughout the wacky show? **25-minute show including preshow.**

LIGHTS, MOTORS, ACTION! EXTREME STUNT SHOW

Movie stunts are the highlight of Disney–MGM Studios' newest attraction, a thrill- a-minute show of super-fast, high-flying stunt cars, screaming motorcycles, and wild Jet-Skis with a cast of more than thirty. Located in the former residential street of the Backlot, this 5,000-seat theater has a 6½-acre stage set in a quiet French village that suddenly becomes crazy with action. Extra highlights include pyrotechnic effects, ramp jumps, high-falls, even a stuntman engulfed in flames. The premise is the filming of a European spy thriller complete with production crew, director, and stunt coordinator who detail how stunts are created, designed, and filmed. After completion, each scene is edited with the addition of "real" actors,

DINING WITH
AN IMAGINEER

Join an Imagineer, a member of the creative team behind Disney's latest theme park and resort projects, for an informal four-course lunch at the Hollywood Brown Derby's private Bamboo Room. A group of no more than eight people will talk about the creative process and what it's like for the Imagineer to work at such a magical place. Each person will receive a personalized souvenir dinner plate signed by the Imagineer. This program is mostly of interest to those age fourteen and older. It normally takes place Monday, Wednesday, and Friday at 11:30 A.M.; $61 for adults and $35 for children ages three through eleven plus park admission (price includes gratuity).

and then shown with close-up detail on a giant video screen. **FASTPASS. 35-minute show.**

WHO WANTS TO BE A MILLIONAIRE—PLAY IT!

In Disney's version of *Who Wants to Be a Millionaire,* a Philbinesque host leads contestants who vie for points to earn small prizes (no cash awarded here) while the audience plays along on individual keypads for a chance to be next to fill the "hot seat" (the trick is to correctly answer the questions and be quick about it). Those few making it to 1 million points are rewarded with a grand prize the likes of a three-night Disney cruise. Contestants may ask for help in the form of "50–50," "Ask the Audience," even "Phone a Complete Stranger" out on Mickey Avenue. It really is quite fun! **30-minute show occurs once each hour; see your guidemap for times.**

VOYAGE OF THE LITTLE MERMAID

Journey under the sea at one of Disney–MGM Studios' most beloved attractions. This tribute to the raven-haired mermaid Ariel combines puppetry, live actors, animated film, and delightful music with the adorable sidekicks Flounder and Sebastian and the not-so-adorable sea witch Ursula. Favorite songs from the movie, such as "Under the Sea," "Part of Your World," and "Poor Unfortunate Souls," along with great special effects including black lights, lasers, rain showers, bubbles, and lightning make this show quite a hit with children. Besides, how often do you have the opportunity to behold a seemingly live mermaid with a flopping tail? **FAST-PASS. 17-minute show.**

NOTE: Don't skip this wonderful attraction simply because you don't have small children in tow. If you would like a center seat, stand back a bit when the doors open into the theater from the preshow holding room and allow about half the crowd to enter before you. And plan on using a FASTPASS; your chances of getting in without one can be slim.

The Very Best Dining in Disney–MGM Studios

Hollywood Brown Derby. Re-creation of the famous Hollywood dining spot; lunch and dinner; best food and most sophisticated atmosphere in the park. (See full description in the Disney–MGM Studios Dining section of the Dining chapter.)

50s Prime Time Café. Dine in a 1950s sitcom where Mom is your waitress and all vegetables must be consumed; lunch and dinner. (See full description in the Disney–MGM Studios Dining section of the Dining chapter.)

Sci-Fi Dine-In Theater Restaurant. Relive the drive-in of your youth at this most unusual restaurant; lunch and dinner. (See full description in the Disney–MGM Studios Dining section of the Dining chapter.)

Mama Melrose's Ristorante Italiano. New York–style Italian restaurant with the best pizzas around; lunch and dinner. (See full description in the Disney–MGM Studios Dining section of the Dining chapter.)

Studio Catering Company. Great new counter-service concept offering fast casual, prepared-to-order food. Offerings include ground lamb kabobs with eggplant spread and chili sauce; marinated chicken with yogurt, cucumber, and tomato; steak gyro with hummus and tomato relish; Greek salad; chicken stew with saffron rice; vanilla panna cotta; fresh fruit éclair; honey almond stick; *children's menu:* chicken wrap with cream cheese spread; smoked ham wrap.

Special Entertainment

Disney Stars and Motor Cars Parade. Relive the glamorous days of Hollywood each afternoon when more than 100 characters in fifteen customized vintage cars based on Disney films are led by the wail of a police motorcycle escort. Cars are filled with the Playhouse Disney friends, Snow White and Dopey, the Little Mermaid, Lilo and Stitch, Aladdin and Jasmine, the Muppets, and more. The tail end of the character cavalcade is Mickey and Minnie chauffeured by Goofy and Donald Duck in a 1929 Cadillac. **15-minute parade.**

FANTASMIC! Sorcerer Mickey's fantasies soar to new heights in the 7,000-seat Hollywood Hills Amphitheater (with standing room for another 3,000). Each evening the mouse himself orchestrates this extravaganza atop a 40-foot mountain on his lagoon-bound island. While Mickey struggles with the forces of good and evil in a series of lavish dreams and wild nightmares, guests thrill to the sight of walls of dancing water and wild, windy storms accompanied by stirring music, choreographed laser effects, and projecting flames. A favorite segment is the procession of floats representing the best of Disney happy endings, quickly followed by a bevy of Disney villains. Of course, Mickey wins out and, to the delight of the audience, a steamboat stuffed with Disney characters sails past in anticipation of the grand finale of water, lasers, and fireworks.

For guaranteed seating with no waiting, book a FANTASMIC! Dinner Package available at Hollywood Brown Derby, Mama Melrose's, and Hollywood and Vine. Reservations can be made as early as ninety days in advance by calling (407) WDW–DINE, or (407) 939–3463, and must be prepaid at time of booking, with a forty-eight-hour cancellation policy for a full refund. The package is a fixed-price dinner that varies in cost according to the restaurant. After your meal you'll receive a seat ticket in a special reserved area on the far right of the theater, making it possible to arrive only thirty minutes prior to showtime. Reservations fill up quickly, so book as early as possible. **25-minute show.**

NOTE: I know it sounds tedious, but it's necessary to arrive about one hour prior to snare a seat; once the theater is full, you're out of luck. If you wait until twenty minutes prior, you have a good chance of a standing-room-only spot whose only advantage is a quick dash out once the show is over. In busy season when there are two shows, opt for the less crowded, final performance. If you'd like to be among the first out of the theater, take a seat in one of the back rows (really some of the better seats; the front rows can be a bit soggy). On windy or rainy nights, the show is sometimes canceled.

Special Events

ESPN the Weekend. It's the ultimate sports fan's weekend in February with star athletes, ESPN telecasts, ESPN personalities and sports celebrity motorcades and chats, plus *Who Wants to Be a Millionaire*—Play It! sports editions. Included in regular park admission.

***Star Wars* Weekend.** For five weekends in May and June, Disney–MGM Studios is filled with dozens of *Star Wars* characters, heroes, and villains. More than forty characters sign autographs, pose for pictures, and participate in motorcades and special editions of *Who Wants to Be a Millionaire*—Play It! Other activities include a talk show, question-and-answer sessions, and a child-oriented Jedi Training Academy. For updated information visit disneyworld.com/starwars. Included in regular park admission.

ABC Super Soap Weekend. More than thirty top stars from favorite ABC soaps are on hand one weekend in mid-November to sign autographs and pose for pictures as well as participate in special editions of the *Who Wants to Be a Millionaire*—Play It! game show, star motorcades, talk shows, and casting calls. If you're not a soap enthusiast, strongly consider steering clear of the park on this crazy weekend when the streets are jam-packed with fans running from one event to another. Included in regular park admission. Call (407) 397–6808 for up-to-date information.

Osborne Family Spectacle of Lights. From late November until early January, the park's Streets of America are dusted with "snow" and lit by 5 million colorful lights. It's quite a sight to see. Included in regular park admission.

Disney's Animal Kingdom

"We inherited this earth from our parents and are borrowing it from our children." This is the important message Disney strives to convey in its environmentally conscious theme park, the Animal Kingdom. It's quite a beauty with more than four million lush, towering plants, making it difficult to believe the park has only been open since 1998. Although the Animal Kingdom is five times the size of the Magic Kingdom, don't panic; it won't take two days to see everything. Remember much of the land is an enclave for the animals; the rest is easily conquered in a day.

The beauty of the Oasis hits you square in the face as you enter the park, a tropical jungle of flowering plants, cooling waterfalls, and overgrown plant life thriving with a menagerie of fascinating creatures. A cool mist pervades the air amid a cacophony of chattering birds and the aroma of fragrant trees and flowers on the variety of pathways leading to hidden grottoes, rushing streams, and towering vegetation. Critters housed in replicas of their natural habitats include macaws, an iguana, an exotic boar, a giant anteater, sloths, pig deer, and swan. They are surrounded by colossal banana trees, swaying palms, massive bamboos, and flowering orchids.

After making your way through the Oasis, cross the bridge over the Discovery River into the park's central hub, Discovery Island. Here visitors congregate to wander streets filled with lampposts, benches, and storefront facades carved with folk art animals. And here, all eyes are immediately drawn to the focal point of the park, the awesome Tree of Life.

Along with the main attractions are great hidden nooks and mysterious trails just waiting to be discovered. If you see a path leading off the main walkway, by all means follow it; it may just take you to a place of sheer enchantment. Take time to explore and discover the many marvelous natural settings throughout or risk leaving a bit disappointed when you haven't gasped the true significance of this magnificent theme park.

Park Basics

GETTING THERE

Those driving to Walt Disney World should take exit 65 off Interstate 4 and follow the signs to the Animal Kingdom.

USING WALT DISNEY WORLD TRANSPORTATION

From all Disney Resorts, Disney–MGM Studios, and Epcot: Board the bus marked ANIMAL KINGDOM.

From the Magic Kingdom: Take the monorail or ferry to the Ticket and Transportation Center (TTC) and then transfer to the bus marked ANIMAL KINGDOM.

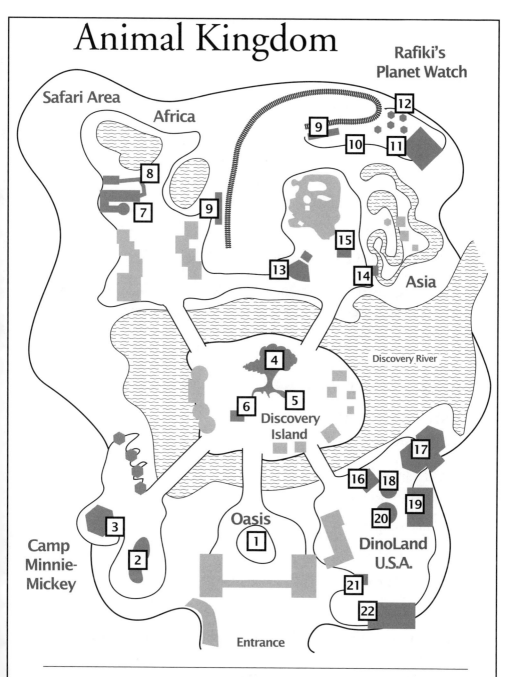

Animal Kingdom

Rafiki's Planet Watch

Safari Area

Africa

Asia

Discovery River

Discovery Island

Oasis

Camp Minnie-Mickey

DinoLand U.S.A.

Entrance

1. The Oasis Exhibits
2. Pocahontas and Her Forest Friends
3. Festival of the Lion King
4. The Tree of Life
5. It's Tough to be a Bug
6. Discovery Island Trails
7. Kilimanjaro Safaris
8. Pangani Forest Exploration Trail
9. Wildlife Express Train
10. Habitat Habit!
11. Conservation Station
12. Affection Section
13. Flights of Wonder
14. Kali River Rapids
15. Maharajah Jungle Trek
16. The Boneyard
17. Tarzan Rocks!
18. Fossil Fun Games
19. Primeval Whirl
20. Triceratop Spin
21. Dino-Sue
22. Dinosaur

PARKING

Cost is $8.00 per day; free to Walt Disney Resort guests and Annual Pass holders. Keep your receipt, good for parking at the Magic Kingdom, Epcot, and Disney–MGM Studios on that day only. Parking is conveniently located in front of the park. Trams circulate throughout the parking area for easy transportation to the entry gate. Make a note of what aisle and section you have parked in.

OPERATING HOURS

Open from 8:00 or 9:00 A.M. until around dark. Call (407) 824–4321 or log on to www.disneyworld.com for updated park hours.

The Oasis and Discovery Island normally open a half hour prior to official opening time. Arrive at least thirty to forty-five minutes early, allowing time to park, buy tickets, purchase a snack or cup of coffee, wander through the Oasis, and be one of the first to hit the big attractions. I recommend heading straight to Kilimanjaro Safaris. After Expedition Everest has opened (it is scheduled to debut in early 2006), head there first.

FASTPASS ATTRACTIONS

- DINOSAUR

- It's Tough to Be a Bug!

- Kali River Rapids

- Kilimanjaro Safaris

- Primeval Whirl

See the introduction to this chapter for FASTPASS details.

WHAT TO WEAR

This is the only Disney park that requires a bit of forethought in clothing. If you plan on riding the Kali River Rapids ride, be sure to wear fast-drying clothes and bring water footwear of some sort. You will more than likely become thoroughly soaked, and if you haven't dressed properly, you'll feel soggy for hours afterward.

PARK SERVICES

ATMs. A cash-dispensing bank machine is located just outside the park entrance.

Baby care center. An infant facility located behind the Creature Comforts shop on Discovery Island is outfitted with changing tables, high chairs, and a room for nursing mothers. Disposable diapers, bottles, formula, and baby supplies can be purchased. All restrooms throughout the park are outfitted with changing tables.

Cameras and film processing. Look for cameras, film, camcorder tapes, memory cards, and batteries at Garden Gate Gifts. Download your images from a digital media card to a CD here.

First aid. For minor medical problems head to the First Aid Center located behind the Creature Comforts shop on Discovery Island.

Guest Relations. Located just inside the park on the left is Guest Relations, where a knowledgeable staff is ready to assist with general information, advance reservations, ticket information, guidemaps, entertainment schedules, information for guests with disabilities, and more.

Guests with disabilities. A guidebook for guests with disabilities is available at Guest Relations. Guests with mobility disabilities should park adjacent to the Entrance Complex (ask at the Auto Plaza for directions). Wheelchairs and ECVs are available for rent. Most restaurants and shops at Animal Kingdom are accessible to guests with disabilities, although some counter-service locations have narrow queues with railings (ask a host or hostess for assistance). Companion-assisted restrooms are located at First Aid, Discovery Island opposite Flame Tree Barbecue, Africa in the Mombasa Marketplace, at Chester and Hester's Dinosaur Treasures in Dinoland, and in Asia near Maharajah Jungle Trek. Most attractions provide access through the main queue while others have auxiliary entrances for wheelchairs and service animals along with as many as five members of your party. Certain attractions require guests to transfer from their wheelchair to a ride system. Service animals are welcome in most locations of the park.

Braille guidebooks, assistive listening devices, video captioning, and audiotape guides are available at Guest Relations for a $25 refundable deposit. The attraction It's Tough to Be a Bug has reflective captioning.

DISCOVERY ISLAND CHARACTER LANDING

Immediately before crossing the bridge from Disney Island to Dinoland U.S.A., look for a pathway on the right leading to a boat dock on the Discovery River where Winnie the Pooh characters from the Hundred Acre Wood sign autographs and pose for pictures.

With seven-day notice, a sign language interpreter will be provided at live shows on Saturdays. Call (407) 824–4321 for more information.

Lockers. Lockers are located just outside the park entrance and just inside on the left for $7.00 per day, including a $2.00 refundable key deposit. If you're park-hopping, keep your receipt for another locker at the three other Disney theme parks for no extra charge.

Lost and Found. Located at Guest Relations or call (407) 824–4245.

Lost children. Locate lost children at the Baby Care Center or Guest Relations.

Package pickup. Purchases may be sent to Garden Gate Gifts for pickup at the end of the day. Allow three hours for delivery. Disney resort guests may send packages directly to their hotel for next-day arrival.

Pet kennel. A kennel is located just outside the park entrance. Daily rate is $6.00. Call (407) 824–6568 for information. Proof of vaccination is required.

Strollers and wheelchairs. Rentals are located next to Garden Gate Gifts on the right as you enter the park. Single strollers are $8.00 per day, double strollers $15.00, and wheelchairs $8.00 inclusive of a $1.00 refundable deposit. Electric convenience vehicles are $40.00, inclusive of a $10.00 refundable deposit. If you're park-hopping, keep your receipt for a same-day replacement at the three other Disney theme parks and Downtown Disney Marketplace.

The Lay of the Land

The Animal Kingdom's Main Street of sorts is the Oasis, a winding series of pathways leading to the hub, Discovery Island, whose focal point is the Tree of Life. The Animal Kingdom lands—Camp Minnie-Mickey, Africa, Asia, and Dinoland are accessible by crossing one of the bridges spanning the Discovery River that encircles Discovery Island. Africa, Asia, and Dinoland are interconnected by back pathways. Africa and Rafiki's Planet Watch are connected to one another by train tracks.

The Very Best Attractions in Disney's Animal Kingdom

IT'S TOUGH TO BE A BUG!

On the winding walkway leading to this attraction is a menagerie of wildlife, lush foliage, waterfalls, caves, and most importantly, an up close view of the marvelous animal carvings that make up the Tree of Life. It's always twilight in the low-ceilinged waiting area underneath the Tree, where chirping crickets sing Broadway tunes from such insect shows as *The Dung and I* (featuring the hit song "Hello Dung Lovers"), *Beauty and the Bees,* and *A Cockroach Line.* Flik (the star of *A Bug's Life*) is the host of this creepy-crawly 3-D movie of assorted bugs who only want humans to understand them. But much to the glee of the audience seated in the theater, they just can't help misbehaving. A favorite opening act is the stinkbug who accidentally lets his smelly, gaseous fumes rip right into the audience. As the show progresses you'll seem to be doused with bug spray, stung sharply in the back, and showered with termite acid, all innocently achieved through special effects. Receive one final surprise as the beetles, maggots, and cockroaches exit safely ahead of you. What a great show, a highlight of the park! **FASTPASS. 8-minute show.**

NOTE: Definitely one attraction too intense for young children, particularly when Hopper, the despicable grasshopper from *A Bug's Life,* scares the dickens out of every child under age five. If you'd like to sit in the center of the auditorium, hang back a little in the waiting area and allow some of the audience to enter ahead of you.

FESTIVAL OF THE LION KING

The all-important message of the continuing "circle of life" is wonderfully portrayed in this sensational stage extravaganza of Broadway-caliber song

DISCOVERY ISLAND TRAILS

Find time to walk the trails encircling the remarkable Tree of Life. You'll find cascading waterfalls, verdant gardens, animal habitats, and quiet resting spots among the pathways meandering along the Discovery River.

and dance. The story of the Lion King is told through a combination of elaborate costumes, wild acrobatic tumble monkeys, daring fire-twirlers, and massive Audio-Animatronics animal floats accompanied by the beat of tribal drums and jungle noise. Don't worry if you're not acquainted with the music; you'll be an expert by the time you leave. Plan your day around this don't-you-dare-miss-it show. **Check your guidemap for show-times. 30-minute show.**

NOTE: All 1,400 seats are great in this circular, now enclosed theater; however, arrive early in busy season to guarantee your party a spot. The first show of the day has the least attendance and requires less of an advance arrival. Children who would like to be chosen to participate in the closing parade should try to sit in the bottom section of the bleachers.

KILIMANJARO SAFARIS

You'll quickly discover Animal Kingdom's most popular attraction when almost every visitor makes a beeline straight to Africa at park opening. Load into safari vehicles for your trip around the 110-acre African savanna brimming with baobab trees, waterfalls, rivers, watering holes, and rickety bridges. Each excursion is different and depends entirely upon which animals decide to make an appearance. As you rumble across the authentic-looking landscape, your driver will assist in locating the wide assortment of wildlife including lions, cheetahs, warthogs, elephants, gazelles, crocodiles, wildebeests, exotic birds, giraffes, even white rhinos. Those with luck might encounter a male lion, rare because they sleep about eighteen hours a day. Some animals may come close to your vehicle, while predators and more perilous species only look as if they could from behind their seem-

SPECIAL PLACES IN ANIMAL KINGDOM

Discovery Island:

- Pathways surrounding the base of the Tree of Life.

- Shady seating area behind Flame Tree Barbecue where visitors can dine among waterfalls and lotus-filled ponds with prime views of the Discovery River.

Africa:

- Courtyard filled with covered tables, perfect for a cooling drink, behind Dawa Bar and Tusker House.

- Delightful shady patio behind Tamu Tamu Refreshments.

Asia:

Asia has some of the best hidden paths and secret places, all leading off the walkway in both directions. Just follow anything that looks like fun and see where it takes you.

- Path across the walkway from Flights of Wonder leading to a peaceful pagoda where there's usually a cooling breeze accompanied by prime views of the Discovery River and the Tree of Life.

- Secret path paralleling the main walkway between Asia and Africa with waterfalls and lush foliage.

- Lovely pagoda behind the multicolored ice cream truck.

- Short pathway leading to the banks of the Discovery River and the best views of the Tree of Life (take the first right after leaving Africa on your way to Asia).

ingly invisible barriers. The calm, soothing portion of the ride ends when ivory poachers are discovered, resulting in a wild, crazy chase. Of course, in Disney fashion, the bad guy has to pay. **Not recommended for expec-**

tant mothers or people with heart, back, or neck problems. **FASTPASS. 20-minute ride.**

NOTE: Don't run for cover during an afternoon thundershower; it's the animals' favorite time to come out for a rain bath.

PANGANI FOREST EXPLORATION TRAIL

Many people walk right past this self-guided trail and only when it's too late find out what they've missed. There are colobus monkeys at the Endangered Animal Rehabilitation Center and naked mole rats at the Research Center. Then on to a beautiful aviary holding birds native to Africa, a cooling waterfall (complete with faux mist), and an aquarium overflowing with kaleidoscopic fish. Soon all visitors are drawn to a terrific underwater observation tank of swimming hippos before hitting the real highlight—lowland gorillas. You'll find a family of six on the right side of the pathway and a group of four bachelors on the other side. Take time to search for them; it can sometimes be difficult to spot them in the profuse vegetation. Experts are scattered throughout to answer questions and give short, informative talks about each exhibit.

NOTE: Go early after the safari or late in the afternoon when crowds are low. It can be difficult to spot wildlife from behind rows of human heads.

EXPEDITION EVEREST

Disney is really getting on the bandwagon when it comes to thrilling coasters combined with innovative story lines. This 200-foot, high-speed train adventure set to open in 2006 is designed to climb through bamboo forests, past waterfalls and glacier fields, and then up to snowcapped peaks. The excitement truly begins when the train races forward as well as backward through icy caves and canyons until the inevitable meeting with Yeti!

KALI RIVER RAPIDS

Take a white-water rafting escapade down the churning waters of the Chakranadi River in Asia after boarding your twelve-seater circular raft. Float peacefully through a misty bamboo forest, past crumbling temples and cascading waterfalls, until the shocking devastation of old-growth rain forests destroyed by loggers appears. Soon your raft is speeding along

ANIMAL KINGDOM'S BEHIND-THE-SCENES TOURS

Fifteen percent discounts on tours are available to Annual Pass holders, Disney Vacation Club members, and AAA cardholders. Call (407) WDW–TOUR, or (407) 939–7687, for reservations.

Backstage Safari. On this three-hour tour, guest explore the animal housing areas, meet the keepers, and learn how the animals are cared for. Visit the nutrition center where animal food is prepared, and see the backstage area of the Veterinary Care Hospital at Conservation Station. Finish with a special tour through Kilimanjaro Safaris. *$65 plus park admission. Starts at 8:30 A.M. Monday, Wednesday, Thursday, and Friday. Guests must be age sixteen or older to participate.*

Wild By Design. Discover how the park's designers combined ethnic art and artifacts, authentic architecture, and story line to create the Animal Kingdom park on this three-hour tour. *$58 plus park admission. Starts at 8:30 A.M. Thursday and Friday. Guests must be age fourteen or older to participate. Those ages fourteen or fifteen must be accompanied by a participating adult.*

through wild water until everyone onboard is thoroughly drenched. Watch out for two stone elephants that love to squirt unsuspecting travelers. **Minimum height requirement 38 inches (3 feet, 2 inches). Not recommended for expectant mothers or those with heart, back, or neck problems. FASTPASS. 7-minute ride.**

NOTE: Don't miss this ride just because you don't like getting wet. Wear a rain poncho or lightweight, fast-drying clothing and footwear; on hot summer days you'll welcome the soaking. If you like water play, look for a button in the center of the bridge as you exit the attraction; push it to spray unwary rapids riders with streams of water shot from two stone elephants.

MARAJA JUNGLE TREK

Once again Disney has outdone itself with this sensational self-guided trail. Wander the grounds of the Anandapur Royal Forest through the ruins of a crumbling palace where you'll encounter spectacular wildlife beginning with the Komodo dragon, a giant lizard (look hard because it's in there somewhere). Next are Dracula-like flying foxes and Rodrigues fruit bats with 6-foot wingspans. Then the walk's highlight—Bengal tigers roaming the grasslands, surrounded by gentle deer and blackbucks, a type of antelope. This remarkable journey ends in the Asian bird sanctuary filled with the most exotic varieties imaginable.

NOTE: Take time to gaze at the marvelous details along the trail such as walls of fading murals, flapping Tibetan prayer flags, abandoned rickshaws, and authentic-looking pagodas.

DINOSAUR

Face fiery meteors and voracious predators on a trip back 65 million years to retrieve a 16-foot, plant-eating dinosaur and return with it before the big asteroid hits the earth. Load into twelve-passenger, all-terrain Dino Institute Time Rovers that rock, tilt, twist, and turn as they move through a dense, dark, prehistoric forest teeming with shrieking dinosaurs, giant lizards, and massive insects. When a hail of meteors strikes, off you go on a wild ride dodging shrieking, nostril-flaring Audio-Animatronics dinosaurs until the big scream encounter with a huge carnosaurus (the only meat-eating dinosaur) who'd like *you* for his dinner. **Minimum height 40 inches (3 feet, 4 inches). Not recommended for expectant mothers or those with heart, back, or neck problems. FASTPASS. 4-minute ride.**

NOTE: This ride is pretty intense for children not only because of massive, screaming dinosaurs but the scary anticipation in an extremely dark attraction.

The Very Best Dining in Disney's Animal Kingdom

What the Animal Kingdom lacks in full-service restaurants, it more than makes up for in some of the most visually delightful dining spots in all of Walt Disney World. Favorites are the Flame Tree Barbecue for its amazing and extensive, terraced seating overlooking the Discovery River and the Tusker House with its decent counter-service food. The park's only full-service restaurants are the Rainforest Café, with access from both outside and inside the park, and Restaurantosaurus, featuring a character buffet for breakfast only; the rest of the day it turns into a fast-food spot with McDonald's fare.

Rainforest Café. Enter through a thundering waterfall to dine among screeching and roaring jungle animals; breakfast, lunch, and dinner; priority reservations advised for lunch. (See full description in the Animal Kingdom Dining section of the Dining chapter.)

Tusker House. Dine in the Safari Orientation Centre or out back along the Discovery River (too bad a wall blocks the view); *breakfast:* scrambled eggs served with sausage, ham, or bacon and a biscuit, biscuits and gravy, fruit cup with yogurt, cereal, cinnamon roll, muffins, Danish pastry; *lunch and dinner:* grilled salmon, fried chicken sandwich, vegetable sandwich, grilled chicken salad, smoked turkey wrapped in flour tortilla with corn chowder; rotisserie chicken served with lovely mashed potatoes, savory gravy, and fresh green beans; cheesecake, chocolate cake, carrot cake; Budweiser and Safari Amber beer; *children's menu:* macaroni and cheese, chicken drumstick with mashed potatoes.

Restaurantosaurus. Dino Institute summer camp lodge cafeteria with mounted dinosaur heads, rustic twig chairs, and rock fireplaces; on balmy days head for the nifty screened-in porch for a quiet meal; *breakfast:* Donald's Breakfastosaurus, a character breakfast buffet hosted by Donald Duck himself; *lunch and dinner:* McDonald's with a twist; Chicken McNuggets, Happy Meals, burgers, hot dogs, Mandarin grilled chicken salad (quite good!), vegetarian burgers, fixings bar with sautéed onions, sauerkraut, and mushrooms; chocolate chip cookies, brownies; Budweiser and Safari Amber beer.

Special Entertainment

Mickey's Jammin' Jungle Parade. Carousing around the Tree of Life each afternoon is an island street party procession featuring Mickey and his gang joined by a bevy of giant rolling animal sculpture drums sounding out an energetic beat. Mickey, Minnie, Goofy, and Donald overload zany safari vehicles with their idea of exactly what should be taken on an extended vacation. They're accompanied by lofty animal puppets on stilts and rickshaws filled with lucky visitors chosen from the crowd, all adding up to one wacky parade. **15 minutes.**

NOTE: A great place to watch the parade is from the bridge between Africa and Discovery Island, quite often almost empty of people.

5

BEYOND THE THEME PARKS

Disney's Boardwalk

Inspired by the Mid-Atlantic wooden seaboard attractions of the 1930s, Disney's Boardwalk offers dining, shopping, and entertainment on the shores of Crescent Lake. Situated in front of the Boardwalk Inn and Villas and just outside of Epcot's International Gateway, it's the perfect destination for a before or after-Illuminations dinner at Spoodles or the Flying Fish, or a place to party down at Jellyrolls and Atlantic Dance, two very different nightclubs. The Boardwalk is at its best in the evening hours, when all the restaurants are open and entertainment in the form of arcades, midway games, musical performers, magicians, fortune-tellers, sword swallowers, caricature artists, and more is in high gear; don't bother during the daytime, when many of the restaurants are closed and entertainment is nil. Although Jellyrolls charges a small cover, there's no admission fee to walk the Boardwalk. For up-to-date information call (407) 939–3492.

Getting There

The Boardwalk is about a five-minute walk from Epcot's International Gateway; a short stroll from the Yacht and Beach Club, Beach Club Villas, and the Walt Disney World Swan and Dolphin; and a boat ride or twenty-minute walk from Disney–MGM Studios. If traveling from a Disney resort during park hours, take transportation to the closest theme park and then a bus to the Boardwalk Inn. After park hours it requires a trip to Downtown Disney's Pleasure Island bus stop and then a transfer to the Boardwalk Inn; a much less frustrating choice is to either drive a car and park it at the Boardwalk Inn or simply cab it.

Parking

Park in the complimentary self-park lot in front of the Boardwalk Inn. Valet parking is available for $6.00.

Hours

Dining hours vary, with some spots open as early as 7:00 A.M. for breakfast and others not closing until after midnight. Shop from 10:00 A.M. to 10:00 P.M. with the exception of the Screen Door General Store, open from 8:00 A.M. to midnight.

The Very Best Dining at the Boardwalk

Boardwalk Bakery. A good stop in the mornings on your way to Epcot or after Illuminations fireworks; open early morning until late night; sugar-free cheesecake, margarita pie, eclairs, tiramisu, napoleans, fruit tarts, cakes, cinnamon rolls, turnovers, muffins, cupcakes, cookies, doughnuts; specialty coffees, beverages, smoothies; roast beef and watercress, smoked Gouda and ham, smoked turkey, and Italian Muffuletta sandwiches; chicken Caesar salad; fruit; *breakfast:* egg, ham, and cheese burritos or breakfast sandwiches with cheese, egg, and Canadian bacon on an English muffin.

Boardwalk Pizza. Spoodles pizza whole or by the slice, calzone, meatball sandwich, garden salad, breadsticks; beer, wine, sangria, nonalcoholic beverages.

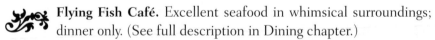 **Flying Fish Café.** Excellent seafood in whimsical surroundings; dinner only. (See full description in Dining chapter.)

Seashore Sweets. Ice cream and sweetshop; extremely popular after the Epcot fireworks; hand-dipped ice cream, cotton candy, confections, saltwater taffy, bulk candy, caramel apples; specialty coffees.

Spoodles. Mediterranean-inspired cuisine served in a family atmosphere; breakfast and dinner; convenient walk-up pizza window perfect for takeout. (See full description in Dining chapter.)

Nightclubs at the Boardwalk

Atlantic Dance. Video DJ nights on Tuesday, Wednesday, and Saturday, with music videos on a giant screen; mix of today's hits on Thursday and Friday; arrive at opening time and make a quick dash upstairs to the outdoor terrace for an excellent view of the Illuminations fireworks. Open 9:00 P.M. to 2:00 A.M.; guests must be at least twenty-one years old for admittance; closed Sunday and Monday. No cover charge.

Jellyrolls. Extremely popular dueling pianos and sing-along bar. Open 7:00 P.M. to 2:00 A.M.; guests must be twenty-one or older for admittance; $7.00 cover charge.

Downtown Disney

The addition of the West Side and Pleasure Island to Disney Marketplace created what is now known as the wildly successful Downtown Disney, a combination of more than seventy scene-setting restaurants, shops, and nightclubs. During the day it's a perfect getaway from the parks, but at night after the parks close, Downtown Disney truly comes alive.

At Disney Marketplace you'll find the largest Disney Store in the world, plenty of shopping, and the volcano-smoking Rainforest Café. Pleasure Island is a party lover's mecca with eight clubs and a nightly New Year's Eve celebration. And then there's the West Side, loaded with dining and entertainment venues including Wolfgang Puck Café, House of Blues, Gloria Estefan's Bongos, Cirque du Soleil, and DisneyQuest.

Getting There

Those driving should take Interstate 4 to exit 67 and follow the signs to Downtown Disney. Direct buses operate from all Disney resort hotels, with additional boat service from Old Key West and Saratoga Springs Resorts. Buses stop first at the Marketplace and then at Pleasure Island.

Parking

Parking here can prove difficult, particularly during busy season and weekend evenings when both locals and visitors alike jam Downtown Disney. If you're a guest of a Disney resort, consider using Disney transportation to avoid the hassle of parking. Self-parking is free; valet parking is no longer available.

Hours

Shops at Downtown Disney Marketplace are open Sunday through Thursday from 9:30 A.M. to 11:00 P.M. and Friday to Saturday and from 9:30 A.M. to 11:30 P.M. Pleasure Island clubs are open from 7:00 P.M. to 2:00 A.M., shops from 7:00 P.M. to 1:00 A.M. Downtown Disney's West Side shops are open Sunday through Thursday from 10:30 A.M. to 11:00 P.M. and Friday and Saturday from 10:30 A.M. to midnight. Restaurant hours vary; see specific restaurants for exact times.

Guest Relations

Stop here for advance reservations, lost and found, wheelchair and stroller rental, park passes, and services for guests with disabilities, along with general information. Facilities are located at both the West Side and the Marketplace.

ATMs

Withdraw cash from your bank account at ATMs located at Wetzel's Pretzels on the West Side, under the Rock 'n' Roll Beach Club at Pleasure Island, at the World of Disney, and at Guest Relations in the Marketplace.

Downtown Disney Marketplace

From its own marina offering boat rentals and fishing trips to a wide variety of shopping (including the largest Disney Store in the world) along with the ever-popular Rainforest Café and its rumbling volcano, this is one popular spot.

Marina and Boat Rental. Sea Raycers; pontoon boats; Boston Whaler Montauks; morning and afternoon two-hour guided fishing trips for as many as five people includes boat, guide, and equipment; specialty cruises for as many as twelve people. Call (407) WDW–PLAY, or (407) 939–7529, for reservations.

SHOPPING AT THE MARKETPLACE

Arribas Brothers. Crystal art in the form of vases, bowls, and other sparkling items; limited-edition jeweled crystal Mickey and Minnie; Swarovski crystal; on-the-spot engraving; glass blower.

Art of Disney. Disney collectibles; animation cells; watches personalized by a Disney artist; Lenox and Goebel Disney character figurines; Disney collectible dolls; Mickey and Minnie–etched Bohemia crystal flutes.

Disney's Days of Christmas. Whopper of a Disney Christmas store; Disney character ornaments and stockings; Victorian Disney character plush toys; tree skirts and toppers; Disney Spode Christmas plates; Christmas cards; have your purchases personalized on the spot.

Disney's Wonderful World of Memories. Disney scrapbooking materials, stickers, stationery, office and school supplies; cameras, film, and memory cards; photo albums; books about Disney.

Disney Tails. Store catering to pampered pets; Disney character costumes for pooches; Mickey ID tags; collars and leashes; treats; pet visors and hats; *fun find:* dog sofas in leopard or checked fabric.

Goofy's Candy Company. Cookies, fudge, Rice Krispies Treats, bulk candy, boxed and individual chocolates, candy apples, lollipops, muffins, cinnamon rolls; interactive candy show kitchen.

Lego Imagination Center. Giant Lego sculptures; 3,000-square-foot outdoor play area; every Lego set imaginable.

Mickey's Pantry. Unusual collection of Disney bed and bath items; Mickey logo dinnerware, cookie jars, and bath accessories; character aprons and oven mitts; Tigger plush pillows; Princess lamp, TV, and CD player; Mickey-etched martini shaker and glasses.

Once Upon a Toy. 16,000 square feet of Disney and Hasbro toys, many of them exclusive; bulk Lincoln Logs; build-your-own Mr. Potato Head station; Adventure Playset models of the monorail, Contemporary and Grand Floridian Resorts, Cinderella's Castle, Space Mountain, and more.

Team Mickey Athletic Club. Huge assortment of sports-related merchandise and clothing; Nike athletic shoes.

Summer Sands. Casual resort clothing and swimwear for all ages.

World of Disney. Largest Disney merchandise store in the world; 50,000 square feet crammed with just about every Disney item imaginable; elaborate displays in twelve themes.

THE VERY BEST DINING AT DOWNTOWN DISNEY MARKETPLACE

Portobello Yacht Club. Italian food in a nautical atmosphere; lunch and dinner. (See full description in Dining chapter.)

Rainforest Café. Follow the sound of a rumbling volcano to this extremely popular hot spot; lunch and dinner; dine amid waterfalls and exotic Audio-Animatronics jungle animals. (See full description in Dining chapter.)

Wolfgang Puck Express. Counter-service taste of Wolfgang Puck's inventive cuisine for breakfast, lunch, and dinner; pizza, Caesar and chinois salads, rotisserie chicken, quesadillas, pasta, soup, sandwiches, dessert; wood-fired breakfast pizzas, pancakes, waffles, French toast, pastries, fruits, cereals, omelets, bagels, muffins, cinnamon buns; coffee, juice.

Pleasure Island

It's New Year's Eve every night of the year at this six-acre playground for adults. Wall-to-wall clubs, a nightly street party with live entertainment, and a midnight fireworks presentation make this the party lover's choice for nighttime entertainment. You're welcome to stroll through for free, but a cover charge of $21 is imposed to enter into the eight clubs. You can also opt to purchase a Single Club Ticket for $10, only good for Rock'n'Roll Beach Club, BET SoundStage Club, Mannequins Dance Palace, Motion, or 8TRAX. No need to purchase a club ticket for admission to the Raglan Road Irish Pub; admission is complimentary. Children under eighteen are welcome here when accompanied by someone twenty-one years of age; however, only those eighteen years or older may visit Motion. Admission is limited to those older than eighteen at Mannequins Dance Palace Sunday through Wednesday, and twenty-one years of age and older Thursday through Saturday. While BET Soundstage Club has no age restrictions for admission Sunday through Wednesday, admission is limited to those twenty-one years of age and older Thursday through Saturday. All clubs are open from 7:00 P.M. until 2:00 A.M. daily.

NOTE: Unless you're in your twenties or love a crowd, avoid Thursday night, when the place is swamped with young Disney cast members who make this their night to party.

THE VERY BEST NIGHTCLUBS AT PLEASURE ISLAND

Adventurers Club. Improvisational and interactive comedy club where a costumed cast of veteran world travelers gets the crowd involved in shenanigans; rooms adorned with funky artifacts, silly photos, and quirky trophies and treasures circa 1930, some of which come to life when you least expect it; continuous entertainment, each act a bit more off-the-wall than the last.

Comedy Warehouse. Improvisational comedy delivered by the remarkably talented Who, What, and Warehouse players; several thirty-minute shows occur nightly, with no two exactly alike; arrive early for a seat, particularly on weekends and Thursday nights.

Mannequins Dance Palace. Award-winning dance club sporting the latest in DJ-driven dance music; dramatic state-of-the-art lighting and super sound system; rotating dance floor; three stories of contemporary furnishings and sleek bars; performances by the Explosion Dancers; must be age twenty-one or older to enter on Friday and Saturday.

Motion. Top 40 music club; two levels of DJ-driven music, blue lights, and big-screen music videos; guests must be at least eighteen years old to enter.

Pleasure Island Jazz Company. Sophisticated club with a New Orleans feel; live jazz and blues performers nightly; long list of cocktails, specialty coffees, and wines by the glass; four shows nightly beginning at 8:15 P.M.

THE VERY BEST SHOPPING AT PLEASURE ISLAND

Changing Attitudes. Disney logo merchandise geared to the teen set.

DTV. Disney logo sports clothing; golfing accessories.

Reel Finds. Hollywood motif T-shirts, mugs, refrigerator magnets, and postcards.

Downtown Disney's West Side

Perhaps the most popular area of Downtown Disney is the West Side. Some big names are here, including the House of Blues, Wolfgang Puck Café, and Gloria Estefan's Bongos together with big entertainment in the form of Cirque du Soleil, a twenty-four-screen AMC movie theater, and DisneyQuest. It's always hopping, but those preferring a bit of peace and quiet can opt for a quiet stroll along the pleasant promenade running beside the Buena Vista Lagoon. This is the perfect place to allow teens to assert their independence with an evening out on the town minus the parents.

AMC THEATERS

Watch newly released flicks in this state-of-the-art, twenty-four-screen theater. Call (407) 827–1308 for movie listings and showtimes.

CIRQUE DU SOLEIL

The tent-shaped building overpowering the West Side of Downtown Disney is none other than Cirque du Soleil, the most talked about entertainment venue in town. Although I've heard it described as a type of circus, it's actually a mixture of circus, dance, drama, and street entertainment, more than worth the hefty price of admission. And because of its immense popularity, think about booking your seats way in advance.

It's difficult to explain this extraordinary event. The show, entitled *La Nouba*, has more than sixty mesmerizing human performers (no animals) in outrageous costumes entertaining in the midst of exciting live music (not one syllable is uttered throughout the show) and surrealistic choreography. Witness daring, gravity-defying acts, each one more outlandish and bizarre than the next. Two showstoppers are the young Chinese girls who perform a routine with a diabolo, a Chinese yo-yo (You won't believe it!), and a trampoline finale with power men literally running up the sides of a wall. The sheer physical strength of these performers is absolutely amazing and quite a sight to see. Tickets can be purchased up to 180 days in advance by calling (407) 939–7719, or going online at www.cirquedu soleil.com or www.omniticket.net/wdwcds; there are two ninety-minute performances Tuesday through Saturday, at 6:00 and 9:00 P.M.; no shows Sunday and Monday; three levels of ticket prices according to seating.

NOTE: Although some seats are better than others, there really isn't a bad seat in the house. You may want to avoid the first row of the highest tier; the wheelchair-accessible seats in front block your view a bit.

DISNEYQUEST

With five floors of virtual games and interactive adventures diverse enough to entertain the entire family, this indoor theme park offers a multitude of attractions (including more than 180 video games) that can be played over and over for the single cost of admission. Become a swashbuckling pirate in a fierce battle for treasure at the virtual, 3-D adventure **Pirates of the Caribbean: Battle for Bucaneer Gold;** watch a large projection screen while paddling with motion-sensor oars on a prehistoric, white-water adventure with the **Virtual Jungle Cruise;** fly through the ancient city of Agrabah on your magic carpet in search of precious jewels in a virtual reality setting on **Aladdin's Magic Carpet Ride;** design your own thrilling roller-coaster ride with **Cyberspace Mountain** (perhaps the most popular attraction); play space-age bumper cars with **Buzz Lightyear's AstroBlaster;** or soar through a 3-D comic book while fighting supervillains sword-to-sword in virtual reality with **Ride the Comix.** Upstairs are two stories of food choices including a food court of sorts run by the Cheesecake Factory. Open Sunday through Thursday from 11:30 A.M. to 11:00 P.M. and Friday and Saturday from 11:30 A.M. to midnight. Admission prices are $34 for adults and $28 for children ages three through nine; same-day reentry allowed with ticket and hand stamp; Annual Pass holders and Disney Vacation Club members receive a discount. Guests age nine or younger must be accompanied by someone age sixteen or older, all of whom must pay admission.

NOTE: Come during the daytime on weekdays and avoid rainy days. Although DisneyQuest is mainly geared to kids and adolescents, it's a great place for quality family time. Adults traveling alone may want to pass unless they really enjoy this type of entertainment.

THE VERY BEST SHOPPING AT DOWNTOWN DISNEY'S WEST SIDE

Disney's Candy Cauldron. Scrumptious candy made on the spot; candy and caramel apples, chocolates, chocolate-covered strawberries, fudge, cookies, cotton candy, lollipops, Rice Krispies Treats, chocolate-covered pretzels, bulk candy.

Guitar Gallery by George's Music. Electric and acoustic guitars; collectible instruments (some as high as $20,000); guitar books and accessories.

Hoypoloi. Beautiful glass items for the home; sculpture in glass, metal, and wood; Zen-inspired gifts; scented candles; whimsical lamps; indoor water sculptures.

Magic Masters. Magic emporium filled with all the trappings needed for hocus-pocus fun; magic tricks, kits, and books; continuous demonstrations, many of which are explained behind the store's bookcase.

Magnetron. Every refrigerator magnet imaginable.

Mickey's Groove. Everything Mickey Mouse, including clothing, hats, and merchandise, even a Mickey TV; *fun find:* set of hors d'oeuvres plates, each with a different Mickey figure.

Sosa Family Cigars. Fine cigars; smoking accessories; master cigar roller in action Thursday through Saturday evenings.

Starabilias. Nostalgic star memorabilia; autographed LPs; signed movie posters; huge assortment of collectibles, the most expensive being a $250,000 guitar signed by forty-two of the greatest musicians ever to play; CD jukebox.

Virgin Megastore. Home to a mammoth selection of music; books, magazines, software, videos; great children's section; Coco Moka Café serving coffee, beverages, and pastries, with an outdoor patio high above the West Side.

THE VERY BEST DINING AT DOWNTOWN DISNEY'S WEST SIDE

Bongos. Cuban-themed restaurant and entertainment spot owned by Latina pop star Gloria Estefan; lunch and dinner. (See full description in Dining chapter.)

House of Blues. Mississippi Delta–style dishes for lunch and dinner; Sunday Gospel Brunch; live blues Thursday through Saturday nights; those dining at the restaurant the day of a concert can bypass the concert line. (See full description in Dining chapter.)

Wolfgang Puck. Four separate dining concepts in one facility: cafe with both indoor and patio seating; upscale dining room on second floor (dinner only); Lounge Sushi Bar; express patio dining. (See full description in Dining chapter.)

Water Parks

Choose from two Disney water parks, each with its own brand of entertainment. At Blizzard Beach you'll find the exhilarating 120-foot Summit Plummet slide, and at the tropical Typhoon Lagoon there's a whopper of a surf pool. Both parks are beautifully themed and landscaped, and each offers something for just about everyone. And because the pools are heated in the cooler months, it's a year-round playground.

During the sizzling summer months, it's important to arrive early in the morning if you want to avoid the long lines that start forming at almost every attraction by midday; in fact, parks are sometimes filled to capacity by midmorning, and new guests are kept from entering until late in the afternoon. Weekends are the worst, when the locals add to the swell. Be sure to bring water footwear to protect tender feet from the scorching hot pavements.

Locker and towel rentals are available at both parks; life jackets are complimentary. Ice chests are allowed as long as they don't contain alcoholic beverages or glass containers (alcoholic drinks may be purchased at the parks). An adult must accompany children ages nine or younger, and all swim attire must be free of rivets, buckles, or exposed metal. Parking is free. Both parks are on a rotating schedule of refurbishment in the winter months, so check ahead.

NOTE: In the busy summer months when the water parks are open until 8:00 P.M., think about arriving in mid- to late-afternoon when the morning guests are beginning to depart. It's the best time to enjoy the attractions minus the crowds.

Blizzard Beach

Disney's largest water park features the strange theme of a melting alpine ski resort in the middle of the hot Florida sunshine. The thaw has created a watery "winter" wonderland where chairlifts carry swimmers instead of skiers up a 90-foot-high mountain to slalom bobsled runs that are now thrilling waterslides. Although you'll find plenty of tame attractions, this is Disney's water park for daredevils, with wild, rushing water and death-defying slides. Upon arrival head straight for Summit Plummet to avoid huge lines later in the day.

Hours vary according to the season but are usually 10:00 A.M.–5:00 P.M., with extended hours until 8:00 P.M. in summer. In cooler months the two water parks are open on a rotating basis, with one open and the other closed for refurbishment. Call (407) 560–3400 for up-to-date information. Admission prices are $34 for adults and $28 for children ages three through nine. Tots ages two or younger get in free.

GETTING THERE

Blizzard Beach is located in the Animal Kingdom area on West Buena Vista Drive. If using Disney transportation, direct buses depart from all resorts. Those driving should take exit 65 off Interstate 4.

THE VERY BEST ATTRACTIONS AT BLIZZARD BEACH

Meltaway Bay. One-acre wave pool with "melting snow" waterfalls. Swells here are not as intense as those at Typhoon Lagoon.

Runoff Rapids. Those in search of a thrill-but-not-a-scare will love this attraction. Tube down your choice of three runs (one is enclosed, the others open) for blast of a ride. To reach this attraction, go behind Mt. Gushmore to pick up a tube at the bottom of a tall flight of stairs and start climbing.

Summit Plummet. The king of water park attractions. From the top is a 120-foot plunge at speeds of up to 55 mph. The slide itself is a 350-foot speed trap where daredevils body slide so fast they don't know what hit them as they plummet to the bottom.

Teamboat Springs. One of the most popular rides in the park, this 1,200-foot attraction is the longest white-water raft ride in the world. Accommodating anywhere from three-to-five-people per raft, it twists and turns through a fun-filled succession of rushing waterfalls.

Toboggan Racers. If you're looking for a challenge on this eight-lane mat slide, go headfirst down the steep slope.

THE VERY BEST DINING AT BLIZZARD BEACH

Avalunch. Foot-long hot dogs, barbecue pork, turkey, and ham and cheese sandwiches; ice cream, cookies; *children's menu:* PB&J sandwiches.

Lottawatta Lodge. Ski lodge–style eatery, the largest in the park; burgers, pizza, fried chicken sandwiches, turkey sandwiches, chicken wrap, Southwest chicken salad, chili dogs; ice cream, cookies; *children's menu:* chicken strips, hot dog.

Warming Hut. Hot dogs, barbecue pork sandwiches, chicken wrap, ribs, smoked turkey legs; ice cream, cookies.

THE VERY BEST SHOPPING AT BLIZZARD BEACH

Beach Haus. Swimsuits and cover-ups; water footwear.

Typhoon Lagoon

At this beauty of a water park, you'll find a 56-acre tropical fantasyland. The premise is that a great storm swept everything in its path to a once sleepy resort town that became Typhoon Lagoon. The shipwrecked shrimp boat, *Miss Tilly*, perched atop the 95-foot-high summit of Mount Mayday, creates a ruckus every half hour when it tries in vain to dislodge itself by spewing a geyser of water high above the park. Geared toward a bit tamer crowd than Blizzard Beach, only one waterslide here is a daredevil's delight. The park's main draw is the 2.75-million-gallon wave pool that boasts some of the tallest simulated waves in the world (some as high as 6 feet tall).

Before park opening on Monday, Tuesday, and Friday is your chance to take surfing lessons in the huge wave pool with surfboards provided. Participants must be at least eight years old and must be strong swimmers. Cost is $135 per person. Call (407) WDW–SURF, or (407) 939–7873, for reservations.

Hours vary according to the season but are usually 10:00 A.M.–5:00 P.M. with extended hours until 8:00 P.M. in summer. During the cooler months, the two parks open on a rotating basis with one always closed for refurbishment. Call (407) 560–4141 for up-to-date information. Admission prices are $34 for adults and $28 for children ages three through nine. Tots ages two and younger get in free.

GETTING THERE

Typhoon Lagoon is located across Buena Vista Drive from Downtown Disney's West Side just off Interstate 4, exit 67. If using Disney transportation, the bus to catch is marked DOWNTOWN DISNEY/TYPHOON LAGOON.

THE VERY BEST ATTRACTIONS AT TYPHOON LAGOON

Crush'n'Gusher. This new attraction billed as a water coaster thrill ride is the only one of its kind in Central Florida. Whisk along a series of flumes and spillways, experiencing torrents of water while weaving in and out of a rusty old tropical fruit factory. Choose from three different spillways ranging between 410- and 420-feet long with a variation of slopes and turns.

Humunga Kowabunga. This trio of 214-foot speed slides is only for the most daring of thrillseekers. Fly along at speeds around 30 mph, a feat for those with strong hearts. Lines can be excruciatingly long, so head for this attraction first thing in the morning.

Shark Reef. Pick up your snorkeling gear and prepare yourself for the bracingly cold saltwater of Shark Reef. Instructors are on hand to help guide inexperienced snorkelers as they swim through a short-but-sweet pool of tropical fish, stingrays, and harmless sharks.

Storm Slides. Corkscrew through 300 feet of caves and waterfalls at speeds of 20 mph. Try all three slides—each offers a different experience than the one before it.

Typhoon Lagoon Surf Pool. This is the park's main attraction. What sounds like a typhoon warning is a foghorn announcing the impending wave soon to follow; some waves are as high as 6 feet. Separate but nearby, you'll find a lagoon made for children too small to handle the big waves.

THE VERY BEST DINING AT TYPHOON LAGOON

Leaning Palms. Hot dogs, chili dogs, cheeseburgers, hot deli sandwiches, fried chicken sandwiches, cheese and pepperoni pizza, grilled chicken Caesar salad; ice-cream novelties, cookies; *children's menu:* grilled cheese pretzel, hot dog, PB&J sandwich.

Typhoon Tilly's. Fish-and-chips, chicken wrap, chicken Caesar salad, barbecue pork sandwiches, ribs, hot dogs, chicken tenders; chocolate chip cookies, ice cream; *children's menu:* grilled cheese pretzel, hot dog, PB&J sandwich.

THE VERY BEST SHOPPING AT TYPHOON LAGOON

Singapore Sal's. Swimwear; resort clothing; beach towels; hats; water footwear; sandals; sunglasses; sunscreen; Typhoon Lagoon logo merchandise.

Spas

When your muscles are aching and your body is screaming for rest after days at the parks, soothe your jangled nerves at one of Orlando's spas. Immerse yourself in luxury with a feel-good treatment or two guaranteed to rejuvenate and swiftly get you back on your feet and ready for another long day of walking the parks.

Grand Floridian Spa

A 9,000-square-foot spa and health club offering a broad range of treatments and packages along with an adjoining health club. Using citrus products in its sixteen treatment rooms, the spa is known for its excellent therapists who vie to work at "the Most Magical Place on Earth." Separate women and men's locker rooms are equipped with whirlpools, Turkish steam baths, saunas, robes, slippers, hot tea, coffee, and fruit. For a true royalty treatment consider the Ultimate Day Spa Package, a full day of pampering. Open 6:00 A.M. to 9:00 P.M., with treatment hours from 8:00 A.M. to 8:00 P.M. daily. Guests ages ten and older are welcome in the spa, although an adult must accompany those under age eighteen. Call (407) 824–2332 for information and reservations.

Don't leave without buying: Jurlique Herbal Recovery Gel with plant-derived essential oils of grape seed, green tea, and turmeric.

Must-have treatment: Two-hour Aromatherapy Massage and Body Wrap, a calming Swedish aromatherapy massage followed by warm compresses and heat while wrapped to encourage absorption of healing essential oils. Finish with a scalp massage.

SAMPLE SERVICES

Citrus Zest Therapies. An aromatherapy massage using the spa's signature ruby red grapefruit body oil, finished with reflexology to restore balance and relieve stress.

Grand Romantic Evening. In a candlelit couples room, each person receives an aromatherapy massage.

My First Facial. Designed for children age twelve or younger to introduce the basics of skin care.

O.C. Exfoliating and Detoxifying Body Masque. Begin with a warm aromatherapy bath followed by an herbal gel exfoliation. Your body is then covered in detoxifying clay.

Peaceful Nights Bath. Candlelight bath with essential oils and bubbling jets, perfect after a day in the parks.

Spa at Disney's Saratoga Springs Resort

Well, the old Disney Institute Spa has been revamped, updated, and renamed, and aren't we glad! The Adirondack stone therapy massage, using heated stones and aromatherapy oil to massage the entire body, is terrific—the effects lasted for days (ask for Natalie). There are ten treatment rooms plus a spa lounge for tea (I wish Disney would lose the

Styrofoam cups) and fruit. Each locker room has steam, sauna, and whirlpool. Within the spa is a fitness center with an exclusive line of Life Fitness and Hammer Strength equipment. Open from 6:00 A.M. to 9:00 P.M., with treatment hours from 8:00 A.M. to 8:00 P.M. daily. Call (407) 827–4455 for reservations.

Don't leave without buying: The maple–brown sugar exfoliating polish used in the body polish treatment at the spa.

Must-have treatment: One of the hydromassage therapies using a hydrotherapy tub with jets that gently massage your entire body.

SAMPLE SERVICES

Couple's Relaxation. One person receives a forty-five-minute aromatherapy massage while the other is in the hydrotherapy tub in the same room. Then they switch, with tea in between.

Geyser Spring Hydro Massage Therapy. An herbal mixture of birch and amica in the hydrotherapy tub for soothing muscular aches and pains, soreness, and overexertion combined with an antioxidant scrub and lemongrass mineral salts.

Marine Algae Body Masque and Wrap. A nourishing sea treatment formulated from algae grown along the Brittany coast of France to hydrate the skin and stimulate natural detoxification.

Mystical Forest Therapies. A signature treatment that combines reflexology and Swedish massage.

Saratoga Springs Deluxe Facial. Two masks and a hand and foot massage.

Canyon Ranch SpaClub at Gaylord Palms Resort

Gaylord Palms Resort has a winner with its superluxurious, 20,000-square-foot spa facility run by the renowned Canyon Ranch. With an emphasis on mind, body, and spirit, the twenty-five soothing treatment rooms, tea-and-relaxation room, and men's and women's locker rooms, each with steam and sauna, make this one place to write home about. On the way out, check out the makeup and skin care products at the Spa Boutique. There's an adjoining fitness club as well as a full-service salon. A full menu of services is available online at www.canyonranch.com. Open from 8:00 A.M. to 9:00 P.M. daily. Call (407) 586–2051 for spa reservations.

Don't leave without buying: *The Canyon Ranch Guide to Living Younger Longer,* available only at Canyon Ranch Spas.

Must-have treatment: The Euphoria, a one hundred-minute, total relaxation experience with scalp massage, body mask and buff, tub soak, and light massage.

SAMPLE SERVICES

Ayurvedic Facial. Holistic facial that uses five ancient beauty techniques to cleanse, detoxify, and nourish the system.

Canyon Ranch Massage. Full-body massage to aid circulation, relieve tension, and promote relaxation.

Canyon Ranch Stone Massage. Therapist applies essential oils and uses heated and cooled basalt stones as extensions of his or her hands for massage.

Mango Sugar Glo. A conditioning body scrub derived from natural sugars, jojoba esters, and beta-carotene for radiant skin, followed by immersion in a whirlpool tub and then application of moisturizer.

Udvartana. The body is coated with herb-enhanced oil, a herbal body mask applied, then buffed off, ending with an oil application to hydrate and balance.

Mandara Spa at Portofino Bay Hotel

Mandara Spa has taken over the facilities at Portofino Bay Hotel, where you'll find fourteen treatment rooms as well as two Spa Suites with a Vichy shower and hot tub. The specialty here is the Balinese service, a traditional healing system passed down from mothers to daughters. An adjoining fitness center, complimentary with a spa treatment, has a full gym with sauna and locker facilities. In-room or in-cabana massage is available as well. Open from 6:00 A.M. to 10:00 P.M., with personal services and salon available from 7:00 A.M. to 10:00 P.M. daily. Call (407) 503–1244 for an appointment.

Don't leave without buying: Elemis Skin Nourishing Milk Bath.

Must-have treatment: Mandara Four Hands Massage, with two therapists working on you simultaneously in synchronicity and silence.

SAMPLE SERVICES

Balinese Massage. A combination of stretching, acupressure, and Swedish massage.

Elemis Aroma Stone Therapy. Small heated stones placed on key energy points are used to massage the body.

Elemis Exotic Coconut Rub and Milk Ritual Wrap. Warm milk bath poured over your entire body and then a cocoon foil wrap.

La Thérapie HydraLift Facial. Antiaging lifting and hydrating facial using Galvani Stimuli and Hi-Frequency.

Traditional Javanese Lulur. A traditional cleansing ceremony with a polish of turmeric, red rice, fenugreek, cempak, and ylang-ylang, finished by a massage.

Ritz-Carlton Spa

Hands down, this is the most luxurious spa in all of Orlando. A 40,000-square-foot, Mediterranean palazzo-style facility, it's an exquisite oasis of soothing perfection. *Citrus* is the word here, with citrus-inspired products used in the spa's forty treatment rooms where you're lavishly pampered and indulged. For the ultimate in luxury, book one of the VIP suites offering half- or full-day programs along with a spa lunch, served on the suite's elegant balcony. Another bonus is the exclusive use of the spa's outdoor heated lap pool. Open from 8:00 A.M. to 9:00 P.M. daily. Call (407) 393–4200 for treatment reservations.

The 6,000-square-foot Wellness Center within the spa is phenomenal, with each Movement Studio's cardiovascular equipment sporting its own personal fan, TV monitor, and headset. Classes are available for a fee, including yoga, Pilates, indoor cycling, cardio-muscle mix, and total body conditioning. Open from 5:00 A.M. to 11:00 P.M. daily.

The Carita Salon features stylist consultations and scalp massage, aromatherapy manicures and pedicures, volcanic stone manicures, and makeup application and lessons along with traditional hair services. The Retail Store sells Carita products, candles, casual clothing, and lingerie. And if hunger pains strike, try the Vitale Spa Café offering healthy appetizers, sandwiches, salads, and low-fat desserts.

Don't leave without buying: A Ritz-Carlton brushed doeskin spa robe.

Must-have treatment: Ashiatsu Massage, an ancient form of body work where therapists use their feet to perform deep compression to bring about a change in soft tissue damage as well as provide deep relaxation and stimulation to the lymphatic system.

SAMPLE SERVICES

East Indian Lime Scalp and Body Massage. A scalp and full body massage using a recipe of avocado, macadamia, and hazelnut oils blended with wild lime blossom, ginger, and sandalwood.

Four Hands Massage. Full-body Swedish massage performed simultaneously by two therapists.

Rain Forest Stones. Begin with a light exfoliation followed by a Vichy waterfall and an application of tropical passion fruit extracts and heated stones.

Thai Massage. Combines shiatsu with yoga stretches for a deep, energetic experience.

Tuscan Citrus Cure. Begin with a citrus scrub and lime shower followed by a massage using Italian extracts of bergamot, green mandarin, and lemon. End with a citrus hydrosoak and sweet orange body wrap.

Special Excursions

Although everything at Walt Disney World seems special, a handful of experiences really take the cake. Plan on at least one of the following excursions to make your stay extra-unique, a memory to last a lifetime.

Catch a Wave

Learn to surf before park opening hours at Typhoon Lagoon. Guests must furnish their own transportation to the park, because buses are not up and running that early in the morning. Cost is $135. Offered Monday, Tuesday, and Friday at 6:30 A.M. Participants must be at least eight years old and strong swimmers. Maximum of thirteen people per class. Surfboards provided. Call (407) 939–7529 for reservations up to sixty days in advance.

Celebrate Your Special Day

Step aboard a pontoon boat complete with driver, birthday cake, and beverages at any of the Walt Disney World marinas for an especially memorable birthday. $207 for as many as twelve people. Call (407) WDW–PLAY, or (407) 939–7529.

Enjoy a Picnic Cruise

Book a picnic cruise on a pontoon boat from any Disney marina, including boat, driver, sandwiches, soda, and snacks. It's a perfect way to spend an afternoon in the Florida sunshine. Prices begin at $188 for four plus $19 for each additional person for as many as twelve people total. Call (407) WDW–PLAY, or (407) 939–7529, for reservations.

Hit the Water

For true action head to the Contemporary Resort, where waterskiing, wakeboarding, and tubing are offered for $140 per hour including boat, driver, and instruction. Personal watercraft cost $65 for thirty minutes. Regular parasailing packages begin at $90 per flight for a single and $140 for a tandem, including eight to ten minutes in the air and 450 feet of line. Premium packages begin at $105 for a single and $155 for a tandem, including ten to twelve minutes in the air and 600 feet of line. Participants must weigh at least a total of 100 pounds and no more than 300 pounds. For reservations call (407) WDW–PLAY, or (407) 939–7529, up to ninety days in advance.

Hunt for Buried Treasure

Children ages four through ten sail from the dock of the Grand Floridian Resort on a two-hour Pirate's Cruise to a deserted island. The $30 fee includes snacks, bandanas, and treasure. Starts at 9:30 A.M. Monday, Wednesday, Thursday, and Saturday. Call (407) WDW–DINE, or (407) 939–3463, for reservations.

Indulge in Your Very Own Yacht

For the ultimate in luxury, charter Disney's 45-foot Sea Ray yacht, the *Grand I*, moored at the marina at the Grand Floridian Resort. Accommodating as many as twelve people, it includes a captain and a deckhand. Private butler service, food, and cocktails are available for an additional charge. Basic cost is $375 per hour. Call (407) 824–2439 for reservations up to ninety days in advance.

Play Cowboy

Disney's Fort Wilderness offers many opportunities for the frustrated cowboy. Book a ride in an antique carriage for a spin around the 700-acre resort (available from 6:00 to 10:00 P.M. daily, $30 for thirty minutes; call (407) 824–2832 for reservations). Or perhaps an old-fashioned, horse-drawn wagon ride, departing nightly at 7:00 and 9:30 from Pioneer Hall on a first-come, first-served basis (forty-five-minutes; $8.00 per adult and $4.00 per child). Group wagon rides are available for $125 per hour (call 407–824–2832 for reservations). Cowhands should consider a guided trail ride ($30 per person with a minimum age of nine and height of 48 inches [4 feet] and a maximum weight of 250 pounds; call 407–WDW–PLAY, or 407–939–7529). Younger children can opt for a $2.00 pony ride at the Fort Wilderness Petting Farm.

Saddle Up

Equestrian enthusiasts should head to the Villas of Grand Cypress Equestrian Center, an excellent facility open to the public just down the road from Downtown Disney. Featured are trails rides, pony rides, junior and adult riding camps, and private instruction. Call (407) 239–1938 or go online at www.grandcypress.com/equestrian_center for more information.

Take Tea with Alice

Children simply love the Wonderland Tea Party held at the Grand Floridian Resort, hosted by *Alice in Wonderland* characters. The one hour, fifteen-minute party includes games, storytelling, and apple juice "tea." $30. Held Monday through Friday at 1:15 P.M. Strictly for children ages three through ten. Call (407) WDW–DINE, or (407) 939–3463, for reservations.

Watch Disney's Nighttime Extravaganzas on a Fireworks Cruise

Depart from the docks of the Boardwalk, Yacht Club, and Magic Kingdom Resorts for a special viewing of either the Wishes fireworks display at the

Magic Kingdom or Illuminations at Epcot. Your captain will cruise Disney's waterways before anchoring at a prime viewing spot. Illumination cruises are offered nightly with your choice of either a 24-foot pontoon boat seating ten or a beautiful 24-foot reproduction of a 1930s Chris Craft, the *Breathless*, accommodating six or seven people. Reservations can be made up to ninety days in advance and sometimes sell out on the first day. Approximately $141–$211. Call (407) WDW–PLAY, or (407) 939–7529.

6

SPORTING DIVERSIONS

I f you love the outdoors, Orlando is definitely the place to head. In addition to an overabundance of theme parks, you'll also find a wealth of sporting activities—golf courses everywhere you turn, tennis courts at almost every resort, plenty of pathways for bicycling and jogging, and miles of waterways for boating and fishing. Those with a bigger appetite for adventure can even try driving a race car. The sunny Florida weather almost guarantees year-round access, with the exception of an occasional cold snap or two. And if spectator sports are your thing, there's the Wide World of Sports located right on Disney property.

Golf

Disney Golf

There's certainly no lack of choice when it comes to playing a round of golf while visiting Mickey Mouse. In fact, some people have been known to never quite make it to the parks, so intent are they on playing all of Disney's ninety-nine holes. Each course offers full-service clubhouse facilities, including pro shops, driving ranges, locker rooms, on-course beverage service, snack bars and restaurants, and equipment rentals. Guests of Disney resorts receive complimentary taxi transportation and special rates. For up-to-date information and fees, visit the Disney golf Web site at www.golf.disneyworld.com.

Instruction. Available from the PGA Professional Staff at any course. Half-hour private lessons are $50 per adult and $30 for youths age seventeen and under.

Tee times. Reservations may be made up to ninety days ahead by calling (407) 938–4653.

OSPREY RIDGE AND EAGLE PINES

These two courses are located between the Magic Kingdom and Downtown Disney. Golf carts at both courses are equipped with a Global Positioning System (GPS) featuring detailed 3-D renderings of golf holes and course features, exact distances from the golf ball to the flagstick, and tips from professionals with helpful strategies for each hole. Back at the clubhouse the Sand Trap Bar and Grill offers light choices for breakfast and lunch with indoor and outdoor dining along with a full bar.

Osprey Ridge is a peaceful course in a remote woodland and wetland setting. Here you'll find uncharacteristically rolling Florida terrain, dramatically raised greens and tees, seventy bunkers, and nine water holes, making this Tom Fazio–designed course Disney's most challenging. *7,101 yards. Slope: 131.*

Eagle Pines, quite a contrast to Osprey, features a different type of challenge with its flat terrain and vast sand beds. In its nature preserve setting, this Pete Dye–designed course boasts low, dish-shaped fairways separated by sand and native grasses, sixteen holes with water, and strategically placed bunkers. *6,772 yards. Slope: 135.*

PALM AND MAGNOLIA

Located near the Magic Kingdom within the grounds of the Shades of Green Resort (an armed forces resort on Disney property) are the first courses ever opened at Walt Disney World, both designed by Joe Lee. Part of the PGA Tour is held here each October, and the eighteenth hole of the Palm is rated as one of the toughest on the tour.

The heavily wooded Palm is one of Disney's most difficult courses, with fairways cinched by tall trees and lovely, elevated tees and greens; nine water holes; and ninety-four bunkers. *6,957 yards. Slope: 138.*

At Magnolia, the longest of all Disney's courses, wide fairways are framed magnificently by more than 1,500 magnolia trees. It too doesn't lack for challenge, with twelve holes of water and ninety-eight bunkers in the midst of large, undulating greens. Check out the sixth-hole hazard in the shape of Mickey Mouse. *7,200 yards. Slope: 136.*

OAK TRAIL

In a corner of the Magnolia course, this nine-hole, par 36 walking course is a good choice for family fun. With its small, rolling greens, it's an ideal course for beginners; however, it does pose a few challenges for the serious golfer or a quick round of golf for those who want to get on to the parks. *2,913 yards.*

LAKE BUENA VISTA GOLF COURSE

Located in the Downtown Disney area within the grounds of the Saratoga Springs and Old Key West Resorts (the pro shop is at Saratoga Springs Resort) is this Joe Lee–designed course in a country club setting. Wandering through pine forests and tall cypress, this shortest of Disney's eighteen-hole courses sports small, elevated greens with plenty of bunkers, narrow fairways, and an island green on the seventh hole. This is a great place for beginners but challenging enough for the more experienced. *6,749 yards. Slope: 133.*

Golfing Beyond Disney

The Orlando area is bursting at the seams with many excellent golf courses. In fact, there are about 150 courses within a forty-five-minute drive from downtown Orlando. Following are several great choices close to Walt Disney World.

CELEBRATION GOLF CLUB

Just ten minutes away from Walt Disney World in the town of Celebration is this course with rolling terrain winding through picturesque lakes and a landscape of native oak, pine, and magnolia. The course was designed by Robert Trent Jones Sr. and Jr. Featuring demanding greens along with strategic hazards, it also sports five sets of tees on every hole. The Celebration Golf Academy offers group and private lessons as well as junior academies. A full-service restaurant, the Windmill Tavern, serves breakfast and lunch daily. Call (407) 566–GOLF, (407) 566–4653, (888) 2PLAY18, or (888) 275–2918 for tee time reservations, or go online at www .celebrationgolf.com. *6,792 yards. Slope: 135.*

FALCON'S FIRE GOLF CLUB

This Rees Jones–designed, eighteen-hole course features beautiful scenery and plenty of challenges, with loads of bunkers and deceptive greens. Located close to Disney in Kissimmee, you'll find a well-stocked pro shop and the Falcon's Nest Restaurant. Carts come with the Pro Shot Digital Caddy System in which monitors give distances to the pin and suggestions on each hole. For information call (407) 239–5445, (877) 878–FIRE, or (877) 878–3473, or go online at www.falconsfire.com. *6,901 yards. Slope: 138.*

GRAND CYPRESS GOLF CLUB

The Grand Cypress Resort, consisting of the Hyatt Regency Grand Cypress and the Villas of Grand Cypress, boasts four Jack Nicklaus– designed golf courses: the nine-hole North, the nine-hole South, the nine-hole East, and the eighteen-hole, St. Andrews–style New Course. The North and South courses are marked by sharply ledged fairways, tall shaggy mounds, and plateau greens. The wooded East has less bunkering. And for a full round of eighteen, courses can be combined as North-South, South-East, or East-North. The New Course comes with steeper and more challenging bunkers and slopes complete with double greens, stone bridges and walls, long grassy mounds, pot bunkers as deep as twelve feet, very little water, and few trees.

At the Golf Club, located on the grounds of the Villas of Grand Cypress, the Golf Academy offers lessons under the guidance of PGA and LPGA certified professionals in a twenty-one-acre practice facility. Also available is CompuSport, which uses video teaching technology in an innovative way to perfect your game. Call (800) 835–7377 or (407) 239–1909 for information and reservations.

RITZ-CARLTON GOLF CLUB AT GRANDE LAKES

This Greg Norman–designed course set on Shingle Creek, the headwaters of the Florida Everglades, is one of the most beautiful and certainly unique golf courses in central Florida. Just off the John Young Parkway about fif-teen minutes from Walt Disney World and down the road from SeaWorld, guests play through a scenery of wetlands and woodlands of palms, pal-mettos, and oaks to three snaking finishing holes just across the lake from the resort.

The Golf Club features clinics, a driving range, a 55,000-square-foot practice tee, a 15,000-square-foot teaching tee, a practice putting green, and club and shoe rentals. Amenities include a restaurant with indoor and outdoor service, a golf retail store, and locker rooms for men and women.

An innovative Golf Caddy-Concierge Program allows for a profes-sional attendant to accompany each twosome or foursome on all eighteen holes, catering to the group's every need, including cleaning clubs, locating golf balls, recommending strategy, raking bunkers, repair-ing divots, explaining course history, and handling special requests such as ordering food, making dinner reservations, and so on.

The Golf FORE Kids etiquette class is offered twice weekly for chil-dren ages five through twelve. The kids learn game fundamentals, sports-manship, and RESPECT (responsibility, etiquette, sensitivity, pace, education, conditions, and tradition). Call (407) 393–4900 for further information and reservations. *7,122 yards, Slope:139.*

Miniature Golf

Miniature golf fans have four courses to play at Disney, each sporting eighteen fun-filled holes. Fees are $10.00 for adults and $8.00 for children ages three through nine; receive a 50 percent discount on a second round played the same day. Open from 10:00 A.M. to 11:00 P.M. daily, subject to weather and seasonal changes. Reservations for tee times available in per-son only. For more information call (407) WDW–PLAY, or (407) 939–7529.

FANTASIA GARDEN AND FAIRWAYS

Two eighteen-hole miniature golf courses, Fantasia Garden and Fantasia Fairways, are located across Buena Vista Drive from the Swan Hotel near Epcot, Disney–MGM Studios, and the Boardwalk. Play amid tutu-clothed hippos, silly alligators, and cavorting fountains ending with Sorcerer Mickey splashing guests with his mop and buckets at the *Fantasia*-inspired Fantasia Garden course. The more challenging Fantasia Fairways, designed as a pint-size golf course, is great for those who like a more traditional round amid sand traps, water hazards, doglegs, roughs, and lush putting greens. A limited snack bar with small arcade is on-site.

WINTER SUMMERLAND

Designed for Santa and his elves as an off-season vacation spot, this hot-and-cold, sand-and-snow miniature golf course is a kick. Sitting adjacent to Blizzard Beach, guests play either the Snow course—amid Christmas music, ice hockey rings, snowmen, ice castles, and igloos—or the Sand course, where Caribbean music plays while Santa grills turkey outside his mobile home surrounded by sand castles and surfboards. A limited snack bar is on the premises.

Tennis

Nearly all of Disney's deluxe hotels (with the exception of the Polynesian Resort, Animal Kingdom Lodge, and Wilderness Lodge) have tennis courts with a professional tennis staff offering lessons at either the Contemporary Resort or the Grand Floridian Resort. Courts can be found at the Contemporary (six clay), the Grand Floridian (two clay), Yacht and Beach Club (one hard), Old Key West (three hard), Boardwalk Inn and Villas (two hard), the Swan and Dolphin (four hard), and Saratoga Springs (two clay). Bring your own racket; no rentals are available.

Serious tennis players may want to consider staying at the Contemporary Resort, where Disney's Racquet Club boasts the best facilities on property, with six lighted Hydrogrid clay courts. Its pro shop offers private lessons, a play-the-professional and tennis-pro-fill-in programs, tennis togs, and restringing services. For Disney court information or to book tennis lessons, clinics, and private instruction, call (407) WDW–PLAY, or (407) 939–7529. Call (407) 824–3578 for the courts at the Swan and Dolphin. Courts are complimentary and are available on a first-come, first-served basis.

Outside of Walt Disney World consider the excellent tennis facility at the Hyatt Regency Grand Cypress Racquet Club. It features eight Har-Tru and four Deco-Turf II courts along with clinics, private and semiprivate lessons. The Grand Cypress Tennis Academy offers five hours of instruction with videotaped analysis, match strategy, and play, along with a written evaluation and a guaranteed game match service. For further information and reservations, call (407) 239–1234. You'll also find three lighted courts at the JW Marriott Grande Lakes.

Biking

Bicycles for all ages are available for rent at the Boardwalk Inn and Villas, Wilderness Lodge and Villas, the Polynesian, Saratoga Springs, and Old Key West. At the Boardwalk Inn, bikers can pedal their way around the walkway surrounding the 0.75-mile Crescent Lake or the pathway that circles to Disney–MGM Studios. Wilderness Lodge guests should take advantage of the adjoining Fort Wilderness and its miles of pine forests. At the Polynesian Resort take a spin around the property on a surrey, and at Old Key West and Saratoga Springs you'll find trails running throughout the property. Bicycles rent for approximately $8.00 per hour or $21.00 per day. Surreys (four-wheeled, canopy-covered cycles perfect for families or friends who want to ride together) rent for $17.00 per half hour for a two-seater and $21.00 for a four-seater. Helmets are provided free of charge. Young people under the age of eighteen must have a signed waiver from a parent or legal guardian.

Off-property you'll find bicycles at the Hyatt Grand Regency Cypress and the Villas of Grand Cypress with two bike paths, one 3.2 miles and the other 4.7 miles. The JW Marriott and the Ritz-Carlton have bicycles available for a spin around a 1.3-mile pathway encircling the resort.

Jogging

Those amazing folks with enough energy to jog after traipsing through the parks day after day will be glad to know that a nice variety of pathways are to be found throughout the Walt Disney World property. Information and jogging maps are available at the front desk of each resort. At the Polynesian a path is laid out through the tropical grounds; the Grand Floridian has a pathway along the Seven Seas Lagoon; and the Wilderness Lodge offers miles of trails winding through the adjoining Fort Wilderness among pines and cypress trees. Epcot Resort guests should take advantage of the boardwalk-style walkway surrounding the twenty-five-acre Crescent Lake or the path encircling the canal leading to Disney–MGM Studios. Old Key West and Saratoga Springs have picturesque pathways that meander throughout the property.

The Grand Cypress Resort has jogging courses ranging from 1.3 miles to 4.7 miles that wind through the extensive property. Celebration Hotel's beautiful jogging paths begin just outside the front door and encircle Celebration Lake. The Hard Rock, Royal Pacific, and Portofino Bay Hotels are connected by attractive pathways to and from the theme parks. The Ritz-Carlton and JW Marriott resort area has a 1.3-mile path encircling the property.

Boating and Waterways

With 850 acres of lakes, 130 feet of shoreline, 66 miles of canals, and more than 500 watercraft, boating is a major pastime at Walt Disney World. And with some of the most incredible weather in the nation, water sports are an important draw. Most resorts as well as Downtown Disney have their own marina with a variety of boats available for hire (see individual resort listings for specific details). Boating takes place on the following waterways:

Seven Seas Lagoon, accessed from the Grand Floridian and Polynesian Resorts and connected to Bay Lake.

Bay Lake accessed from the Contemporary Resort and the Wilderness Lodge and connected to the Seven Seas Lagoon.

Crescent Lake, around whose shores sit the Epcot resorts of the Yacht and Beach Club, the Beach Club Villas, the Boardwalk Inn and Villas, and the Swan and Dolphin.

Buena Vista Lagoon fronting Downtown Disney and Saratoga Springs, leading down the Sassagoula River to Old Key West.

Boating choices include canopy boats, a luxury yacht, pedal boats, pontoon boats, sailboats, and Sea Raycers.

Boston Whaler Montauks

These 17-foot, canopy-covered, motorized boats accommodate as many as six adults and are available at the Grand Floridian, Contemporary, Yacht and Beach Club, Beach Club Villas, Wilderness Lodge, Old Key West, and Downtown Disney. *Approximately $31 per half hour.*

Luxury Yacht

For the ultimate in indulgence, charter the 45-foot Sea Ray, the *Grand I*, docked at the Grand Floridian Resort. Accommodating ten to twelve people, it includes a captain and deckhand. Food and cocktails are available at an additional charge. For reservations call (407) 824–2439. *Basic cost is $375 per hour.*

Pedal Boats

Available at the Swan and Dolphin (swan pedal boats) and Old Key West. *$6.00 to $13.00 per half hour.*

Pontoon Boats

SunTracker 21-foot canopied pontoon boats holding as many as ten people are perfect for those who want a nonthrill ride around Disney's waterways. Available at the Grand Floridian, Contemporary, Polynesian, Yacht and Beach Club and Beach Club Villas, Old Key West, Wilderness Lodge, and Downtown Disney. *Approximately $40 per half hour.*

Sailboats

The Grand Floridian, Polynesian, Contemporary, and the Wilderness Lodge rent sailboats in various sizes accommodating from two to six people. Catamarans are available at the Grand Floridian, Polynesian, and Contemporary, but they do require a bit of sailing experience. Approximately $19–$23 per hour.

Sea Raycers

What could be more fun than renting a Sea Raycer, a two-seater minipowerboat perfect for zipping around Disney's waterways and lakes. You'll get the most bang for your buck at one of the resorts near the Magic Kingdom, where there are miles of recreation on the Seven Seas Lagoon and Bay Lake. At the Magic Kingdom resort area marinas, at least one person in the boat must have a valid driver's license (those under eighteen must bring along a parent to sign a waiver). All other marinas permit guests at least twelve years old and 5 feet tall to operate independently as long as the parent or legal guardian signs for the child. Sea Raycers are available at the Contemporary, Polynesian, Grand Floridian, Yacht and Beach Club and the Beach Club Villas, Downtown Disney, Old Key West, and Wilderness Lodge. *Approximately $23 per half hour.*

🌿 *Waterskiing and Parasailing*

Head to the Contemporary Resort for waterskiing and parasailing action. Sammy Duvall Water Sports offers waterskiing, wakeboarding, and tubing at the Contemporary Resort for $140 per hour including boat, driver, and instruction. Personal watercraft rent for $65 per half hour. Parasailing packages begin at $90 per flight for a single and $140 for a tandem, including eight to ten minutes in the air and 450 feet of line. Premium parasailing packages begin at $113 for a single and $163 for a tandem, including ten to twelve minutes in the air and 600 feet of line. Participants must weigh at least a total of 100 pounds and no more than 300 pounds. For reservations call (407) WDW–PLAY, or (407) 939–7529, up to ninety days in advance.

Fishing

Walt Disney World's stocked fishing lakes are filled with plenty of large-mouth bass, perfect for the amateur as well as the seasoned angler. In fact, the largest bass caught at Walt Disney World weighed in at 14.25 pounds. Boats departing from the marinas of the Contemporary, Polynesian, and Grand Floridian Resorts and the Wilderness Lodge and Villas fish the waters of Bay Lake and the Seven Seas Lagoon from pontoon boats with an experienced guide. The waterways surrounding Epcot and Disney–MGM Studios are your fishing holes from boats departing the Yacht and Beach Club, Beach Club Villas, and Boardwalk Inn and Villas. From Downtown Disney angle for bass on Lake Buena Vista. Fish in the Sassagoula River from Old Key West. No fishing license is required, and it's strictly catch-and-release.

Two- and four-hour trips (maximum of five people) cost $200 to $395 per boat. That price includes an experienced guide, Bassmaster equipment, tackle, artificial bait, one-year BASS membership, and nonalcoholic beverages. Excursions may be prearranged up to two weeks in advance by calling (407) WDW–BASS or (407) 939–2277, and must be made at least twenty-four hours in advance.

Special one-hour excursions for children ages six through twelve leave the marinas of the Contemporary, Polynesian, Grand Floridian, Wilderness Lodge, Boardwalk Inn and Villas, Old Key West, and the Yacht and Beach Club. The cost is approximately $30. Kids also love shore fishing at Fort

Wilderness, where cane poles and rods and reels may be rented at the Bike Barn in the Meadow Recreation Area.

Guests of the Hyatt Regency Grand Cypress Resort and the Villas of Grand Cypress can fish from the shores of Lake Windsong. The JW Marriott and the Ritz-Carlton at Grande Lakes offer fly fishing on private charter boats from Shingle Creek, the headwaters of the Everglades.

Richard Petty Driving Experience

Those who dream of sitting behind the wheel of a race car can have their chance here. Lying next to the Magic Kingdom is this sometimes very loud speedway where white-knuckle rides in a NASCAR Winston Cup–style race car are offered. Each experience begins with a one-hour training session. All driving participants must have a valid driver's license and must know how to operate a stick shift. Spectators are welcome for no charge. Since the track sometimes closes due to inclement weather, it's always best to call ahead. Call (800) BE–PETTY, or (800) 237–3889, for information.

Getting There

With its location virtually in the parking lot of the Magic Kingdom, it's necessary to either make your way to the Ticket and Transportation Center (TTC) and take the shuttle located near the kennels or enter the Magic Kingdom parking lot and follow the signs, driving through the tunnel to the infield.

Programs

RIDE-ALONG PROGRAM

For $99, ride shotgun at speeds of up to 145 mph for three laps around the track with an experienced driving instructor. You must be at least age sixteen to participate (riders age seventeen or younger must be accompanied by a parent or guardian). This is the only program not requiring reservations.

ROOKIE EXPERIENCE

Those age eighteen or older can drive the car themselves for eight laps around the course. That is, of course, after an introductory class out on the speedway. The three-hour program costs $379.

KING'S EXPERIENCE

You'll feel like a king after five hours of driving eighteen laps (one eight-lap and one ten-lap session) around the speedway for the princely sum of $749. Only those age eighteen or older may participate.

EXPERIENCE OF A LIFETIME

For $1,249, drive three ten-lap sessions, improve your skills, and maybe change careers. Only for those age eighteen or older.

Disney's Wide World of Sports

In the heart of Walt Disney World is a 200-acre complex devoted exclusively to sports. Built for both professional and amateur events and more than thirty types of sporting activities, this vast development holds a 9,500-seat baseball stadium, a nine-lane track-and-field complex, and the 30,000-square-foot Milk House accommodating basketball courts, volleyball, wrestling, martial arts, and in-line hockey. A ten-court tennis complex accommodates up to 17,500 spectators. The baseball quadruplex along with the stadium compose the spring training ground for the Atlanta Braves; there are youth baseball fields as well at the softball quadruplex. The new Hess Sports Field added twenty more acres of fields and diamonds, including multisport fields for soccer, football, and lacrosse as well as new diamonds for baseball and softball.

The Sports Experience, a multisport challenge for guests, offers a variety of activities including hockey, football, baseball, basketball, soccer, and volleyball. It's included in the price of general admission but only open on select days when Wide World of Sports events are scheduled.

General admission costs $10.00 for adults and $7.00 for children ages three through nine and covers all nonpremium events. Advance tickets for premium events are available through Ticketmaster at (407) 839–3900 or www.ticketmaster.com as well as at the box office on the day of the event. For further information call (407) 828–FANS, or (407) 828–3267, or go online at www.disneyworldsports.com.

Getting There

Bus transportation can be time-consuming with a transfer at Disney–MGM Studios; consider a taxi instead of the lengthy bus ride. By car take exit 65 off Interstate 4 and follow the signs. Parking is free.

7

SHOPPING

For many people, shopping is the best part of a vacation. The parks are loaded with something for everyone in just about every price range. But those who would like to bring home something minus a Mickey Mouse or Cinderella motif will want to check out Orlando's best shopping options away from the parks.

Belz Factory Outlet World

There are 170 stores at this indoor, mega–outlet mall, including Izod, Wolf Camera and Video, Harry and David, Gap, Woolrich, Foot Locker, Mikasa, Nautica, Birkenstock, and Sunglass Hut. Located 12 miles from Disney World just across the Interstate 4 and Kirkman Road interchange from Universal Orlando fronting I–4 (exit 75A) and the Florida Turnpike. Open Monday through Saturday from 10:00 A.M. to 9:00 P.M. and Sunday from 10:00 A.M. to 6:00 P.M.; (407) 352–9611.

Celebration

Small-town America is alive and well in Celebration, Disney's perfectly planned community located just minutes from the parks. Filled with a mix of delightfully nostalgic homes, palm tree–lined boulevards, great restaurants ringing a picture-perfect lake, and charming retail shops in its compact village, it's a perfect afternoon getaway or a great alternative to Disney lodging.

Several streets of shopping go along well with the great ambience. Some of the stores you'll find are Orvis; Market Street Gallery for collectibles; Jerard International, carrying home decor items; Soft as a Grape for casual clothing; White's Books and Gifts; Village Mercantile, specializing in resort clothing along with Celebration logo merchandise; and Goodings Food Market, perfect for picnic items.

Crossroads at Lake Buena Vista

The closest shopping center to Disney has a Sunglass Gallery for great prices on designer sunglasses, Sony, Goodings Market (the closest grocery store to Disney), Foot Locker, and Hallmark. Located at the intersection of State Road 535 and Hotel Plaza Boulevard, just off I–4 close to Downtown Disney.

Florida Mall

This 260-store mall is a bit less upscale than the Mall at Millenia but just as much fun with anchors like Saks, Lord & Taylor, Nordstrom (shoe heaven), Burdines, JC Penny, Dillards, and Sears. Other stores include Williams-Sonoma, Pottery Barn, Brookstone, Brooks Brothers, Abercrombie & Fitch, Guess, Ritz Camera, Sharper Image, Waldenbooks, Harry and David, MAC Cosmetics, and Sephora. Located at the corner of South Orange Blossom Trail and Sand Lake Road. From Disney take I–4 East to Sand Lake Road and go east for 4 miles. From Universal take I–4 West to Sand Lake Road. Open Monday through Saturday from 10:00 A.M. to 9:00 P.M. and Sunday noon to 6:00 P.M.; (407) 851–6255.

Groceries

Goodings at Crossroads at Lake Buena Vista near Downtown Disney has a full line of groceries and will deliver to your resort for a $10 fee with a minimum $50 order; forty-eight hours notice required; phone (407) 827–1200, fax (407) 827–1219; online at http://shop.goodings.com.

For a better selection and lower prices, drive down the road about five minutes to the Publix at Vineland and International Drive near the Orlando Premium Outlets. Albertsons and another Publix are located near the intersection of Sand Lake Drive and Dr. Phillips Boulevard near Universal Orlando.

Mall at Millenia

If you have time for only one mall, make it this one. Close to Universal Studios and only a fifteen-minute drive from Disney, this high-end shopping experience is Orlando's best. Anchored by Bloomingdale's, Macy's, and Neiman Marcus, other shopping choices include Chanel, Tiffany and Co., Gucci, Louis Vuitton, Burberry, Hugo Boss, Cartier, St. John, Furla, Jimmy Choo, and Cole Haan. When the shopping gets too much for you, rest your feet at some great restaurants including P.F. Chang's China Bistro, Brio Tuscan Grill, McCormick & Schmick's, and the Cheesecake Factory. From Walt Disney World and Universal take I–4 East to exit 78 (right on Conroy Road). Open Monday through Saturday from 10:00 A.M. to 9:00 P.M. and Sunday noon to 7:00 P.M.; (407) 363–3555.

Orlando Premium Outlets

This 127-store designer outlet mall is a gem. Here you'll find stores like Burberry, Ermenegildo Zegna, Escada, Armani, Hugo Boss, Salvatore Ferragamo, Versace, and Barney's New York Outlet. Located at 8200 Vineland Avenue just off I–4 (exit 68 or SR535) close to Downtown Disney. Open Monday through Saturday from 10:00 A.M. to 10:00 P.M. and Sunday 10:00 A.M. to 9:00 P.M.; (407) 238–7787.

Winter Park

This quaint village of beautiful gardens and three notable art museums is only a twenty-five-minute drive from Disney. Shop along Park Avenue in the historical district, where blocks of small boutiques, jewelry stores, and art galleries are scattered among well-known names like Ann Taylor and Banana Republic. Relax along the way at any number of sidewalk cafes and restaurants.

The Charles Hosmer Morse Museum of American Art has an excellent Tiffany glass collection, including an exquisite Tiffany chapel interior built for the 1892 Chicago World Columbian Exposition. There's also a 12-mile scenic boat tour on the town's chain of lakes. To reach downtown Winter Park take I–4 East to exit 87 and go east on Fairbanks Avenue for 3 miles.

8

DINING

Pomegranate-glazed quail stuffed with North African–style colusari rice on Swiss chard. Grilled buffalo sirloin with sweet potato-hazelnut gratin. Sesame-crusted ahi seared rare with sticky rice, stir-fried vegetables, wasabi cream, and Tobiko caviar. That's just a sampling of some of the incredible meals found at Walt Disney World restaurants, where a remarkable culinary transformation has taken place since the mid-1990s. Extraordinary cuisine is especially evident in such renowned dining establishments as the California Grill at the Contemporary Resort, Flying Fish Café at Disney's Boardwalk, and Victoria and Albert's at the Grand Floridian, winner of the AAA Five-Diamond Award.

Disney's guests are becoming more sophisticated and demanding in their search for creative and sumptuous cuisine, and this challenge has been met quite nicely with the opening of many serious, fine-dining venues, particularly at the resort hotels. Top-notch chefs are now the norm, creating exciting menus at some of the highest-rated restaurants in the country. First-rate sommeliers (almost 300 on Disney property, more than any other company in the world) have fashioned outstanding wine lists, particularly at Victoria and Albert's, California Grill, Citricos, Jiko, and the Flying Fish. In fact, Disney sells over a half million bottles of wine every year.

Even Disney's reputation for dreadful theme park food has changed. Once just a hot dog and hamburger haven, it's now quite possible to find pleasurable choices ranging from fine dining to more-than-palatable counter-service food. Though you'll always find burgers and chicken tenders, you'll also discover restaurants with outstanding cuisine and unique atmosphere. Children are always treated as special guests; almost every restaurant along with all counter-service spots offer a menu just for kids. Meals are delivered quickly, so if a speedy dinner is not your cup of tea, stretch it out a bit by ordering an appetizer only and then your entree when you are finished with that first course.

Those in need of vegetarian meals will find something for them in both full-service restaurants and many counter-service spots where at least one vegetarian option is usually available; vegetarian choices are included in the sample entrees in this chapter. Those with special needs—such as low-fat, no sugar added, low-carb, and kosher—can be accommodated at full-service restaurants as long as they receive a twenty-four-hour notice (it's probably best to do this when making your advance reservations). Special dietary requests such as allergies to gluten or wheat, shellfish, soy, lactose, peanuts, or other substances will be accommodated at all full-service restaurants as long as Disney is notified at least seventy-two hours in advance.

As for dress code, *casual* is the word. Theme park restaurants are extremely informal; however, you'll find that in many resort restaurants, dress is a bit more sophisticated. Smart casual clothing is usually fine, but I have noted the usual dress at each restaurant outside the theme parks.

Reservations, particularly in busy season, are very important. Advance reservations are available at Disney's theme parks, resorts, and most Downtown Disney full-service restaurants by calling (407) WDW–DINE, or (407) 939–3463. Same-day advance reservations may be made at each park, at the restaurant itself, through Guest Relations, or by picking up any public phone in Disney and dialing *88. Those staying in a Disney concierge room or suite may make reservations through the concierge staff. Non-Disney restaurants' reservation phone numbers are listed with their full descriptions.

Although there are many excellent restaurants in the city center of Orlando, I have not reviewed them. Most visitors to Walt Disney World or even Universal will probably not want to drive the thirty minutes or so it would take to reach these commendable dining spots. Instead, I've concentrated on the many excellent choices closer to the parks.

A wealth of admirable restaurants have sprung up near Universal Studios, particularly in the area of Sand Lake Road and Dr. Phillips Boulevard. Here you'll find Timpanos, Roy's, Seasons 52, and Christini's. Vito's Chop House is just around the corner on International Drive. All are worth the short drive from Disney and are only a hop away from the hotels near Universal. And you mustn't forget Emeril's at CityWalk and Tchoup Chop at Universal's Royal Pacific Resort, two wonderful restaurants.

If you would like to preview the menus of many of these restaurants, go online to www.luxurydisneyguide.com/disneymenus.htm. Another Web site with Disney menus is http://allearsnet.com/menu/menus.htm.

Advance Reservations

Advance reservations are Disney's answer to long waits. It requires planning ahead, but it is well worth the extra thought. You can call anywhere from a month to up to two years in some cases ahead of your trip and reserve a place. When you arrive, the dining facility won't actually have a table waiting for you, but you'll be seated as soon as they can set a table to accommodate your party, ahead of any walk-ins.

I cannot emphasize enough how important it is to secure advance reservations; without them, you'll be spending way too much time cooling your heels waiting for a table, particularly at Epcot and the better resort restaurants where demand is high. This is especially true in the busier times of the year and for the more popular spots like Victoria and Albert's, California Grill, Citricos, and the Flying Fish, along with all character breakfasts. For advance reservations call (407) WDW–DINE, or (407) 939–3463, unless otherwise noted.

A handy tool that allows you to enter in a date in order to learn when and where you can get your advance reservations at Walt Disney World can be found at www.pscalculator.net.

Advance reservations available two years in advance: Hoop-Dee-Doo Musical Revue; Spirit of Aloha Dinner Show.

Advance reservations available one year in advance: Mickey's Backyard Barbeque.

Advance reservations available 180 days in advance: Victoria and Albert's.

THE BEST OF THE BEST

Best Italian: Palio at the Walt Disney World Swan, where the Tortellini con Aragosta topped with enormous amounts of lobster is amazing, or Portobello Yacht Club at Downtown Disney for a fantastic, superthin pizza followed by the Rigatoni alla Calabrese with Italian sausage, cremini (mushrooms), plum tomatoes, black olives, and escarole. Watch for Bice, the new restaurant at the Portofino Bay Hotel, to be part of this list.

Best seafood: Flying Fish at Disney's Boardwalk for Potato Wrapped Red Snapper with creamy leek fondue and red wine reduction, or the newcomer on the block, Todd English's Bluezoo at the Walt Disney World Dolphin, where seafood is taken to new heights. Off Disney property it's got to be Roy's on Sand Lake Road near Universal for Roy Yamaguchi's remarkable Hawaiian fusion cuisine.

Best steak: Shula's at the Walt Disney World Dolphin, a standout for sensational Angus steaks cooked to perfection, or Vito's Chop House on International Drive for the filet mignon stuffed with gorgonzola.

Best for romance: Victoria and Albert's at Disney's Grand Floridian Resort, where you'll savor a sumptuous six-course meal served on elegant fine china to the accompaniment of enchanting harp music. Or Normans at the Ritz-Carlton for fine dining in plush surroundings all enveloped in the grandeur of an amazing resort.

Best for kids: Children love the Rainforest Café at the Animal Kingdom or Downtown Disney, where they're bombarded with thunderstorms and noisy Audio-Animatronics wildlife. A close runner up is Whispering Canyon Café at Disney's Wilderness Lodge; come prepared for plenty of whoopin' and hollerin', and please, whatever you do, don't ask for the ketchup—unless, that is, you like a lot of attention.

Best character meal: Cinderella's Royal Table at the Magic Kingdom, a chance to breakfast in a fairytale castle with Cinderella, Jasmine, Aladdin, Belle, and Snow White. Or try the Crystal Palace at the Magic Kingdom for a tasty, bountiful buffet hosted by Winnie the Pooh and his friends.

Best hip atmosphere: Todd English's Bluezoo at the Dolphin, the coolest spot this side of South Beach, or Tchoup Chop at Universal's Royal Pacific Resort, a knock-'em-dead, Asian-inspired beauty.

Best Disney view: Arthur's 27 at the Wyndham Palace, with drop-dead views of Downtown Disney and the surrounding area; or California Grill at Disney's Contemporary Resort, with its picture-perfect views of the Magic Kingdom, the Seven Seas Lagoon, and the Wishes fireworks presentation.

Best Disney resort restaurant: Tough call. My favorites are the California Grill at the Contemporary Resort (just about anything on their exceptional menu is fantastic), or Victoria and Albert's at the Grand Floridian Resort (particularly the Chef's Table, where Chef Scott Hunnel oversees an eleven-course meal designed especially for you).

Best Downtown Disney restaurant: Wolfgang Puck's Upstairs Dining Room for dishes such as Szechuan marinated "chinois" rack of lamb served with a spicy cilantro-mint sauce or the restaurant's exceptionally great Wiener schnitzel.

Best Universal resort restaurant: Tchoup Chop at the Royal Pacific Resort for wonderful Asian and Polynesian-influenced cuisine in a stunning setting, but look for Bice, the newly opened restaurant at Portofino Bay Hotel, to give Tchoup Chop a run for its money.

Best CityWalk restaurant: Emeril's for its justifiably famous Creole-Cajun food.

Best Epcot Illuminations view: Rose and Crown in World Showcase's United Kingdom. Set your priority seating for about one hour prior to showtime and pray for a lagoonside table with a good view.

Best milk shake: Beaches and Cream at Disney's Beach Club Resort serves oh-so-delicious thick shakes and malts in a frosty fountain glass with the extras on the side in the stainless steel shaker.

Best pizza: You can't beat the pizzas at Downtown Disney's Wolfgang Puck Café (choose the house-made fennel sausage pizza), Downtown Disney's Portobello Yacht Club (thin-crusted and smoky flavored), or Mama Melrose's at Disney–MGM Studios (don't miss the grilled chicken pizza with sun-dried tomato pesto, pancetta, and Asiago cheese).

Best breakfast: Spoodles at Disney's Boardwalk. I love the Egg Rotollo, scrambled eggs with chorizo, onions, peppers, and cheddar cheese rolled in *lavosh* (flatbread).

Best food at the Magic Kingdom: *Restaurant:* Crystal Palace or Cinderella's Royal Table; *fast food:* Pecos Bill Café.

Best food at Disney–MGM Studios: *Restaurant:* Hollywood Brown Derby; *fast food:* Studio Catering Company.

Best food at Epcot: *Restaurant:* Bistro de Paris; *fast food:* Tangierine Café in Morocco.

Best food at the Animal Kingdom: *Restaurant:* Rainforest Café; *fast food:* Tusker House.

Best food at Universal Studios: *Restaurant:* Finnegan's Bar and Grill; *fast food:* Classic Monster Café.

Best food at Islands of Adventure: *Restaurant:* Mythos; *fast food:* Thunder Falls Terrace.

Advance reservations available ninety days in advance: All Walt Disney World restaurants except Wolfgang Puck Café and Epcot's Bistro de Paris.

Advance reservations available sixty days in advance: Wolfgang Puck Café.

Advance reservations available thirty days in advance: Bistro de Paris at Epcot.

Special Dining Shows

Combining dining with a show is a Disney specialty that's particularly popular with the little ones. Families love the Hoop-Dee-Doo Revue, Mickey's Backyard Barbeque, and Spirit of Aloha Dinner Show, shows so popular that reservations are taken two years in advance! Advance reservations are a must and can be made by calling (407) WDW–DINE, or (407) 939–3463 (payment in full is required at time of booking, with a full refund if canceled forty-eight hours in advance). For a more adult change of pace, consider the House of Blues Gospel Brunch on Sundays offering a Southern-style buffet along with foot-stomping gospel music.

Hoop-Dee-Doo Revue

Daily at 5:00 and 7:15 P.M.; in the busier months a third show is offered at 9:30 P.M.; price includes tax and gratuity. $$$$
For thirty years at the Fort Wilderness Pioneer Hall, an old-fashioned hoedown dinner has been on the agenda, with live entertainment in the form of country-and-western music, cancan dancers, and slapstick comedy. The down-home chow served family style includes fried chicken, smoked pork ribs, corn, baked beans, salad, bread, strawberry shortcake, nonalcoholic beverages, beer, and sangria. Since no parking is allowed at Pioneer Hall, those driving should park in the Fort Wilderness lot and take an internal bus to the Settlement Depot. Buses run from the Ticket and Transportation Center (TTC), but it will still be necessary to take an internal bus. Those staying at the Contemporary Resort or Wilderness Lodge can take a boat to Fort Wilderness with a short walk to Pioneer Hall.

Mickey's Backyard Barbecue

Tuesday and Thursday at 6:30 P.M., early March through late November and Tuesday only in December. Price includes tax and gratuity. $$$$

Have a rootin'-tootin' time chowin' down on barbecue to the tunes of a live country-and-western band. The picnic-style festivities take place in an open-air, covered pavilion near Fort Wilderness and Pioneer Hall. Line dancing and games are led by your hosts Mickey, Minnie, Chip 'n' Dale, and Goofy. The fare is an all-you-care-to-eat buffet of barbecue pork ribs, baked chicken, hot dogs, baked beans, macaroni and cheese, corn on the cob, potato salad, corn bread, watermelon, cake, draft beer, wine, ice tea, and lemonade. If you're mainly interested in seeing Mickey Mouse, a better and less expensive choice would be one of the excellent character meals held at the resorts or parks. If barbecue and country music are your thing, this might be the place for you. Allow plenty of time to take the internal resort bus from the Fort Wilderness parking lot or bus stop to the Pioneer Hall area (see previous directions to Hoop-Dee-Doo Revue).

Spirit of Aloha Dinner Show

Tuesday through Saturday at 5:15 and 8:00 P.M.; price includes tax and gratuity; subject to cancellation in inclement weather. $$$$

Disney's version of a luau can be found at the Polynesian Resort. Hosted by Aunt Winnie, the show features music from the Disney movie *Lilo and Stitch* along with traditional Polynesian song and dance. It's an all-you-care-to-eat Polynesian-style meal served family style featuring mixed greens with mango–poppy-seed dressing, pineapple coconut bread, roasted chicken, barbecued pork ribs, Polynesian rice, seasonal vegetables, volcano cake, and unlimited beverages, including beer and wine. Children have additional options of macaroni and cheese, chicken nuggets, hot dogs, or PB&J sandwiches.

House of Blues Gospel Brunch

Sundays at 10:30 A.M. and 1:00 P.M. For reservations call the House of Blues box office at (407) 934–BLUE, or (407) 934–2583. $$$$

On Sundays there's plenty of foot stomping and good old soulful music in the House of Blues at Downtown Disney. The bountiful Southern-style buffet includes pastries, fresh fruit, chilled prawns with cocktail sauce, smoked catfish, potato salad, Caesar salad, macaroni and cheese, omelets, scrambled eggs, barbecue chicken, biscuits and gravy, prime rib of beef, honey-baked ham, chicken jambalaya, apple cobbler, banana bread pudding, and cookies.

Dining with the Disney Characters

If you have a child in tow, at least one or two character meals are a must. These extremely popular dining spots, offered both at the theme parks and at many of the Disney resorts, are a perfect way for children to spend extra time with their favorite characters. Meals are all-you-care-to-eat, offered in one of three ways: buffet-style, family-style, or as preplated meals. Characters work the room, stopping at each table to interact with guests, pose for photos, and sign autographs (it's a good idea to pick up an autograph book for your child right away at one of Disney's gift shops). Book advance reservations early (ninety days out), particularly for Cinderella's Royal Table, Restaurant Akershus's Princess Storybook Dining, and Chef Mickey's by calling (407) WDW–DINE, or (407) 939–3463. Characters available may vary somewhat each day.

Magic Kingdom

Cinderella's Royal Table. Breakfast and lunch; breakfast is a preplated meal; lunch is a family-style salad, your choice of five entrees, and dessert; Disney's most popular character meal served high atop Cinderella's Castle; Cinderella, Jasmine, Snow White, Belle, Aurora, Fairy Godmother.

Crystal Palace. Breakfast, lunch, and dinner buffet; Pooh, Eeyore, Piglet, Tigger.

Liberty Tree Tavern. Dinner family-style; Pluto and friends.

Epcot

Garden Grill. Lunch and dinner; family-style starter and dessert, and your choice of five entrees; Farmer Mickey, Chip 'n' Dale, Pluto; afternoon ice cream social at 3:00 with ice-cream sundaes along with Mickey.

Restaurant Akershus. Pre-plated breakfast; family-style lunch and dinner; appetizers, your choice of five entrees, and dessert; on a rotating schedule are Disney characters Belle, Jasmine, Snow White, Sleeping Beauty, Mary Poppins, Pocahontas, and Mulan.

SUE SAYS: DISNEY'S MAGIC YOUR WAY DINING PLAN IS A DELICIOUS DEAL!

By Sue Pisaturo, Owner of Small World Vacations, www.wdwvacations.com

When something seems too good to be true it usually is, right? Well, it's not the case with Disney's new Magic Your Way Dining Plan. It truly is a great deal! Add it along with your Magic Your Way package for just $35 per night for adults and $10 per night for children ages three through nine. Choose from over one hundred participating Disney restaurants. View a detailed list at www.wdwvacations.com/MagicYourWayDiningLocations.htm. Prices and locations are subject to change.

Each night you'll enjoy:

- One table-service meal including appetizer, entree, dessert, nonalcoholic beverage; includes gratuity or service charge.

- One counter-service meal including entree and nonalcoholic beverage.

- One snack, such as a snack-cart ice cream, fruit, chips, popcorn, apple juice, or another nonalcoholic beverage.

I checked some menu prices and was amazed that many table-service restaurants total much more than $35 per night. So you're already ahead before even using the counter-service and snack selections! Here are some of the best values for an adult character meal or one meal including appetizer, entree, dessert, nonalcoholic beverage, tax, and tip.

Table-Service Locations

$70 Alfredo's at Italy in Epcot

$65 Cap'n Jacks at Downtown Disney

$57 Chefs de Paris at France in Epcot

$56 Spoodles on the Boardwalk

$55 Concourse Steakhouse at Disney's Contemporary Resort

$51 Cinderella's Royal Table Dinner in the Magic Kingdom

$50 Teppanyaki at Japan in Epcot

$48 Tony's Town Square in the Magic Kingdom

Signature Table Locations (requires two table-service options)

$95 Yachtsman Steakhouse at Disney's Yacht Club

$92 Narcoossee's at Disney's Grand Floridian

Character Meals

$34 Cinderella Gala Dinner at Grand Floridian Resort

$33 Chef Mickey's Dinner at Contemporary Resort

$27 Cinderella's Royal Table Breakfast in the Magic Kingdom

$27 Storybook Princess Breakfast in Norway

Animal Kingdom

Donald's Prehistoric Breakfastosaurus. Breakfast buffet; Donald Duck, Goofy, Mickey, Pluto.

Disney Resorts

Chef Mickey's. Breakfast and dinner buffet; Contemporary Resort; Mickey, Goofy, Chip 'n' Dale, Minnie (with Donald Duck at dinner).

Cape May Café. Breakfast buffet; Beach Club Resort; Goofy, Minnie, Chip 'n' Dale.

Garden Grove (becomes **Gulliver's Grill** in the evening). Characters at breakfast on Saturday and Sunday and at dinner nightly; Walt Disney World Swan; *breakfast:* a la carte or buffet dining with Goofy, Pluto, Chip 'n' Dale; *dinner:* buffet and a la carte dining with visits by Timon and Rafiki on Monday and Friday and Goofy and Pluto the other evenings of the week.

1900 Park Fare. Breakfast and dinner buffet; Grand Floridian Resort; *breakfast:* Mary Poppins, Pooh, Tigger, Alice in Wonderland, Mad Hatter; *dinner:* Cinderella, Prince Charming, Fairy Godmother, Suzy and Perla, Lady Tremaine.

Ohana. Breakfast family-style; Polynesian Resort; Mickey, Chip 'n' Dale.

Magic Kingdom Dining

Cinderella's Royal Table

American cuisine. Breakfast, lunch, and dinner. $$$–$$$$
Those who want to feel like a six-year-old again should definitely plan to dine in Cinderella's fairytale castle, a medieval dream with thick stone floors, shining shields, dazzling suits of armor, and resplendent banners. Up a spiral staircase is the grand dining room where through glittering leaded-glass windows is a bird's-eye view of Fantasyland. It's a great respite from the throngs below with satisfying food, where everyone is a prince or princess waited on by "royal attendants" clad in Renaissance clothing.

The restaurant's most popular meal has always been the plated all-you-care-to-eat character breakfast, delicious and well worth the high price tag if little ones are part of your vacation. Summer 2005 brought a big-hit character lunch featuring a family-style salad and dessert, and a choice of five entrees to the agenda. To ensure a seat for these highly coveted meals, it's essential to call (407) WDW–DINE, or (407) 939–3463, at 7:00 A.M. eastern standard time exactly ninety days prior. Reservations are sometimes gone in a matter of minutes. A $10.00-per-adult and $5.00-per-child deposit is required at time of advance reservation booking (cancellations must be made 48 hours prior in order to ensure refund).

Best known for: Major Domo's Favorite Pie of prime rib in a rich cabernet sauce with mashed potatoes and sautéed vegetables topped with a light pastry.

SAMPLE MENU ITEMS

Preplated breakfast: Juice; fresh fruit; cheese Danish pastry; scrambled eggs; bacon; sausage; French toast; potato casserole; waffles for children; *healthy choice:* granola, low-fat yogurt, caramelized bananas.

Lunch entrees: Pasta al pomodoro; grilled salmon with saffron risotto and lemon beurre blanc; herb-crusted pork tenderloin with mustard-cheese grits and cabernet sauce; focaccia sandwich; Major Domo's Favorite Pie.

Dinner entrees: Roasted chicken breast on spinach and garlic bread pudding with red onion marmalade; seafood cioppino; pork tenderloin on a cassoulet of baked pasta, sun-dried tomatoes, gruyère cheese, and pesto; spice-crusted ahi with tomato fennel relish and cannellini mash; roasted prime rib of beef served with mashed potatoes; grilled portobello mushroom and roasted asparagus with quinoa falafel and ranch dipping sauce.

Crystal Palace

American buffet. Breakfast, lunch, and dinner. $$$

Winnie the Pooh and his friends Eeyore, Piglet, and Tigger are your hosts in this sunlight-drenched, conservatory-style restaurant found at the castle end of Main Street. Patio-style wrought-iron furnishings, lofty windows, and ceilings hung with baskets of greenery create an alfresco atmosphere. A surprisingly good and bountiful buffet is the fare, definitely one of the better spreads in the park. This is a popular dining choice, so make advance reservations and on arrival ask for the dining room closest to Main Street with its charming view of Cinderella's Castle.

Best known for: Breakfast lasagna made of waffles, pound cake, and fruit topped with custard and pastry cream.

SAMPLE MENU ITEMS

Breakfast buffet: Juice, fresh fruit; pastries, muffins, croissants, biscuits and gravy, cereal, oatmeal, sweet breakfast lasagna; breakfast meats, prime rib hash; made-to-order omelets, scrambled eggs, frittata; roasted potatoes; puff French toast, pancakes.

Lunch buffet: Sliced roast beef, salami, turkey, ham, and cheeses; Caesar, chicken, tuna, tomato and mozzarella, coleslaw, and fruit salads; assorted breads; soup; ham roll-ups, chicken Caesar pasta, barbecue chicken, sausage with onions and peppers, shepherd's pie; mashed and roasted potatoes, rice, vegetables; make-your-own sundae bar, cupcakes, brownies, cookies, peach cobbler, fruit; *children's buffet:* little hot dogs, macaroni and cheese, chicken nuggets, cheese pizza.

Dinner buffet: Peel-and-eat shrimp; assorted cheeses; salads the same as lunch; assorted breads; barbecue chicken, arroz con pollo, carved ham and prime rib, seafood Caesar pasta; roasted red potatoes, grilled vegetables, rice medley; desserts and children's buffet same as lunch.

Liberty Tree Tavern

American cuisine. Lunch and dinner. $$$
In an atmospheric tavern of period charm, dining rooms christened with the names of early American patriots are filled with colonial American reproductions. Planked flooring, thick lead glass windows, dark-paneled walls, servers in period attire, even squeaky wooden stairs lend an air of authenticity to the cozy restaurant. Lunch features updated American comfort food and a cool break from the park, but dinner turns into a standard fare, family-style meal hosted by patriots Chip 'n' Dale, Minnie, Goofy, and Pluto.

NOTE: Even though Cinderella's Castle is more popular, this is a good place for a sit-down meal. Lunch is especially nice for adults, with not a Mickey or Pluto in sight.

Best known for: Pilgrims' Feast of roast turkey served with herb dressing, mashed potatoes, and vegetables.

SAMPLE MENU ITEMS

Lunch entrees: Colony Salad of rotisserie chicken, Washington apples, sweet pecans, and applewood-smoked cheddar tossed with field greens in a honey-shallot vinaigrette; cider-cured salmon on griddled pumpkin bread with butternut vinaigrette; field greens and market vegetables tossed with strawberry vinaigrette; savory rigatoni with grilled chicken breast, apple-wood-smoked bacon, mushrooms, and spinach in creamy marinara sauce; Tri-Corner Sandwich of rare roast beef and Swiss cheese with coleslaw, horseradish cream sauce, and arugula on marble rye bread.

Family-style character dinner: Tossed salad; roasted turkey breast, carved beef, smoked pork loin; mashed potatoes, market vegetables, herb bread stuffing, macaroni and cheese.

Plaza Restaurant

American cuisine. Lunch and dinner. $
A pleasant ambience permeates this informal restaurant located at the castle end of Main Street. Servers in Victorian dress mill about the art nouveau dining room serving simple but tasty sandwiches, hamburgers, and salads. If not for a meal, stop in for one of the famous ice cream specialties.

Best known for: Delicious ice cream creations.

SAMPLE MENU ITEMS

Lunch and dinner entrees: Grilled Reuben; cheesesteak sandwich; chicken and pear salad with garden greens, grilled chicken breast, fresh pears, gorgonzola cheese, and red onions tossed in a white zinfandel vinaigrette; create-your-own hamburger; fresh vegetable sandwich.

Tony's Town Square Restaurant

Italian cuisine. Lunch and dinner. $$$
At the end of Main Street nearest the park entrance sits Disney's delightful re-creation of Tony's Italian Restaurant as portrayed in the animated movie *Lady and the Tramp.* Romantic accordion music sets the mood in a Victorian-era trattoria of marble-topped tables, black-and-white checked flooring, gaslights, and colorful stained glass. Dinner is the key here (lunch is pretty unimaginative) beginning with tasty sun-dried tomato sauce in which to dip soft Italian bread. Amazingly enough, it seems that every other dish coming out of the kitchen is spaghetti and meatballs (actually it's pretty good); I prefer the tasty Chicken Fiorentina topped with prosciutto,

spinach, and melted cheese. If you can time it right for the afternoon parade or Spectromagic, the outdoor porch overlooking the Main Street square is the best seat in house.

Best known for: Spaghetti and meatballs.

SAMPLE MENU ITEMS

Lunch entrees: Tony's pizza (smoked chicken, spinach, caramelized onions, fontina cheese, and red pepper sauce); grilled chicken breast pressed panini sandwich with bacon, asiago cheese, and red onions; baked ziti with meat sauce and ricotta; pasta primavera; meatball sub.

Dinner entrees: Pork osso buco; twelve-ounce New York strip, truffled fontina macaroni and cheese and caramelized onion veal reduction; roulade of eggplant and ricotta, tomato sauce, and mozzarella cheese; clams, mussels, shrimp, and calamari with baby vegetables in spicy tarragon-tomato broth; grilled veal chop on wild mushroom bread pudding and shallot-balsamic demi-glace.

Epcot Dining

Biergarten Restaurant

German buffet at the Germany Pavilion in World Showcase. Lunch and dinner. $$$

It's a year-round Oktoberfest at this festive restaurant set in a faux Bavarian courtyard. Musicians clad in traditional Alpine clothing entertain with live oompah music accompanied by yodelers and folk dancers while guests feast on a German food buffet. Drinking giant steins of beer encourages introductions all around at communal dining tables with plenty of singing and clapping and the occasional round of "Ticky, Tacky, Ticky, Tacky, Oy, Oy, Oy! Prost!" I resisted dining here for quite some time and was actually pleasantly surprised by the fun atmosphere and tasty food.

Best known for: The oompah band.

SAMPLE MENU ITEMS

Lunch buffet: Chicken soup; cheese and cold cuts; rotisserie chicken, assorted sausage, roasted pork with mustard sauce, bratwurst; mushroom, potato, sliced beet, and bean and carrot salads; roasted red potatoes, braised red cabbage, *wein kraut,* spaetzle; apple strudel with vanilla sauce, Black Forest cake, cheesecake, raspberry almond cookies.

Dinner buffet: Same as lunch with the addition of sauerbraten, *frikadelle* (meatballs), and fish.

Bistro de Paris

French cuisine at the France Pavilion in World Showcase. Dinner only. $$$$

Upstairs from Chefs de France is a charming belle epoque dining room with an air of exclusivity. Gilded mirrors, white linen tablecloths, crimson banquettes, and billowy white drapes framing windows overlooking the World Showcase Lagoon provide the perfect setting for delicious French accents and luscious dishes prepared simply in tantalizing sauces. Favorites include a savory rack of lamb or one of the restaurant's lobster dishes. After dinner a dessert of crepe suzette prepared and flamed tableside while lingering over cordials and coffee is definitely my idea of a nightcap.

NOTE: Request a window table (most are for two) to receive a nice view of the lagoon.

Best known for: Flaming entrees and desserts.

SAMPLE MENU ITEMS

Dinner entrees: Maine lobster bisque flavored with sweet Vouvray wine; pan-seared young pheasant accompanied by savoy cabbage stuffed with foie gras and chestnuts, apple cider demi-glace; seared scallops with braised endives, citrus and truffle ravioli, and creamy white wine sauce; grilled tenderloin of beef, potato Emmentaler gnocchi, served with mushroom jus and green asparagus.

Chefs de France

French bistro cuisine at the France Pavilion in World Showcase. Lunch and dinner. $$–$$$$

This Left Bank–style bistro will transport you to the Paris of your dreams. In a fun and festive atmosphere, white-aproned waiters with romantic accents bustle about the glass-enclosed veranda-style restaurant. At lunch choose a bowl of onion soup crusty with bubbly gruyère accompanied by an excellent salade niçoise (ask them not to overcook the tuna). A nice ending is a traditional tart *tatin*.

NOTE: This is one of World Showcase's most popular restaurants, and advance reservations are highly recommended. The lunch menu is less expensive; however, the ambience is nicer in the evening. A veranda table for the fireworks is relaxing, but don't expect a perfect view.

Best known for: Filet au Poivre Noir, grilled tenderloin of beef with black pepper sauce and potato gratin.

SAMPLE MENU ITEMS

Lunch entrees: *Croque monsieur,* the classic French toasted ham and cheese sandwich; quiche lorraine; zucchini, eggplant, and tomato lasagna; seafood brochette of shrimp, scallops, and salmon served with paella; grilled hanger steak with black pepper sauce served with *pommes frites* (french fries).

Dinner entrees: Stuffed, baked codfish wrapped in potato slices with a lobster demi-glace, served on a bed of leeks; roast breast of duck and confit leg with cherries, *haricots verts* (green beans), and sweet potato puree; half of a farm-raised rotisserie chicken, panfried red potatoes, and braised tomato; baked macaroni with cream and gruyère cheese.

Coral Reef Restaurant

Seafood at the Living Seas Pavilion in Future World. Lunch and dinner. $$$–$$$$

Feel like the Little Mermaid in this one-of-a-kind, softly lit dining room of tiered leather banquettes lined with shimmering blue mosaic tiles. Dominating the restaurant and just a trident's throw away from all seats is the Living Seas' six-million-gallon aquarium rife with coral reefs and sea life; use the handy reference guide at your table to help identify the wide assortment of underwater creatures. Superfresh seafood is deliciously prepared with a flair, including a delicate grilled mahimahi with creamy garlic mashed potatoes and shiitake broth sauce. Skip the blackened catfish on smoked tomato compote with balsamic glaze (a specialty of the house); it's overseasoned with just too much going on, although the accompanying Pepper Jack cheese grits are to die for. Personally, I think the view of the aquarium alone is worth the price of a meal.

Best known for: Creamy lobster soup and Pepper Jack cheese grits.

SAMPLE MENU ITEMS

Lunch entrees: Grilled Atlantic salmon with sautéed corn, coriander, caramelized onions, asparagus, and smoked tomato broth; beef bourguignon lasagna; pan-seared chicken breast with curry risotto, cremini and lobster mushrooms, and curried ginger sauce; tofu, eggplant, and grilled vegetables with balsamic glaze.

Dinner entrees: Grilled scallops with Pepper Jack cheese polenta and lobster sauce; roasted lamb stuffed with sautéed spinach and andouille sausage with vegetable ravioli; seared South African lobster tail; pan-seared tilapia, crab cake, asparagus, hollandaise sauce, and tomato oil.

Garden Grill

American cuisine at the Land Pavilion in Future World. Lunch and dinner. $$$

Slowly revolve through views of the ecosystems seen in the Living with the Land attraction while seated in comfortable lime green– and carrot-colored booths. The previous all-you-care-to-eat skillets have been replaced by a family-style appetizer and dessert with your choice of five entrees. All meals begin with a platter of breadsticks accompanied by a trio of dipping sauces including roasted red pepper hummus, sharp cheddar cheese sauce, and a garlic and herb olive oil. Entrees are tasty but certainly not anything special, even though Disney has tried to modernize the menu. Perhaps the best part of the meal is the creamy orzo and pearl-barley risotto accompanying the chicken and fish entrees. I can't help but question, though, where are the vegetables that the Garden Grill is supposed to represent (a salad comes with dinner only)? End with a family-style dessert of yummy chocolate fondue with marshmallows, mini Toll House cookies, pound cake, fruit, and gummy worms for dipping. Farmer Mickey still hosts along with Chip 'n' Dale and Pluto, all dressed in jeans, overalls, and bandanas. And take the boat ride before your meal so you'll know what you're looking at from above.

NOTE: Request a booth in the bottom-seating tier for the best panorama.

Best known for: The view of the Living with the Land ride.

SAMPLE MENU ITEMS

Lunch and dinner entrees: Slow-roasted beef strip loin with natural au jus and carmelized-shallot mashed potatoes; seafood cioppino; mushroom ravioli and vegetables; chipotle-rubbed rotisserie chicken with orzo and pearl-barley risotto; grilled red snapper with orzo and pearl-barley risotto with a coconut-lime essence.

Le Cellier Steakhouse

Steaks at the Canada Pavilion in World Showcase. Lunch and dinner. $$–$$$$

A wine cellar setting with low ceilings and snug fireplaces makes for cozy dining in the Canada pavilion. Although the food is tasty, with steaks as the house specialty, you'll find nothing unusually memorable with the exception of the outstanding porcini-dusted mushroom filet mignon served atop a creamy wild mushroom risotto, with truffle and beurre blanc sauce topped with fried parsnips. With a dessert of maple crème brûlée or the Canadian Club cake, you'll have the makings of a perfect meal. And try a choice from the cellar, showcasing a nice selection of Canadian wines, Old World–style craft ales, and Canadian apple cider. At the very least, stop in for a bowl of the best cheddar cheese soup on the planet, and don't hesitate to request the recipe before leaving.

Best known for: Canadian cheddar cheese soup.

SAMPLE MENU ITEMS

Lunch entrees: Grilled steak burger topped with your choice of cheddar, gruyère, or blue cheese; ten-ounce New York strip steak finished with veal demi-glace; grilled chili-spiced jumbo shrimp and *tasso* ham tossed with linguine, basil, and wilted rapini in a roasted tomato broth.

Dinner entrees: Sterling salmon with maple butter; herb-crusted prime rib finished with veal demi-glace; grilled portobello and sweet potato stack served on roasted tomato and eggplant sauce; grilled double bone Hatfield pork chop over sweet potato bacon hash and black mission figs; seared free-range chicken breast over cream cheese mashed potatoes with roasted onion broth.

L'Originale di Roma Ristorante

Italian cuisine in the Italy Pavilion in World Showcase. Lunch and dinner. $$$–$$$$

In the waiting area of this elegant World Showcase dining spot you'll find photos of celebrities feasting at Alfredo de Lelio's original eatery in Rome, whose claim to fame was fettucine Alfredo. This ornate restaurant is a beauty, with blazing chandeliers, trompe l'oeil walls, and white-coated waiters parading with giant silver trays of steaming food. Alas, the fare, mediocre at best, doesn't live up to the atmosphere. Food here is totally inconsistent, with meat sometimes cooked until dry and pasta often mushy (it used to be too al dente—go figure!). But I can't fault them on service. The all-Italian staff is ultrafriendly and super efficient. Additional patio dining is a pleasant alternative, offering views of the piazza and its sparkling fountain of Neptune.

Best known for: Fettucine Alfredo.

SAMPLE MENU ITEMS

Lunch entrees: Lasagna with veal bolognese and cream sauce, mozzarella, and Parmesan cheese; slow-roasted half chicken with aged white grape sauce served on gorgonzola polenta; Italian sausage, onion, and green peppers in tomato sauce.

Dinner entrees: Gnocchi a la bolognese; lamb roast cooked with wild herbs in its own juices and served with garlic and rosemary roasted potatoes and fresh vegetables; fettucine noodles in a traditional Italian tomato, cream, and vodka sauce, served with jumbo shrimp; osso buco, slow-roasted pork shank in a sauce of demi-glace, porcini mushroom, Barbera wine, tomato and *gremolata* served with fresh garlic mashed potatoes and *peperonata* (sautéed sweet peppers).

Nine Dragons

Chinese cuisine at the China Pavilion in World Showcase. Lunch and dinner. $$–$$$$

Rich in beautifully carved rosewood decor, Oriental carpets, and lantern-style lighting, this elegant restaurant serves typical Chinese dishes inspired by five provinces. Lunch brings an assortment of just so-so dim sum choices along with fairly good a la carte selections. But don't really expect anything much different than the standard fare at one of your better local Chinese restaurants with a gracious staff.

Best known for: Peking duck dinner.

SAMPLE MENU ITEMS

Lunch dim sum: Sweet rice *shai mai;* steamed dumplings with peanuts and Chinese vegetables; steamed chicken and shrimp balls coated with pearls of sweet rice; *Xiao* long buns; roast duckling; pork pot stickers; savory beef shank in spicy dressing; seafood noodle bowl.

Lunch and dinner entrees: Rainbow kung pao chicken; scallops with black bean sauce; beef with spicy *sha cha* sauce; stir-fried shrimp with garden vegetables; stir-fried seasonal Chinese vegetables; lobster and sea treasure casserole (lobster tail, shrimp, scallops, and squid sautéed with ginger and scallions in white sauce).

Restaurant Akershus

Scandinavian cuisine at the Norway Pavilion in World Showcase. Breakfast, lunch, and dinner. $$$

Those traveling with their own little princess should definitely book a meal at this fairytale dining spot. Housed in a replica of Oslo's Akershus Castle, the dining room sparkles with massive iron chandeliers, high-beamed ceilings, lovely, cut-glass windows, and a friendly waitstaff clothed in traditional Norwegian dress. Disney Princesses and other characters are in attendance for all meals and may include Belle, Jasmine, Snow White, Ariel, Sleeping Beauty, Mary Poppins, Pocahontas, or Mulan. Breakfast is a standard, American, family-style meal, but where Akershus really shines is at dinner. Begin with a platter of unusual but tasty cold selections including mackerel, gravlaks, smoked salmon, chilled scrambled eggs, and a variety of cheeses, all followed by your choice of an entree accompanied with a side platter of mashed rutabaga (really quite good), meatballs, and boiled potatoes. I was quite pleased with my entree choice, an excellent piece of grilled salmon served over celery root mashed potatoes. Your meal ends with a family-style dessert platter of traditional rice cream, chocolate mousse, and lingonberry tart. An excellent way to sample a bit of unfamiliar Scandinavian fare.

NOTE: A $10.00-per-adult and $5.00-per-child credit card deposit is required to guarantee a reservation. Cancellations must be made forty-eight hours in advance.

SAMPLE MENU ITEMS

Family-style breakfast: Pastries and breakfast bread; fruit; bacon, sausage; scrambled eggs; French toast; breakfast potatoes.

Lunch entrees: Braised lamb and cabbage; grilled chicken salad; salmon niçoise salad; vegetable tart served on top of salad greens drizzled with balsamic reduction; pasta Akershus tossed in a Chardonnay cream sauce with seasonal vegetables topped with Jarlsberg cheese.

Dinner entrees: Grilled chicken with pasta Akershus; braised lamb and cabbage; fresh poached cod with seafood and shrimp, julienne vegetables, and horseradish mashed potatoes; grilled salmon with celery root mashed potatoes topped with corn and caper relish; venison stew.

Restaurant Marrakesh

Moroccan cuisine at the Morocco Pavilion in World Showcase. Lunch and dinner. $$$–$$$$

The soul of Morocco is certainly captured in one of World Showcase's best dining venues. With the feel of a lavish palace, its lacelike walls, carved columns, and graceful arches are interspersed with vibrant mosaic tiles and a lofty inlaid ceiling. Agreeable waiters in colorful silk clothing and fez hats work the two-tiered dining room around the hip-wiggling belly dancer and Middle Eastern musicians; it's even more entertaining when members of the audience get involved. The Moroccan cuisine is extremely appetizing with its many exotic spices and delicate accompanying couscous that's part of each meal. Choosing a dish is difficult, so take a crack at one of the combination meals offering a little of everything. This is one of the best and certainly the most authentic attempts in Epcot to re-create the atmosphere of international dining.

NOTE: This is usually an easy place to dine without advance reservations.

Best known for: The belly dancing and spicy cuisine.

SAMPLE MENU ITEMS

Lunch and dinner entrees: Marrakesh Feast and the Royal Feast (family-style meal with a sampling of appetizers, entrees, and dessert from the entire menu); roasted lamb; shish kebab of beef; lemon chicken (braised half chicken seasoned with garlic, green olives, and preserved lemons); broiled salmon marinated in Moroccan herbs and spices; vegetable couscous.

Rose and Crown Pub and Dining Room

Pub food at the United Kingdom Pavilion in World Showcase. Lunch and dinner. $$–$$$

Nestled on the banks of the World Showcase Lagoon is an English pub with snug dining rooms and a rich wood bar. Old-fashioned etched-glass windows, dark beams, gleaming brass, and pressed tin ceilings are surrounded by walls loaded down with dartboards and family pictures. The delightful English accent of your server is worth the hefty price of the simple food the likes of tasty, thickly battered fish and fat chips or yummy cottage pies. Unlike most places in England, here you'll find soft drinks served with plenty of ice and beer served frosty cold. Outside dining affords the best panorama of the Illuminations fireworks.

NOTE: Most, but not all, of the outdoor tables come with a view of the Illuminations fireworks.

Best known for: Harry Ramsden's famous fish-and-chips.

SAMPLE MENU ITEMS

Lunch entrees: Cottage pie (ground beef with carrots, topped with mashed potatoes and cheddar cheese); Guinness beef stew; bangers and mash (traditional English sausage, sautéed cabbage, mashed potatoes, and onion gravy); chicken pastry (chicken and vegetables wrapped in a pie dough topped with a cream sauce); curried vegetables served with jasmine rice.

Dinner entrees: English pie sampler (chicken and leek, pork, and cottage pies); roasted chicken with sage-onion stuffing; pan-seared steak with batter-fried prawns; pan-seared salmon filet with jasmine rice and barley, green beans, and caper relish; twelve-ounce rib eye with Yorkshire pudding and scotch mushroom sauce.

San Angel Inn

South-of-the-border cuisine at the Mexico Pavilion in World Showcase. Lunch and dinner. $$$

It's hard to find a more romantic restaurant than San Angel, where it's perpetual nighttime alongside the inky Rio del Tiempo (River of Time). Having grown up near the U.S.–Mexico border, I consider myself a Mexican food aficionado, and I must say that the traditional dishes here are good. The combination plates are the most popular and very tasty, but consider branching out to the meat and seafood dishes prepared in a variety of piquant sauces. Those not used to spice may be in for a bit of a surprise— a pleasant one, I hope—however, not all dishes are prepared with chiles (your waiter can recommend a dish without the heat). Margaritas here are only passable but, if you're in luck, the fabulous Mariachi Cobre will be performing during your meal. My only quibble is the basket of store-bought tostadas served upon arrival; however, the yummy red salsa accompanying it makes up for any lack of authenticity in the chips.

Best known for: The romantic atmosphere.

SAMPLE MENU ITEMS

Lunch entrees: Sample several items by ordering the *plato nacionale* featuring a beef burrito, tamale, and beef flauta (beef rolled in a corn tortilla and crispy fried) each topped with a different tasty sauce; tacos *al carbon* (flour tortillas filled with grilled chicken or beef with peppers, onions, guacamole, and pico de gallo relish); *pollo a las rajas* (grilled chicken breast served over red peppers, onions, poblano chiles, Mexican sausage, and melted cheese).

Dinner entrees: Mahimahi à la Veracruzana (grilled fish fillet prepared with capers, olives, onions, and tomatoes) served with chipotle mashed potatoes; *plato Mexicano* featuring beef tenderloin *tampiquena* style, chicken enchilada, and beef burrito; beef tenderloin tips sautéed with onions and poblano chiles covered with roasted chile *pasilla* sauce; grilled shrimp served over angel-hair pasta with tomatoes and chipotle peppers.

Tempura Kiku

Japanese cuisine at the Japan Pavilion in World Showcase. Lunch and dinner. $$–$$$

Devotees of tempura will love this delightfully cozy space where they'll find the lightly battered, deep-fried meats and vegetables so popular in Japanese restaurants. Compensating for its compact size is charming bar-style seating around a U-shaped counter rimming the cooking space, allowing guests a view of the chefs as they prepare the tasty tidbits. Also on the menu is a small offering of sashimi and sushi along with Kirin beer, sake, wine, and green tea.

SAMPLE MENU ITEMS

Lunch and dinner entrees: Tempura choices—chicken, shrimp, scallops, fish, and skewered beef served with tempura vegetables, *sumashi* soup, green salad, and steamed rice.

Teppanyaki

Japanese cuisine at the Japan Pavilion in World Showcase. Lunch and dinner. $$–$$$$

A smoking-hot teppan grill is the centerpiece of each black-lacquered counter around which guests are seated to watch the show provided by a lightning-quick, multitalented Japanese chef. In his tall white chef's hat, he chops, slices, and dices while stir-frying the meats and vegetables for his table of eight guests. Similar to the Benihana restaurants found around the United States, it is well worth the money for the delicious yet simple food and the unforgettable show that goes along with it.

Best known for: The performance put on by the chefs.

SAMPLE MENU ITEMS

Lunch and dinner entrees: All entrees prepared on the teppan grill accompanied by grilled vegetables, mixed green salad, and steamed rice; *entree choices:* chicken, shrimp, scallops, sirloin, tenderloin, or simply a large portion of vegetables as well as numerous combinations; *everyone's favorite:* lobster and tenderloin steak.

Disney–MGM Studios Dining

50s Prime Time Café

American cuisine. Lunch and dinner. $$–$$$

Pass through a time warp into a 1950s family kitchen where guests dine while watching *Leave It to Beaver* and *Topper* on black-and-white TVs sitting on the counter between the toaster and the blender. Linoleum floors, Formica tables, pull-down lamps, and windows covered in venetian blinds and tacky drapes are accompanied by a menu of savory renditions of good old American comfort food. "Mom" herself is your server, making sure everyone in the "family" observes good manners. No fighting at the table! No throwing spitballs! Mustn't forget to eat your vegetables! Our "mom" told us to set our own table; she didn't do chores. Check out the adjoining Tune-In Lounge for an appetizer and drinks before dinner.

Best known for: Great golden fried chicken.

SAMPLE MENU ITEMS

Lunch entrees: Caramelized salmon served with roasted potatoes and mushrooms; vegetarian stuffed pepper; traditional meat loaf; old-fashioned pot roast; chicken pot pie; seafood primavera; stacked sandwich.

Dinner entrees: Charbroiled pork tenderloin glazed with chipotle barbecue sauce and served with cheddar and bacon mashed potatoes; New York strip steak topped with roasted mushrooms; grilled tuna salad; barbecue spiced grilled chicken breast.

Hollywood and Vine

American buffet. Dinner only. $$$

In this art deco diner at Hollywood and Vine are Naugahyde banquettes and Formica tables accented by shiny chrome serving counters where buffet lovers choose from an array of pretty standard but homey items. Ask to dine outside on the veranda if it's afternoon parade time for a nice view of the festivities. This is one of three restaurants here offering the Fantasmic Dinner Package (full details on page 210).

Best known for: Roasted sweet potatoes with root beer–bourbon glaze.

SAMPLE MENU ITEMS

Dinner buffet: Salad bar; sage-rubbed rotisserie turkey, grilled flank steak, oven-baked chicken, chef's catch of the day, shrimp Alfredo penne pasta, vegetable lo mein; mashed potatoes, roasted sweet potatoes with root beer and bourbon glaze, curry rice, corn with roasted peppers, marinated tomatoes with buffalo mozzarella; soft-serve ice cream with toppings, cookies, assorted cakes and tarts, Snickers cheesecake; *children's buffet:* barbecue meatballs, hot dogs, macaroni and cheese, chicken strips.

Hollywood Brown Derby

Contemporary cuisine. Lunch and dinner. $$$–$$$$
The best food at Disney–MGM Studios is to be found at the illustrious Brown Derby, perfectly re-created right down to the collection of celebrity caricatures hanging on just about every square inch of wall space. It's sheer 1930s Hollywood glamour, seen everywhere from the rich mahogany walls and furnishings to the sway of potted palms. Massive cast-iron chandeliers, crisp white tablecloths, snug ruby red banquettes, and derby-shaped art deco lamps all set the mood for a sentimental waltz through the heyday of Hollywood. You can't go wrong with any of the fish dishes—on my last visit I tried a lightly breaded and sautéed grouper with a lemon butter sauce; simply perfect. The wine list is exceptionally good for a theme park, with many types available by the glass. Of course, there's the famous Brown Derby cobb salad (so finely chopped, the lettuce resembles parsley) along with the signature grapefruit cake for dessert (a must-try). This is also one of three restaurants here offering the Fantasmic Dinner Package (full details on page 210).

NOTE: Your server won't mind providing you with the recipe for the cobb salad and grapefruit cake; just ask.

Best known for: Brown Derby cobb salad.

SAMPLE MENU ITEMS

Lunch entrees: Sesame-seared yellowfin tuna cobb salad with avocado, chives, and cucumber tossed in wasabi vinaigrette with sweet and spicy noodles; Thai noodle bowl with coconut-crusted tofu, edamame, bok choy, and shiitake mushrooms in red curry broth; grilled New York strip marinated in ale with *chimichurri* and boniato mashed potatoes; grilled Atlantic salmon "bruschetta" with chilled marinated seasonal vegetable, lemon aioli, toasted fennel oil, and white balsamic syrup.

Dinner entrees: Sesame seared ahi with wasabi whipped potatoes, sugar peas, ginger soy reduction, and coriander lime essence; roasted pork tenderloin with tomato napoleon, butter bean succotash, and Madiera-sage pan juices; mustard-crusted rack of lamb with potatoes gratin, rosemary garlic fusion, and port wine; grilled Atlantic salmon on creamy polenta, gorgonzola, oven-dried tomatoes, arugula, and balsamic butter sauce.

Mama Melrose's Ristorante Italiano

Italian cuisine. Lunch and dinner. $$–$$$
Frank Sinatra and Tony Bennett music sets the tone at this New York–style Italian restaurant. It's actually a warehouse scene in Hollywood with ceilings dripping in grape-laden vines, long salamis, strings of garlic, straw-wrapped Chianti bottles, and strands of twinkling lights. The redbrick walls are covered in vintage LP record albums, old movie posters, and Hollywood street signs. Food is tasty but not memorable, with the exception of the wood-oven, thin-crusted flatbreads for which Mama Melrose's excels. This is one of three restaurants here offering the Fantasmic Dinner Package (full details on page 210).

Best known for: Veal osso buco with risotto Milanese.

SAMPLE MENU ITEMS

Lunch entrees: Grilled chicken flatbread with sun-dried tomato pesto, pancetta, Asiago cheese, and fresh chives; penne alla vodka with pancetta, sweet onion, and tomato basil cream; eggplant napoleon; Tuscan chicken bruschetta; oak-grilled tuna with sun-dried tomato pesto in tomato broth.

Dinner Entrees: Oven-baked chicken Parmesan over pasta; Fra Diavolo with clams, shrimp, mussels, and calamari tossed in a spicy marinara sauce over spaghetti rigati; oak-grilled salmon basted with sun-dried tomato pesto over fire-roasted vegetables; charred sirloin steak over roasted red pepper polenta with gorgonzola butter and red wine reduction.

Sci-Fi Dine-In Theater Restaurant

American cuisine. Lunch and dinner. $$–$$$
Anyone lonesome for the drive-ins of their youth will go mad for this

place. Load into sleek, 1950s-era convertibles to watch B-movie sci-fi and horror trailers amid roller-skating waiters who carhop the darkened, starlit theater. Speaker boxes hang on the side of your car and, of course, popcorn and hot dogs dance on the screen during intermission. Though the food is just so-so, who cares when Godzilla is your entertainment!

NOTE: If you want to be seated quicker, let them know you're willing to sit at one of the picnic tables instead of in a car. Stop in during nonprime hours for dessert and soak up the surroundings in one of Disney's best themed restaurants.

Best known for: The atmosphere, certainly not the food.

SAMPLE MENU ITEMS

Lunch entrees: Reuben sandwich; slow-roasted barbecue ribs cooked in Coca-Cola; flatiron steak sandwich; all-American burger; barbecue chicken breast sandwich topped with Gouda.

Dinner entrees: Shrimp penne pasta with garlic, capers, tomatoes, and spinach; vegetable potato bake; panfried catfish with Cajun remoulade; pan-seared salmon and lemon caper butter; chicken Caesar salad.

Animal Kingdom Dining

Donald's Prehistoric Breakfastosaurus

American buffet in Dinoland. Breakfast only. $$$
Start your day at the Animal Kingdom with a tasty character breakfast buffet hosted by Donald Duck himself. He brings along fisherman Goofy and scout troop leader Mickey with his dog Pluto in tow to this dig site base camp for student paleontologists (your waitstaff). Eat on rustic tables stacked with Melmac camping mugs in barracks-style dining rooms among dinosaur fossils, but beware of waiters who love to tease and play tricks on unsuspecting visitors. After breakfast this place reverts to a fast-food spot with burgers and Happy Meals from McDonald's.

Best known for: Being one of the few character meals featuring Donald Duck.

SAMPLE MENU ITEMS

Breakfast buffet: Frittatas, omelets, scrambled eggs; hash browns, skillet potatoes, pancakes, cinnamon French toast, oatmeal, grits, cereal, breakfast pizza; sausage, bacon; fresh fruit, juice; biscuits and gravy, muffins, doughnuts, coffee cake, bagels.

Rainforest Café

American cuisine at the Entrance Plaza. Breakfast, lunch, and dinner. Call (407) WDW–DINE, or (407) 939–3463, or (407) 938–9100 for advance reservations. $–$$$$
Dine among the beasts of the jungle surrounded by crashing waterfalls, lush tropical foliage, dripping vines, and giant aquarium tanks while being bombarded with thunderstorms and noisy Audio-Animatronics wildlife. Although the atmosphere outweighs the food, it certainly is a delightful place, one that should definitely be on your Disney agenda. If you'd like a sampling of the ambience without a meal, stop for a drink at the cafe's Magic Mushroom to sip on specialty drinks, smoothies, juice, and coffee under a towering toadstool roof. An outside-the-park entrance allows dining without admission to the park.

NOTE: Priority reservations are taken and are highly recommended for lunch. Breakfast service begins a half hour before park opening time. Mammoth portions require either a big appetite or the need to split an entree.

Best known for: Audio-Animatronics jungle beasts.

SAMPLE MENU ITEMS

Breakfast entrees: Tonga toast (baked cinnamon French toast surrounded by fresh strawberries and bananas); eggs Benedict; warm tortilla wrapped around scrambled eggs sautéed with peppers, andouille (spicy pork sausage), and Creole sauce; waffle served with fresh strawberries, bananas, and maple syrup.

Lunch and dinner entrees: Hong Kong stir-fry; pot roast; cobb salad; buffalo fried chicken salad; shrimp, penne pasta, mushrooms, sun-dried tomatoes, and sweet peas tossed in Alfredo sauce; slow-roasted pork ribs basted with barbecue sauce, served with coleslaw and fries; Rainforest natural burger; Maine lobster filled with crabmeat.

Walt Disney World Resort Dining

The best dining experiences in the "World" are to be found at Disney's deluxe resorts. Back in 1996, the California Grill set the pace when it opened to rave reviews with an ever-changing menu of New American cuisine. One by one the deluxe hotels have launched a new breed of dining venues offering innovative cuisine and superior wine lists, one of which, Victoria and Albert's, boasts a AAA Five-Diamond Award rating, the only such restaurant in central Florida.

Artist Point

Pacific Northwest cuisine at the Wilderness Lodge. Dinner only; casual dress. Open daily 5:30–10:00 P.M. $$$–$$$$
The rustic, U.S. National Park theme of the Wilderness Lodge continues into this attractive dining establishment where the intoxicating aroma of cedar wafts among the expanse of fat ponderosa pine columns, vaulted ceilings, and Old West murals. Oversize windows overlook sparkling Bay Lake and the hotel's enchanting courtyard of giant boulders and cascading waterfalls; on pleasant days request a table on the outdoor terrace. The decor does, however, take a backseat to the Pacific Northwest cuisine of fresh seafood and game meats. I couldn't have been happier with my divine smoky portobello soup, grilled buffalo sirloin with sweet potato–hazelnut gratin, and a nice glass of Washington State wine. And don't even think of leaving without trying the decadent Coffee Two Ways dessert of mochaccino bread pudding and vanilla latte crème brûlée—it's worth every calorie.

NOTE: Before dark ask for a view of Bay Lake. After dark request the knockout view of the illuminated courtyard waterfall. Then take a romantic postdinner walk through the property to the edge of Bay Lake and wait for the geyser to erupt (every hour on the hour until 10:00 P.M.).

Best known for: Cedar plank roasted salmon with truffle-honey-brown butter.

SAMPLE MENU ITEMS

Dinner entrees: Pan-seared tuna with roasted parsnips, shallots, chanterelle mushrooms, escarole, and sherry *gastrique* (reduction glaze); roasted free-range chicken breast with fennel-russet potato hash; potato-

DISNEY RESORTS'
BEST RESTAURANTS

- California Grill, perched high atop the Contemporary Resort with its picture-perfect views of the Magic Kingdom.
- Citricos at the Grand Floridian Hotel, featuring innovative Mediterranean cuisine.
- Flying Fish at Disney's Boardwalk, specializing in seafood and everything whimsical.
- Victoria and Albert's at the Grand Floridian for a special evening of romance and fantastic food.
- Artist Point at the Wilderness Lodge for exceptional Pacific Northwest cuisine.
- Shula's at the Walt Disney World Dolphin for the best steaks around.
- Bluezoo at the Walt Disney World Dolphin for great seafood in a hip setting.
- Jiko at the Animal Kingdom Lodge, an atmospheric restaurant with an African flair.

chive pot stickers with soybeans, spinach, mizuna, and soy vinaigrette; Hatfield pork chop on Tillamook cheddar macaroni and cheese with Maytag blue-cheese crust; pan-seared scallops on red flannel hash with parsley emulsion.

Beaches and Cream
American cuisine at the Beach Club Resort. Lunch and dinner; park casual dress. Open daily, 11:00 A.M.–11:00 P.M. $
Sit in one of the marble-topped booths or at the hopping counter in this vintage-style soda shop and listen to the old-fashioned jukebox (the one on your table is just for looks) while dining on tasty burgers and the best

crispy onion rings around. But I say forget the food, and just go for a thick, icy malt served in a frosty fountain glass with the extras on the side in the stainless steel shaker; it's the best I've had anywhere. Whatever, do not neglect to find your way to this adorable place, just a quick walk away from Epcot's International Gateway. A walk-up counter allows for a speedy stop for ice cream or menu takeout.

NOTE: This very small place can really become crowded after the Epcot fireworks; come in the afternoon when it's not hopping with hungry, exhausted diners.

Best known for: The Kitchen Sink, eight scoops of ice cream smothered with every topping on the menu.

SAMPLE MENU ITEMS

Lunch and dinner entrees: Hamburgers and cheeseburgers; grilled roast beef sub with provolone, grilled peppers, and onions; grilled chicken sandwich; deli turkey sandwich; veggie burgers; hot dogs; chicken Caesar salad; chili.

Desserts: Fudge Mud Slide (gooey chewy brownie covered with hot fudge, ice cream, Oreos, and whipped cream); classic banana split; Coke or root beer float; old-fashioned sundaes; Milky Way Sundae (Bundt cake topped with ice cream, hot fudge, butterscotch, whipped cream, and a cherry).

Boma

African-inspired buffet at the Animal Kingdom Lodge. Breakfast and dinner; casual dress. Open daily, 7:30–11:00 A.M. and 5:00–10:00 P.M. $$$
The essence of Africa is potent beneath Boma's circular thatch roof where hearty foods prepared with an African flair (and a dash of American cuisine for the picky eater) are the fare. Even if you're just a bit adventuresome, you'll like this most interesting of Disney buffets. Earthy colors are dominant in the appealing but noisy dining room filled with hardwood chairs adorned with fanciful African-style designs and green leather booths topped with kraal fences. Breakfast is quite good, with plenty of great American favorites along with delicious African specialties like *bobotie,* a custard made with ground lamb. Evenings the place comes alive with a bountiful spread of African soups and stews, savory wood-roasted meats, and an entire section (or pod) of meatless dishes, all served in a lively buffet setting. It's the perfect place to try a different and exciting cuisine.

NOTE: If you're in luck you'll be around during breakfast or late in the evening when the African staff sing rhythmic songs from their homelands.
Best known for: Tasty wood-roasted meats.

SAMPLE MENU ITEMS

Breakfast buffet: Orange juice or Frunch (a blend of lemonade, pineapple, guava, papaya, and orange juices); fresh and dried fruit; pastries, brioche, cereal, oatmeal, quinoa porridge, pap (an African cornmeal dish), pancakes, waffles, breakfast pizza; carving station with roasted ham and cured pork loin, bacon, sausage; made-to-order omelets, scrambled eggs; roasted potatoes with peppers.

Dinner buffet: Mixed field greens, Moroccan seafood, watermelon rind, black-eyed peas with ginger juice, spinach and quinoa, fried plantain, corn; avocado, papaya, and grapefruit salads; hummus; chicken corn porridge, chicken pepper pot, smoked tomato soup, curried coconut seafood stew; African breads; coconut curried salmon, whole spiced chicken, African-spiced center cut top sirloin, crusted prime rib with sauces; *bobotie* (custard made with ground lamb); *fufu* (mashed yams), Jollos rice, couscous Marrakesh, falafel, roasted vegetables; zebra domes (ganache-covered chocolate-coffee mousse), brownies, banana bread pudding, pineapple cheesecake, coconut pudding; *children's buffet:* macaroni and cheese, chicken tenders, penne pasta and meatballs.

California Grill

Contemporary American cuisine at the Contemporary Resort. Dinner only; smart casual dress. Open nightly, 5:30–10:00 P.M. $$$–$$$$
This sensational restaurant should be at the top of every visitor's list to Walt Disney World. I am a view fanatic, and this drop-dead-gorgeous setting on the fifteenth floor of the Contemporary Resort enjoys the most mesmerizing panorama in all of Disney. From its lofty heights diners can see the Magic Kingdom, the sparkling Seven Seas Lagoon, and, best of all, a picture-perfect view of the Wishes fireworks. From exemplary sushi to the exceptional New American cuisine to sensational desserts and the outstanding California wine list each available by the glass, this place has it all. It's a kick to watch the kitchen action from the dining room, and the cocktail lounge has some of the best vistas in the house. Procuring a window seat can be tough, but don't be discouraged; time your meal around

the fireworks and head outside to the super observation platform for a bird's-eye view of the extravaganza.

NOTE: Reservations here go quickly, so plan ahead. A new check-in procedure is now in force—head to the third floor, where you'll check in and be escorted upstairs.

Best known for: Grilled pork tenderloin with creamy polenta, cremini (mushrooms), and Zinfandel glaze.

SAMPLE MENU ITEMS

Dinner entrees: Chili-rubbed free-range chicken breast with braised bean medley, smoked bell peppers, and jicama slaw; sturgeon steamed with banana leaf, basmati rice, macadamia nuts, cucumbers, and Hong Kong vinaigrette; pumpkin lasagna with brown butter-sage vinaigrette, spinach, dried cranberries, and pistachios; oak-fired beef filet with three-cheese potato gratin and tamarind barbecue sauce; roasted wild striped bass with chanterelle (mushroom) risotto, braised oxtails, and red wine sauce.

Cape May Café

Seafood buffet at the Beach Club Resort. Breakfast and dinner; casual dress. Open daily, 7:30–11:00 A.M. and 5:30–9:30 P.M. $$$
Colorful beach umbrellas and Victorian seaside murals create a New England seaside atmosphere that is bright and cheerful at Cape May Café. Goofy's Beach Bash is a popular character breakfast buffet with his friends Minnie and Chip 'n' Dale, all clad in bathing attire. However, the all-you-can-eat seafood buffet in the evenings is one of my least favorite Disney dining experiences, a New England–style clambake featuring a steam pit full of tasty but overcooked mussels, clams, and shrimp accompanied by unexciting sides. Your best bet is to head across the Boardwalk to the Flying Fish, where you'll find exemplary cuisine.

Best known for: The all-you-can-eat steamed mussels, shrimp, and clams (why, I don't know.)

SAMPLE MENU ITEMS

Breakfast buffet: Juice, fresh fruit, yogurt; scrambled eggs, omelets, and eggs to order; bacon, sausage; Mickey waffles, French toast, pancakes, biscuits and gravy, potatoes, oatmeal, cereal; pastries, breakfast bread pudding with vanilla sauce.

Dinner buffet: Peel-and-eat shrimp; clam chowder, tomato bisque; mixed green, Caesar, potato, seafood, broccoli, and ambrosia salads; coleslaw; steamed mussels and clams, baked fish, barbecue ribs, hand-carved prime rib; pasta of the day; mashed red-skinned and steamed red bliss potatoes, corn on the cob, vegetables; corn bread; key lime pie, cookies, chocolate cake, brownies, flan, cheesecake, cupcakes, Oreo bonbons; *children's buffet:* fish nuggets, chicken strips, macaroni and cheese, kid-size hot dogs.

Chef Mickey's

American buffet at the Contemporary Resort. Breakfast and dinner; casual dress. Open daily, 7:00–11:30 A.M. and 5:00–9:30 P.M. $$$$
Join Mickey, Goofy, Minnie, and Chip 'n' Dale (with Donald Duck in the evening) for a lively buffet on the fourth-floor Grand Canyon Concourse of the Contemporary Resort. The decor here follows the mood of the resort with intense colors of purple and teal, sharp angles, and plenty of chrome with supersize flatware lining the noisy, bright dining room. The characters, attired in chef's clothing, schmooze with guests below the gliding monorail, and every forty minutes or so it's a party when they lead diners in a cheerful song accompanied by plenty of dancing and napkin waving. Food is home-style cooking with lots of choices, but nothing stands out unless you count a heaping serving of the best Parmesan mashed potatoes around. If children are not a part of your vacation and steam tables leave you cold, I would definitely skip this one. Make early reservations for this extremely popular feast.

Best known for: Parmesan mashed potatoes.

SAMPLE MENU ITEMS

Breakfast buffet: Scrambled eggs, egg and sausage roulade, three-cheese omelet; bacon, sausage links; Mickey waffles, vegetable lasagna, cheese potatoes, breakfast pizza, cinnamon-sugar French toast, pancakes made to order with a variety of toppings, buttermilk biscuits and gravy; bagels, chocolate croissants, muffins, cinnamon rolls, Rice Krispies Treats, peach cobbler, warm bread pudding, Danish pastry.

Dinner buffet: Soup and premium salad bar; chef-carved prime rib and oven-roasted ham, adobo roasted chicken, baked cod with dijon tarragon butter, beef tips with mushrooms, penne pasta with seafood; Parmesan mashed potatoes, Spanish vegetable rice, Mickey cheese ravioli and marinara sauce; broccoli with black olives and feta, orange-glazed carrots; make-your-own sundaes and cupcakes, lemon meringue pie, chocolate mousse cake, carrot cake, brownies, cobbler, cheesecake, cookies; *children's buffet:* macaroni and cheese, pizza, chicken tenders, tiny hot dogs.

 Citricos

Contemporary Mediterranean food at the Grand Floridian Resort. Dinner only; smart casual dress. Open Wednesday through Sunday, 5:30–10:00 P.M., lounge 5:30–11:00 P.M. $$$–$$$$

An ambitious, ever-changing menu delivers innovative Mediterranean cuisine with admirable results. Combined with a sophisticated, contemporary dining room and exhibition kitchen reminiscent of the California Grill, this is a not-to-be-missed spot. Starched white linens emblazoned with Citricos's logo, rich silk curtains, mosaic tiles, and swirling wrought iron are enhanced by immense windows affording views of the charming resort courtyard and, in the distance, the Magic Kingdom fireworks. The standouts: a sautéed shrimp appetizer with lemon, white wine, and feta cheese, the warm goat cheese salad, and a tender duck loin with a ragout of spinach, shiitake, and white beans. A *Wine Spectator* Restaurant Award winner, its over 200 selections of international offerings shine in every category, making it possibly the best in "the World."

Best known for: Braised veal shank.

SAMPLE MENU ITEMS

Dinner entrees: Sautéed salmon fillet with black olive butter and roasted fennel; seared tuna, saffron *pappardelle,* tomatoes, olives, and capers; grilled pork tenderloin, celery root mash, and red wine jus; roasted free-range chicken with vegetable quinoa and tomato cilantro sauce; braised autumn vegetables with goat cheese, pesto, and beurre blanc.

Concourse Steakhouse

Steak at the Contemporary Resort. Breakfast, lunch, and dinner; casual dress. Open daily, 7:30–11:00 A.M., noon–2:00 P.M., and 5:30–10:00 P.M. $$–$$$

This space-age-looking steak house is open to the soaring Grand Concourse with nice views of the monorail gliding overhead. Simple but not spectacular grilled steaks are the specialty here; nothing fancy, just decent, fresh food. However, it's not simple enough that you can just show up after the Magic Kingdom fireworks and expect a seat—come prepared with advance reservations or be willing to fight it out with droves of diners. Breakfast features the usual suspects with the addition of yummy smoothies and shakes in eight varieties. Lunch, just a monorail ride away, is a good choice for a quiet respite from the Magic Kingdom.

Best known for: Hickory-smoked prime rib.

SAMPLE MENU ITEMS

Breakfast entrees: Steak and eggs; challah French toast with mixed berry sauce; eggs Benedict; Western omelet; steak house platter with two eggs any style, French toast, bacon, sausage, and biscuit; blueberry pancakes.

Lunch entrees: Blackened salmon sandwich; ten-ounce New York strip steak with roasted garlic smashed potatoes and cabernet sauce; chicken and spinach pizza; spicy buffalo chicken sandwich; chicken quesadilla.

Dinner entrees: Herb-crusted Atlantic salmon with creamy saffron sauce; barbecue pork ribs with smashed boniato (sweet potatoes) and onion rings; herb-crusted salmon; sixteen-ounce T-bone with cabernet sauce and red wine butter; barbecue half chicken and napa cabbage slaw; penne and oven-roasted mushrooms tossed with sun-dried tomatoes, asparagus, basil pesto, and Parmesan.

Flying Fish Café

Seafood at the Boardwalk. Dinner only; smart casual dress. Open Sunday through Thursday, 5:30–10:00 P.M., Friday and Saturday, 5:30–10:30 P.M. $$$–$$$$

Contemporary and trendy, yet whimsical, this restaurant will absolutely delight the senses with its flying fish mobiles, sparkling sea blue mosaic floors, and golden fish scale pillars. As fanciful as it might be, the food, however, is serious. Starters like the Caesar salad or a giant-size "peeky toe" crab cake are great choices. Follow that with just about any of the excellent fish entrees, or perhaps an astonishingly good oak-fired veal chop accompanied by a champion variation of melting risotto. A *Wine Spectator* Restaurant Award winner, the cellar here boasts an excellent international list. And don't forget to save room for the unforgettable desserts, in particular the banana napoleon with warm caramel sauce.

Best known for: Potato wrapped red snapper with creamy leek fondue and red wine butter sauce.

SAMPLE MENU ITEMS

Dinner entrees: Oak-grilled Columbia River salmon, chanterelle mushrooms, artichokes, pearl onions, celeriac-potato puree, warm bacon vinaigrette; spinach-ricotta ravioli with toasted pine nuts, stewed grape tomatoes, Parmigiana Reggiano, and microbasil; char-crusted New York strip with roasted potatoes, button mushrooms, bacon lardoons, and sauce *foyot*.

Fresh Mediterranean Market

Mediterranean cafe and buffet at the Walt Disney World Dolphin. Breakfast and lunch; casual dress. Open Monday through Friday 6:30–11:00 A.M. and 11:30 A.M.– 2:00 P.M.; buffet only Saturday and Sunday. $$–$$$
At Fresh Mediterranean Market, the concept of a buffet takes a giant leap. Simple in decor but not in taste, when they say fresh, they mean *fresh!* There are two parts to the restaurant, one a sit-down cafe, the other a buffet of sorts but so much better. Food is served from stations with chefs busy at work whipping up entrees and tossing fresh salads, the result being everything freshly prepared (and delicious) at all times. While the breakfast buffet is tasty, it doesn't work as efficiently as lunch; way too much time is spent waiting for prepared-on-the-spot omelets and pancakes; a better choice is the cafe service weekday mornings.

Best known for: Breakfast juicing station with detox, antioxidant, and wheatgrass choices.

SAMPLE MENU ITEMS

Breakfast buffet: Fresh fruit; breakfast potatoes; bacon, bangers (sausage rolls); hot and cold cereals; made-to-order omelets; rotisserie ham and turkey; pancakes, waffles, stuffed French toast; pastries, bagels, muffins, croissants, biscuits; Starbucks or French pressed coffee; juice.

Breakfast Café entrees: Spiced oatmeal, grits; oven-baked quiche of the day; three-egg omelet with crabmeat, sun-dried tomatoes, spinach, and brie; belgian waffle with fresh whipped cream and seasonal berries; oven-baked crepes filled with mascarpone, apples, and cinnamon baked in a vanilla bean custard; yogurt parfait cart.

Lunch buffet: Tossed green, chicken orzo, chicken curry, and Mediterranean rice salads; sliced meats, feta-stuffed red peppers; beef or lamb gyros, panini sandwiches; swordfish kebabs, shrimp penne pasta, rotisserie chicken, roast lamb, paella; roasted vegetables, scalloped potatoes; *desserts:* crème brûlée, flan, chocolate mousse cake, key lime pie, carrot cake, chocolate mousse.

Lunch Café entrees: Israeli couscous chicken salad; seared tuna niçoise; rotisserie chicken salad sandwich; shrimp and artichoke sandwich; Mediterranean pulled pork sandwich; herb-marinated chicken panini with sun-dried tomato pesto, caramelized onions, and smoked mozzarella; sliced lamb panini with charred red pepper and roasted eggplant garlic spread; grilled vegetable panini.

Grand Floridian Café

American cuisine at the Grand Floridian Resort. Breakfast, lunch, and dinner; casual dress. Open daily, breakfast 7:00–11:00 A.M., lunch 11:45 A.M.–2:00 P.M., dinner 5:00–9:00 P.M. $–$$$

With an appealing view from its large picture windows of the Grand Floridian Resort's courtyard and pool area, this cheerful, airy cafe of Victorian floral wallpaper, tufted banquettes, and a peaches-and-cream color scheme is a great choice for lunch away from the Magic Kingdom. I wouldn't make a special trip here for dinner, but don't hesitate to hop on a boat from the park to enjoy one of the terrific oversize sandwiches or the excellent cobb salad. Those with smaller appetites will enjoy finishing with one of the minidesserts.

Best known for: The Grand Sandwich, an open-faced hot turkey and ham sandwich topped with a rich Boursin cheese sauce and French onion straws.

SAMPLE MENU ITEMS

Breakfast entrees: Southern-style breakfast of scrambled eggs, ham, and biscuits with sausage gravy; salmon eggs Benedict; steak and eggs; corned beef hash and poached eggs; Belgian waffles with fruit.

Lunch entrees: Philly cheesesteak sandwich with shaved rib eye steak; New York–style Reuben sandwich; Asian grilled chicken salad; shrimp and penne pasta with prosciutto and asparagus in a creamy Asiago sauce;

seared corvina with baby bok choy and spring vegetables in lemongrass broth.

Dinner entrees: Prime rib with roasted garlic mashed potatoes and creamy horseradish; New York strip steak topped with blue cheese butter and cabernet sauce; Asian noodle bowl, seared tofu with noodles in ginger broth; roast chicken, kalamata olives, and squash in Provençal tomato broth.

Jiko

Contemporary cuisine with an African flair at the Animal Kingdom Lodge. Dinner only; smart casual dress. Open daily, 5:30–10:00 P.M. $$$–$$$$

Jiko, a AAA Four-Diamond Award–winning restaurant, richly deserves kudos for its innovative and consistently great cuisine, seductive atmosphere, and one-of-a-kind all–South African wine list. The lovely dining room is furnished with massive, mosaic tile columns surrounded by floor-to-ceiling windows, blue leather banquettes, honey-colored walls, and gleaming wood floors. Soft, contemporary lighting shaped in the guise of bird wings hangs from a rich, blue ceiling, giving the feeling of open space. Giant, twin clay ovens draw the eye to the open kitchen where an eclectic blend of creations, prepared with an African flair in terms of spices and ingredients, is turned out in attractive presentations. Nosh on the off-the-menu sampler platter of appetizers, move on to the smoky wood-grilled pork tenderloin with sweet potato dumplings and a brothy mushroom ragout, and don't leave without ordering the unbelievably wonderful chocolate-filled Beggars' Purses, one of Disney's best desserts. In the tiny, adjoining Cape Town Lounge and Wine Bar, knowledgeable bartenders are happy to convey the finer points of the Wine Spectator Award–winning, all-South African list, the largest in North America.

Best known for: Berber braised lamb shank.

SAMPLE MENU ITEMS

Dinner entrees: Oak-grilled filet mignon with macaroni and cheese and red wine sauce; pan-roasted monkfish with tomato butter sauce, served with vegetables and crispy sweet potatoes; pomegranate-glazed quails stuffed with North African–style colusari rice on Swiss chard, braised carrots and parsnips with pomegranate dressing; *chermoula* roasted chicken with mashed potatoes, garlic, olives, *harissa,* and preserved lemons; black garbanzo peas, *kamut,* quinoa, black and pearl barley, wheat berries with roasted vegetables and seared tandoori tofu.

Kona Café

Pan Asian cuisine at the Polynesian Resort. Breakfast, lunch, and dinner; casual dress. Open daily, 7:30–11:30 A.M., noon–2:45 P.M., and 5:00–9:45 P.M. $$–$$$

This simple dining room is extremely popular with repeat customers who return time and time again for the reasonably priced, tasty food. Adorned with intricate ironwork, amber-colored pod lighting, and paddle fans that softly turn to the relaxing strains of South Seas music, it overlooks the tropical profusion so common at the Polynesian resort. Come at breakfast for the famous Tonga Toast or the macadamia pineapple pancakes, but lunch and dinner's refreshing, Asian-inspired cuisine will surely please.

NOTE: Another great getaway from the Magic Kingdom for an appetizing alternative to park fare.

Best known for: Breakfast Tonga Toast, batter-fried, banana-stuffed sourdough bread rolled in cinnamon sugar.

SAMPLE MENU ITEMS

Breakfast entrees: Eggs Benedict; ham and cheese omelet; beef tenderloin filet and eggs; Calabash Breakfast, a melange of ham, scallions, mushrooms, and home-fried potatoes in a cheddar cheese sauce topped with two eggs.

Lunch entrees: Blackened mahimahi sandwich; Asian deli sandwich of Hawaiian sweet bread layered with salami, ham, and turkey, pickled carrots, cucumber, red onions, cilantro, and mayo; Asian noodle bowl of spiced beef broth with strip steak, snow peas, carrots, celery, and rice noodles garnished with chili garlic sauce and lime; barbecue pork sandwich with Asian barbecue sauce.

Dinner entrees: Coconut almond chicken served with Asian greens tossed with honey-lime vinaigrette, pineapple, strawberries, and toasted almonds; pan-Asian pasta, Asian noodles with chicken, vegetables, and vegetarian stir-fry sauce; macadamia mahimahi with mushroom risotto, lime beurre blanc, and crispy fried onions; vegetable rice bowl; blackened ahi Oscar served rare with asparagus, grilled tomatoes, tempura jumbo lump crab-meat, and wasabi hollandaise.

Narcoossee's

Seafood at the Grand Floridian Resort. Dinner only; smart casual dress. Open daily, 5:30–10:00 P.M. $$$–$$$$
Nestled on the shores of the Seven Seas Lagoon is this gazebo-shaped din-ing establishment featuring a tranquil setting, an inventive North Ameri-can seafood menu, and a glorious view of Cinderella's Castle and the Magic Kingdom fireworks. The softly lit, two-level space offers a pleasant nautical atmosphere, but come prepared for quite a din—this is one noisy restaurant. With a new chef in residence, the cuisine here just gets bet-ter and better; you really can't go wrong with the in-season, fresh fish selec-tions. I thoroughly enjoyed every bite of a grilled wahoo and rock shrimp in sage butter broth served on a pillow of pumpkin risotto topped with fried parsnips. Fantastic! And beef lovers will delight in the filet mignon with potato gratin and a mushroom-cabernet sauce.

For a perfect culmination of your evening, step outside to the restau-rant's wraparound deck or the adjoining boat dock for prime fireworks viewing. Then stick around for an after-dinner drink in the bar and a per-formance of the Electrical Light Parade.

NOTE: Request a window table with a view of Cinderella's Castle along with your necessary advance reservations, and then rerequest it on arrival. The best strategy is to time your meal around the fireworks, mov-ing outside to the deck or the adjoining boat dock for a great view.

Best known for: Always-on-the-menu Key Lime Crème Brûlée.

SAMPLE MENU ITEMS

Dinner entrees: Sesame-crusted ahi seared rare with sticky rice, stir-fry vegetables, wasabi cream, and Tobiko caviar; grilled chicken breast on cele-riac mashed potatoes, roasted onions, and caramelized onion gravy; jumbo seared scallops and angel-hair pasta tossed with a bacon tomato broth; steamed whole Maine lobster; grilled wild salmon with crushed fingerling potatoes, wilted chard, toasted pistachios, and Madeira-saffron sauce.

1900 Park Fare

American buffet at the Grand Floridian Resort. Breakfast and dinner; casual dress. Open daily, 8:00–11:10 A.M. and 4:30–8:20 P.M. $$$$
Breakfast here is a great start to your morning. Bright and whimsical kaleidoscopic hot-air balloons are your table's centerpiece, and the brightly striped walls are accented by carousel horses and framed Victorian circus prints. While the turn-of-the-century French band organ, Big Bertha, plays overhead, Disney characters roam the room signing autographs and taking pictures at each table. Mary Poppins, Pooh, Tigger, Alice in Wonderland, and the Mad Hatter appear at breakfast. In the evening hours the characters from Cinderella are in attendance for a bountiful dinner buffet.

Best known for: Breakfast, one of the best morning feasts at Disney.

SAMPLE MENU ITEMS

Breakfast buffet: Fresh fruit, yogurt; cereal, house-made granola, grits, oatmeal; croissants, muffins, bagels, pecan sticky buns, strawberry and apple turnovers, Danish pastry, blueberry muffins; bacon, sausage links; mini-pancakes, waffles, challah bread French toast, biscuits and gravy, shredded triangle potatoes; scrambled eggs, made-to-order omelets; strawberry melba, apple cobbler, bread pudding with vanilla sauce.
Dinner buffet: Mixed green, Caesar, Greek, broccoli, fruit, German potato, beet, roasted vegetable, and macaroni salads; cream of mushroom, tomato Florentine, and chilled strawberry soups; sweet potato mash, glazed carrots, creamed spinach, broccoli, niblet corn; chef's pasta, carved roasted prime rib of beef au jus, carved ham, fish du jour, chicken piccata, Cajun Parmesan-crusted cod, paella, steamed mussels in garlic white wine, five-cheese lasagna, Jamaican jerk pork, vegetable lo mein, curry beef pie; apple cobbler, key lime tart, warm bread pudding with vanilla sauce, Linzer torte, brownies, Rice Krispies Treats, chocolate chip cookies, soft-serve ice cream with toppings; *children's buffet:* chicken and fish nuggets, macaroni and cheese, little hot dogs and hamburgers, pizza.

Ohana

Polynesian cuisine at the Polynesian Resort. Breakfast and dinner; casual dress. Open daily, 7:30–10:45 A.M. and 5:00–9:45 P.M. $$$
Although I'm not a big fan of all-you-can-eat meals or even Polynesian food, I like Ohana. The food is bountiful and the atmosphere is simply a

hoot. The way-too-bright dining room is decorated with batik fabric ceilings, banana-shaped upholstered rattan chairs, and torchlit tiki statues, but best of all are the massive picture windows with pleasant views of the Seven Seas Lagoon, the Magic Kingdom fireworks, and the Electrical Water Pageant. The restaurant's focal point is an 18-foot, semicircular fire pit where 3-foot skewers of marinated meat are grilled for the evening meal. Miraculously, given the amount of meat flaming away, nothing is overcooked or dry.

Each evening brings entertainment in the guise of broomstick coconut races, hulahoop contests, and ukulele music. Adults looking forward to a quiet meal should arrive after 9:15 P.M., when the hullabaloo is over, or request a seat in the side dining room away from the action. Breakfast is a family-style feast with Mickey, Goofy, and Chip 'n' Dale dressed in Polynesian regalia.

NOTE: Request a window seat overlooking the lagoon when making your advance reservations, and then rerequest it on arrival.

Best known for: The delicious pit-fired meats and shrimp.

SAMPLE MENU ITEMS

Family-style breakfast: Juice; scrambled eggs; fried potatoes with caramelized onions and scallions; pork sausage links; bacon; buttermilk biscuits and sausage gravy; fresh fruit.

Family-style dinner: Stir-fried green beans and onions, green salad with honey-lime dressing; shrimp and vegetable wontons, honey-coriander chicken wings, stir-fried rice; barbecue pork loin, mesquite-seasoned turkey breast, marinated sirloin steak, grilled tiger shrimp; pineapple spears with caramel dipping sauce.

Olivia's Café

Florida cuisine at Old Key West Resort. Breakfast, lunch, and dinner; park casual dress. Open daily, 7:30–10:30 A.M. and 11:30 A.M.–10:00 P.M. $$–$$$$

What you'll find here is a simple, cheerful cafe with an Old Key West atmosphere. Soft pastel walls are covered with family photos and canoe oars, and overhead paddle fans turn gently on white pressed tin ceilings to the beat of soft Caribbean music. Lunch and dinner bring reasonably priced food with an interesting Floridian flair, but best is breakfast with huge omelets, fluffy biscuits, and irresistible hot cinnamon rolls.

Best known for: Buttermilk chicken breast, deep-fried and served with mashed potatoes, white gravy, and sautéed vegetables.

SAMPLE MENU ITEMS

Breakfast entrees: Poached eggs over sweet potato and ham hash; steak and eggs; pancakes and eggs; three-egg omelet chock-full of your choice of numerous items; buttermilk pancakes with blueberry sauce.

Lunch entrees: Cuban sandwich; grilled Monte Cristo sandwich; baked mahimahi on a bed of warm greens with sun-dried tomato caper vinaigrette and fried sweet potato curl; garden veggie wrap; shrimp po'boy sandwich.

Dinner entrees: Jumbo shrimp Alfredo over fettucine; penne pasta tossed with Asiago cheese, sun-dried tomatoes, spinach, olive oil, and garlic; baked lobster tail with sirloin steak; grilled filet mignon paired with shrimp scampi with a mushroom and burgundy wine sauce; slow-roasted prime rib.

Palio

Italian cuisine at the Walt Disney World Swan. Dinner only; smart casual dress. Open daily, 6:00–11:00 P.M. $$$–$$$$
Often overlooked, this atmospheric restaurant in the Swan Hotel certainly deserves attention. The draw of gratifying Tuscan cuisine along with a softly lit dining room filled with friendly waiters and the festive banners of "il Palio" (the drapes presented to the winner of Siena's famous horse race) makes for pleasurable dining. What more could anyone want than to begin with a complementary head of roasted garlic served with foccacia bread, exquisite antipasti of giant sautéed shrimp in garlic, white wine sauce over cannellini beans finished with truffle butter, and the house specialty of osso buco perfectly prepared with white instead of red wine? Pasta lovers won't want to miss the outstanding Tortellini con Aragosta topped with an enormous amount of lobster tossed with garlic and basil in a light cream sauce. The strolling musicians are a nice touch—they take requests, so think of a great Italian song or two beforehand to avoid the "Volare" syndrome. And dessert? Go for the chocolate *tartufo,* a sinfully rich, giant ball of chocolate filled with vanilla gelato surrounded by fresh berries. Yum!

NOTE: Because it's open until 11:00 P.M., this is a great dining choice after Epcot closes; however, you might be more comfortable changing out of park clothing.

Best known for: Osso buco, a braised veal shank with white wine vegetable sauce served over saffron risotto.

SAMPLE MENU ITEMS

Dinner entrees: Yellowtail snapper topped with black olive *tapenade* and herbed bread crumbs over *haricots verts* (green beans) and leeks in a Vernaccia wine sauce; rack of lamb, wood-oven-roasted on a bed of fresh mint, served over bell pepper and chanterelle mushroom ragout; *fazzoletti* stuffed with farmer cheese and black truffles in a wild mushroom broth; cioppino, a hearty fish stew with calamari, scallops, shrimp, lobster, clams, mussels, and vegetables.

Shula's Steakhouse

Steaks at the Walt Disney World Dolphin. Dinner only; business casual dress. Open daily, 5:00–11:00 P.M. $$$–$$$$
This handsome restaurant's theme is based on the Miami Dolphins' 1972 undefeated season, well depicted in attractively framed black-and-white pictures embellishing the rich wood-paneled walls. The dimly lit, dark-hued interior is comfortably outfitted in elegant cherrywood, loads of shiny brass, cushy high-backed chairs, leather banquettes, and white linen–covered tables. What doesn't fit the sophisticated atmosphere is a menu printed on a football and the rolling tray of raw meat explained in detail (a la Morton's) by a member of the knowledgeable and friendly waitstaff. But you don't have to be a quarterback to enjoy the sensational Angus beef steaks, cooked to perfection, accompanied by mouthwatering sourdough bread. Order a bottle from Shula's outstanding California wine list, winner of the Wine Spectator Restaurant Award of Excellence, to round out the evening.

Typical steak house side dish standards include sharing portions of Caesar salad, creamed spinach, oversize baked potatoes, great hash browns, or broccoli with hollandaise sauce. And with Frank Sinatra on the soundtrack, what else could you ask for? Oh, and don't leave without lingering over a chocolate soufflé or stopping in the adjoining clubby lounge, perfect for an after-dinner drink.

NOTE: Those traveling with small children should take advantage of the two hours of complimentary child care at Camp Dolphin. Be sure to reserve ahead and enjoy your time alone. Valet parking is complimentary when dining at Shula's.

Best known for: Monster-size forty-eight-ounce porterhouse.

SAMPLE MENU ITEMS

Dinner entrees: Steak Mary Anne, beef tenderloins prepared in a creamy rich butter sauce; twelve-ounce filet mignon; twenty-four-ounce porterhouse; thirty-two-ounce prime rib; twenty-two-ounce lamb loin chops; four to five pound lobster surf and turf; herb-crusted chicken breast; Norwegian salmon; ten-ounce Florida snapper.

Spoodles

Mediterranean cuisine at the Boardwalk. Breakfast and dinner; park casual dress. Open daily, 7:30–11:00 A.M. and 5:00–10:00 P.M. $$$–$$$$
Walls adorned with Italian ceramics, glossy hardwood flooring (making this one noisy spot), a blend of earthy colors, and a wood-burning pizza oven in an enormous open kitchen set the stage for robust Mediterranean food and family fun. Sharing an appealing assortment of tapas (Spanish-style appetizers) and thin-crusted savory pizza is the thing here; the peasant salad combined with a tapa or two (try the lemon garlic shrimp or the Spoodles sampler platter) is a meal in itself. Entrees are heartily prepared with robust sauces and sides. The seafood paella is one of the best dishes on the menu.

In the mornings, fuel up on such specialties as French toast made with challah bread topped with banana nut brittle, roasted vegetable frittata, or the excellent egg rotollo, *lavosh* filled with scrambled eggs, chorizo, onions, peppers, and cheddar cheese.

NOTE: Another great alternative to Epcot dining, just a ten-minute walk from the International Gateway.

Best known for: The wide variety of tapas on the menu.

SAMPLE MENU ITEMS

Breakfast entrees: Breakfast platter (all-you-care-to-eat scrambled eggs, breakfast potatoes, French toast, bacon, sausage, and breakfast bread); calzone stuffed with scrambled eggs, smoked ham, and mozzarella; breakfast flatbread topped with scrambled eggs, Italian sausage, and mozzarella cheese.

Tapas: Fried calamari with orange oil drizzle; crispy grouper cheeks with pureed sweet peas, lemon aioli, and buttered crisp capers; selection of Mediterranean dips; potato *keftedakia,* a potato cake with chopped mint, feta, and mint crème fraîche.

Dinner entrees: Grilled salmon "Provençal" butter-basted with a vegetable caponata; rigatoni with Italian sausage, tomatoes, and portobello mushrooms; Italian gnocchi with oven-roasted wild mushroom medley, mushroom jus, and gorgonzola cheese; oak-grilled pork loin chop basted in fig port butter with rosemary feta cheese spoon bread; oak-fired New York strip steak basted with sun-dried tomato butter, served with smashed potatoes and a horseradish chive cream drizzle.

Todd English's Bluezoo

Contemporary seafood at the Walt Disney World Dolphin. Dinner only; business casual dress. Open daily, 5:30–11:00 P.M.; raw bar and lounge open daily, 3:30–11:00 P.M. $$$–$$$$

There's plenty of buzz surrounding celebrity chef Todd English's dreamy outpost at the Walt Disney World Dolphin. I have to say that it's worth the cost of dinner just to check out this stunning, underwater-like fantasyland adorned with air bubble light fixtures, shimmery silver-blue organza curtains, and carpeting mimicking an expanding drop of water. Seductive seating of chocolate brown leather booths interspersed with mango orange chairs completes the picture.

The menu, as captivating as the surroundings, is fresh, inventive, and ultramodern. Awarded a AAA Four-Diamond Award in 2005, meals here begin with a basket of savory house-made bread such as onion foccacia, sourdough, whole grain, or black olive, accompanied by garlic butter. A good starter is something from the raw bar accompanied by a choice from the extensive and sophisticated international wine list. My favorite entree? The crispy-skinned, teppanyaki-grilled salmon (one of several nightly selections offered as the Fish Grilled Simply choices) accompanied by a baby copper pot of dijon mustard and chive sauce, artfully presented with a side of whipped potatoes topped with a Tuscan crouton, shaved fennel, and asparagus. Another delicious selection is the miso-glazed Chilean seabass, wonderfully moist, and wrapped in a banana leaf with sticky rice and served with a rich sesame spinach, and light pea tendril salad. But restrain yourself so you can sample one of Disney's best desserts, a warm molten chocolate banana cake nestled in a dollop of malted cream with banana ice cream on the side. Simply heavenly!

NOTE: For a light meal and cocktails, head to Bluezoo's divine lounge. Those traveling with small children should take advantage of the two hours of complimentary child care at Camp Dolphin. Be sure to reserve ahead and enjoy your time alone. Valet parking is complimentary when dining at Bluezoo.

Best known for: Dancing Fish, fresh market fish whole-roasted on a rotisserie.

SAMPLE MENU ITEMS

Dinner entrees: Sashimi-grade tuna steak wrapped in bacon with herb whipped potatoes, sautéed spinach, chanterelle mushrooms, and port reduction; lobster bolognese (rigatoni pasta, lobster tail, sherry-infused sauce) and marscapone and fennel salad; flame-grilled beef tenderloin with horseradish fingerling potatoes, charred frisée, and balsamic veal jus; Simply fish with your choice of sauces (warm crabmeat, dijon mustard and chives, warm foie gras apple vinaigrette, or baby shrimp, parsley, and lemon); spice route salmon with curried beluga lentils, red-pepper paint, warm-roasted carrot salad, and a cool yogurt spill.

🎀 *Victoria and Albert's*

American cuisine with classical influences at the Grand Floridian Resort. Dinner only; reservations mandatory; jackets required for gentlemen (tie optional), dinner attire for women. Call (407) 824–1089 for reservations. Open daily with two seating times: 5:45 to 6:30 P.M. and 9:00–9:45 P.M.; July and August one seating daily, 6:45 to 8:00 P.M. $$$$
Fine dining in a stunning setting combined with virtually flawless service sets Victoria and Albert's apart. Year after year awarded the AAA Five-Diamond Award and the Wine Spectator Best of Award of Excellence, this is Disney's best dining experience. Here you'll find tables set with Wedgwood china, Christofle silver, Frette linens, and Riedel crystal. Dinner is served by your own maid and butler—who are all, by the way, named Victoria and Albert—with the strains of a lovely harpist to accompany the meal. A seasonal prix fixe menu includes six sumptuous courses, all small,

allowing enough room for a sensational dessert accompanied by a pot of coffee brewed at the table in an amazing vacuum pot.

Those seeking a special evening should book the chef's table set in an alcove in the kitchen, a spot perfect for an up close, behind-the-scenes look at Disney's top chef in action. The most outstanding meal around, up to thirteen spectacular courses are served, each more fantastic than the last, all overseen by the brilliant Chef de Cuisine Scott Hunnel. I can't recommend it highly enough and beg you to consider adding the wine pairing to make this a meal of a lifetime. It books up quickly, up to 180 days in advance.

NOTE: This is no place for children; be sure to book a babysitter.

Best known for: The only AAA Five-Diamond restaurant in central Florida.

SAMPLE MENU ITEMS

Appetizers and first course: Lemongrass poached lobster with pickled papaya and tatsoi; herb-cured *poulet* (chicken) with pumpernickel curls and miniature romaine lettuce; roasted quail with heirloom tomatoes, candied potatoes, and tomato water vinum; serrano ham–wrapped gulf shrimp with chilled canary melon coulis; brie leek Maui onion cream soup.

Entrees: Jamison Farm rack of lamb with mushroom "cannelloni" and truffle jus; roasted duck with mission figs and consomme with foie gras tortellini; grilled prime filet with Brentwood corn risotto au jus.

Desserts: Pyramid of Tanzani chocolate mousse; Plant City strawberry ice cream gâteau; Hawaiian Kona chocolate soufflé; caramelized banana gâteau; vanilla bean crème brûlée; Grand Marnier soufflé.

Sample ten-course Chef's Table offerings: Tasting course of Osetra and Beluga caviar, miniature stuffed blue crab blossom, and batter-poached Florida shrimp; Maine lobster "cannelloni" in jicima with Bibb lettuce and cannellini beans; Florida blue crab stuffed squash blossoms with summer squash ragout; carrot-ginger cream with carrot royale; *poulet* (chicken) with Scottish chanterelles and mushroom flan; terrine of sorbet with pickled watermelon; herb-crusted veal tenderloin, gnocchi and ratatouille, grilled prime filet with sweet onion puree and Burgundy reduction sauce, foie gras garnish; Colston Bassett stilton with black mission figs; miniature crème brûlée and strawberry with chocolate fondue; Hawaiian Kona chocolate soufflé.

Whispering Canyon Café

Barbecue and smoked meats at the Wilderness Lodge. Breakfast, lunch, and dinner; casual dress. Open daily, 7:30–11:00 A.M., noon–3:00 P.M., and 5:00–10:00 P.M. $$$
Come prepared for plenty of hootin' and hollerin' and please, whatever you do, don't ask for the ketchup—unless, that is, you like a lot of attention. Dedicated to hearty, not haute, cuisine, it's an all-you-care-to-eat blowout of rib-stickin' barbecued and wood-smoked vittles served piping hot in iron skillets. For those with smaller appetites, there's the option of an a la carte menu. In a setting reminiscent of *Bonanza* is the dining room of rustic lodgepole pines, metal wagon-wheel light fixtures, and tables laid with bandana napkins, jelly jar glasses, and lazy Susan barrelheads perfect for skillet sittin'. Here it's always a show, where hobbyhorse-racing waiters in Western attire love to make a huge production out of serving food, birthday celebrations, and those unfortunate enough to leave for the restroom. And the outside view of a cozy log cabin nestled in the woods only adds to the Old West atmosphere.

NOTE: Dinner here is extremely popular with families, so make your advance reservations early. Or beat the crowd and take the boat over from the Magic Kingdom at high noon, a time when the silliness is at a minimum. Those desiring a more grown-up meal should request the smaller, more intimate room with its own cozy fireplace tucked away in the back of the restaurant.

Best known for: All-you-care-to eat skillet barbecue meals.

SAMPLE MENU ITEMS

Breakfast entrees: Skillet meal (scrambled eggs, hash brown rounds, bacon, sausage, buttermilk biscuits, sausage gravy, waffles); steak and eggs; Kansas City hash (corned beef sautéed with home fries, onions, and peppers, topped with Tillamook cheddar cheese, spicy barbecue sauce, and two scrambled eggs); French toast topped with cinnamon icing; flapjacks.

Lunch entrees: Skillet meal (smoked pork ribs, oven-roasted chicken, pork sausage, cowboy beans, corn on the cob, coleslaw, mashed potatoes, corn bread); smokehouse stack sandwich of turkey, ham, cheese, and bacon on Asiago focaccia bread; little nutty chicken and cheese salad; fried chicken; pulled pork sandwich; meat loaf; vegetarian pasta.

Dinner entrees: Skillet meal (mixed greens with apple vinaigrette, smoked pork ribs, pulled pork, oven-roasted chicken, pork sausage, mashed potatoes, cowboy beans, coleslaw, corn on the cob, corn bread); New York strip steak; maple-ancho-glazed pork chops; oven-roasted chicken; sautéed grouper with oven-dried tomatoes and cannellini bean salad.

Yacht Club Galley

American cuisine at the Yacht Club Resort. Breakfast, lunch, and dinner; casual dress. Open daily, breakfast 7:00–11:00 A.M., lunch 11:30 A.M.–2:00 P.M., dinner 6:00–10:00 P.M. $$–$$$

This casual dining spot is a good place for a quick dinner without advance reservations after the Epcot fireworks. Nothing fancy, just a basic but tasty menu of sandwiches, salads, and such at reasonable prices. A great light meal choice is the open-faced steak "sandwich" consisting of a top sirloin steak on a grilled baguette surrounded by a wilted arugula salad chock-full of blue cheese, sautéed onions, and portobello mushroom, corn, and tomato, all drizzled with a balsamic-bourbon reduction.

Best known for: House-made garlic potato chips served with smoked bacon-jalapeño dip.

SAMPLE MENU ITEMS

Breakfast entrees: Crab cake Benedict; three-egg omelet; ham and eggs with biscuits and breakfast potatoes; cinnamon raisin French toast; oatmeal brûlée; breakfast buffet of fruit, yogurt, Danish pastry, muffins, pancakes, French toast sticks, oatmeal, cereal, bacon, sausage, potatoes, scrambled eggs, frittata, and juice.

Lunch entrees: Crab and shrimp cake sandwich; char-grilled cheeseburger; fish-and-chips; Italian sausage grinder; portobello mushroom grinder; club sandwich.

Dinner entrees: Herb-roasted pork chop served with spiced baked apples and mashed sweet potato butternut squash; honey-glazed salmon with a ragout of tomatoes, onions, and corn; *pappardelle* pasta with sautéed rock shrimp and broccoli, tomato-garlic broth, fresh herbs, and Asiago cheese.

Yachtsman Steakhouse

Steak at the Yacht Club Resort. Dinner only; casual dress. Open daily 5:30–10:00 P.M. $$$–$$$$

An atmospheric steak house setting of white linen–topped tables, red leather chairs, and walls of framed pictures depicting the cattle drives of the Old West makes up for the too-bright lighting and loud hubbub of this bustling but pleasant dining room. Now my question is, "What happened here?" This was one of Disney's best places for steak, but my last visit proved to be quite a disappointment when two out of three steaks at the table were as tough as shoe leather and not even cooked according to our request. For over $30 a steak, I certainly expect better. Non–beef eaters will be glad to know there are seafood (including Maine lobster) and poultry choices. Some of the better sides have been eliminated, such as the yummy au gratin potatoes, but thankfully the fantastic creamed spinach is still on the menu. Let's just hope the steaks return to their former excellence.

NOTE: Ask to sit in the circular dining room overlooking Stormalong Bay, the Yacht Club Resort's incredible pool.

Best known for: Charred Angus bourbon strip steak.

SAMPLE MENU ITEMS

Dinner entrees: Twin beef medallions and a warm-water lobster tail with mashed potatoes, Maytag blue cheese, and cabernet wine sauce; New Zealand rack of lamb with mint reduction; Angus prime rib with horse-radish mashed potatoes and merlot jus; Maine Diver scallops with wild mushroom risotto, roasted portobello mushrooms, and lobster cabernet sauce; winter squash ravioli with chanterelle mushrooms and sautéed spinach in a white wine mushroom broth topped with Camembert cheese.

Downtown Disney Dining

Bongos

Cuban cuisine at Downtown Disney's West Side. Lunch and dinner; advance reservations sometimes taken the same day at (407) 828–0999; casual dress. Open Sunday through Thursday, 11:00 A.M.–11:00 P.M., and Friday and Saturday, 11:00 A.M.–midnight, with dancing until 2:00 A.M. $$–$$$$
Easily spotted by its three-story pineapple, this cafe is one of Downtown Disney's most defining landmarks. A rose-colored version of 1950s Havana, it features soaring palm tree columns and walls glowing with glittering mosaics representing things Cuban: Latino music, tourism, and Bacardi

rum. Sip on a *mojito,* Cuba's classic cocktail, while relaxing on conga drum stools at the bamboo bar (one of three). In the dining room, whopping platters of decent Cuban food are served with mounds of white rice and black beans. And on weekend nights the place goes loco courtesy of a Ricky Ricardo–style band blasting out pulsating music for dance floor revelers.

Best known for: Pollo Asado, a slow-roasted half chicken marinated in lemon, garlic, and white wine tomato Creole sauce.

SAMPLE MENU ITEMS

Lunch entrees: Cuban sandwich; *pan con bistec,* a thin Cuban steak with grilled onions and mozzarella served on Cuban bread; *media noche,* sweet midnight bread with ham, pork, swiss cheese, and pickles; fruit salad topped with raisins, grated coconut, and coconut sauce.

Dinner entrees: *Ropa vieja,* shredded beef in a light tomato sauce with onion and peppers; *churrasco,* tenderized skirt steak grilled and served with a side of *chimichurri* sauce; *zarzuela de mariscos,* sautéed lobster, shrimp, scallops, calamari, fish, baby clams, and mussels in creole sauce; *arroz con pollo,* chicken breast served on a bed of yellow saffron rice; *masitas de puerco,* deep-fried pork chunks marinated in Cuban mojo served with grilled onions and moro rice.

Fulton's Crab House

Seafood at Downtown Disney's Marketplace. Lunch and dinner; call (407) WDW–DINE, or (407) 939–3463, for advance reservations; casual dress. Open daily, 11:30 A.M.–11:00 P.M. $$$–$$$$
Don't expect wildly inventive dishes at Fulton's, but do expect fresh seafood served in a Mississippi riverboat docked in the Lake Buena Vista Lagoon. Nautical treasures abound throughout the three-story boat in the form of buoys and lobster traps, ship wheels, and mounted fish. Seating is either inside at one of the window-filled dining rooms or outside on the deck with great water views. Your best bet here is a platter of simply steamed crab, lobster, mussels, and clams or some of the freshly shucked oysters. A quick dining choice is Fulton's Stone Crab Lounge, where the crowd is lively and a full menu is served.

Best known for: Alaskan king crab claws.

SAMPLE MENU ITEMS

Lunch entrees: Dungeness crab club sandwich; shrimp Caesar salad; grilled rib eye steak sandwich; grilled sea scallops; yellowfin tuna charcoal grilled rare with jasmine rice cake, oriental slaw, and sweet soy glaze; seafood salad.

Dinner entrees: Char-grilled, pan-blackened grouper and beef filet; steamed twin Maine lobsters; grilled gulf shrimp; charcoal-grilled whole yellowtail snapper; fried rock shrimp; cioppino; seafood boil of whole Maine lobster, clams, mussels, and Dungeness crab with corn and potatoes.

House of Blues

Cajun-Creole cuisine at Downtown Disney's West Side. Lunch and dinner; call (407) WDW–DINE, or (407) 939–3463, for advance reservations; casual dress. Open daily, Sunday and Monday 11:00 A.M.–11:00 P.M.; Tuesday and Wednesday 11:00 A.M.–midnight; Thursday through Saturday 11:00 A.M.–1:30 A.M. $–$$$$
Behind the rusty tin facade of the House of Blues is a funky dining room of wall-to-wall and floor-to-ceiling folk art, good old blues music, and some of the heartiest Mississippi Delta–style dishes around. Stick with the specialty recipes—a mean jambalaya full of shrimp, chicken, and fantastic andouille sausage topped off with a screaming hot habañero pepper, the down-home ribs slowly smoked with Jim Beam barbecue sauce, and HOB's white chocolate banana bread pudding, one of the best desserts this side of the Mississippi. Thursday through Saturday the pulse moves up a notch with live blues beginning at 11:00 P.M., and on Sundays they pack 'em in at the popular Gospel Brunch, where plenty of foot stomping and good old soulful music is accompanied by a bountiful Southern-style buffet (see full description in the Special Dining Shows section earlier in this chapter).

NOTE: On balmy days request a table outside on the pleasant back porch with perfect views of the Buena Vista Lagoon. Those interested in attending a concert should consider the Pass the Line program, an exclusive queue to enter the show five to ten minutes prior to the scheduled door time; each ticket holder must purchase one dinner entree or spend $35 in the House of Blues Company Store. Not available for all shows or events. For information about applicable shows, call the box office at (407) 934–BLUE, or (407) 939–2583, or the restaurant at (407) 934–2623.

Best known for: Slow-smoked Tennessee-style baby back ribs with Jim Beam barbecue sauce and mashed sweet potatoes.

SAMPLE MENU ITEMS

Lunch and dinner entrees: Grilled flatiron steak salad; shrimp po'-boy sandwich; salmon with shrimp and eggplant stuffing, crab claws, and balsamic butter; fried buttermilk-battered chicken breast with country gravy and mashed potatoes; Cajun meat loaf; penne pasta with wild mushrooms, chicken, and smoked Gouda.

Portobello Yacht Club

Italian cuisine at Downtown Disney's Marketplace. Lunch and dinner; call (407) WDW–DINE, or (407) 939–3463, for advance reservations; casual dress. Open daily, 11:30 A.M.–11:00 P.M. $$–$$$$
Excellent Northern Italian food in a warm and friendly nautical ambience attracts a loyal following at this Downtown Disney restaurant. The food consistently lives up to its good reputation, with pasta and pizza being the restaurant's best offerings; you can't go wrong ordering my all-time favorite, Rigatoni alla Calabresse, with Italian sausage, mushrooms, plum tomatoes, black olives, and escarole. On pleasant evenings ask to dine on the outdoor patio overlooking the lake. And be sure to choose something from Portobello's excellent wine list, a Wine Spectator Restaurant Award winner, featuring domestic and Italian vintages.

Best known for: Spaghettini alla Portobello, made of scallops, shrimp, clams, and Alaskan king crab with tomatoes, garlic, olive oil, wine, and herbs lightly tossed with spaghettini pasta.

SAMPLE MENU ITEMS

Lunch entrees: Seafood stew; Insalata Rustica, grilled asparagus, prosciutto, roasted peppers, artichokes, fresh mozzarella, and olives served over field greens in a Mediterranean vinaigrette; Quattro Formaggi, white pizza with sun-dried tomatoes and four types of cheese; Panino di Bistecca, rib eye steak served on a grilled Italian baguette with caramelized onions and spinach; Baci di Formaggi, cheese-filled pasta purses served with sautéed spinach, plum tomatoes, brown sage butter, and Parmigiana cheese.

Dinner entrees: Charcoal-grilled center-cut fillet of beef and gulf shrimp topped with white truffle butter sauce; wood-roasted prosciutto and sage-wrapped yellowfin tuna steak with aged balsamic vinegar; charcoal-grilled swordfish with butternut squash, whipped potatoes, and garlic wilted spinach and balsamic reduction; linguine with fresh Manila clams in garlic white wine sauce.

Rainforest Café

American cuisine at Downtown Disney's Marketplace. Lunch and dinner; call (407) 827–8500 for advance reservations; casual dress. Open Sunday through Thursday, 11:30 A.M.–11:00 P.M., and Friday and Saturday, 11:30 A.M.–midnight. $–$$$
Of the two Rainforest Cafés at Disney (the other is located at the Animal Kingdom), this one's the most popular with its prime Downtown Disney location and its rumbling and smoke-spewing 60-foot-high volcano. Visitors ooh and aah over the dining room's lush canopy of foliage, gushing waterfalls, massive aquariums, and menagerie of Audio-Animatronics wildlife that screech and growl when intermittent "thunderstorms" pass over. Waits here can be ridiculous, so stop by and put your name on the list before browsing the Marketplace or checking out the Rainforest Café retail store filled with ecological souvenirs and clothing. For menu specifics see previous Rainforest Café listing in the Animal Kingdom section.

Wolfgang Puck Café

Contemporary cuisine at Downtown Disney's West Side. Lunch and dinner downstairs, dinner only upstairs; casual dress downstairs and smart casual upstairs; call (407) WDW–DINE, or (407) 939–3463, for advance reservations. Open Sunday and Monday 11:30 A.M.–10:30 P.M.; Tuesday through Thursday 11:30 A.M.–11:00 P.M.; Friday and Saturday 11:30 A.M.–11:30 P.M. $$–$$$ (downstairs); $$$–$$$$ (upstairs)
Gastronomic fires are out of control at the exciting, ultramodern Wolfgang Puck Café. Long known for its innovative cuisine, savory thin-crust pizza, and inventive pasta, the food here is always delicious and one of Disney's best dining bets. It's a four-restaurant complex featuring the B's Lounge & Sushi Bar, a downstairs Café with additional outdoor dining, a Wolfgang Puck Express, and an upstairs Dining Room serving an ever-changing

menu of fusion cuisine in a more formal, sophisticated atmosphere. With so many choices it's hard to decide which delectable dining venue to choose from.

The downstairs Café serves up Wolfgang Puck's specialties, such as wood-fired pizzas, fresh hand-tossed salads, zesty pastas, savory sandwiches, and decadent desserts. With its boldly colored, contemporary design and energetic atmosphere, it's always a favorite of Downtown Disney diners. Too bad a lack of decent wine choices by the glass almost forces you to pay for a bottle.

Upstairs, the Dining Room, created after the fashion of Wolfgang's famous Spago, offers black linen, bone china, fine wineglasses, subdued lighting, and a nice view from many tables of Downtown Disney and the lagoon. The noise level here can be irritating, a detriment considering the high prices. Start with something from the excellent but small sushi menu, then move on to the Italian Green Salad topped with proscuitto da Parma, white truffle oil, eight-year-old balsamic vinegar, and toasted pine nuts. The restaurant's best entree is the excellent Szechuan marinated "Chinois" lamb rack served with a spicy cilantro-mint sauce and wasabi mashed potatoes. And if risotto is on the menu, go for it, always one of Disney's best.

Best known for: Wolfgang's famous wood-fired pizzas.

SAMPLE MENU ITEMS

Café lunch and dinner entrees: Smoked salmon pizza; pumpkin ravioli with brown butter, port wine glaze, pine nuts, Parmesan, and crispy sage; herb goat cheese stuffed chicken breast; "Chinois" chicken salad with spicy honey-mustard dressing and crispy wontons; bacon-wrapped meat loaf served with garlic mashed potatoes.

Dining Room entrees: Rare ahi, wasabi-infused potatoes, miso vinaigrette, and seaweed salad; pan-seared half chicken, wood-roasted wild mushrooms, jus with potato puree; filo-wrapped Atlantic salmon, Boursin cheese and spinach stuffing, basil beurre blanc; scallops with pancetta and spring pea pasta, fire-roasted tomato-Parmesan coulis; Wiener schnitzel with warm potato salad.

Other Notable Restaurants Near Disney

 *Arthur's 27*

Contemporary cuisine at the Wyndham Palace Resort near Downtown Disney. Dinner only; business dress; call (407) 827–3450 for reservations. Open Monday through Saturday, 6:00–10:00 P.M. $$$$

In a drop-dead setting high atop the Wyndham Resort is Arthur's 27, enjoying a scene-stealing backdrop of Disney and the surrounding area along with fine dining in a sophisticated atmosphere. Tuxedoed waiters, soft lighting, classical music, pale pink linens, fine china, and gleaming crystal add to the romance of the evening. Even though the restaurant was awarded a AAA Four-Diamond rating in 2005, my last time here left me not as enamored with the food as in previous visits. While extremely creative, nothing quite lived up to its exotic description. Perhaps it was the large group dining at the same time that may have caused a slip in the normally great kitchen. If only for the view and the excellent service, it's certainly a restaurant that shouldn't be crossed off the list. The pricey wine list is small but interesting, and a four- or five-course prix-fixe menu is offered for those with a larger appetite.

NOTE: Valet parking is complimentary for those dining at Arthur's 27. When making reservations (highly suggested) ask for a table with a view of Downtown Disney. From this vantage point you can see Spaceship Earth glowing in the fiery sunset along with the evening fireworks display at both Epcot and the Magic Kingdom. The view from the other side of the room, though very nice, also contains a not-so-lovely look at Interstate 4. If you'd like the panorama without dinner, have drinks in the adjoining sophisticated bar.

Best known for: Arthur's 27 Lobster Bisque.

SAMPLE MENU ITEMS

Dinner entrees: "Free range" breast of capon, applewood-smoked bacon risotto, celery root conserve, and apple ginger sauce; pepper-seared sea bass, roasted corn, potato leek fondue, and tomato ver jus; tenderloin of beef, Syrah-braised short ribs, roasted parsnips, and sauce Marchand du Vin; soba (Japanese noodles), roasted garlic tofu, edamame, wild mushrooms, truffles, and basil ginger bouillon.

Black Swan

Contemporary cuisine at the Villas of Grand Cypress. Dinner only; business casual dress; jackets recommended for men but not mandatory; call (407) 239–4700 for reservations. Open daily, 6:30–10:00 P.M. $$$$
I've always felt a bit smug that I was one of the few tourists who knew about the almost secret Black Swan restaurant located at the Villas of Grand Cypress. Well, I'm not feeling so smug anymore! Not that the food is exactly bad, it just doesn't seem to live up to the almost $40 per entree price tag, and with sometimes snooty service to boot. I've checked to see if a new chef was in the kitchen, but no. I'm not sure what happened to the almost divine food I've so enjoyed in the past, but it seems to be gone. The great pianist is still around nightly to entertain, and I still love the intimate dining room and sweeping views of the golf course, but I have a hard time recommending this restaurant as one of the best spots around. The kitchen always seems to redeem itself with amazingly good desserts— if it's on the menu, try the Chocolate Wonton, a toasted wonton stuffed with chocolate and banana, served with ice cream.

NOTE: A mandatory 18 percent service charge is added to the bill regardless of table size.

Best known for: Honey-mustard coated rack of lamb with a rosemary demi-glace.

SAMPLE MENU ITEMS

Dinner entrees: Washington State wild salmon en croute with a tiger shrimp mousse drizzled in a sauvignon beurre blanc; pan-seared veal chop smothered with caramelized Vidalia onions and a red wine Zinfandel sauce with creamy cheese risotto infused with Australian goat cheese; sesame-crusted jumbo Maine scallops and a ginger-garlic beurre blanc served with cucumber slaw and lemongrass-infused jasmine rice.

Café D'Antonio

Italian cuisine at 691 Front Street in the town of Celebration. Lunch and dinner; call (407) 566–2233 for reservations; casual dress. Open Monday through Friday, 11:30 A.M.–3:00 P.M. and 5:00–10:00 P.M., Saturday, 11:30 A.M.–10:00 P.M., Sunday, 11:30 A.M.–9:00 P.M. $$–$$$$
As unassuming as the dining room is at Café D'Antonio, the food can be

surprisingly delicious. Start your meal with fantastic foccacia bread and a perfectly crisp Caesar salad before choosing from a tempting menu of authentic Italian recipes and brick-oven pizzas; if al dente isn't the way you like pasta, say so, or you may come away unhappy. The linguine mounded with fresh, succulent clams can't be beat; vegetarians should try the mouthwatering Quattro pizza loaded with mushrooms, artichokes, pepperonata, and mozzarella. On my last visit the pasta arrived cold, but it was swiftly and pleasantly replaced in record time by my apologetic waiter. Opt for the outside tables on balmy days for a view of the surrounding town of Celebration.

Best known for: Lombata al Forno, a veal chop stuffed with proscuitto San Daniele, fontina, and spinach, sautéed, deglazed with white wine, topped with mozzarella cheese, and finished in the wood-burning oven.

SAMPLE MENU ITEMS

Lunch entrees: *Pappardelle alla bolognese;* ravioli filled with lobster and tossed in a brandy tarragon cream sauce; rotisserie half chicken basted with fresh rosemary, garlic, olive oil, and kosher salt; veal scallopine piccata; salmon filet brushed with olive oil and fresh herbs and grilled over a wood fire.

Dinner entrees: Chicken roasted over a wood fire served on mixed greens with mushrooms, fontina cheese, and roasted peppers; risotto porcini; penne pasta in a sauce of portobello and porcini mushrooms, pancetta, cream, and tomato; *pappardelle* tossed with fresh North Atlantic salmon, sweet peas, brandy, and mascarpone; Black Angus filet mignon sautéed with pink peppercorns and brandy, finished with a touch of demi-glace.

Colombia Restaurant

Cuban-Spanish cuisine at 649 Front Street in the town of Celebration. Lunch and dinner; call (407) 566–1505 for reservations; casual at lunch, smart casual at dinner. Open daily, 11:30 A.M.–10:00 P.M. $$$
This fourth generation family-operated restaurant opened in 1905 in Tampa's Ybor City and has since become a legend, expanding throughout Florida and, lucky for us, to the town of Celebration. Decor here runs to white tablecloths, cane chairs, snug booths, warm Spanish lantern lighting, lush palm trees, and languidly turning wood fans. The delightful

atmosphere along with superb service and exceptional Spanish and Cuban cuisine are certainly the ingredients for success.

Start with several platters of tapas, little dishes of appetizers that are a Spanish tradition, or a bowl of tasty Cuban black bean soup followed by a must-have, tableside-tossed, original "1905" salad of lettuce, smoked ham, swiss cheese, tomato, olives, Romano cheese, and tangy garlic dressing. Entree choices include a hard-to-beat paella, and be sure to order an accompanying pitcher of the specialty sangria or a bottle of rich Spanish red wine. A popular seating choice is the pleasant patio. The adjoining cigar and tapas bar is a fun alternative to the main restaurant where you can catch live music on Friday and Saturday nights.

Best known for: Paella "a la Valenciana" with clams, mussels, shrimp, scallops, grouper, calamari, chicken, and pork.

SAMPLE MENU ITEMS

Lunch entrees: Cuban sandwich; Havana club sandwich; *arroz con pollo,* chicken baked with yellow rice, green peppers, onion, tomatoes, and spices; *palomilla,* thinly sliced marinated top sirloin, quickly grilled and topped with a *mojo crudo* of chopped onion, parsley, and lime juice; deviled blue crab–filled pastry turnover; chicken *salteado,* boneless chicken sautéed with garlic, green peppers, onions, mushrooms, potatoes, chorizo, and red wine.

Dinner entrees: Roast pork a la Cubana; sea bass Bilboa baked with tomatoes, potatoes, onions, olive oil, garlic, and white wine; a good *boliche criollo,* eye round of beef stuffed with chorizo and roasted in a flavorful gravy; red snapper "Alicante" baked in a casserole with sweet onions, green peppers, rich gravy, olive oil, garlic, and sauterne wine, topped with sliced roasted almonds.

Hemingways

Seafood at the Hyatt Regency Grand Cypress Resort. Dinner only; call (407) 239–3854 for reservations; smart casual dress. Open daily, 6:00–10:00 P.M. $$$–$$$$
A lovely waterfall greets you on arrival at Hemingways, where several small dining rooms adorned with brass hurricane lanterns and vases of fresh orchids are surrounded by long, narrow windows overlooking the lush

grounds of the Hyatt Regency. The casual Key West atmosphere is enhanced by Hemingway-style memorabilia. Welcoming waiters happily advise guests to start with the stone crabs when in season and to order Orlando's best crab cakes, composed of only prime crabmeat and a smidgen of filler.

NOTE: The front room is not as nice as the back two dining areas that overlook the giant boulders forming the waterfalls above the resort's fantasyland pool. Try to make it before dark to enjoy the lovely view.

Best known for: Maryland-style crab cakes.

SAMPLE MENU ITEMS

Dinner entrees: Feast of the Sea, a two-pound Maine lobster, broiled, steamed, or stuffed with crab cake; seared diver scallops crusted with lemongrass, spiced plum tomatoes, and linguine; beer-battered macadamia and coconut shrimp served with pineapple guava sauce; filet mignon with wild mushroom ragout, roasted garlic crushed potatoes, and béarnaise sauce; fresh catch, flame-grilled, blackened, or pan-seared, served with your choice of Cajun tartar, Creole, béarnaise, or wasabi soy and ginger sauce.

Old Hickory Steakhouse

American cuisine at the Gaylord Palms Resort. Dinner only; call (407) 586–0000 for reservations; smart casual dress. Open daily, 5:30–10:00 P.M. $$$–$$$$

For sheer atmosphere, this restaurant can't be beat. Dine in a rustic, tin-roofed hideaway over the swamps of the misty Everglades in the extraordinary Gaylord Palms Resort while feasting on Black Angus steak and excellent fresh seafood. While the steaks are the restaurant's claim to fame, fish or lobster is also a good choice, followed by an array of artisanal cheeses from farms across Europe and North America. Try to stop in early for a drink at the rustic, candlelit bar with views over the swamp.

NOTE: Those in the know will request one of the tables on the decks overlooking the swamp.

Best known for: The sixteen-ounce Certified Black Angus naturally aged prime center-cut New York strip steak.

SAMPLE MENU ITEMS

Dinner entrees: All steaks are served with your choice of béarnaise, au poivre, Bordelaise, or diabolo sauces; twenty-four-ounce porterhouse steak; surf and turf of beef tenderloin and lobster tail; twenty-one-ounce bone-in rib eye steak; tenderloin of American buffalo; rack of lamb; sea scallops with American caviar and beurre blanc; twin medallions of venison with huckleberry sauce; Maine lobster served with drawn butter and lemon; boneless free-range chicken with citrus Chablis sauce.

Universal Orlando Dining

Finnegan's Bar and Grill

Irish food at Universal Studios. Lunch and dinner; call (407) 224–3613 for reservations. $–$$$
Although Lombard's Landing is considered the premier restaurant at Universal Studios, stop here for a pint, much better food, and a bit of live entertainment. The casual, boisterous surroundings of an Irish pub make this the favored establishment for party goers. Roost around an aged, dark-paneled bar with a pint in hand, reveling in the live music (not necessarily Irish) amid old family photos and memorabilia. A full pub menu—consisting of hearty, traditional Irish food along with some American choices—is served in the bar as well as in the adjoining, more serene dining room of scuffed flooring, wooden booths, dingy pressed tin ceilings, and vintage sports memorabilia.

Best known for: Great Cornish pasties and a yard of ale served in a glass so tall you'll need to stand up to drink it.

SAMPLE MENU ITEMS

Lunch and dinner entrees: Celtic chicken salad; Dublin pie (potpie baked with chicken, mushrooms, and leeks); shepherd's pie (casserole of ground beef and vegetables topped with a crust of potatoes); fish-and-chips; corned beef and cabbage; bangers and mash; Irish stew; corned beef, sautéed onions, and swiss cheese served on a pretzel roll; steak sandwich topped with sautéed peppers and onions; gardenburger.

Lombard's Seafood Grille

Seafood at Universal Studios. Lunch and dinner; call (407) 224–3613 for reservations. $$–$$$
Dine in a Victorian-style warehouse reminiscent of old San Francisco among redbrick walls, rich stained glass, and plenty of green cast iron. A Captain Nemo–looking aquarium sits center stage in the comfortable dining room where oversize picture windows afford a great view of the lagoon; in warm weather opt for the pleasant outdoor deck. Although the menu is agreeable, it isn't spectacular and certainly not a bargain. If you really need a quiet break, go for it; if not, opt for one of the nearby counter-service spots where the same fried seafood baskets can be had for around $10 less if you're willing to forgo table service.

Best known for: Daily fresh fish specials.

SAMPLE MENU ITEMS

Lunch and dinner entrees: Seafood cobb salad; charbroiled chicken sandwich; fried snapper sandwich; stir-fried lo mien noodles with grilled chicken breast, crispy vegetables, and fresh ginger served with a shrimp and pork egg roll; fresh catch fry basket; cioppino; lobster risotto.

Mythos Restaurant

Contemporary American cuisine at Islands of Adventure. Lunch (dinner only in busier seasons); call (407) 224–3613 for reservations. $–$$$
Inside this stone sea cave of a dining room are dreamlike, undulating rock walls interspersed with bubbling streams and fountains, carved ironwork railings, and red velvet chairs and banquettes. The food is exceptional by park standards, certainly worth a gold star in Universal's crown. If you want to eat quickly, Mythos offers an Express Lunch Menu that will get you in and out in a half hour. And those following the Atkins routine will appreciate the Low Carb Cuisine; try the excellent Cedar Plank Salmon accompanied by rich-tasting spaghetti squash and crisp asparagus.

Best known for: Cedar Plank Salmon with citrus butter.

SAMPLE MENU ITEMS

Lunch and dinner entrees: Chinese chicken salad; pasta with chicken and mushrooms in roasted garlic and sherry cream sauce; grilled chicken club with applewood-smoked bacon and cheddar; pan-seared mahimahi with sweet plantain and black bean sauce; coq au vin; risotto of the day.

CityWalk and Universal Resorts Dining

 *Emeril's*

Contemporary Cajun-Creole cuisine at CityWalk; lunch and dinner; call (407) 224–2424 for reservations; smart casual dress. Open daily, 11:30 A.M.–2:00 P.M. and 5:30–10:00 P.M. (Friday and Saturday until 11:00 P.M.) $$$$
CityWalk is lucky enough to have an outpost of one of the hottest restaurants in the nation, one that is absolutely intoxicating, from the friendly waitstaff to the trendy decor to the exceptional food. Reminiscent of the New Orleans warehouse district, the vibrant dining room is comprised of exposed pipe, stone walls adorned with contemporary art, sleek hardwood flooring, a circular slate bar, and a two-story, 12,000-bottle wine display (awarded the Wine Spectator Best of Award of Excellence).

The beautifully presented and innovative Cajun-Creole cuisine explodes with flavor and creativity. I can never resist starting with the spicy smoked wild and exotic mushrooms in a home-cured *tasso* cream sauce over angel-hair pasta, but a bowl of the spicy gumbo is always tempting. Move on to a perfectly prepared roasted rack of lamb with a zesty Creole mustard crust, and then consider skipping dessert. What, are you kidding! Emeril's is known for its extraordinary homemade desserts; try whatever form of always superb bread pudding is on the menu.

The best seats in the house are in the Julia and Tchoupitoucas Room, a glass-enclosed space facing CityWalk, or the coveted counter seats perched in front of the exhibition kitchen. This is one restaurant that will leave you yearning for another night and yet another terrific meal. It is simply the best.

NOTE: Although no one would raise an eyebrow, you won't feel comfortable in park clothes. If you must come without changing, try sitting at the bar for your meal (the easiest way to eat without a reservation). Speaking of reservations, they are almost mandatory, even at lunchtime. Children are scarce here, so consider getting a babysitter. At lunchtime, use CityWalk's valet parking and have the restaurant validate your ticket (good for up to two hours).

Best known for: Pecan-crusted Texas redfish in a Creole meunière sauce.

SAMPLE MENU ITEMS

Lunch entrees: Mississippi farm-raised quail with Crystal hot sauce butter, Southern cooked greens, sweet potato spoon bread, and duck confit étouffée; grilled pork chop with caramelized sweet potatoes, essence of tamarind glaze, and green chile mole; smoked and grilled filet of beef served with smoked Gouda creamed potatoes, flash fried spinach, and brandy au poivre sauce.

Dinner entrees: Pan-seared grouper with sautéed rapini, pearl onion, grape tomato, and mixed baby herb salad; cedar plank-roasted portobello mushroom with garlic crust, toasted red bell pepper, asparagus, and herb salad with a drizzle of truffle oil; grilled veal chop with homemade ricotta cheese–vegetable gratinée and balsamic reduction sauce; sauté of gulf shrimp and wild and exotic mushroom open-faced ravioli.

Emeril's Tchoup Chop

Contemporary Asian-Polynesian cuisine at the Royal Pacific Resort; lunch and dinner; call (407) 503–2467 for reservations; smart casual dress. Open daily, 11:30 A.M.–2:00 P.M. and 5:30–10:00 P.M. (Friday and Saturday until 11:00 P.M.) $$$–$$$$

Think Pacific Rim with Emeril's flair in a drop-dead gorgeous setting. Begin with a mai tai (the best I've had outside of Hawaii) at the restaurant's superchic bar while gazing in awe at the dreamy contemporary Polynesian setting of massive cast-glass chandeliers, a Zen-inspired waterfall wall, and the restaurant's centerpiece, a dreamy zero-edge river rock reflecting pool filled with floating lotus blossoms. What's more, the food is terrific! Try the Crunchy Shrimp served with butter lettuce and a hot-and-sour chile glaze or the fantastic warm spinach salad with homemade croutons, goat cheese, toasted pecans, cherry tomatoes, and chorizo vinaigrette. For an entree consider the Tempura Firecracker Fish served with steamed rice, papaya-serrano salsa, Asian pesto drizzle, and coconut-lemongrass sauce. And everyone's favorite dessert is the somewhat stiff but oh-so-tasty banana cream pie topped with chocolate shavings and caramel sauce. Personally I'd go for a creamy coconut crème brûlée or the warm pineapple upside-down cake served with caramelized ginger ice cream.

NOTE: Self-parking (a bit of a walk) is free. Valet parking is $5.00 (at the Pacifica Ballroom Entrance next to the restaurant). Both require a stamped ticket from the restaurant. Request one of the booths surrounding the reflecting pool.

Best known for: Hawaiian-style plate of Kiawe smoked ribs, Kahlua pork and noodle sauté, teriyaki grilled chicken, and braised Chinese broccoli.

SAMPLE MENU ITEMS

Lunch entrees: Seared yellowfin tuna with baby lettuces, avocado-wasabi vinaigrette, radish sprouts, enoki mushrooms, and sesame crackers; macadamia nut-crusted salmon served with ginger-soy butter, steamed rice, and stir-fry vegetables; grilled Kobe beef burger; pineapple chicken salad.

Dinner entrees: Grilled double-cut pork chop with ginger-roasted sweet potatoes, tamarind barbecue glaze, and five-spice green apple chutney; pan-roasted filet mignon with red bliss potatoes, Long Chong–port wine–anise reduction sauce, melting brie cheese, and sweet onion crisp; clay pot of the day: Thai spiced tomato broth, bay scallops, shrimp, little-neck clams and Prince Edward Island mussels with green tea soba (Japanese noodles); banana leaf steamed fish of the day with charred onion vinaigrette and sake-soy glaze; Moo Shu–style vegetable plate with spicy eggplant, snow peas, shiitake mushrooms, vegetable fried rice, spicy garlic glaze, butter lettuce leaves, and sesame pancakes.

Mama Della's Ristorante

Italian cuisine at Portofino Bay Hotel. Dinner only; call (407) 503–3463 for reservations; casual dress. Open daily, 5:30–10:00 P.M. $$$–$$$$
Dine well on Old World, hearty Italian food presented in the festive atmosphere of Mama Della's home. Mama herself roams the family-style restaurant of gaudy, flowery wallpaper and mismatched chairs encouraging guests to "eat, eat." Many of the earthy appetizers and entrees can be enjoyed family-style on huge platters, with each additional portion at a bargain price. While excellent strolling musicians entertain, feast on my favorite, rigatoni with crumbled Italian sausage, fresh tomatoes, and broccoli rabe, an impeccable dish with light garlic broth and perfectly cooked al dente pasta. There's lovely outdoor dining on the piazza, great on a balmy night, but it's much more fun inside where the action is.

Best known for: Frutti di Mare alla Griglia Grouper, consisting of grilled shrimp, scallops and grouper with roasted tomatoes, angel-hair pasta, spinach, garlic, and olive oil, and creamy beurre blanc.

SAMPLE MENU ITEMS

Dinner entrees: Linguine with red or white clam sauce; lasagna made with ricotta, meat sauce, and béchamel; veal medallions with either Marsala or lemon caper sauce; chicken cacciatore; gnocchi with bolognese, roasted eggplant, mushrooms, and mozzarella; seared rib eye steak with sun-dried tomato and goat cheese polenta.

Palm Restaurant

Steak house at the Hard Rock Hotel. Dinner only; call (407) 503–PALM, or (407) 503–7256, for reservations; smart casual dress. Open Sunday, 5:00–9:30 P.M.; Monday through Thursday, 5:00–10:00 P.M.; and Friday and Saturday, 5:00–11:00 P.M. $$$–$$$$

Orlando's branch of the famous New York steak house sits in the trendy Hard Rock Hotel, but fortunately the blasting music from the hotel's public areas doesn't travel quite this far. Rich wood surroundings, private booths, and walls plastered with caricatures of local celebrities (a Palm trademark) exude a clubby and sophisticated steak house atmosphere. Long known for specialties of divine but pricey jumbo lobsters and prime aged steaks and chops, additional choices include pasta, seafood, veal, and chicken dishes with sometimes disappointing and too-greasy sides of creamed spinach, string beans, hash browns, and fried asparagus. Stick with the steak, lamb, or lobster, and you won't go wrong. And head elsewhere for dessert.

Best known for: Jumbo Nova Scotia lobster.

SAMPLE MENU ITEMS

Dinner entrees: Double-cut lamb chops; swordfish steak; prime aged porterhouse; prime rib of beef; veal milanese; linguine with red or white clam sauce; thirty-six-ounce New York strip steak for two.

Notable Restaurants Near Universal

Christini's

Italian cuisine at 7600 Dr. Phillips Boulevard. Dinner only; call (407) 345–8770 for reservations; business casual. Open daily, 6:00–11:00 P.M. $$$–$$$$

For wonderful Old World Northern Italian food and personalized service, head straight to this gem. Don't be put off by its location in a strip mall or its easygoing, classic menu; every morsel is exceptional, prepared perfectly with the best and freshest of ingredients. Since 1987 Chris Christini has wowed the locals with his award-winning restaurant; however, here tourists are treated as if they frequent the place on a regular basis. Expert tuxedoed waiters and a strolling musicians roam the three intimate dining rooms of black tablecloths, soft banquettes, and frosted glass. Have Mauricio, Christini's expert and amiable wine steward, help you pick the perfect bottle from among 400-plus selections to accompany your meal. You'll leave with a feeling of total contentment as well as a long-stemmed red rose for the ladies.

NOTE: Request a booth and leave young children with a sitter.

Best known for: The veal chop broiled and seasoned with fresh sage served with Calvados applesauce, a dish first raved about by Bob Hope on the *Tonight Show* when Johnny Carson was the host.

SAMPLE MENU ITEMS

Dinner entrees: Rigatoni in a Parmesan fennel cream sauce with shredded sweet Italian sausages; fresh Maine lobster flambé with brandy and vodka simmered in a spicy pescatore sauce garnished with shellfish, served over linguine; fresh littleneck clams over linguine with red or white clam sauce; chicken Marsala; jumbo shrimp flambé with cognac in light dijon mustard garlic cream sauce, served with risotto; rack of lamb seasoned with fine herbs and served with balsamic-mint sauce.

Normans

Contemporary New World Cuisine at the Ritz-Carlton Grande Lakes. Dinner only; call (407) 393–4333 or go online at www.normans.com; resort casual. Open Sunday through Thursday, 6:00–10:00 P.M. and Friday and Saturday, 6:00–10:30 P.M. $$$$

For fine dining in ultrasophisticated surroundings, head to celebrity chef-restaurateur Norman Van Aken's outpost at the Ritz-Carlton Grande Lakes Resort. The seductive, octagonal dining room is accented by caramel-hued marble walls and floors, lofty windows covered in dreamy raw silk drapery, leather banquettes in warm black and chocolate brown, and iron chandeliers with Venetian glass shades. All this as well as wonderfully attentive but not fawning service in an unbeatable atmosphere.

The daring menu consists of an extraordinary fusion of Caribbean, Southern U.S., Latin American, and Asian cuisines with the food almost but not quite living up to the original Normans located in Miami. What used to be a mandatory three-course meal is now an a la carte menu (much better for those with smaller appetites), where insiders know to order the long-standing signature dishes of Roasted Pork Havana in Mole Sauce or the oh-so-popular Key West Yellowtail in Citrus Butter Sauce. Or consider the five-course tasting menu that changes monthly; the only hitch is that it must be ordered by the entire table. Those with smaller appetites may want to consider a light meal in the gorgeous cocktail salon where anything can be ordered off the regular menu. Whatever you choose, you really can't go wrong here at one of the best dining spots in Orlando.

NOTE: Tables overlooking the lush golf course or in the center of the dining room are the places to be—steer clear of those that come with a vista of the parking lot; well, at least it's valet parking!

Best known for: Pan-cooked fillet of Key West yellowtail on a "belly" of garlicky mashed potatoes with citrus butter.

SAMPLE MENU ITEMS

Dinner entrees: Escabeche roasted sweetbreads on jalapeño corn bread, black trumpet mushrooms, and ancho-pomegranate jus; chicory-dusted Cervena venison on vanilla-braised belgian endive, brandied chestnuts, Asian pear, and gingersnap venison jus; "Mongolian" barbecued marinated and grilled veal chop with Chinese eggplant and Thai fried rice; Florida black grouper on Peruvian purple potatoes and oxtail hash with onion rings and Rioja jus; wood-oven-roasted glazed breast of duck with bok choy, daikon, ginger tomato chutney, and five spices jus.

Primo

Contemporary Mediterranean cuisine at the JW Marriott Grande Lakes. Dinner only; call (407) 393–4444 for reservations; smart casual dress. Open daily, 6:00–9:30 P.M. $$$–$$$$

JW Marriott's signature restaurant is quite the star. Executive chef Melissa Kelly, a James Beard Foundation award winner, and chef de cuisine Kathleen Blake are passionate about fresh, organic produce and believe in offering it in the ever-changing, Mediterranean-influenced menu. Every dish here is masterful—nothing in heavy sauces, no one flavor dominating another. Service is extremely efficient and delightfully friendly. Don't get relegated to the side dining area, an uninteresting, almost windowless space that seems like an afterthought. Instead, ask for the softly lit main dining room surrounded by floor-to-ceiling windows or the candlelit terrace.

Best known for: Scallopine of Niman Ranch Pork Saltimbocca in a sage-infused mushroom-Madeira jus with prosciutto and olive oil mash.

SAMPLE MENU ITEMS

Dinner entrees: Diver scallops on handmade chestnut taglietelle tossed with wild mushrooms, celeriac, roasted chestnuts, and truffles; grilled swordfish with a warm ragout of white beans, green olives, preserved lemon and arugula, and Meyer lemon-butter sauce; Maine monkfish medallion in a rich tomato *brodetto* with semolina gnochetti and *gremolata;* Grimaud Farm duck two ways—grilled breast and confit leg tossed with organic red rice, winter fruits, and port jus; porcini-rubbed and aged New York strip steak with greens, garden vegetables, and truffle butter.

Roy's

Contemporary cuisine at 7760 West Sand Lake Road. Dinner only; call (407) 352–4844 for reservations; business casual dress. Open Sunday through Thursday, 5:30–10:00 P.M.; Friday and Saturday, 5:30–10:30 P.M. $$$–$$$$

Roy Yamaguchi originated Hawaiian fusion cuisine in Honolulu and has spread his worldwide dining experience to a stretch of West Sand Lake Road near Universal. This is no tacky tiki lounge with drinks in coconut shells or Don Ho look-alikes, only a sleek, contemporary dining room washed in soft amber light attracting a stylish crowd of in-the-know locals. The best starters are a wonderfully fresh ahi poke salad and the lemon-grass-crusted tiger prawns with pad thai noodles in a Malaysian golden curry sauce. Although beef is on the menu, go for one of the many fresh fish choices, always cooked just so and set off by delectable sauces; my favorite is the gorgonzola spinach crusted, wood-grilled swordfish accompanied by a blue crab chardonnay sauce. End with the restaurant's signature chocolate soufflé or a yummy slice of the macadamia nut tart. Many of the wines are Roy's private labels, most of which are served by the glass. And make sure you know that what Roy's calls butterfish is actually cod supersoaked in a miso and sake marinade, not the best thing on the menu unless your tastes run to the very different.

Best known for: Roy's original blackened island ahi with spicy soy mustard butter, and the melting hot chocolate soufflé with vanilla bean ice cream.

SAMPLE MENU ITEMS

Dinner entrees: Roasted macadamia nut–crusted mahimahi with lobster butter sauce; charbroiled garlic-honey-mustard beef short ribs; Kabayaki-seared deep-sea scallops with wasabi sweet ginger butter; hibachi-style grilled salmon with Japanese vegetables and citrus ponzu sauce; cast-iron skillet seared venison loin with organic blueberry chili *gastrique*.

Seasons 52

New American cuisine at 7700 West Sand Lake Road. Dinner only; call (407) 354–5212 for reservations; smart casual. Open Sunday through Thursday, 4:30–10:00 P.M. and Friday and Saturday, 4:30–11:00 P.M. with flatbreads and desserts served in the lounge one hour after dinner ends. $$–$$$

A welcome addition to the Orlando culinary scene is this restaurant featuring contemporary, high-style food blessedly low in calories at gentle prices. The handsome, Frank Lloyd Wright–chic dining room is a happening spot, but on balmy nights the outdoor veranda with views of Little Sand Lake beckons. Because the menu changes each week, the proprietors (Darden Restaurants, which also happens to own the Olive Garden, Red Lobster, and Bahama Breeze chain restaurants, but don't let this fact put you off) use fifty-two in the name. Just a few of the terrific appetizers—such as the superthin vegetable flatbread or goat cheese ravioli in a light broth with tomatoes, basil, and vegetable truffle essence—could make a meal, but don't stop there. Choose something from the wide assortment of entrees, all uncomplicated and quite delicious, with nothing over 475 calories. The under-100 calorie, $1.95 minidesserts served in oversize shot glasses offer just a few bites of perfection. Orlando's chic crowd flocks to the buzzing bar scene here where they vie for one of sixteen booths, order up a few small plates, pick a glass of wine from the more than sixty choices, and enjoy the live piano music.

NOTE: Unless you like waiting for an hour or two, don't come here without reservations, particularly on the weekend. And don't wait until the last minute to make reservations; I delayed until the week of my stay, and there were none to be had.

Best known for: Cedar planked salmon and the luscious low-cal minidesserts.

SAMPLE MENU ITEMS

Dinner entrees: Jumbo crab-stuffed shrimp; citrus grilled chicken breast with spinach Parmesan pearl pasta and spring market vegetables; grilled vegetable stack sandwich with melted mozzarella and roasted red pepper dressing; ahi grilled rare, served over udon noodles with miso broth, shiitake mushrooms, and bok choy; mesquite-roasted pork tenderloin over soft herb polenta with leaf spinach and grilled mushrooms.

Timpano Italian Chophouse

Italian steaks, seafood, and pasta at 7488 West Sand Lake Road. Lunch and dinner; call (407) 248–0429 for reservations; smart casual dress. Open for lunch Monday through Friday, 11:00 A.M.–4:00 P.M., and Saturday and Sunday, noon–4:00 P.M.; for dinner Sunday through Thursday, 4:00–10:00 P.M. (Friday and Saturday until 11:00 P.M.). $$–$$$$
There are several good reasons to come to this retro-swank throwback to a Manhattan-style, 1950s supper club: first of all, for a great martini; second, for dreamy Frank Sinatra music; and last but not least, for a dandy of a grilled chop. Tourists mingle with smartly dressed locals in this atmospheric restaurant of rustic wood floors, black leather booths, white linen tablecloths topped with butcher paper, a poised and professional staff, and first-rate food. Begin with a martini that's shaken tableside accompanied

by a basket of to-die-for foccacia bread. Choose one of the excellent seafood or meat dishes, and don't even think about not ordering the gorgonzola gratin, the most decadent potato dish I've ever put in my mouth. And whatever you do, stop in at the restaurant's intimate Starlight Lounge, the most seductive bar around, with live music Tuesday through Saturday.

Best known for: Grilled ahi served rare with tomato-basil vinaigrette.

SAMPLE MENU ITEMS

Lunch entrees: Herbed chicken breast flatbread with basil pesto marinated chicken, goat cheese, sun-dried tomato pesto, and *grana padana* cheese; turkey club panini; lasagna bolognese; wild mushroom pasta with herbs and garlic in a light sauce; ravioli with lobster and shrimp filling, sautéed shrimp, and tomato-basil sauce; veal piccata with caperberries, artichokes, fresh herbs, lemon juice, and butter.

Dinner entrees: Wild mushroom ravioli; shrimp *fra diablo;* crispy half chicken with mashed potatoes and lemon garlic sauce; veal Marsala with mushrooms, Marsala wine, herbs, and diced tomatoes; seafood cioppino; grilled swordfish with potato puree and truffle hollandaise sauce; sixteen-ounce veal chop, sixteen-ounce pork chop, eight-ounce filet mignon, twenty-ounce bone-in rib eye, all available either "Al Forno" with creamy peppercorn sauce or "Al Balsamico."

Vito's Chop House

Steak house at 8633 International Drive. Dinner only; call (407) 354–2 467 for reservations; smart casual dress. Open Sunday through Thursday, 5:00–10:30 P.M., and Friday and Saturday 5:00–11:00 P.M. $$–$$$$
Ignore the fact that it's located on tacky International Drive and plan an evening at Vito's, a sophisticated steak house with an Italian flair and loads of ambience. Melt into one of the red leather banquettes to enjoy the intimate, brick-walled dining room decorated with fish tanks and stacks of wine (from my perch I sat staring at a case of Opus One). Excellent service (ask for James) is provided by tuxedoed waiters who present enormous and succulent aged steaks and impeccably fresh, perfectly prepared seafood. And with a 1,200-label, 18,000-bottle-strong award-winning wine list (*Wine Spectator's* Best of Award of Excellence winner many years in a row), it's a wine lover's dream come true.

You'll realize this is not your average chophouse when you take one taste of Vito's marvelous filet mignon stuffed with gorgonzola or its lean and flavorful, 2½-inch-thick veal chop. Feast on great side choices including my favorite, potatoes rapini smashed and then pan-sautéed with bacon and broccoli rabe, or perhaps creamed spinach, green fried tomatoes, or fresh oak-grilled vegetables. Better bring a hungry friend or two along to share one of Vito's colossal desserts (it's hard to resist the chocolate cake as big as a serving platter). And consider coming early or lingering after dinner for drinks and a cigar in the restaurant's atmospheric lounge.

Best known for: Thirteen-ounce filet mignon stuffed with gorgonzola.

SAMPLE MENU ITEMS

Dinner entrees: Twenty-four-ounce prime rib eye; the ultimate surf and turf of a fifty-ounce porterhouse with a one-and-a-half-pound lobster; thirty-two-ounce Tuscan porterhouse seasoned with garlic and herbs, served with gorgonzola butter; linguine and clam sauce en papillote; wood-grilled pork chops; king salmon cedar plank roasted; lobster *fra diablo*, twin lobster tails, fried and placed atop linguine and then topped with marinara and an assortment of peppers.

9

UNIVERSAL ORLANDO

J ust 12 miles north of Walt Disney World is this whopper of a destination composed of two side-by-side theme parks, Universal Studios and Islands of Adventure; a dining, shopping, and entertainment venue, CityWalk; and three themed resorts where a few nights of pampering could only add to your vacation experience. (The three resorts—the Hard Rock Hotel, the Portofino Bay Hotel, and the Royal Pacific Resort—are described in the Universal Orlando Resorts section of the Accommodations chapter.) Universal's rapid expansion has certainly given Walt Disney World a run for its money, and what it lacks in magic it more than makes up for in its certain brand of frenzied, high-speed intensity. Although Disney has the edge in service, attractions, and plain old customer satisfaction, the compact Universal Orlando is a great two- or three-day excursion.

With more thrill rides at Islands of Adventure theme park than Walt Disney World will probably ever have, a trip here is a must if you have a teenager or coaster addict in your party. Although it will never live up to the Magic Kingdom in the eyes of small children, Universal does have fascinating child-oriented areas in each theme park as well as the fun Nickelodeon Studios. Low-key adults love the working studio aspect of Universal Studios and are simply wowed by the creativity invested in Islands of Adventure. Take Universal for what it is, try not to compare it to Disney, and just enjoy.

Universal Orlando Admission

Take into account the variety of options when purchasing park passes. The Universal multipark passes never expire and with only a few dollars difference between the two- and three-day pass, even if your plans only include two days at Universal, buy the three-day pass if a return trip is a strong possibility. Consider how many days will actually be spent at the Universal theme parks and whether visiting SeaWorld, Wet 'n' Wild, or Busch Gardens in Tampa are to be part of your plans. If many of these parks are of interest to you, buy one of the Orlando Flex Tickets, remembering that they expire in fourteen days.

To avoid a lengthy (and I mean *lengthy!*) wait in line your first morning at Universal, prepurchase your passes by calling (800) 711–0080 or going online at www.universalorlando.com, where a slight discount is usually offered. New automatic ticketing machines at both park entrances are another option as long as you're paying by credit card. If you're staying at a hotel on Universal property, purchase your tickets at the concierge desk. The following prices will most likely change, given that price increases occur regularly, so be sure to check for current rates. AAA members receive a discount on multiday tickets. Florida residents should always inquire about any special discounts offered.

- *1-Day/1-Park Ticket:* Good for one day at either Universal Studios or Islands of Adventure. No park-hopping allowed.

- *1-Day/2-Park Ticket:* Good for one day at both parks, with park-hopping privileges.

- *2- and 3-Day Multipark Pass:* Admission to both Universal Studios and Islands of Adventure, with park-hopping privileges and a free CityWalk Party Pass.

- *4-Park Orlando Flex Ticket:* Unlimited admission with park-hopping for as many as fourteen consecutive days to Universal Studios, Islands of Adventure, SeaWorld, and Wet 'n' Wild. Also includes a free City-Walk Party Pass. Parking fee is required only once a day at the first park visited. Pass expires fourteen days after first use.

- *5-Park Orlando Flex Ticket:* Unlimited admission with park-hopping for fourteen consecutive days to Universal Studios, Islands of Adven-

PRICE WITHOUT TAX

	Adult (ages 10+)	Child (ages 3–9)
1-Day/1-Park Ticket	$60	$48
1-Day/2-Park Ticket	$79	$67
2-Day Multipark Pass	$100	$90
3-Day Multipark Pass	$106	$95
4-Park Orlando Flex Ticket	$185	$151
5-Park Orlando Flex Ticket	$225	$190
Preferred Annual Pass	$189	N/A
Annual Power Pass	$120	N/A

ture, SeaWorld, Wet 'n' Wild, and Busch Gardens Tampa Bay. Parking fee is required only once a day at the first park visited. Also includes a CityWalk Party Pass and a complimentary Busch Gardens Express Bus. Pass expires fourteen days after first use.

■ *Preferred Annual Pass:* Includes 365 days of admission to Islands of Adventure and Universal Studios, along with free self-parking and free admission to select special events as well as discounts on separately ticketed events. Special discounts are offered on multiday and single tickets, merchandise, restaurants, VIP tours, CityWalk Party Passes, and seasonally up to 30 percent at the Loews Universal hotels. No child rate available for annual passes.

■ *Annual Power Pass:* Less expensive than the Preferred Annual Pass, good for 365 days of admission to both Islands of Adventure and Universal Studios but minus the extra benefits of free parking, free admission to special events, and discounts. Blackout dates when admission is not allowed include several weekends in the summer, Christmas, and Easter week. Quite a bargain when you consider that an adult two-day Multipark Pass is only $20 less. No child rate available for annual passes.

Getting There

From the airport take Highway 528 west (the Bee-Line Expressway) then Interstate 4 east to exit 75A, Universal Boulevard, and follow the signs. From Walt Disney World take I–4 east to exit 75A and follow the signs.

Parking

Parking is $9.00 per day, $13.00 per day for preferred parking closer to the main entrance (although it is still a five- to ten-minute walk), $16.00 for valet parking, and free to Preferred Annual Pass holders. Instead of wide-open lots like those at Walt Disney World serviced by a shuttle, Universal Studios, Islands of Adventure, and CityWalk all share two gigantic high-rise parking facilities. The result is quite a jam-up in the mornings; more-experienced people or simply more people (believe it or not, many times only one person is moving all those cars along) directing traffic could certainly improve matters. From the parking lot proceed on long walkways (some of which are moving sidewalks) to CityWalk and then either straight ahead to Islands of Adventure or to the right for Universal Studios. Either way it is about a ten- to fifteen-minute walk to the parks from your parking space. No trams are available.

Operating Hours

Both parks operate 365 days a year. They normally open at 9:00 A.M. and close at 6:00 or 7:00 P.M., with extended hours during holidays and busy season. For special events the park may close as early as 4:00 or 5:00 P.M. Go online to www.universalstudios.com or call (800) 837–2273 for up-to-date operating hours and information.

Basic Universal Orlando Reference Guide

Alcohol. Alcohol is sold at both parks and CityWalk.

Child-Switch Program. Available at most attractions is a child-swap area allowing parents to take turns staying with a child while the other parent rides without losing their place in line.

Pets. A day kennel, located in the parking structure, is $11 per day. No overnight boarding. Guests must provide proof of vaccination and food as well as return periodically to walk their dogs.

Loews loves pets. Guests of the Portofino Bay, Hard Rock, and Royal Pacific Hotels can have their pets in the room. Offered are special pet menus, pet walking and sitting services, and pet amenities. A veterinarian certificate no more than ten days old is required, and no more than two pets are allowed per room.

Smoking. Smoking is permitted in designated areas only.

Transportation to Universal. From the airport use the same town car, limousine, and shuttle services as for Disney for a slightly lower fee. From Walt Disney World either take a taxi or for $14 round-trip per person utilize Mears Transportation shuttles (407–423–5566). From the Universal resorts, board the convenient water taxi or bus shuttle to reach the parks and CityWalk.

Universal Express. Similar to Disney's FASTPASS, the Universal Express system has literally taken over, with almost every major attraction offering front-of-the-line access by reserving a time to return and ride. Simply take your park pass to the Universal Express Distribution Center found somewhere near each Express attraction and receive a time slot in which to return for less than a fifteen-minute wait in line. There's no charge for the service. Only one Express pass at a time; get another once you've used your existing pass, the time slot to return has passed, or two hours have elapsed since the transaction time. Registered guests at the Loews Universal hotels may use their room key for all-day front-of-the-line access at both parks.

Consider paying an extra $15 to $35 per person (price varies according to season) for a Universal Express Plus pass for front-of-the-line access. It does, however, limit you to one time only per participating attraction.

VIP Tours. For $100 per person, a Universal guide will take you and as many as twelve people on a five-hour tour with no wait in line on at least eight attractions; departures at 10:00 A.M. and noon daily. A 1-Day/2-Park six-hour VIP tour is $125.

For a real splurge, opt for the $1,400 (per tour group) private Exclusive VIP Tour, an eight-hour behind-the-scenes tour of the park of your choice, with front-of-the-line access to the rides of your choice. A 1-Day/2-Park Tour is $1,700 and a 2-Day/2-Park Tour is available for $2,600. Park admission is included along with bilingual guides, a VIP gift bag, and priority seating at restaurants. Call (407) 363–8295 or e-mail to viptours@universalorlando.com for information and reservations. Reservations must be made at least seventy-two hours in advance.

Universal Studios Florida

This 100-acre theme park based entirely on the movies is actually a working motion picture studio with more than one hundred back lot locations and excellent attractions. Here you'll find realistic facades and sets intermixed with an array of rides and live shows including stage sets and props, film production, mind-blowing pyrotechnics, even tornado reenactments. Its immense appeal to adults sets it apart from many of Orlando's other theme parks, but child-oriented features such as Woody Woodpecker's Kidzone and Nick Live will certainly charm the little ones. However, realize that many attractions outside those areas can be intense and not appropriate for small children.

Park Services

ATMs. Four automated teller machines are located at the park: just outside to the right of the main entrance, two just inside on the right, and one in the San Francisco/Amity area near Lombard's Landing.

Baby facilities. A nursing room and companion restroom are located at Family Services. Diaper-changing facilities are available in all restrooms.

Cameras and film processing. On Location located in the Front Lot near the main entrance sells cameras, film, and batteries. One-hour film processing is available.

Dining reservations. Make same-day dining reservations for Lombard's Landing and Finnegan's Bar and Grill at the dining kiosk in Production Central. If you'd like to plan ahead, call (407) 224–3613.

First aid. First aid stations are located across from Beetlejuice's Graveyard Revue as well as near Guest Services just inside the main entrance.

Guest Services. Located just inside the park entrance on the right is the place for information on studio production and special dining assistance along with guides for guests with disabilities, assistive listening devices and captioning services, and foreign language maps.

Guests with disabilities. Guests with disabilities may park in a special parking area; ask for directions at the toll plaza. All attractions, shopping and dining facilities, and restrooms are wheelchair accessible; however, several rides require the ability to transfer from the wheelchair to the ride's seating (check the guidemap for details). A companion restroom is

Universal Studios Florida

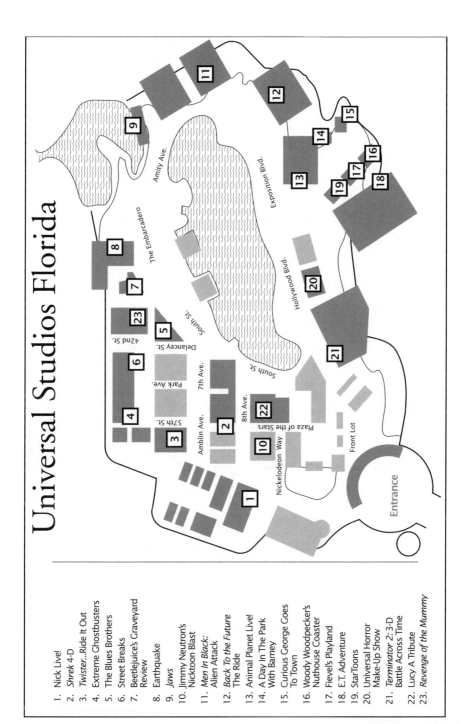

1. Nick Live!
2. *Shrek 4-D*
3. *Twister...Ride It Out*
4. Extreme Ghostbusters
5. The Blues Brothers
6. Street Breaks
7. Beetlejuice's Graveyard Review
8. Earthquake
9. *Jaws*
10. Jimmy Neutron's Nicktoon Blast
11. *Men In Black:* Alien Attack
12. *Back To the Future* The Ride
13. Animal Planet Live!
14. A Day In The Park With Barney
15. Curious George Goes To Town
16. Woody Woodpecker's Nuthouse Coaster
17. Fievel's Playland
18. E.T. Adventure
19. StarToons
20. Universal Horror Make-Up Show
21. *Terminator 2:* 3-D Battle Across Time
22. Lucy A Tribute
23. *Revenge of the Mummy*

located at Family Services. Call (407) 224–5929 at least two weeks in advance to reserve a sign language interpreter. Closed captioning, braille guides, assistive listening devices, a guidebook for guests with disabilities, and attraction scripts are available at Guest Services. Guide dogs are allowed in the park.

Locker rental. Located on both the right and left sides of the Front Lot for $7.00 per day. Additional lockers are located outside the *Men in Black* and *Revenge of the Mummy* attractions for $2.00 per hour, with the first forty-five minutes free.

Lost and found. Located at the Studio Audience Center just inside the main entrance.

Lost children. Look for a lost child at Guest Services.

Package pickup. Purchases may be sent to the Universal Studios Store for pickup before leaving the park. Registered guests of Loews Universal hotels may have purchases sent directly to their room.

Production information. Call the Studio Audience Center at (407) 224–6355 or the Nickelodeon Production Hotline at (407) 363–8000 for upcoming production schedules.

Readmission. Have your hand stamped before leaving the park and retain your ticket for same-day readmission.

Stroller and wheelchair rentals. On your left as you pass through the turnstiles are stroller and wheelchair rentals for $10; ECVs are $40 (with a $50 refundable deposit). Call (407) 224–6350 at least forty-eight hours in advance for ECV reservations.

Studio Audience Center. Located next to the bank on your right upon entering the park. Stop here for complimentary tickets to most studio productions, distributed on a first-come, first-served basis. Tickets for Slime Time Live are usually only obtainable at Nickelodeon Studios, but check here for times.

Universal Orlando Vacations Services. The place for ticket upgrades, hotel and dining reservations, movie tickets for Cineplex at CityWalk, and special event passes. Located on the left as you enter the park.

The Lay of the Land

The Universal Studios layout can be a bit confusing. Just beyond the park's main entrance you'll encounter a wide boulevard with attractions on either side making up Production Central. Branching off to the right are four main streets leading to the other areas of the park: New York, San Francisco/Amity, World Expo, Woody Woodpecker's Kidzone, and Hollywood, all of which partially encircle a large lagoon.

The Very Best Attractions at Universal Studios

SHREK 4-D

Picking up where the first *Shrek* movie left off, Shrek, Princess Fiona, and Donkey depart on a honeymoon adventure with plenty of mishaps along the way. If you're not familiar with the movie, don't worry; it will be recapped in the silly preshow. Now, don't expect to see your typical, run-of-the-mill 3-D film; this one adds an extra dimension of awesome special effects. You can see, hear, and really feel what the characters are experiencing from seats that move along with the action. Get ready for lots of laughs with squirts of water, creepy-crawly things under your rear end, and more. Unquestionably this show one-ups any other 3-D theme park movie around. **Those with back, heart, or neck problems or families with small children may want to take advantage of the stationary seats available. 12-minute show.**

REVENGE OF THE MUMMY

Located in Universal's New York City is a new super attraction featuring a combination flat-track and dark coaster with loads of special effects. After working your way in line through a tomblike setting, board your "mine car" and blast off through scene after scary scene; you'll even travel backward and rotate 180 degrees encountering ghouls, mummies, walls of scarab beetles, and fog and flame effects along the way. If it makes you feel any better, there are no loops or big dips, just speed. Just as you think this hair-raising ride is almost over, think again—the mummy doesn't let you off that easily! It certainly plays with your mind; you'll find yourself close to freaking out at every turn. Don't miss this unique attraction, one of Orlando's best. **Minimum height 48 inches (4 feet). Not recommended for expectant mothers or those with heart, back, or neck problems. 3-minute ride.**

UNIVERSAL STUDIOS CHARACTER GREETING SPOTS

Check your guidemap for specific greeting times or changes.

- Front Gate appearances with such characters as the Rugrats and Woody Woodpecker in the morning hours.
- Nickelodeon character appearances with SpongeBob and Jimmy Neutron at the Nickstuff Store.
- Meet Barney after each A Day in the Park with Barney show.
- Shrek at Shrek's Ye Olde Souvenir Shoppe at various times throughout the day.
- Character meet and greet after the Star Toons show in Woody Woodpecker's Kidzone.

NOTE: If you don't mind riding without other members of your party, go for the singles line, a process used to fill empty seats, which will greatly cut your time in line. Carry-on bags are not allowed; use the free (for the first forty-five minutes) lockers out front to store your gear.

TWISTER: RIDE IT OUT

In the waiting area for this hair-raising attraction is film footage of actual twisters wreaking their devastation. Move inside a soundstage to view clips of *Twister* narrated by stars Helen Hunt and Bill Paxton, who relay many of the frightening experiences they encountered during the filming of the movie. Walk through the set of a twister-ripped house where another video explains the logistics of some of the more intense portions of the film. Then on to the grand finale, a re-creation of a scene set in a small Midwestern town, one in which visitors will actually feel the power of a five-story twister. The wind and pelting rain build and darkness and cold descend as the funnel cloud approaches. The entire set begins shaking as trees tear apart, power lines fall, a gas tank explodes, and a drive-in screen, truck, and cow go flying through the air. Just a small testimony to the majesty and mystery of nature. **15-minute attraction.**

NOTE: Rated PG-13 due the intensity of the twister demonstration. Those in the back and immediate front get the wettest, although no one actually gets drenched. If you stand too far to the side, you might not get the full effect of the wind and rain—which can be a good or bad thing, depending on your taste for thrills.

JAWS

The coastal New England town of Amity seems calm enough as you load into forty-passenger boats. Of course, something is amiss in Amity. A crackly distress call from another tour boat sounds over the radio, warning of a shark sighting; soon your boat is jarred and the dorsal fin of a great white shark is spotted. The guide makes a quick decision to escape into the so-called safety of a gloomy boathouse, but Jaws soon finds you; his huge head and sharp, jagged teeth pierce the water, scaring the daylights out of everyone on board. There's barely enough time to recover before onshore gas tanks explode into a 30-foot wall of fire, resulting in a massive fish fry when Jaws bites a dangling high-voltage wire. It's guaranteed to get a few giggly screams out of even the most daring of adults. **Not recommended for expectant mothers. 7-minute ride.**

NOTE: Although too frightening for young children, adults find it to be quite a riot. You'll most likely get wet on this one, but the right side of the boat is usually a bit drier. Most of the action takes place on the left, for those who dare. For heightened enjoyment try it at night when the special effects really dazzle the eye.

BACK TO THE FUTURE: THE RIDE

When you catch sight of the silver DeLorean parked outside, you'll know you've made it to one of the best rides Universal has to offer. Meet up again with crazy Doc Brown and bully Biff at the Institute of Future Technology, where Biff wants to return to the 1950s via a stolen test DeLorean with a bit of a joyride on the way. Doc Brown asks you to save the universe by catching Biff before he alters the past. Your mission is to bump his car and send him reeling back to the institute.

Strap into an eight-passenger DeLorean-style motion simulator vehicle and prepare yourself for the ride of your life. Suspended above an IMAX-size screen, you'll fly back to the Ice Age (get ready for a blast of cold air), have a run in with a man-eating dinosaur, and take a plunge down a fiery volcano. As your body jerks, dips, and dives, your brain is thinking you're flying through space at heart-stopping speeds. **Minimum height 40 inches (3 feet, 4 inches). Not recommended for expectant mothers, those with heart, neck, and back problems; and those susceptible to motion sickness. 5-minute ride.**

NOTE: This ride really jerks you around and is probably not for those who tend to get motion sickness. And don't eat before riding unless you possess a stomach of steel. If you start to feel sick, take your eyes off the screen and look at the cars on either side (your attention is so affixed to the screen, you won't even notice them at first), immediately easing the nausea.

MEN IN BLACK: ALIEN ATTACK

The MIB training facility is searching for several good agents to protect Earth from the galaxy's evil aliens in this interactive, video-game thrill ride. Two six-passenger cars depart together and meet up again several times as they speed through New York streets and alleyways playing laser tag along the way, blasting away at as many lifelike aliens as possible. The team that creams the most extraterrestrial creatures is the winner. Look up, down, and sideways for the little green guys: in trash cans, Dumpsters, hot dog stands, and upstairs windows, on top of buildings, and hanging from lampposts; there's even a baby alien in a carriage. Zip, tilt, and spin as your score builds. What makes this ride interesting is that contestants find themselves in battle with the other vehicle as well as the aliens themselves who react when they are shot and even shoot back; when your vehicle is zapped it goes into a 360-degree spin. The last creature you encounter is a 50-foot-wide, 30-foot-tall alien bug. **Minimum height 42 inches (3 feet, 6 inches); children between 42 and 48 inches (4 feet) tall must be accompanied by an adult. Not recommended for expectant mothers, those with heart, neck, and back problems; and those susceptible to motion sickness. 5-minute ride.**

NOTE: If you don't mind riding without other members of your party, go for the singles line, a process used to fill empty seats, which will greatly cut your time in line. Carry-on bags are not allowed; use the free (for the first forty-five minutes) lockers out front to store your gear.

TERMINATOR 2: 3-D BATTLE ACROSS TIME

You're on a tour of Cyberdyne's corporate headquarters when, during a briefing on the new SkyNet program, John Conner and his mother, Sarah, from *Terminator 2* seize the video screen. They're here with a warning that SkyNet's newest scheme is a threat to the human race and must be destroyed before it destroys us. Only five minutes remain to get out before the building is obliterated. The video is quickly stopped and the ditzy tour guide smoothes over the interruption by escorting visitors into the huge Cyberdyne theater.

Slip on your special glasses and be prepared to watch one of the best 3-D shows around. The original stars of *Terminator 2* appear on giant screens along with 8-foot Cinebotic T-70 Soldiers and stunt actors. Fantastic 3-D special effects and colossal explosions accompanied by loads of smoke and a rocking theater will leave you reeling. I guarantee your mouth will be hanging open when it's all over. **Expectant mothers or those with heart, neck, or back problems may sit in stationary seats. 20-minute show.**

NOTE: Rated PG-13 and a pretty darn intense show for young children due to loud and startling noise. All seats are decent, but hang back a little and enter the doors on the right to sit front and center. At one point all the seats in the theater jerk abruptly; people with back or neck problems may want to sit this one out.

The Very Best Dining at Universal Studios

Monster's Café. Saturday afternoon fiends from baby boomers' childhoods are glorified here at this special counter-service cafe for monster movie fans; purchase your frightfully decent grub in Frankenstein's lab and proceed to your preference of monster dining rooms; cream of broccoli soup, chopped chef's salad, chicken Caesar salad, penne primavera, spaghetti bolognese, wood-oven pizza, rotisserie chicken; devil's food cake, deep-dish apple pie, strawberry shortcake, butterscotch chocolate parfait, fresh fruit cup.

Finnegan's Bar and Grill. Irish pub dining with live entertainment; lunch and dinner. (See full description in the Universal Orlando Dining section of the Dining chapter.)

Lombard's Seafood Grille. Seafood is the specialty here in a San Francisco warehouse setting; lunch and dinner. (See full description in the Universal Orlando Dining section of the Dining chapter.)

Richter's Burger Co. Good burgers complete with all the trimmings; single and double hamburgers, grilled chicken sandwiches, gardenburgers, chili cheese fries, toppings bar; shakes, root beer floats; apple or cherry turnovers, fruit cup, chocolate chip cookies.

Mel's Drive-In. Authentic-looking 1950s-style burger joint a la *American Graffiti;* bright vinyl booths, curved picture windows, vintage jukebox; counter service instead of gum-smacking waitresses; burgers, chicken "fingers," chicken sandwiches, crispy fried chicken salad, onion rings, chili cheese fries; apple pie; shakes, root beer floats.

Special Entertainment in Universal Studios

Blues Brothers. This hopping street show on the corner of Delancey Street in Universal Studios' New York really gets the crowd rocking. Jake and Elwood Blues sing and dance accompanied by a piped-in soundtrack, a talented sax player, and a one-woman showstopper with an Aretha Franklin–like voice. The Blues Brothers renditions of "Soul Man," "Everybody Needs Somebody to Love," even "Rawhide," all sung in the movie *The Blues Brothers,* entertain the hand-clapping crowd.

Special Events

For information and tickets call the Special Events hotline at (407) 224–5500.

Mardi Gras. Late winter into early spring, experience the festivity of New Orleans with nightly parades, live music, street entertainment, and Cajun and Creole food. Included in the price of admission.

Fourth of July. Colossal fireworks show accompanied by an orchestra playing America's favorite music can be seen throughout the Universal Orlando area.

Rock the Universe. For two nights on a weekend in early September, the latest in contemporary Christian music is on the agenda. Requires purchasing a separate ticket.

Halloween Horror Nights. Experience your favorite rides and attractions along with a spooky evening on selected nights during October. This is a very popular event for teens and adults, featuring seven haunted houses, Scare Zones, Bill and Ted's Excellent Halloween Adventure Show, ghouls and monsters roaming the park, and a Festival of the Dead parade. The party extends to both parks. Young children are encouraged not to attend. No costumes allowed. Requires purchasing a separate ticket. Call (407) 22–HORROR, or (407) 224–6776, or go online at halloweenhorrornights.com.

Holiday Festivities. The park is merry with plenty of Christmas decorations, a Macy's holiday parade with floats and giant helium balloons direct from New York's Macy's Day Parade, carols, Santa Claus sightings, and a holiday food festival.

Islands of Adventure

When Islands of Adventure opened in 1999, it was an immediate hit, with more state-of-the-art attractions and amazing thrill rides than any other park in Orlando. Totally different from its next-door sister park Universal Studios, it's worth the price of admission simply for a glimpse of its five distinctive islands, each more imaginative and outrageous than the next. Everywhere the eye rests, there's a barrage of zany color and immense creativity.

Although the park has something for every age, it's a sure lure for coaster junkies and the teenage set. Many of the attractions have height restrictions; however, with Seuss Landing and Camp Jurassic, there's plenty to keep the little ones happy. And if roller coasters are not your thing, you'll be more than thrilled with the variety of attractions for the tamer crowd.

Park Services

ATMs. Three automated teller machines are located at the park: just outside the park's entrance, on the right after entering the park next to the restrooms, and in front of the Enchanted Oak Tavern in the Lost Continent.

Baby facilities. A nursing facility and companion restroom is located at Family Services within Guest Services. Diaper changing facilities are available in all major restrooms.

Cameras and film processing. Cameras, film, and batteries are available at De Foto's Expedition Photography just inside the entrance on the right.

Islands of Adventure

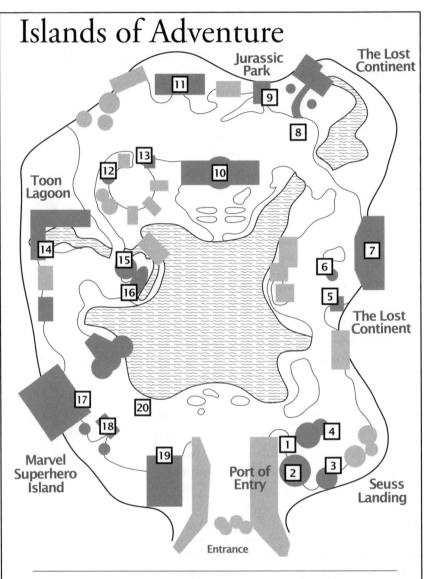

Jurassic Park

The Lost Continent

Toon Lagoon

The Lost Continent

Marvel Superhero Island

Port of Entry

Seuss Landing

Entrance

1. If I Ran the Zoo
2. *The Cat In The Hat*
3. One Fish, Two Fish, Red Fish Blue Fish
4. Caro-Seuss-el
5. Poseidon's Fury
6. The Mystic Fountain
7. The Eighth Voyage of Sinbad
8. Dueling Dragons
9. The Flying Unicorn
10. Jurassic Park Discovery Center
11. Jurassic Park River Adventure
12. Camp Jurassic
13. Pteranodon Flyers
14. Dudley Do-Right's Ripsaw Falls
15. Popeye and Bluto's Bilge-Rat Barges
16. Me Ship, The Olive
17. The Amazing Adventures of Spider-Man
18. Doctor Doom's Fearfall
19. Incredible Hulk Coaster
20. Meet Spider-Man and the Marvel Superheroes!

Dining reservations. Make same-day dining reservations at Vacation Services on your left as you enter the park. If you would like to plan ahead, call (407) 224–3613.

First aid stations. Located near the Eighth Voyage of Sinbad in the Lost Continent.

Guest Services. Located on the right-hand side of Port of Entry in the Open Arms Hotel building for information, special dining assistance, guides for guest with disabilities, assistive listening devices and captioning services, and foreign language maps.

Guests with disabilities. Special parking areas for guests with disabilities are available; ask for directions at the toll plaza. All shops, dining facilities, attraction queues, and restrooms are wheelchair accessible; however, many rides require the ability to transfer from the wheelchair to the ride's seating (check the guidemap for details). Wheelchair-accessible restrooms are located throughout the park, and companion-assisted restrooms can be found near Guest Services and next to the Eighth Voyage of Sinbad in the Lost Continent. Call (407) 224–5929 at least two weeks in advance to reserve a sign language interpreter. Closed captioning, Braille guides, assistive listening devices, a guidebook for guests with disabilities, and attraction scripts are available at Guest Services. Guide dogs are allowed in the park.

Lockers. Located on the left upon entering the park, available for $7.00 per day. Lockers are also located at the entrance to Incredible Hulk, Dueling Dragons, and Jurassic Park River Adventure for $2.00 per hour, with the first forty-five minutes free.

Lost and found. Located at Guest Services.

Lost children. Locate lost children at Guest Services.

Readmission. Have your hand stamped before leaving the park and retain your ticket for same-day readmission.

Strollers and wheelchairs. Rentals are located on the left-hand side as you pass through the turnstiles. Strollers and wheelchairs rent for $10, ECVs for $40 (with a $50 deposit). Call (407) 224–6350 at least forty-eight hours in advance for ECV reservations.

Universal Orlando Vacations Services. Annual Pass processing, Express Plus purchase, and ticket upgrades.

When to Come and What to Wear

Because of the popularity of this park with local teenagers, avoid the weekends. Even in the fall when most parks are slow, this park is crowded Saturday and Sunday with locals who receive special end-of-the-year discounts for Florida residents beginning in September.

This is one park that requires a bit of forethought in park attire. If you plan on riding Popeye and Bluto's Bilge-Rat Barges you will, and I repeat, *will* become thoroughly soaked. Depending on where you sit, Dudley Do-Right's Ripsaw Falls and Jurassic Park River Adventure can cause quite a drenching. Come wearing fast-drying clothing, water footwear of some sort, and in cooler months perhaps a rain poncho to remain somewhat dry. A change of clothing (easily stowed in a locker) might also be helpful. And remember, if you're a coaster fan, flip-flops cannot be worn on Dueling Dragons.

The Lay of the Land

This park is laid out in a more traditional fashion than Universal Studios. A main street, Port of Entry, leads from the entrance and dead-ends into a large lagoon, with the islands arranged in a circular fashion around it. Moving clockwise you'll first find Marvel Super Hero Island, then Toon Lagoon, Jurassic Park, the Lost Continent, and finally Seuss Landing.

The Very Best Attractions at Islands of Adventure

THE AMAZING ADVENTURES OF SPIDER-MAN

Hands down, this is the most remarkable attraction in the Orlando area, the first to combine 3-D film, special effects, and moving vehicles. On your long wait, snake your way through the office of the *Daily Bugle* where you'll find that the dastardly Sinister Syndicate has absconded with the Statue of Liberty. Since all of the staff reporters have mysteriously disappeared, you are recruited by the gruff editor, J. Jonah Jameson, to go out into the devastated streets of New York and get the big scoop.

Board your twelve-passenger, state-of-the-art "scoop vehicle," actually a 3-D simulator that moves along a track and rotates 360 degrees, for the ride of your life. You'll scream with delight at each encounter with Spider-Man and his foes as they spring onto the hood of your car in amazing 3-D, causing your vehicle to gyrate and pitch off to the next crazy commotion. Move through more than a dozen New York scenes, plowing through warehouses, dropping below the streets to the city sewers, and flying above towering skyscrapers. Feel the heat of mind-boggling 3-D explosions accompanied by a state-of-the-art sound system (each vehicle has its own proprietary system) offering intense audio along with the excitement of the ride. The most amazing scene is the 400-foot simulated drop (pure illusion but scary just the same). Don't worry, Spider-Man plans on catching you in his net at the bottom. **Minimum height 40 inches (3 feet, 4 inches); children 40 to 48 inches (4 feet) tall must be accompanied by an adult. Not recommended for expectant mothers, those with back or neck problems, or those prone to motion sickness. 5-minute ride.**

NOTE: This is the most popular ride in the park. Show up early and go directly to this attraction or be ready for a long wait in line. If you want to save huge amounts of time, use the singles line; just don't expect to ride in the same vehicle with your party. Ask to sit in the front seat. This is an intense ride for young children; even though there are no actual drops, it certainly feels as if you're falling at a high rate of speed.

INCREDIBLE HULK COASTER

An eruption of gamma rays from the studio of Bruce Banner (better known as the Hulk) launches you straight up from a near standstill to a whiplashing 40 mph in just two seconds on this green giant of a steel coaster. Immediately roll into a gut-wrenching 128-foot, zero-G dive, accompanied by a feeling of weightlessness and an adrenaline rush beyond belief, straight down toward a misty lagoon. With speeds of up to 60 mph, loop through inversion after giant inversion and twice underground before you finally come to a halt on this unbelievable monster. This is one of America's most thrilling rides and not to be missed if you are a fan of big, bad coasters. **Minimum height 54 inches (4 feet, 6 inches). Not recommended for expectant mothers or those with heart, back, or neck problems. 2-minute ride.**

NOTE: This is another extremely popular ride, so try for first thing in the morning after riding Spider-Man. You can't possibly hold on to your valuables; make use of the short-term lockers located at the attraction entrance, free for the first forty-five minutes. If you'd like to ride in the front seat, there's a line just for that purpose, but be ready for a long wait. To save huge amounts of wait time, use the singles line; just don't expect to ride in the same row as the rest of your party.

POPEYE AND BLUTO'S BILGE-RAT BARGES

This is perhaps the funniest barge ride you'll ever have the pleasure of encountering. You can't help but get entirely soaked on this absolutely hilarious attraction as you swirl and twist over white-water rapids in twelve-passenger circular rafts accompanied by the tooting and bellowing of boat horns, renditions of "Blow the Man Down," and Popeye's theme song. Sail through scenes of Popeye and Bluto fighting for Olive Oyl's love while water swirls close to your knees. You'll rendezvous with a squirting, giant octopus and ride through Bluto's Boat Wash for a good cleaning. Of course, Popeye saves Olive Oyl in the end but is none the drier in the process. Don't miss this enjoyable attraction, even if you have to wear a rain poncho to keep dry. **Minimum height 42 inches (3 feet, 6 inches); children 42 to 48 inches (4 feet) tall must be accompanied by an adult. Not recommended for expectant mothers. 5-minute ride.**

NOTE: Place your valuables in the watertight containers located in the center of the raft, and make sure the snaps are tightly shut. You must wear footwear to ride, so come prepared in fast-drying shoes or water sandals; even if you prop your feet off the floor, they'll still get soaked from above.

JURASSIC PARK RIVER ADVENTURE

This ride brings you gently into the middle of a lost world and then roughly lets you out. In oversize, twenty-five-person rafts, travel deep into the lush rain forest of Jurassic Park as you float past gentle five-story-tall dinosaurs (some of the largest Audio-Animatronics in any theme park) who ignore the passing traffic as they breathe, roar, and munch on plants. Soon, however, the sweetness turns to fighting when visitors come across the more aggressive breeds (even a few that spit!), particularly a nasty T. rex that forces the raft into the Raptor Containment Area where a few hairs might rise on the back of more than one passenger's neck. The only way out of this mess is up and over, and by over I mean by way of a pitch-dark, 80-foot, very steep plunge at speeds of 50 mph ending in a tremendous splash guaranteed to douse each and every person in the boat. **Minimum height 42 inches (3 feet, 6 inches); children 42 to 48 inches (4 feet) tall must be accompanied by an adult. Not recommended for expectant mothers or those with back or neck problems or medical sensitivity to dizziness and fog or strobe effects. 6-minute ride.**

NOTE: Use the short-term lockers, free for the first forty-five minutes, for loose articles or valuables. To the right of Thunder Falls Terrace Restaurant is a walkway leading to a great splash zone and observation spot where the chicken hearted can watch as others drop down the final descent. If you want to save huge amounts of wait time, use the singles line; just don't expect to ride in the same vehicle with your party.

DUELING DRAGONS

You'll notice as you board either one of these two terrifying roller coasters, named Fire and Ice—surprise! surprise! Your feet dangle free. On the world's first inverted, dual-track, near-miss coasters, two dragons are in a dogfight and you're along on the back of one for the battle. As you loop and twist along you'll swear your feet almost touch those of the opposite dragon as it goes roaring by (supposedly they're only a scant foot apart). Ride one first and then the other for comparison; they are two different experiences. This ride is not for the fainthearted. **Minimum height 54 inches (4 feet, 6 inches). Not recommended for expectant mothers or those with heart, back, or neck problems. Flip-flop footwear not permitted. 2-minute ride.**

NOTE: If waits are short, it won't be necessary to go all the way back to the entrance to ride the other coaster; just look for an opening on the way out for the turnaround to the second coaster. Daredevils should try for the front row in order to get a clear shot of the oncoming train. Use the short-term lockers (free for the first forty-five minutes) for loose articles or valuables. If you want to save huge amounts of wait time, use the singles line; just don't expect to ride in the same row as the rest of your party.

THE CAT IN THE HAT

Anyone who's ever enjoyed Dr. Seuss's book *The Cat in the Hat* will love this amusing ride. Sit on powder-blue sofas and ride, spin, and swoop along to the hilarious story of the famous cat that comes to visit two children home alone for the day. Your journey includes the Cat along with the naughty Thing One and Thing Two and the tormented family goldfish who tries but fails to keep order while the parents are away. Every creature and object moves, flies, and bounces along to the frenzied beat of the crazy narration. Laughingly move through scene after scene of this celebrated children's book and be enchanted with the re-creation of a simply great story. **Children under 48 inches (4 feet) tall must be accompanied by an adult.**

ot recommended for expectant mothers, those with back or neck problems, or those prone to motion sickness. 3-minute ride.**

NOTE: Regrettably, this ride seems to break down with frequency; if so, don't wait it out, since it usually takes quite a bit of time to restart.

The Very Best Dining at Islands of Adventure

Islands of Adventure with their huge array of food choices have one-upped the image of park food. Creative dining areas, many with delightful views, offer plenty to eat besides the typical hot dog and burger meals.

Confisco Grille. Full-service restaurant serving breakfast (Thursday through Sunday only), lunch, and dinner; character breakfast buffet with Spider-Man, the Grinch, a Super Hero, and the Cat in the Hat; *lunch and dinner:* buffalo wings with blue cheese dipping sauce, ribs, wood-oven pizza, nachos, chicken Caesar salad, cobb salad, fajitas, burgers, grilled mahimahi, chicken wrap.

Burger Digs. Indoor seating overlooks the Discovery Center's huge T. rex skeleton while outdoor balcony tables come with excellent views of the lagoon and park; burgers, grilled chicken sandwiches, chicken tenders, gardenburgers, toppings bar; milk shakes, deep-dish apple pie.

Thunder Falls Terrace. A jungle lodge setting with huge picture windows affording views of the final plunge of the Jurassic Park River Adventure; rotisserie chicken platter or salad, char-grilled ribs, chicken tortilla wrap, roasted corn and potatoes, cream of chicken soup, tortilla and roasted tomato soup, green salad; chocolate cake, key lime cheesecake.

Enchanted Oak Tavern. Cavernous counter-service restaurant in the base of a gnarly, ancient tree; delightful eating terrace out back with lagoon views; smoked chicken, ribs, and turkey legs, bacon cheeseburgers, smoked chicken salad, corn chowder, roasted corn, corn muffins; warm caramel apple pie, Black Forest cake.

Mythos. Remarkable sea cave dining room offering the best food in the park; lunch (and dinner only in busy seasons). (See full description in the Universal Orlando Dining section of the Dining chapter.)

Special Events

Halloween Horror Nights. See previous listing in Universal Studios section for details.

Grinchmas. From mid-December until the beginning of January, Seuss Landing is transformed into the Christmas town of Whoville, featuring the Grinch and live stage shows. Included in the price of admission.

CityWalk

Universal's energetic answer to Downtown Disney is quite a good one. Though not as extensive, it's a nice alternative to park food for day-trippers and a sparkling mirage of twinkling lights, fun dining and shopping, and unique and happening nightclubs for evening partygoers (come prepared for a much younger and local crowd than at Downtown Disney). The thirty-acre complex, conveniently positioned between Universal Studios and the Islands of Adventure, is a definite lure for those making their way to and from the parks, and the picturesque lagoon running through it offers an opportunity for a boat ride to the Universal resort hotels where even more dining and entertainment possibilities exist.

CityWalk Basics

ADMISSION

There's no charge to enter CityWalk; however, there are individual cover charges at each club. If you plan to party in several spots, consider the

CityWalk

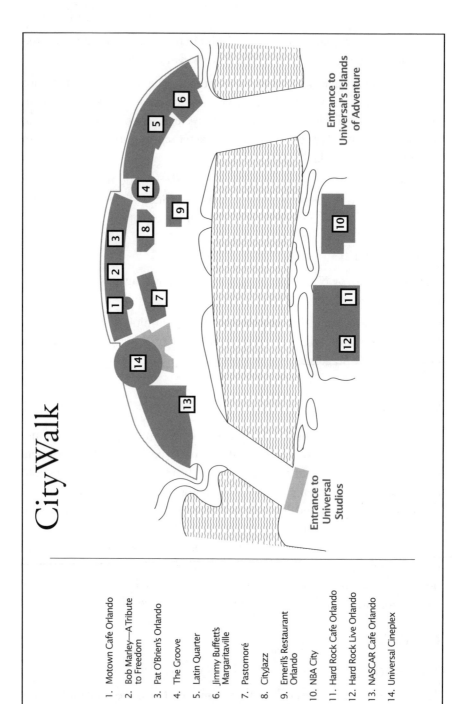

Entrance to Universal Studios

Entrance to Universal's Islands of Adventure

1. Motown Cafe Orlando
2. Bob Marley—A Tribute to Freedom
3. Pat O'Brien's Orlando
4. The Groove
5. Latin Quarter
6. Jimmy Buffett's Margaritaville
7. Pastomoré
8. CityJazz
9. Emeril's Restaurant Orlando
10. NBA City
11. Hard Rock Cafe Orlando
12. Hard Rock Live Orlando
13. NASCAR Cafe Orlando
14. Universal Cineplex

CityWalk Party Pass for $10 allowing unlimited entry for one night to all clubs (excluding Hard Rock Live). Any Universal Multiday Pass comes with a CityWalk Party Pass. The $13 CityWalk Party Pass and Movie buys unlimited one-night club admission plus a movie at Universal Cineplex. Purchase a Meal and Movie Deal for $20 to receive dinner at one of several CityWalk restaurants and a movie. A Meal and Party Deal is $19.

PARKING

Parking is $9.00 during the day, free after 6:00 P.M.; valet park for $16.00. At lunchtime most full-service restaurants will validate your valet parking ticket for two hours or less.

UNIVERSAL CINEPLEX MOVIE THEATER

When you weary of walking and are ready to relax, head here for your choice of twenty extra large screens of entertainment. Along with stadium seating and high-backed rocking seats are wine and beer at the refreshment stand.

Dining at CityWalk

MAKING RESERVATIONS

Call (407) 224–3663 for priority seating or stop by the CityWalk Information kiosk on the walkway in front of the movie theater. Registered guests of Loews Universal hotels can show their room key for the next available table at all CityWalk restaurants excluding Emeril's (not available on Friday and Saturday). Call (407) 224–2424 for Emeril's reservations.

THE VERY BEST FULL-SERVICE RESTAURANTS AT CITYWALK

Emeril's. CityWalk's best dining spot, a spin-off of the hot New Orleans' restaurant. (See full description in the CityWalk and Universal Resorts Dining section of the Dining chapter.)

NBA City. Good food and a nonstop barrage of NBA championship highlights. In the upstairs SkyBox Lounge are twenty TV screens and a view of CityWalk along with a full bar and menu items.

Pastamoré. This restaurant proves that not all dining venues in CityWalk have a party atmosphere. Here meals begin with a wonderful bubble bread chock-full of tomatoes followed by thin-crust pizzas baked in a wood-fired oven or flavorful, creative pastas and wood-roasted meats served a la carte or family style.

THE VERY BEST COUNTER-SERVICE AT CITYWALK

Latin Quarter Express. Counter service window with outdoor seating; mojitos, margaritas, Chilean wine, beer, specialty coffees; empanadas, *papa rellena,* nachos, Cuban sandwiches, tacos, roasted chicken, slow-roasted pork.

Pastamoré Market Café. All-day cafe annex adjoining the main Pastamoré restaurant; *breakfast:* scrambled egg platter, pastries; *lunch and dinner:* chicken Caesar or pasta salad, pasta fagioli soup, pizza, Tuscan chicken breast sandwich, Italian sausage and peppers, meatball sub, lasagna, spaghetti with marinara, bolognese, or Alfredo sauce or meatballs; assorted desserts, ice cream, milk shakes; beer, wine, specialty coffees.

The Very Best Nightlife at CityWalk

Bob Marley—A Tribute to Freedom. There's "No Worries, Mon!" in this replica of Bob Marley's Jamaican home; two levels face an open-air court-yard holding a gazebo-shaped bandstand and dance floor; live reggae on tap every evening along with Red Stripe beer; *appetizers and light meals:* oven-roasted sweet peppers stuffed with fresh vegetables and rice, Jamaican fish stew, jerk mahimahi sandwich, fried red snapper in a Red Stripe tempura batter, smoky white cheddar cheese fondue spiked with Red Stripe, jerk marinated chicken breast with yucca fries. Open 4:00 P.M. to 2:00 A.M.; food served Sunday through Thursday from 4:00 to 10:00 P.M. and Friday and Saturday from 4:00 to 11:00 P.M.; live entertainment nightly 9:00 P.M. to 1:30 A.M.; cover charge after 9:00 P.M., with only those age eighteen and older admitted Sunday through Thursday and twenty-one and older Friday and Saturday.

CityJazz. Live bands play a wide range of music from the 1960s through today's Top 40, Tuesday through Saturday; comedy club Thursday through Saturday followed by a live band; karaoke on Monday; comedy Thursday through Saturday; hypnotist-comedian Sunday; full bar, martinis, coffees, specialty drinks, wine, beer, champagne; hot wings, chicken tenders, arti-choke and spinach dip, Mediterranean salad, chicken Alfredo, burgers, desserts. Open 6:30 P.M. to 2:00 A.M.; open to those age eighteen and older.

The Groove. DJ-driven techno music and live bands; five bars and three specialty lounges spread over two stories; hopping dance floor, terrific sound system, and special effects. Open 9:00 P.M. to 2:00 A.M.; must be age twenty-one or older for admittance except for several nights per month when it's Teen Night for ages fifteen through nineteen.

Hard Rock Live. Live entertainment arena; big names as well as local bands; can be configured as either a large rock concert venue accommodating over 3,000 or converted to an intimate nightclub setting. Ticket prices vary; purchase tickets at Hard Rock Live box office, by calling (407) 351–5483, through Ticketmaster, or online at www.hardrocklive.com.

Pat O'Brien's. Replica of the world-famous New Orleans watering hole; three bars: fun Piano Bar where the concept of dueling pianos originated, laid-back Main Bar with its neighborhood gathering place atmosphere, and the romantic, candlelit courtyard with flaming fountains and famous Hurricane drinks; *light meals:* crawfish nachos, po'boy sandwiches, gumbo, crawfish étouffée, jambalaya, Muffuletta sandwich, beignets, bread pudding. Open 4:00 P.M.–2:00 A.M.; after 9:00 P.M. guests must be age twenty-one or older, with a cover charge for the piano bar only.

10

OTHER NEARBY
THEME PARKS

SeaWorld

Lovingly landscaped and sparkling-clean, this first-rate marine park's 200 acres of fun are certainly worth a day away from Mickey. And if you think Shamu is the only show of real interest here, think again. Show after show and exhibit after exhibit lead you through the fascinating world of marine life and its connection with humankind. And it's all done at a more laid-back pace, a welcome respite from the breakneck speed of Walt Disney World and Universal's theme parks.

Divided into two sections, the North Area and the South Area almost separated by a seventeen-acre lagoon, SeaWorld features live shows and continuous exhibits or rides. With a bit of planning and lots of speed walking, it's possible to go from one show to the next with a short break for lunch, although that doesn't leave much time for seeing the continuous exhibits, many of which are even better than the live shows. If time allows, plan two days for a relaxed tour of the park and all it has to offer.

SeaWorld Basics

GETTING THERE

From Disney take Interstate 4 east to exit 71. From Universal take I–4 west to exit 72 (Beeline Expressway/FL-528/Airport), then once on the Beeline, take the first exit (International Drive). At the traffic light turn left (you'll be driving on International Drive). At the second light turn right onto Central Florida Parkway. SeaWorld's entrance is on the right-hand side of Central Florida Parkway.

OPERATING HOURS

Open at 9:00 A.M. with closing times varying according to the season. Call (407) 351–3600 for up-to-date information.

PARK SERVICES

ATMs. Six automated teller machines are scattered throughout the park: just outside and just inside the main entrance, across from Stingray Lagoon, across from Terrors of the Deep, across from Penguin Encounters, and next to Mango Joe's.

Baby care services. A nursing area is located next to the ladies' restroom near the Penguin Encounter.

Cameras and film. Film and disposable cameras can be found in most stores throughout the park.

First aid. Two locations: behind Stingray Lagoon and in Shamu's Harbor.

Guest relations and information counter. Just past the entrance gate is an information booth with guidemaps and guest information. Make reservations for dining and behind-the-scenes tours, and look for lost children and lost articles here.

Guest with disabilities. Parking for guests with disabilities is located near the main entrance. All exhibits and attractions except Kraken are accessible through the main entrance for guests in wheelchairs. All restrooms, restaurants, and gift shops are accessible to guests in wheelchairs, and companion-assisted restrooms are located near the main entrance next to Exit Gifts, at the Friends of the Wild Gift Shop, in the Village Square across from Polar Parlor, and at Shark Encounter. Guide dogs are permitted. Sign language interpreters for live shows are available for the hearing-impaired with at least a one-week notice; call (407) 363–2414 for reservations. Guides for guests with disabilities and in braille are available at the information booth at the park. Assistive listening devices for many of the live shows are available at guest relations, with a $20 refundable deposit. Call (800) 432–1178 for more information.

PRICE WITHOUT TAX

	Adult (ages 10+)	Child (ages 3–9)	Children (under 2)
1-Day/1-Park Ticket	$60	$48	Free
4-Park Orlando Flex Ticket	$185	$151	Free
5-Park Orlando Flex Ticket	$225	$190	Free
SeaWorld/Busch Gardens Value Ticket (1 day at each park)	$90	$81	Free
Silver Passport (12 months admission)	$90	$80	Free
Gold Passport (24 months admission)	$135	$125	Free

Information and reservations. Go to www.seaworld.com or call (800) 432–1178 for advance information.

Lockers. Located just inside the main gate and near Kraken; available for $1.00 to $1.50 per day depending on the size.

Parking. $8.00 per day; free for Silver and Gold Passport holders. Preferred parking for $10.00 within easy walking distance to the entrance. Rows 1 through 37 are within walking distance; all others serviced by tram.

Pet kennels. Located immediately outside the main gate next to the tram stop for a daily fee of $6.00. Proof of vaccination required.

Soak zones. Some of the live shows have clearly marked soak zones. Avoid them if you wish to stay dry and/or are carrying expensive camera equipment. Believe it when you're warned that you'll get wet; you may even get soaked, and that's with ice-cold salt water.

Stroller and wheelchair rentals. Single strollers rent for $10.00, doubles $17.00, wheelchairs $8.00, and ECVs $35.00.

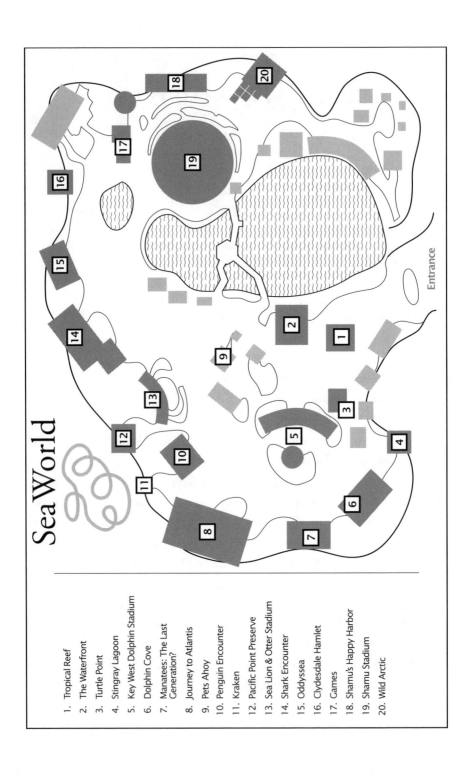

SeaWorld

Entrance

1. Tropical Reef
2. The Waterfront
3. Turtle Point
4. Stingray Lagoon
5. Key West Dolphin Stadium
6. Dolphin Cove
7. Manatees: The Last Generation?
8. Journey to Atlantis
9. Pets Ahoy
10. Penguin Encounter
11. Kraken
12. Pacific Point Preserve
13. Sea Lion & Otter Stadium
14. Shark Encounter
15. Oddyssea
16. Clydesdale Hamlet
17. Games
18. Shamu's Happy Harbor
19. Shamu Stadium
20. Wild Arctic

The Very Best Attractions at SeaWorld

JOURNEY TO ATLANTIS

Travel on water as well as high-speed rails in a special-effects battle between good and evil at this one-of-a-kind attraction. Riders are lured by sirens into the Lost City of Atlantis where, with the use of lasers and holographics, they encounter hundreds of special effects and several surprises along the way including two steep and wet drops, one of which is totally unexpected. Pump up your heart for the final 60-foot plummet and be prepared for a good soaking. **Minimum height 42 inches (3 feet, 6 inches); guests 42 to 48 inches (4 feet) tall must be accompanied by an adult. Not recommended for expectant mothers or those with heart, neck, and back problems. 6-minute ride.**

KRAKEN

A legendary sea monster held in captivity by the sea god Poseidon is released in all its fury at the longest, tallest, fastest, and only floorless coaster in Orlando. All that's holding you in are your bench and shoulder harness. Ascend to the top of the steepest drop in central Florida before plunging 149 feet (fifteen stories) to the bottom at speeds of 65 mph. You'll find yourself upside down seven times and underwater three times before shooting through a tunnel and immediately screeching to a halt. It's so fast you won't know what hit you. **Minimum height 54 inches (4 feet, 6 inches). Not recommended for expectant mothers or those with heart, neck, or back problems. 3½-minute ride.**

CLYDE AND SEAMORE TAKE PIRATE ISLAND

In a live show with a loose plot involving pirates, a treasure map, and a search for gold, Clyde and Seamore, two of SeaWorld's cleverest resident sea lions, entertain while slipping and sliding through their antics as they mimic their way around the stage. A sneaky sea otter only adds to the fun. And if you're in luck, a 2,000-pound walrus will put in an appearance, making the entire show worth the wait. (Be careful, it spits!) **25-minute show.**

PETS AHOY

Worth a bit of planning, this comically entertaining live show set in a harborside village features one hundred animals, including dogs, cats, birds, rats, even a potbellied pig. Considering that most have been rescued from local animal shelters, you'll be amazed at their skillful performance in a variety of fun skits and tricks. You'll see cats walking tightropes, pigs driving cars, dogs jumping rope, and ducks flapping their way across the stage. All in all, one cute act. **25-minute show.**

ODYSSEA

A copycat Cirque du Soleil live show has added a touch of fun to this area of the park. This new performance features colorful sets and costumes along with talented dancers, contortionists, and gymnasts in an underwater fantasy-themed setting. You'll love the ending, a fun trampoline act of playful penguin characters. **30-minute show.**

SHAMU ADVENTURE SHOW

This high-tech killer whale live show is by far the best in the park. A huge "ShamuVision" screen suspended behind the giant pool displays film clips and live footage of the show in progress. On the screen Jack Hanna introduces the audience to the natural habitat of the orca (killer whale) with beautiful footage of the hunting habits of these powerful predators. Then out come the glorious creatures themselves. Listen to the screams of delight that echo throughout much of SeaWorld as the audience watches the black-and-white whales propel their trainers around the pool, riding them 30 feet in the air, leaping and diving as they perform an absolutely amazing show.

Members of the audience who choose to sit in the designated soak zone will indeed get soaked throughout the show; however, nothing compares to the grand finale, when the largest killer whale in any marine life facility in the world—weighing in at over 12,000 pounds—sends enormous waves of ice-cold water (up to thirty rows high) over unprepared spectators. You'll roar laughing as the mind-changing audience runs up the stadium steps to higher and drier ground when they realize the true power in the tail of this huge creature. After leaving the show, walk around the other side of the stadium to Shamu: Close Up! Here you'll find the whales' training facility and a super underwater viewing area. The after-dark show, Shamu Rocks America, is performed to rock 'n' roll music. **35-minute show.**

NOTE: Think twice before seating young children in the soak zone. The water that hits the audience can be quite powerful and could intimidate an adult, much less a small child. A major advantage that might pos-

PARK TOURS AND INTERACTIVE PROGRAMS

Call (800) 432–1178 (press 4) for advance reservations for Sharks Deep Dive or the Marine Mammal Keeper Experience. All other tours can be booked by calling (800) 406–2244 or by e-mailing SeaWorld at education@seaworld.org. Once inside the park reservations may be made at the Guided Tour Counter.

Adventure Express Tour. Enjoy a six-hour guided tour with backdoor access to Kraken, Journey to Atlantis, and the Wild Arctic along with reserved seats at two shows. The tour also includes lunch as well as dolphin, sea lion, and ray feedings plus a chance to go behind the scenes to pet a penguin. $89 for adults, $79 for children ages three through nine. Park admission not included.

Marine Mammal Keeper Experience. Eight-hour program designed for those interested in the care, feeding, rescue, and rehabilitation of SeaWorld's animals. Work alongside marine mammal experts, interacting and caring for dolphins, sea lions, walruses, whales, and manatees. $389 per person including lunch, T-shirt, souvenirs, and seven-day pass to SeaWorld. The program begins at 6:30 A.M. for up to two guests per day; only those age thirteen or older may participate.

Polar Expedition Tour. A one-hour behind-the-scenes tour at the Wild Arctic attraction. Learn about polar bears and beluga whales, even pet a penguin. $15 for adults, $12 for children plus park admission.

Predators. In this one-hour tour, explore the mystery and behavior of sharks, with a chance to touch one. Then move backstage at Shamu Stadium and learn about killer whales. $15 for adults, $12 for children plus park admission.

Saving a Species Tour. For one hour visitors will hand-feed exotic birds in a free-flight aviary and tour SeaWorld's rescue, rehabilitation, and release facilities where endangered and threatened species such as manatees, sea turtles, and birds receive state-of-the-art medical treatment. Generally $15 for adults, $12 for children, but cost varies seasonally; check ahead of time for current price. Park admission is not included and is required. Children must be accompanied by an adult.

Sharks Deep Dive. Two-hour program immersing guests into the fascinating world of the shark. The program begins by exploring shark physiology, conservation, and myths. Then participants don wet suits and either snorkel or scuba dive in a shark cage smack-dab in the middle of more than fifty sharks and thousands of fish. $125 to snorkel, $150 to scuba. Program requires park admission and includes a souvenir T-shirt. Proof of scuba certification is required. Participants must be age ten or older.

sibly overshadow the soaking is the spectacular underwater view of the whales through the glass-walled tank from the lower seats. In busy season arrive thirty minutes prior to showtime to assure yourself a spot for this most amazing of shows.

SHARK ENCOUNTER

This is definitely SeaWorld's best exhibit, fear-inspiring yet fascinating. Begin your exploration by traveling on a moving sidewalk through an amazing underwater clear acrylic tunnel surrounded by fish and moray eels. Look closely at the reef for eels that love to find cozy hiding places. If you're in luck, one might swim slowly over your head.

Proceed to individual tanks filled with scorpion fish, barracuda with razor-sharp teeth, poisonous puffer fish, and the lionfish with its toxic spines, then on to the best part of the exhibit, the shark tunnel. Fifty sharks swim around you, a sight guaranteed to raise the hair on the back of your neck. The accompanying ominous music only adds to the tension. Oftentimes as you move through the tunnel, a sawfish will rest right over your head, quite a sight to behold.

WILD ARCTIC

The fascinating animals of the Arctic have come to sunny Florida. Your adventure begins either by air with a "jetcopter" adventure film in a motion simulator setting or on foot by walking in for a viewing in stationary seats minus the stomach churning (the line for the walking show is always shorter). After the film, proceed to chilly Base Station Wild Arctic where beluga whales, polar bears, and walruses in ice cold pools can be viewed both from above and, after winding your way down ramps, from under the water. **The by-air simulator ride has a 42-inch (3-foot, 6-inch) minimum height. Not recommended for expectant mothers; anyone with heart, neck, or back problems; or those prone to motion sickness.**

NOTE: The simulator ride is pretty gut-wrenching; those with even a bit of motion sickness should beware.

The Very Best Dining at SeaWorld

Seafire Inn. Waterfront counter-service restaurant with a dueling piano show; gourmet burgers, coconut-fried shrimp, tropical chicken stir-fry, Le Cordon Bleu club sandwich, Cuban sandwich, jumbo baked-stuffed potatoes, Greek and antipasto salads; Jell-O, fruit, cannoli, cheesecake; red vel-vet, carrot, or chocolate cake. Join SeaWorld costumed characters Shamu, Dolly Dolphin, and Pete and Penny Penguin for a hearty buffet breakfast Saturday and Sunday from 8:45 to 10:15 A.M.; just show up; no reserva-tions necessary.

Sharks Underwater Grill. Dine in front of the amazing shark tank at Sea-World's only full-service restaurant, featuring a "Floribbean" menu with an accent on seafood; grottolike setting with an amazing dining room of floor-to-ceiling windows peering into the 660,000-gallon Shark Encounter tank; flatbread pizza, pan-seared red snapper served with garlicky creamed spinach and empanada filled with black beans and rice, oak-grilled filet mignon, citrus Caesar salad, *mojo* pork, jumbo lump crab cakes, grilled salmon, chorizo-stuffed chicken breast; *children's meals:* pasta marinara, hot dog, chicken tenders. Open for lunch and dinner; call (800) 327–2420 for priority seating or arrange on day of visit at the information desk.

Spice Mill. The Waterfront's newest counter-service restaurant with both indoor and outdoor dining on the lagoon; chicken tender platter with hick-ory barbacue sauce, jambalaya, grilled steak-and-cheese sandwich, jerk chicken sandwich, Amber Bock chili con carne, saffron chef salad, chicken Caesar salad, muffaletta sandwich; Jell-O, chocolate pudding, chocolate cherry cake, spice cake, cheesecake.

Voyagers Pizza. Waterfront counter-service restaurant; four-cheese, spinach and white cheese, and meat pizzas; grilled salmon, orangewood-smoked chicken, Mediterranean focaccia club sandwich, fettuccine with roasted vegetables and marinara or Alfredo sauce, grilled chicken breast, grilled shrimp; pasta primavera or marinated tomato and cucumber salads; brownie pizza, chocolate cherry cake, cheesecake, watermelon, pudding, Jell-O.

Special Entertainment

Mystify. Summer fireworks show in the lagoon.

Special Events

Halloween Spooktacular. Three-weekend event with costumed charac-ters, Halloween-themed shows, and trick or treat for little goblins. Included in park admission.

Christmas at SeaWorld. From the end of November until the beginning of January the park is decorated in homey Norman Rockwell style.

✿✿ Discovery Cove

Swim with the dolphins at the one-of-a-kind Discovery Cove. Much controversy surrounds this type of park as animal rights activists protest the exploitation of dolphins, making the decision to participate one not to be taken lightly. However, if there is one place to do a dolphin swim, Discovery Cove is it, where extreme caution is taken to ensure the animals' safety.

That said, here is one of the best places to spend your vacation dollars. And dollars you will spend, with a full day costing as much as $259. But it is a chance to get in the water with a dolphin, snorkel in tropical coves loaded with fish and rays (sharks and barracudas are safely behind Plexiglas), and sit on relatively uncrowded white-sand beaches. Only 1,000 guests per day are allowed to enter this thirty-acre park, built at a cost of $100,000,000.

Discover a tropical paradise overflowing with palms and flowering plants, dripping bougainvilleas, crystal clear blue lagoons, waterfalls, aviaries, and marine life galore. Interact with tropical fish, stingrays, colorful birds, and of course, dolphins, or just lie under an umbrella on a white-sand beach fronting the boulder-strewn, sparkling blue dolphin lagoon while sipping tropical drinks to your heart's content. It has all the makings for a great day in the Florida sun.

Discovery Cove Basics

GETTING THERE

From Disney take Interstate 4 east toward Orlando to exit 71 (the same exit as SeaWorld). Turn right on Central Florida Parkway. Discovery Cove is on the right just past the entrance to SeaWorld. From Universal take I–4 west to exit 72 (Beeline Expressway/FL-528/Airport). Once on the Beeline, take the first exit (International Drive). At the traffic light turn left (you will be driving on International Drive), and at the second light turn right onto Central Florida Parkway. The entrance to Discovery Cove is on the left-hand side of Central Florida Parkway.

HOURS

Open from 9:00 A.M. to 5:30 P.M. Doors usually open at 8:30 A.M. for those who would like an early jump on the park. This is definitely one place where the early bird gets the worm, the worm being one of the first in the lagoon with the dolphins. Arriving early assures a dolphin swim first thing in the morning, allowing time to explore the other areas of the park at your leisure.

PARKING

Complimentary parking is just a short stroll away from the lobby. Valet parking for $10 is surely a waste of money given the small size of the parking lot. Those with a disability tag receive free valet parking.

ADMISSION

The cost, depending on the season, is an all-inclusive price of $229 to $259, including a dolphin swim, or $129 to $159 minus the swim. Only those ages six and older may participate in the dolphin swim. I personally do not think the park is worth the money if there is no interest in the dolphins. Although it's certainly a beautiful spot, there really isn't enough activity for a full day unless you love the idea of suntanning on a white-sand beach. Your money would be better spent at one of the many spectacular water parks in the area.

If the price seems unreasonably high, consider what is included: all attractions, lunch, a 5-by-7-inch photo of your party, parking, lockers, snorkeling equipment, wet suit, towels, fish and bird food, and a bonus admission of seven consecutive days at either SeaWorld Orlando or Busch Gardens Tampa Bay. Admission to both parks for fourteen consecutive days is available for an additional charge of $30.

RESERVATIONS

Reservations are a must. In busy season try to plan your visit six months in advance (reservations are taken up to one year prior). Off-season allows for a bit more flexibility. If the day you wish to visit is sold out, keep checking for cancellations. Call (877) 434–7268 or go online at www .discoverycove.com. A 25 percent deposit is required at time of booking, with full payment due forty-five days prior.

CANCELLATION POLICY

Full refund up to thirty days prior, 50 percent refund fifteen to twenty-nine days prior, 25 percent refund eight to fourteen days prior, and no refund if canceled within seven days of your visit.

Discovery Cove only closes in case of lightning; once your payment is made, rain or shine, you'll not receive a refund. Date changes are allowed up to 5:00 P.M. the day before if space is available. So if stormy weather threatens, try for an alternate day. There is no charge for the first date change; after that a $50 fee is assessed.

WHEN TO COME

Discovery Cove is open year-round; however, warmer weather makes it easier to dip into the chilly seventy-degree saltwater pools. Although winter days in Florida can be warm and sunny, some are downright cold, not exactly conducive to relaxing on the beach or swimming in the bracing water. If you want to avoid rain, stay away during the peak hurricane season from August through the end of October. Spring and late fall are the best times to visit.

GENERAL INFORMATION

Dining. Your admission price includes lunch at the Laguna Grill, and that lunch includes an entree, side salad, beverage, and dessert. Entree choices are fajitas, chicken breast, salmon, chicken or vegetarian stir-fry, burgers, roast beef sandwich, chicken or salmon Caesar salad, hot dogs, and chicken "fingers."

Snacks may be purchased at one of two spots, each with a slightly different menu. Choices include nachos, pretzels, cookies, specialty coffees, ice cream, fresh fruit, smoothies, floats, beer, wine, tropical frozen drinks, and sodas. In the morning a breakfast of fresh pastries, cereal, juice, and coffee is available.

Guests with Disabilities. Those who can maneuver up to the wading areas may participate in the dolphin swim as long as they need only limited help or have personal assistance. Specially equipped outdoor wheelchairs with oversize tires for beach maneuvering are available and can be reserved in advance.

Lockers and Changing Rooms. Complimentary lockers are located near the lagoons. Leave your regular sunscreen at home—special dolphin-safe sunscreen is provided. Near the lockers are showers and changing rooms with complimentary towels, toiletries, and hair dryers.

Shopping. Tropical Gifts store offers marine art, island-style housewares, jewelry, bathing suits, caps, sandals, tropical resort clothing, dolphin plush toys, Discovery Cove merchandise, and gifts galore.

"Trainer For a Day" Program. This behind-the-scenes program allows as many as twelve guests per day to work with the trainers in the feeding, training, and caring of the park animals. The price of $399 to $429 (depending on the season) also covers everything included in the cost of regular admission, with the addition of an enhanced dolphin encounter and training session as well as complimentary valet parking. Participants must be in good physical condition and at least six years old. Those age twelve or younger must be accompanied by a paying adult.

"Twilight Discovery" Program. In summer months this evening program offers everything that the day program includes as well as sunset animal interactions, live Caribbean music, hors d'oeuvres and dinner, tropical drinks, dessert on the beach, and valet parking for $259 ($159 without the dolphin encounter).

The Very Best Attractions at Discovery Cove

AVIARY

Almost worth the price of admission is the free-flight aviary where more than 250 tropical birds literally eat right out your hand. A Discovery Cove employee is on hand to distribute bird feed (some of it pretty gross-looking) and offer advice on exactly how to attract these colorful creatures. If you're holding a handful of food, be prepared; the birds seem to come at you from out of nowhere. The large bird area has wonderful and unusual varieties of toucans, pigeons, and doves, but my favorite section is the small bird sanctuary where visitors can hand-feed tiny birds including finches and hummingbirds. Oh, and enter from the Tropical River instead of walking in; it's a kick.

DOLPHIN ENCOUNTER

The superstar of adventures here is the thirty-minute dolphin swim. After a short orientation, visitors are divided into groups of no more than eight people with two trainers to meet their bottle-nosed dolphin. Now the fun begins! What gentle yet unbelievably strong creatures! Your introduction begins with a dolphin rubdown; you'll be amazed at how clean and rubbery their bodies are. Those timid about being in the water with dolphins (as I was) will find that their worries soon evaporate. The trainers do not allow any sudden movements, kicking, or hand slapping that might scare the animal. Continue with hand signals that get an instant reaction, such as chattering, spinning, or flips, and receive a big dolphin hug for a great photo that can be purchased later. A videographer also films the session.

Then comes the part you've been waiting for as two people at a time along with a trainer swim out to deeper water to "play" one-on-one with the dolphin. What you do depends on the trainer but always ends with each person hanging on for dear life to the dolphin's back and a fin for a tow into shore. What a ride! Your session ends with a big smooch on your new friend's nose.

RAY LAGOON

Swim among hundreds of southern and cow-nose rays in this small, shallow water cove. Go ahead and touch them; they're gentle, and most important, have had their barbs removed.

DISNEY CRUISE LINES

Combining a land package with a Disney cruise gives you the best of both worlds. Departing from nearby Port Canaveral are three- and four-night cruises to the Bahamas as well as seven-night cruises to both the western and eastern Caribbean, perfect for extending your vacation on a trip to sea. While mainly geared toward adults traveling with children, the ships do offer many adults-only experiences, including special programs, their own beach at Castaway Cay, and an adults-only dining room and spa. But do come prepared to cruise along with hordes of little ones; it can't be avoided. Those traveling with children can look forward to many shared as well as adults-only activities, and kids will love the supervised children's programs and many character appearances onboard.

Both ships—the *Disney Wonder* and the *Disney Magic*—are lovingly designed in an art deco style, basically identical varying only in itinerary. Each holds 2,400 passengers in 877 staterooms, many with verandas. Staterooms are spacious by cruise standards, with 73 percent of them outside cabins and 44 percent with private verandas. Call (800) 951–3532 or go online to www.disneycruise.com for more information and reservations.

Accommodations

Choose among accommodations ranging from a simple inside cabin to a two-bedroom suite with oversize veranda, media library, walk-in closet, and whirlpool tub. Twelve categories make it easy to choose what's best for you and your family. Of course the larger the staterooms, the higher the price. You'll also pay a premium for outside versus inside rooms, the addition of a balcony, and a higher deck versus a lower one. Always ask about promotions when you call for reservations, or book far in advance and receive an early-booking discount.

Even the least expensive of Disney's staterooms are larger than on most cruise ships. All are nautically decorated with natural woods, brass fixtures, and imported tiles. Bedding is either a queen-size or two twin beds, and all rooms have, at the very least, a sitting area with a sofa and curtained divider. Each room comes with satellite TV, telephone, safe, a minifridge for drinks, and a low-powered hair dryer. No smoking is permitted except on verandas, outside decks, and a few of the lounges. Concierge service is included in the top three categories. It includes full room-service breakfast, snacks throughout the day, CD and video rental, special gifts, and the services of a concierge staff to help with dining, spa, and shore excursion reservations.

ROYAL SUITE WITH VERANDA—CATEGORY 1

Two luxurious suites fit this category, featuring two bedrooms and two-and-a-half baths, with a living area, eight-person dining table, media library, walk-in closets, Jacuzzi, wet bar, and even a baby grand piano. The very spacious veranda runs the length of the cabin. Sleeps seven; 1,029 square feet. Includes concierge service.

TWO-BEDROOM SUITE WITH VERANDA—CATEGORY 2

These two-bedroom, two-and-a-half-bath spacious suites have an extended balcony. The living area has a queen-size sofa bed, six-person dining table, and wet bar. The master bath offers a whirlpool tub, double sink, commode, and walk-in closet. Sleeps five; 945 square feet. Includes concierge service.

ONE-BEDROOM SUITE WITH VERANDA—CATEGORY 3

One-bedroom, two-bath suites offer a separate parlor with double sofa bed as well as a pull-down bed, wet bar, four-person dining table, and extralarge veranda. There are two closets, one a walk-in. Sleeps four or five; 614 square feet. Includes concierge service.

DELUXE FAMILY STATEROOM WITH VERANDA—CATEGORY 4

A large stateroom with a split-configuration bath. The sitting area, separated from the bed by a curtained divider, contains a sofa bed and a pull-down bed. All Category 4 staterooms come with a veranda. Sleeps four or five; 304 square feet.

DELUXE STATEROOM WITH VERANDA—CATEGORY 5 AND 6

Category 5 cabins are located one deck higher than Category 6. Both have a veranda and a curtain-divided sitting area with a vanity, small sofa bed, and pull-down bed. Sleeps three or four; 268 square feet.

DELUXE STATEROOM WITH NAVIGATORS VERANDA—CATEGORY 7

The same as Category 5 and 6 except for a different type of veranda that's enclosed with a large open porthole. Sleeps three; 268 square feet.

DELUXE OCEANVIEW STATEROOM—CATEGORY 8, 9, AND 10

Category 8 staterooms are outside cabins on higher decks than Category 9 cabins, which are outside but on the two lowest decks; neither has a veranda. Category 10 is an inside cabin without a veranda located on the two lower decks. All have a curtain-divided sitting area with small sofa bed, pull-down bed, and vanity. Sleeps three or four; 214 square feet.

STANDARD INSIDE STATEROOM—CATEGORY 11 AND 12

Category 11 accommodations are inside cabins located on the upper decks; Category 12 staterooms are inside on a lower deck. The sitting area has a curtain divider with a small sofa bed, pull-down bed, and vanity. Sleeps three or four; 184 square feet.

Cruise Itineraries

Although Disney has recently offered various change-of-pace itineraries including the Panama Canal, ten-night special cruises, and Mexican Riviera cruises, you'll find that three-, four-, and seven-day cruises from Port Canaveral are the norm, with each itinerary including a stop at Disney's own private island, where an entire day is dedicated to fun in the sun. Here guests can swim, cruise around on paddleboats, sail, sea kayak, snorkel in special Disney-created "shipwrecks," snooze in a hammock, shop a Bahamian marketplace, and dine at a barbecue buffet on the beach. Trails and bike paths are laid out for the exercise-minded, and those who really want to relax can book a massage in one of the private beach cabanas. (Reservations should be made 105 days in advance for concierge cruisers and 75 days in advance for all other cruise passengers.) Castaway Jo Pavilion is the place for pool, foosball, Ping-Pong, shuffleboard, horseshoes, and basketball. Several bars scattered throughout the island sell alcoholic tropical drinks.

Four separate beaches cater to the needs of children, families, teens, and adults. Kids have their own special area called Scuttle's Cove where a program of activities is sure to please. Serenity Bay is the adults-only beach for those age eighteen and older, where private cabana massages can be prearranged. The Family Beach is perfect for those who want to spend the day with their children, and the Teen Beach offers floats and rope swings as well as a supervised activity program.

At each stop a variety of shore excursions is offered, and the good news is that they may now be booked before your cruise begins.

THREE- AND FOUR-NIGHT BAHAMA CRUISES

Sail on the *Disney Wonder* to the Bahamas on a three-night itinerary departing on Thursday with stops at Nassau and Castaway Cay. Four-night cruises depart on Sunday with the same ports and an additional day at sea.

SEVEN-NIGHT CARIBBEAN CRUISES

Seven-night cruises to the western Caribbean alternate weekly with an eastern Caribbean itinerary on the *Disney Magic*. All depart on Saturday, with the western itinerary stopping at Key West, Grand Cayman, Cozumel, and Castaway Cay, and the eastern itinerary stopping at St. Maarten, St. Thomas, and Castaway Cay.

Recreation

Arcade. Quarter Masters, the ship's arcade, features the latest in video games.

Deck fun. All ages enjoy the shuffleboard and Ping-Pong tables, and the exercise-minded will love the outdoor jogging track on Deck 4.

Pools. Three heated pools are found on Deck 9, all with fresh water. Forward is the adults-only Quiet Cove pool with two adjacent whirlpools, amidship is Goofy's Pool, perfect for families with two adjacent whirlpools (one hot and one cold); and aft is the shallow Mickey Pool with a fun waterslide for young children.

Wide World of Sports. Recreation area on Deck 10 featuring basketball, volleyball, and badminton.

Entertainment

Beat Street/Route 66. On the *Disney Magic* you'll find Beat Street, an entertainment area offering three nightclubs for adults (age eighteen and older) only. At the Rockin' Bar D are live bands playing rock 'n' roll in a honky-tonk atmosphere; Diversions, a casual hangout with karaoke, group sing-alongs, and sports events; and Sessions, a jazz club featuring live piano music along with specialty coffees, champagne, wine, liqueurs, even caviar.

On the *Disney Wonder* it's Route 66. Clubs include WaveBands, where dancing to a live band or DJ-driven music playing the hits of a span of generations is the agenda; the Cadillac Lounge for soothing music and a sophisticated setting; and Diversions, similar to the same-named club on the *Disney Magic*.

Buena Vista Theater. Watch Disney classic movies as well as first-run feature films in this 268-seat theater.

Internet Café. Surf the Web, e-mail a friend, or find out more about your cruise activities. A fee is charged for Internet services. Open 24/7.

Promenade Lounge. Lobby lounge featuring live easy-listening music each evening.

Studio Sea. This family nightclub offers game shows, karaoke nights, cabaret acts, and dancing for all ages.

Walt Disney Theater. Three-level, 1,022-seat theater with original live productions each evening. Stage shows on both ships include *The Golden Mickeys,* combining live-action theater with film, music, and pyrotechnics in a tribute to Walt Disney's animated films; *Hercules—A Muse-ical Comedy*; and *Disney Dreams,* a bedtime story with many of the most popular Disney characters.

Dining

Disney's dining system, which rotates through each of three restaurants, is unique. Seating is assigned, and although you'll be moving to a different place each evening, your servers as well as the other table guests travel with you.

At Parrot Cay there's island-style cuisine along with Caribbean music and tropical decor, and at Animator's Palette the room changes as the night progresses from black-and-white to a barrage of color with animated scenes from classic Disney movies. On the *Disney Magic* the third dining room is Lumiere's, offering fine dining and a *Beauty and the Beast* twist on the evening; on the *Disney Wonder* it's Triton's, featuring seafood and a *Little Mermaid* underwater-style setting.

Dinner is served at either 6:00 or 8:30 P.M. Disney tries to put childless adults with other childless adults and families with children with other families. Evening attire for adults in Animator's Palate and Parrot Cay is resort casual (no shorts, T-shirts, or jeans except on young children), while dress shirts and slacks for men and pantsuits and dresses for women are suggested in Lumiere's and Triton's. Aboard the seven-night cruises, one dinner is semiformal, and one requires more formal or black-tie-optional attire.

Breakfast and lunch with open seating are served at Parrot Cay and either Lumiere's on the *Disney Magic* and Triton's on the *Disney Wonder.* A casual breakfast and lunch buffet are offered at Topsider's on the *Disney Magic* and at Beach Blanket Buffet on the *Disney Wonder.* Beverages such as coffee, tea, soda, juice, and milk are complimentary with meals only. Anywhere else beverages, both alcoholic and non, may be charged to your room.

Tables are tough to come by at Palo, the reservations-only, adults-only (age eighteen and over) dining room. Here you'll enjoy Northern Italian cuisine, fine wines, and an air of romance accompanied by 270-degree views of the ocean. Since reservations fill up quickly, make them immediately after boarding. Suggested dress at Palo is a jacket or a button-down shirt and tie for men and a dress or pantsuit for ladies. Dining is from 6:00

to 11:00 P.M. Palo also features a reservations-only champagne brunch on four- and seven-day cruises. For both, an additional $10 service charge per guest is added to your final bill.

Anytime the stomach starts to rumble, head to Pluto's Doghouse for hot dogs, hamburgers, grilled chicken sandwiches, and chicken tenders; Pinocchio's Pizzeria for a slice of pizza; or Scoops for soft-serve ice cream and wrap sandwiches. Room service is offered twenty-four hours a day, with continental breakfast served from 7:00 to 10:00 A.M. and sandwiches, salads, soup, pizza, pasta, and dessert the remainder of the day and into the wee hours of the morning. Those staying in a suite may order a full breakfast.

Services

VISTA POOL AND SPA

This adults-only, 9,000-square-foot spa, salon, and fitness center has a long list of luxurious services perfect for a great day at sea, including many types of massage, body treatments, facials, and hydrotherapy. Couples love the Surial Bath, where they're provided with three types of medicinal mud in a private steam room. The Tropical Rain Forest is a thermal suite with steam, sauna, and water therapy for a nominal fee. A salon offers manicures, pedicures, haircuts, and hair coloring.

At the complimentary fitness center you'll find treadmills, stairclimbers, exercise bicycles, rowing machines, exercise machines, and free weights in a facility that comes with a fantastic ocean view. For an additional fee, personal training, yoga, and lifestyle consultation are available. Pilates, aerobics, and sculpt-and-tone classes are complimentary.

For Adults Only

A third of all guests aboard Disney's ships are adults traveling without children, and there are many areas where no children are to be found: Palo for dining, the adults-only pool on the ship, a separate beach at Castaway Cay, Cove Café for coffee and drinks, and the soothing Vista Spa. On the *Disney Magic* the Art of Entertainment seminar teaches how to plan the perfect dinner party, prepare fancy desserts, and create floral arrangements and beautiful tables. Behind-the-Scenes allows guests a backstage perspective in Disney's global projects, and the Navigator Series is the perfect opportunity to explore the ship's architecture and bridge. On the *Disney Wonder* adults will find culinary demonstrations, wine tastings, and game shows.

Children's and Teens' Programs

With nearly an entire deck dedicated to children, there is a wide range of age-specific programs for kids. We all know what Disney does best, and that is cater to the needs of children. And when children are happy, so are their parents. It's a perfect combination of family time as well as playtime with others their own age. The programs run from around 9:00 A.M. to about midnight and are complimentary (with the exception of Flounder's Reef Nursery). Pagers are provided to parents in case their children need them summoned for any reason.

FLOUNDER'S REEF NURSERY

This is the place for children ages twelve weeks to three years; those three- and four-year-olds who are not potty trained, and therefore not eligible for the Oceaneer Club, also may be accommodated here. The fee is $6.00 per hour per child ($5.00 per additional child per hour) with a two-hour minimum. It's best to make advance reservations since only a limited number of infants and toddlers are accepted at one time. Although hours vary, the service is generally provided from 1:00 to 4:00 P.M. and again from 6:00 P.M. to midnight while in port and 9:30 to 11:30 A.M., 1:30 to 3:30 P.M., and 6:00 P.M. to midnight while at sea.

OCEANEER CLUB

In a setting reminiscent of Never Land, potty-trained children ages three through seven have plenty to keep them occupied and happy. For three- and four-year-olds there are such activities as an "unbirthday" party with *Alice in Wonderland* characters, puppet shows, a Pumba PJ party, and singing with Cinderella. Ages five through seven enjoy a PJ party with Goofy, try out new experiments in the Oceaneer Lab, hear pirate stories with Captain Hook, and participate in detective school. All this plus much, much more. Open from 9:00 A.M. to midnight.

OCEANEER LAB

At Disney's ultramodern Oceaneer Lab, older children enjoy Nintendo played on a giant screen and ten terminals of computer games. Divided into two age groups, children ages eight and nine participate in lab workshops, learn the secrets of Disney animation, race regattas, camp out under the stars, play music trivia, and make radio commercials. Those ages ten through twelve participate in such activities as drawing animation cells, Disney game shows, ghost storytelling, making a mouse pad, and solving mysteries. Open from 9:00 A.M. to midnight.

HANGOUTS FOR TEENS

Teens ages thirteen through seventeen hang out at the Stack on the *Disney Magic* and Aloft on the *Disney Wonder,* where they'll find games, Internet, music, and a big-screen TV. Other activities include pool parties, animation drawing, dance classes, photography and photo album construction, table tennis tournaments, movie parties, filmmaking, karaoke, and trivia games. Open from 10:00 A.M. to 1:00 A.M.

APPENDIX: SUGGESTED ITINERARIES

Suggested One-day Itinerary at the Magic Kingdom for Adults with Young Children

Although this is a suggested one-day itinerary, those with young children may want to plan for two days at the Magic Kingdom. With so many attractions for the little ones, a couple of days spent at a relaxing pace is certainly preferable over a one-day mad dash through the park, allowing time to head back to your resort for a midday nap or a dip in the pool. If a second day can't be spared, get a good rest the night before.

Make a before-park-opening advance reservation (call exactly ninety days prior at 7:00 A.M. Orlando time) for breakfast at Cinderella's Royal Table. Get the earliest seating possible to be finished close to park opening time. Check your guidemap and decide when to work in the Cinderellabration show.

Head straight to Fantasyland, pick up a FASTPASS for Winnie the Pooh, and then ride Dumbo and Peter Pan's Flight and see Mickey's PhilharMagic before your FASTPASS time. Afterward take in Cinderella's Golden Carousel, It's a Small World, Ariel's Grotto, and Snow White's Scary Adventure.

Head to Mickey's Toontown Fair. First visit the Hall of Fame and then the Judge's Tent for multiple visits with Disney characters. Afterward take in both Mickey and Minnie's Homes as well as the Barnstormer, and then have a splashing good time at Donald's Boat.

Time for a late lunch. Eat at one of the many counter-service spots—my favorite is Pecos Bill Café for good burgers.

Pick up a FASTPASS for the Haunted Mansion before finding a place for the Share a Dream Come True Parade.

Return to the Haunted Mansion before moving on to Adventureland. Pick up a FASTPASS at the Jungle Cruise before getting in line for Pirates of the Caribbean and the Magic Carpets of Aladdin. If you're making good time, see the Swiss Family Treehouse, The Enchanted Tiki Room, or Country Bear Jamboree.

Move on to Tomorrowland, pick up a FASTPASS if necessary for Buzz Lightyear, and take in the race cars at Tomorrowland Speedway.

If your kids (or you) are not totally exhausted by now and want to stay for the evening fireworks, have dinner at either the Crystal Palace or the Liberty Tree Tavern (both character meals, so plan ahead with advance reservations) before the evening's festivities.

Suggested One-day Itinerary at the Magic Kingdom for Adults and Older Children

If your kids are older or you're traveling with adults only, try this itinerary.

Have breakfast at your hotel or pick up a quick treat at the Main Street Bakery. Whatever, try to be finished with your meal and in line for the rope drop at park opening time.

Head straight to Splash Mountain in Frontierland, and then take in Big Thunder Mountain next door.

Cut back through the hub to Tomorrowland and ride Space Mountain.

If anyone in your party is interested in the attractions in Fantasyland (as I usually am), go there now. It will probably be necessary to pick up a FASTPASS for either Peter Pan's Flight or Winnie the Pooh, so check that out first before your tour of this land begins. Ride Peter Pan's Flight, Snow White's Scary Adventure, and the Many Adventures of Winnie the Pooh. See Mickey's PhilharMagic and, if you really like torture, It's a Small World.

Have a relaxing lunch at either Liberty Tree Tavern or Tony's Town Square. If fast food is your choice, head to Pecos Bill's for great burgers.

Pick up a FASTPASS at the Haunted Mansion in Liberty Square before settling down for the afternoon Share a Dream Come True Parade at 3:00 P.M.

After the parade head to the Haunted Mansion and then see Pirates of the Caribbean in Adventureland.

Pick up anything of interest to you that you missed during the day. Good choices would be Buzz Lightyear, Stitch's Great Escape! or the Jungle Cruise.

Before leaving take a stroll down Main Street for shopping and a late afternoon snack.

If you decide to stay for the evening's festivities, make advance reservations at Cinderella's Royal Table or Tony's Town Square for dinner (non-character meals) and enjoy the park until the evening's festivities begin, or head back to your hotel (easy to do if you're staying at a monorail-serviced property), freshen up, and have an early dinner before returning for the parade and fireworks.

Suggested One-day Itinerary for Touring Epcot

For optimum enjoyment, Epcot really needs to be seen in one and a half to two days; however, the following itinerary does hit all the highlights. It may be difficult if not impossible to accomplish in busy season but entirely possible in the slower times of the year. Come prepared with plenty of energy and a good pair of walking shoes.

Have breakfast and be at the park a half hour before opening.

Ride Soarin' at the Land then move over to the east side of Future World to first Test Track and then Mission: SPACE.

See the attraction at the Universe of Energy and then ride Spaceship Earth.

See *Honey, I Shrunk the Audience* at the Imagination pavilion.

Hop next door to the Land pavilion where you'll want to ride the Living with the Land attraction.

Move to World Showcase and pick up a late lunch at one of the many fast-food spots.

Work your way around World Showcase for the remainder of the afternoon, making time between stops for shopping as you attempt to take in some of the highlights, including Maelstrom in Norway, the *Reflections of China* film, *The American Adventure* show, *Impressions de France,* and *O Canada.*

Make advance reservations at one of the World Showcase restaurants for 7:00 P.M., have dinner, and then roam or pick up anything you missed until about a half hour prior to the Illuminations fireworks when it's time to search for a nice viewing spot for the show.

Go back to your hotel room and collapse.

Suggested Two-day Itinerary for Touring Epcot

Now this is more like it, a much more relaxing two days at this massive park.

First Day

Your first day of touring will take in all of Future World. Begin by riding Soarin' at the Land, and then see the Living with the Land attraction and the Circle of Life.

Move over to the east side of Future World, pick up a FASTPASS for Test Track, and while you wait ride Mission: SPACE and the Universe of Energy attractions.

Have lunch at the Coral Reef Restaurant; make your advance reservations for around 12:30 P.M. After lunch visit the Living Seas.

Head to the Imagination pavilion to see *Honey, I Shrunk the Audience* and Journey into the Imagination.

Tour Innovations and ride Spaceship Earth.

If the Wonders of Life pavilion is open, experience Body Wars (your food should be sufficiently settled by now), Cranium Command, and *The Making of Me*.

Hang out enjoying Epcot's fun atmosphere before make your way to dinner (remember to make advance reservations weeks ahead of time) at one of the World Showcase restaurants or the Flying Fish at the Boardwalk.

Tomorrow night you'll be staying for the fireworks, so tonight head home for a good night's sleep.

Second Day

Your second day will be a complete tour of World Showcase. Sleep in today because this area of Epcot doesn't open until 11:00 A.M. Begin your tour in Canada, where shopping and the *O Canada* film are in order.

Next tour the United Kingdom's cutesy shops and perhaps have a pint at the pub.

Break for lunch at either Chefs de France or the Marrakesh Restaurant in Morocco; make your advance reservations for around 1:00 P.M. Then see the *Impressions de France* show and do a bit of perfume shopping.

Visit Morocco to walk the interesting bazaars and alleyways.

Japan is next with its serene gardens and the Mitsukoshi Department Store brimming with all kinds of goodies.

Then *The American Adventure* show, a must on every patriotic citizen's list.

After America head to Italy for soft Italian leather and a glass of Chianti.

Take in Germany and its jolly village and then go on to the *Reflections of China* film.

Next Norway and the Maelstrom attraction before your advance reservation time of 7:00 P.M. at the San Angel Inn in the Mexico pavilion. Ride El Rio del Tiempo either before or after dinner and stake out a place for the Illuminations fireworks at least a half hour before the show.

See Illuminations and then head for home.

Suggested One-day Itinerary for Touring Disney–MGM Studios

Arrive thirty minutes before park opening. It is hoped that you've already made your advance reservation for the FANTASMIC! Dinner Package (see Special Entertainment at the end of the Disney–MGM Studios section for full details); if not, do so first thing at the corner of Hollywood and Sunset Boulevards.

Since this park offers scheduled live shows, you'll need to work in the Indiana Jones Epic Stunt Spectacular, *Beauty and the Beast* Live on Stage, and the Lights, Motors, Action! Extreme Stunt Show when your schedule allows during the course of the day. And if you're traveling with toddlers, you'll certainly need to find time to see Playhouse Disney.

Thrill junkies should immediately head down Sunset Boulevard to the Tower of Terror and Rock 'n' Roller Coaster.

If touring with young children or if thrill rides aren't your cup of tea, skip the scary attractions and see the Voyage of the Little Mermaid and Magic of Disney Animation, then head to the Great Movie Ride.

By now it's time for a snack or light lunch. Good choices are the Backlot Express or the ABC Commissary. Advance reservations for the FANTASMIC! Dinner Package can be startlingly early (sometimes as early as 4:00 P.M.), so you won't want to stuff yourself with a big lunch.

Take the Backlot Tour and then head over to MuppetVision 3-D.

Stake out a place for the Stars and Motorcars afternoon parade.

Swing over to *Who Wants to Be a Millionaire*—Play It!

By now it is time for your advance reservation for the FANTASMIC! Dinner Package; if you're smart you've made your reservation for the Hollywood Brown Derby.

After dinner there should be plenty of time to ride Star Tours and see *Sounds Dangerous* before heading over to FANTASMIC! thirty minutes before showtime (even earlier if you haven't made priority seating for the FANTASMIC! Dinner Package).

Suggested One-day Itinerary for Touring Disney's Animal Kingdom

Be at the park gates a half hour before opening, using the time before rope drop to walk the paths of the Oasis. Those with children may want to take in the character breakfast at Restaurantosaurus before park opening.

At rope drop head straight to Kilimanjaro Safaris and then walk the Pangani Forest Exploration Trail. (After Expedition Everest's scheduled opening in 2006, go there first instead.)

Explore Africa before backtracking to Discovery Island to take in the It's Tough to Be a Bug show. Then head to Camp Minnie-Mickey.

Work in the Festival of the Lion King sometime in the morning and, if you have young children, see Pocahontas and Her Forest Friends and stop for a visit at the Character Greeting Trails.

Head to your 1:00 P.M. advance reservation at the Rainforest Café or pick up fast food at the Tusker House.

After lunch it's time for Dinoland. If necessary, pick up a FASTPASS to Dinosaur. During the wait take in the rides at Chester and Hester's Dino-Rama and see Tarzan Rocks if possible. If you have children in tow, make a stop at the Boneyard for playtime.

See the afternoon Mickey's Jammin' Jungle Parade (in slower seasons, the parade is sometimes the last event of the day, in which case it would be necessary to take in Kali River Rapids and the Maharaja Jungle Trek before it begins).

Move on to Asia, pick up a FASTPASS to Kali River Rapids, and while you're waiting walk the Maharaja Jungle Trek and see Flights of Wonder.

After Kali River Rapids you'll be soaked. Either head out to Rafiki's Planet Watch to see the exhibits or head home for a hot shower and dinner at your resort.

Suggested One-day Itinerary at Universal Studios for Adults with Young Children

This park has enough to keep kids busy for part of a day, but remember that many of the attractions with major scare factors are not suitable for little ones.

Those with children who are not too young will want to see *Shrek* 4-D first, then Jimmy Neutron's Nicktoon Blast (younger children can sit in stationary seats).

Next head to Woody Woodpecker's Kidzone and ride the E.T. Adventure followed by Woody Woodpecker's Nuthouse Coaster. Work in the *Animal Planet Live* show and A Day in the Park with Barney when you can during the day.

Break for lunch at the Classic Monster Café and then visit Nick Live!

Return to Woody Woodpecker's Kidzone for wet playtime at Fievel's Playland and *Curious George Goes to Town*.

If your children are not too young and have a high tolerance for scary attractions, you may want to try *Twister:* Ride It Out.

Parents should utilize Universal's Child-Switch Program for rides with a high scare factor, whereby one parent stays behind with the children while the other rides an attraction, then the other parent hops aboard, leaving the first rider with the children.

Suggested One-day Itinerary at Universal Studios for Adults and Older Children

Be at the park before opening time, allowing thirty minutes to park and another thirty to buy tickets (but hope you've prepurchased them). Use Universal Express when needed, but head straight to *Shrek* 4-D and then *Revenge of the Mummy*.

Move on to the World Expo area to take in *Back to the Future* and *Men in Black*: Alien Attack.

Retrace your steps to Hollywood and see *Terminator 2*: 3-D (use Universal Express if necessary), the Gory, Gruesome and Grotesque Horror Makeup Show, and then walk through Lucy—A Tribute.

Sometime during your day pick up lunch at a counter-service spot. My favorites are the Classic Monster Café and Richter's Burger Co. Or head outside the park's gates to one of the CityWalk restaurants.

Move to the New York area and pick up a Universal Express pass to *Twister*: Ride It Out (if necessary) and during your wait see *Earthquake*: The Big One and *Jaws* in the nearby San Francisco/Amity area.

If you like attractions geared to the younger set, swing over to Woody Woodpecker's Kidzone (this might be the time to pick up the *Animal Planet Live* show) and ride the E.T. Adventure. Walk back to the *Curious George Goes to Town* area and get wet if it's a hot and steamy day.

Head back to your hotel or plan for an evening at CityWalk.

Suggested One-day Itinerary at Islands of Adventure for Adults with Young Children

Begin your day at Seuss Landing and make *One Fish, Two Fish, Red Fish, Blue Fish* your first stop. Proceed to the *Cat in the Hat,* then Caro-Seuss-el, and stop to play at If I Ran the Zoo.

Have an early lunch and see the show at Circus McGurkus Café Stoopendous, and then head to The Lost Continent to ride the Flying Unicorn. If your children are not too young for loud noises, work in the Eighth Voyage of Sinbad.

Next comes Jurassic Park, where the Jurassic Park Discovery Center is a must for dinosaur-loving kids, followed by a romp in super Camp Jurassic, one of the best play areas for children in the Orlando area. If lines are short, ride the Pteranodon Flyers.

Work your way over to Toon Lagoon and let the kids have fun at Me Ship, The *Olive.*

Parents may want to utilize Universal's Child-Switch Program for attractions with a high scare factor whereby one parent can watch the children while the other rides, and then the other parent hops aboard, leaving the children with the first rider.

Suggested One-day Itinerary at Islands of Adventure for Adults and Older Children

Be at the park before opening time, allowing thirty minutes to park and another thirty to buy tickets (which I hope you've purchased ahead). Head straight to Marvel Super Hero Island to ride the Amazing Adventures of Spider-Man, then the Incredible Hulk, and finally Doctor Doom's Fearfall before heading over to the Jurassic Park area.

Pick up a Universal Express pass (if necessary) for the Jurassic Park River Adventure. While waiting, take a spin around Camp Jurassic, one of the neatest kid play areas in Orlando (don't miss the cave that leads to the amber mine) and the Jurassic Park Discovery Center. Return to ride the Jurassic Park River Adventure.

Pick up a Universal Express pass for Dueling Dragons if necessary and during your wait have lunch at Mythos Restaurant.

After lunch see *Poseidon's Fury* and then ride Dueling Dragons. If there's time, see the Eighth Voyage of Sinbad.

Walk through quirky Seuss Landing and, if you are still a child at heart, ride the Cat in the Hat and Caro-Seuss-el.

Now that you are hot and sweaty, go back to Toon Lagoon to ride Popeye and Bluto's Bilge-Rat Barges and Dudley Do-Right's Ripsaw Falls before heading home.

INDEX